RED CLAY, WHITE WATER, AND BLUES

Published in association with Georgia Humanities

RED CLAY
WHITE WATER
& BLUES

A HISTORY OF Columbus, Georgia

VIRGINIA E. CAUSEY

THE UNIVERSITY OF GEORGIA PRESS ATHENS

Publication of this book was made possible
in part by generous gifts from
Cecil and Bettye Cheves
Frank and Tammy Lumpkin
Wright and Katherine Waddell
Wyler Hecht
The Loft, Columbus GA

Paperback edition, 2020
© 2019 by the University of Georgia Press
Athens, Georgia 30602
www.ugapress.org
All rights reserved
Designed by Kaelin Chappell Broaddus
Set in 10/13.5 Sentinel Book by Kaelin Chappell Broaddus

Most University of Georgia Press titles
are available from popular e-book vendors.

Printed digitally

The Library of Congress has cataloged the hardcover edition of this book as follows:

Names: Causey, Virginia Estes, author.
Title: Red clay, white water and blues : a history of Columbus, Georgia / Virginia E. Causey.
Description: Athens : The University of Georgia Press, [2019]
| Includes bibliographical references and index.
Identifiers: LCCN 2018049447| ISBN 9780820354996 (hardcover) |
ISBN 9780820355030 (ebook)
Subjects: LCSH: Columbus (Ga.)—History.
Classification: LCC F294.C7 C38 2019 | DDC 975.8/473—dc23
LC record available at https://lccn.loc.gov/2018049447

Paperback ISBN 978-0-8203-5882-6

Title page photo: *Columbus Georgia Downtown* by SeanPavonePhoto/Adobe Stock.

To John Lupold,
Billy Winn, and
Clason Kyle,
who paved
the way.

CONTENTS

Acknowledgments
ix

Notes on the Text
xi

Introduction
1

Chapter 1
"Stepping to the Music of Jingling Dimes"
A Trading Town on the Chattahoochee
5

Chapter 2
The "Last Battle" and "Black Reconstruction"
The Civil War and Its Aftermath
34

Chapter 3
"Plethoric, Laborious, Well-Fed, Jolly, and Complacent"
Politics and Economics, 1880–1920
60

Chapter 4
Lynching, Industrial Education, Babe Ruth,
and Christian Communism
Social Change at the Turn of the Twentieth Century
94

Chapter 5
The Klan and Coca-Cola
The Roaring Twenties
120

Chapter 6
Columbus in the 1930s and 1940s
Depression and World War
144

Chapter 7
Violence, Direct Action, Negotiation
The Struggle for Civil Rights, 1944–1975
172

Chapter 8
From Optimism to Malaise
Economics, Politics, and Culture, 1950s–1980s
202

Chapter 9
Renaissance
Columbus since the 1990s
235

Notes
267

Selected Bibliography
315

Index
319

ACKNOWLEDGMENTS

Deep thanks go to Nick Norwood, the manuscript's first reader, critic, and grammarian. Editing by my husband, Tim Chitwood, and copy editor Ellen Goldlust cut the academic blather and made the book more readable. The archivists who provided invaluable support included Reagan Grimsley, David Owings, Jesse Chariton, and Dalton Royer. The Fussell family helped on several fronts: Cathy by critiquing my analysis of Carson McCullers, Fred by reviewing the section on Ma Rainey, and Jake by sharing his knowledge of Jimmie Tarlton and Tom Darby. Thanks to Columbus State University professors John Ellisor, Gary Sprayberry, and Amanda Rees. Jesse Williams knows more about the river than anyone. He also shared information on the 1934 general textile strike, in which his uncle, Reuben Sanders, was killed. Superior court judge Bobby Peters, councillor Gary Allen, Muscogee tax commissioner Lula Lunsford Huff, Phenix City collector Jim Cannon, Katherine Jordan Waddell, Aflac, and the W. C. Bradley Company allowed me to use rare photographs from their collections.

John Lupold's tremendous body of local scholarship provided the foundation for this book. My appreciation goes to Billy Winn, whose passion for social justice shaped his writing for half a century. Clason Kyle shared his knowledge of Old Columbus families, many of whom are his relatives, and made seminal contributions to historic preservation. And, most of all, thanks to the gazebo sitters, whose discussions of local scandals, lore, history, and myths were sometimes as muddy as the river flowing by but were ever entertaining—Cathy, Fred, Elinor, Billy, John, Nuria, Tim, Mike, and Craig.

NOTES ON THE TEXT

All quotations have been transcribed as they appear in the original. Errors in grammar and spelling are not indicated by [*sic*].

Racial identifiers such as "colored," "Negro," "black," and "African American" are used within their chronological context. The epithet "nigger" in direct quotations reflects the attitudes of the times discussed.

RED CLAY, WHITE WATER, AND BLUES

INTRODUCTION

The red brick matching the oldest buildings in Columbus, Georgia, to its newest comes from clay tinted with iron leached from ancient mountains along a primordial ocean shore. The shoreline's remains underlie the city, which is strategically fixed along the fall line where the Chattahoochee River foams white as it plunges through miles of rapids. The plummeting water powered brick mills that spun white cotton into cloth. The land yielding the clay produced the cotton. City founders drove off indigenous Indians and imported enslaved Africans to work the cotton fields. From those workers' despair came music. In the brick mills, white laborers also helped birth what became known worldwide as the blues. Though there were boom times, the city suffered reversals and conflicts, deepening the people's embrace of the blues.

Red clay, white water, and blues.

Several themes weave through Columbus's history:

Columbus is a city on a physical and a metaphorical fall line. Founded in 1828 as a trading town, Columbus's site at the Chattahoochee's falls made it the lower river valley's economic, political, and social center. At the head of navigation, the town was a collection point for agricultural products, principally cotton from West-Central Georgia and East-Central Alabama used in local textile mills or shipped through the port at Apalachicola to world markets. The falls also powered industry beginning in the 1830s. By 1860 Columbus was the third-largest city in Georgia and a leading commercial and industrial center, especially for textile production. Its antebellum industry was unusual in the South. Though the Civil War's destruction and economic downturns in the late nineteenth century slowed the city's development, textile manufacturing's robust growth dominated the city's economy through the mid-twentieth century.

The city historically teetered on the verge of success but was too geographically isolated or faced too many barriers to achieve the triumphs that local leaders expected. Beginning in antebellum times, promoters branded the city a progressive place with slogans such as the Center of the Sunbelt South; the Electric City; the Brightest Light on the Georgia Horizon; Georgia's West Coast; Georgia's Best Kept Secret; We're Talking Proud!; Alive and Doin' Well!; the Lowell of the South; What Progress Has Preserved; We Do Amazing. Local boosters often wildly overestimated Columbus's potential. Through much of its history, the city remained on the brink of achieving major regional status, but it never quite crossed that threshold.

Power resided in the hands of an often benevolent elite. The city's first settlers were middle- and upper-class entrepreneurs seeking commercial opportunities. The elite dominated civic decision-making, with wealthy business leaders often holding elected and appointed office. African Americans and women had no political voice until well into the twentieth century, and tax and residency barriers often excluded poor whites. The elites were sometimes divided among themselves, with cliques vying for control, but the lower classes rarely influenced decision-making.

Those elites always acted in ways that served their own best interests, which often coincided with those of the city. Banker and industrialist John Winter loaned the city $30,000 to survive the Panic of 1837, consolidating his business interests at the same time. Powerful textile owner William H. Young started a free school for mill children and a savings bank for employees, ensuring their loyalty and providing capital for his enterprise. Textile, real estate, and railroad magnate G. Gunby Jordan donated funds for white and African American industrial schools, not only helping educate the powerless but also training workers for his factories and enhancing the value of his real estate development. W. C. Bradley made a fortune in cotton factoring, steamships, textiles, and Coca-Cola. He and his heirs created the Bradley-Turner Foundation, which has pumped millions of dollars into Columbus institutions and played a prominent role in the revitalization of the downtown in the late twentieth century, which was centered on the river, along which W. C. Bradley Company real estate interests boomed.

Endemic violence has left a bloody trail through Columbus history. In the raw frontier town, elites fought duels in Indian Territory on the

Chattahoochee's west bank, a lawless area known as Sodom. Alcohol fueled much of the bloodshed, including murders of the marshal during Reconstruction and of policemen in 1896 and 1920. White men's concept of honor sometimes underlay violence, including political duels and murders in the 1830s and a spectacular shootout before a thousand onlookers at the racetrack in 1890.

Racial violence was a constant reality. Slavery was incredibly brutal, as interviews of former slaves conducted in the 1930s attest, and racial violence intensified after the Civil War, when African Americans challenged whites for their rights. The Ku Klux Klan assassinated a white Republican advocate of equal rights in 1868 and instituted a reign of terror against outspoken black citizens. In 1896 and 1912, mobs lynched black men believed to have violated the racial code. During the 1920s, the Klan controlled Columbus, including the police department. A courageous newspaper editor and elite leaders battled the group, leading to its decline, but it surged again with the rise of the civil rights movement. The murder of the most prominent local African American civil rights leader prompted many black professionals to flee the city. Firebombings and rioting erupted in 1970 after black policemen lost their jobs for protesting unfair treatment. Deepening the sense of crisis, the 1970s and 1980s witnessed some horrific murders, including those committed by three serial killers. Though crime statistics improved beginning in the 1990s, Columbus remained a violent place.

Isolated on Georgia's western boundary, Columbus has long suffered from a somewhat justified inferiority complex. It clung to river travel when it should have embraced railroads. Paved roads did not connect Columbus to any other significant city until the late 1930s. The interstate highway system bypassed it for decades. But the city's history is unique in many ways, and its past can be quite illuminating. Columbus not only was a textile powerhouse from its antebellum days through the late twentieth century but also has been home to many colorful individuals. Blind Tom Wiggins was an autistic musical genius born into slavery who performed before presidents and crowned heads of Europe. Freed slave and engineer Horace King constructed bridges throughout the South. Augusta Howard founded the Georgia Woman Suffrage Association and hosted Susan B. Anthony at her family's antebellum home. Ma Rainey ranks among the greatest of blues singers. Tom Darby and

Jimmie Tarlton recorded "Columbus Stockade Blues," which remains a bluegrass standard. Renowned author Carson McCullers used her hometown as the basis for much of her fiction, including her best-selling *The Heart Is a Lonely Hunter*. Nunnally Johnson became one of Hollywood's most prolific screenwriters and received an Academy Award nomination for *The Grapes of Wrath*. Columbus remains a major military center. The U.S. Army planted Fort Benning there in 1918, and since the 1940s, hundreds of thousands of troops have passed through, among them George Marshall, Dwight Eisenhower, Joseph Stilwell, George Patton, Omar Bradley, and Colin Powell.

Since the 1990s, Columbus has experienced a renaissance fueled by the revitalization of its downtown. Visionary leaders laid the foundation for cultural growth, economic prosperity, and increased tourism. Columbus returned its focus to the river that birthed it, creating the longest urban whitewater course in the United States and developing commercial and residential riverfront real estate. Though serious problems remain, political and civic leaders are addressing them, and the city's future is bright. Its rich history deserves a wide audience.

CHAPTER 1

"Stepping to the Music of Jingling Dimes"

A Trading Town on the Chattahoochee

Cyprian Willcox, recently graduated from Yale, visited the young town of Columbus, Georgia, from October 1844 through July 1845. Though of Yankee lineage to the core, he liked southern food, especially pork ("how infinitely cookable is he!"), sweet potatoes ("rich and mealy"), and cornbread ("a good pioneer" that "goes so scratchingly down the throat,... clears out the cobwebs, and makes the passage a nicely swept thoroughfare for what's coming"). After being delighted by "the luscious softness" of the spring air, he suffered through summer's oppressive heat. Willcox felt he was in "the centre seed of a red pepper, or the suburbs of Purgatory... fry[ing] in my own oils like dry pork over a slow fire." He found relief in cold watermelon: "How restorative of our prostrate energies on a hot day like this to bathe the countenance in a cool watermelon... the crispy yielding pulp holding in solution the richest saccharine! how it breaks up the fountains of my mouth to talk of them." On balance, however, Willcox viewed antebellum Columbus negatively. Though he foresaw a promising future, the city's newness made it "decidedly rural," with meager buildings "mainly one story, flat roof, unsubstantial, having scarcely form or comeliness." Columbus society "lack[ed] individuality" and was too egalitarian for the elitist Willcox. He wanted a "super-structure" to separate the upper class. "Silk and calico," he declared, should not meet on equal terms. One reason the upper-class residents did not focus on their proper station, Willcox asserted, was their single-minded pursuit of wealth. He wrote in disgust, "The scent of the 'Almighty dollar' is unmistakable.... The Columbians never open their eyes but to describe the size of quarter-dollars; they step to the music of jingling dimes; and always wear faces proportionate to the length of their purses."[1] Willcox's observations were on the mark.

Columbus in 1845 had not planed its raw frontier edges. The city's business elite cared much more about profits than dress and manners.

The Georgia legislature established Muscogee County in December 1826, distributing most of the land by lottery. The next June it "set apart for public purpose" five square miles on the fall line. On Christmas Eve 1827, the General Assembly passed "an act to lay out a trading town... near the Coweta Falls, on the Chattahoochee river." The act named the town Columbus. Why legislators chose this name was never made explicit, but Christopher Columbus was an early nineteenth-century icon representing the nation's fearless expansion into new lands. A mere five years earlier, both Columbus, Mississippi, and Columbus, Indiana, received their names. The 1825 publication of the Navarette manuscripts, a contemporary's account of Columbus's life, caused a sensation and became the basis for Washington Irving's popular *A History of the Life and Voyages of Christopher Columbus* (1828).[2]

Five appointed commissioners established the town: Dr. Edwin L. de Graffenreid, who had moved to the falls in 1825; James Hallam, probably a local Indian trader; and Col. Philip H. Alston, Col. Ignatius Few, and Brig. Gen. Elias Beall from central Georgia, all of whom had fought the Creeks in the War of 1812. On January 16, 1828, the commissioners appointed Edward Lloyd Thomas to survey and lay out the new community. A skilled surveyor who in 1826 marked Georgia's boundary from Miller's Bend near present-day West Point north to Tennessee, Thomas arrived at Coweta Falls on January 27. The site was not an unpopulated wilderness. The Creek town of Coweta, a few miles downriver, was a major political and economic center. The Wewoka settlement on the Georgia side had several hundred white settlers, a ferry, an inn, a few stores, and a post office. Thomas commenced work the next day, creating what would become Georgia's last state-planned city. On February 15, he began laying out the town with his son, Truman, as a chain-bearer. The cold rainy winter weather took its toll. Several of Thomas's crew became ill, including his son, who died on March 26 and was buried in the new graveyard, later named Linwood Cemetery. Thomas marked off 1,614 half-acre residential lots and set aside plots for schools, churches, and municipal offices. Large commons bordered Columbus on the south, east, and north, with the town owning the land along the river. Larger estates were available outside the town limits, current Fourth Street on the south, Tenth Avenue on the east, and Fifteenth Street on the north.[3]

The new town's natural setting was beautiful. Virgin hardwood forests covered high banks overlooking the clear rushing river that dropped 125 feet over two and a half miles of rapids, providing, as an 1829 gazetteer gushed, "freshness to the air and pleasure to the sight, by *jets d'eau*." Thomas's plan called for a promenade along the river, "one of the handsomest and most romantic walks in the State." The town site included huge trees and a large pond near present Thirteenth Street where hunters shot ducks and geese. The Creek Indians spread across the river's shoals using dip nets to catch shad during the spring run. The southern end of town was mostly swamp. The commissioners advertised the July 10, 1828, land auction. Mirabeau Lamar, former secretary to Governor George Troup, set up a press on the northwest corner of future Broad and Eleventh Streets. He printed notices that were sent to newspapers across the South and published in the first issue of his local newspaper, the *Enquirer*. The commissioners praised "the rich and extensive back country [Columbus] has already at command and [the] increasing importance it will derive from the cession of lands on the West of the Chattahoochee River will ensure to it a degree of commercial prosperity not surpassed by any other town in Georgia." The organizers' priorities emerged in their emphasis on an Indian land cession not yet made, rather than the river's potential for trade and industry. Andrew Jackson's election as president that fall made the opening of those Creek lands fairly certain.[4]

Hundreds of buyers poured in for the auction. The *Fanny*, the first steamboat to reach Coweta Falls, arrived in January, followed in March by the *Steubenville*. The commissioners tried to maintain order, prohibiting any permanent buildings or fences and outlawing the cutting of lumber within the town. Six weeks before the auction, retired British naval officer Basil Hall marveled at the bustling nascent community: "Every thing indicated hurry.... As none of the city-lots were yet sold, of course no one was sure the spot upon which he had pitched his house would eventually become his own[, so] many of the houses were built on trucks—a sort of low, strong wheels, such as cannon are supported by—for the avowed purpose of being hauled away when the land should be sold.... Anvils were heard ringing away merrily at every corner; while saws, axes, and hammers, were seen flashing amongst the woods all round." Hall heard that four thousand people were expected in the settlement by the time of the sale, "like birds of prey attracted by the scent of some glorious quarry." The auction drew "men of a speculating disposition." Most were middle- and upper-class planters, merchants, and entrepreneurs with capital to invest. Over nearly two weeks, 488 half-acre lots in town and all of the larger lots outside town sold for a total of $130,991. The most expensive lot, at the southwest corner of Broad and Crawford (now Tenth), went for $1,855, and construction immediately began there on the Columbus Hotel. Seaborn Jones, a prominent Milledgeville lawyer and politician, spent $4,256 on nine lots.[5]

Pleased with the auction's outcome, the commissioners still wanted to restrain rampant development, recommending "preserv[ing] the large trees" along the river, "arresting the mists, and inhaling, as they are known to do, the mephitive exhalatory [foul-smelling vapors] arising from putrid waters." The legislature incorporated the town in December 1828, and in the first election, white male voters chose Ulysses Lewis as the town superintendent, along with six commissioners. In keeping with the appointed commissioners' earlier concerns, the elected officials' first ordinance forbade "all persons to cut down or destroy any tree on the river Common."[6]

Columbus grew quickly, and by December 1829, around one hundred buildings were under construction, most of them frame but two of them brick, and a regular mail stage operated to Montgomery, Alabama. Three months later, a visitor described a flourishing town with "a population of 1500 people, three churches, a post-office, several brick buildings, and above 130 frame buildings of wood, most of them painted." The original town plan set land aside for churches. A Methodist congregation with fifty-four white members and seven black members organized in 1829 and built a log church on the southwest corner of what is now Second Avenue and Eleventh Street. After a revival boosted membership in 1831, the group, which later became St. Luke, built Georgia's first brick Methodist church. Also in 1829, twelve whites and a slave, Joseph, organized a Baptist congregation, which built its first church next to the Methodists the following year. A Presbyterian congregation also formed and initially was located blocks from the town center. In 1831, the commissioners gave the group a new lot close to the other churches, and in 1845, the Presbyterians moved to a larger building at the southwest corner of present-day First Avenue and Eleventh Street. The parishioners of the Roman Catholic Church of St. Philip and St. James settled on their appointed lot on lower Second Avenue in 1831, remaining there until 1880, when they built the Church of the Holy Family uptown across First Avenue from the Baptists. The original plan for Columbus did not reserve a space for an Episcopalian congregation, but Trinity Episcopal Church was founded at the home of Dr. Edwin de Graffenreid in August 1834, and the congregation erected its first church three years later on the west side of what is now First Avenue near Twelfth Street. In 1891, Trinity Episcopal moved across First Avenue to a new Gothic Revival church.[7]

The churches and middle-class residents tried to provide a bulwark against the frontier town's excesses, with mixed success. In 1829, de Graffenreid established a temperance society, much needed in an era when saloons lined Columbus's streets and men commonly drank themselves comatose. A circulating subscription library opened on Broad Street in January 1832. A second newspaper, the *Democrat*, began publication in 1830. The Girls and Boys Academies, attended by middle-class children whose parents could afford the tuition, opened in 1832 on their lots reserved in the original town plan. The first itinerant acting troupe, Sol Smith and His Dramatic Company, arrived in Columbus on Sunday, May 20, 1832. The following day, Smith hired local contractor Asa Bates to build a theater on Broad Street, and Bates completed the structure by opening night on Thursday. It likely resembled the frontier theater described by Joseph Jefferson, who played Columbus's Springer Opera House in 1880: "two log houses joined together with an opening between them which was floored and covered in. The seats were arranged outside in the open air—benches, chairs, and logs."[8]

It was not unusual for a theater troupe to use locals as supporting actors, but Smith got more than he bargained for when he produced *Pizarro in Peru*. He hired twenty-four Creeks as extras for the play, paying each fifty cents and a glass of whiskey. He gave them the whiskey beforehand, "causing a great degree of exhilaration" among the Creeks. When the actors playing the high priest and his half dozen virgins appeared onstage, Smith remembered, the Creeks "raised such a yell as I am sure had never before been heard inside of a theatre." Smith soon heard a mournful low humming, quickly rising in volume "from the stentorian lungs of the savages.... *The Indians were preparing for battle* by executing... the Creek war-song and dance!" The virgins fled, locking themselves in their dressing room. The Indians sang and danced for half an hour and "scalped" one actor by removing his wig. Smith danced along with them, hoping to move them offstage, but the Creeks showed no sign of stopping. Though the curtain fell, the Indians continued to dance until Smith paid them. The Creeks returned the next night and wanted to assist in the performance of *Macbeth*, but Smith adamantly declined their offer.[9]

Horse racing and attendant gambling were popular with both the elites and the masses. Beginning in 1834, a racetrack operated on the South Commons, featuring spring and winter seasons. Planter John Woolfolk also had a track and raised fine horses on his land south of town across Upatoi Creek. In 1857, three of the best horses in the country met on the South Commons for a four-heat match race run in a single day. Each race was four miles long, an unheard-of distance today. The lone mare won the endurance contest, covering the sixteen miles in about 31.5 minutes. One horse was in distress after the third heat and did not compete in the final heat, while the other horse died after the last race. Animal welfare was not a consideration in frontier sport. Dog- and cockfighting were also common, with one epic July 1834 cockfight lasting three days.[10]

The area along Front Avenue near present-day Tenth Street was called Battle Row because it was the site of frequent "trials of manhood"—violent disputes settled outside the law. Passing through in 1833, Swedish scholar C. D. Arfwedson was appalled at Columbus's roughness. No civilized person could remain in the town, he declared, because "the manners of the people were uncouth.... Many individuals, there called gentlemen, would in other places receive a very different appellation." Across the Chattahoochee, Indian Territory was not under the control of law: a "number of dissolute people had founded a village, for which their lawless pursuits and atrocious misdeeds had procured the name of Sodom. Scarcely a day passed without some human blood being shed in its vicinity; and, not satisfied with murdering each other, they cross the river clandestinely, and pursue their bloody vocation even in Columbus." Irish comedian Tyrone Power visited the next year and described the inhabitants of Sodom as "'minions o' the moon,' outlaws from the neighbouring States. Gamblers, and other desperate men, here find security from their numbers, and from the vicinity of a thinly inhabited Indian country, whose people hold them in terror, yet dare not refuse them a hiding-place." These miscreants came into Columbus "in force, all armed to the teeth," got drunk, and then fled back across the river, unmolested by outnumbered local marshals. Arfwedson noted that the resulting insecurity led all men to arm themselves: "Necessity makes it obligatory to obtain justice by personal efforts; and... as a consequence, the contest on both sides too often terminates in blood. The most trifling difference not unfrequently occasions murders of the blackest dye."[11]

Southern men embraced a code of honor emphasizing "justice by personal efforts." Historian Bertram Wyatt-Brown notes that honor was external in nature, considered physically demonstrable. Others' opinions were an indispensable part of individual identity and a measure of self-worth. Violence was an acceptable response to public insult. Working-class men settled slurs on their honor with eye-gouging fights along Battle Row, while the aristocrats fought ritualized duels. Nevertheless, locals were shocked on January 23, 1832, when a young lawyer, Joseph Camp, killed Sowell Woolfolk, a large landowner and state senator who had served as secretary to the original commissioners, in a duel near Fort Mitchell. The two ambitious men had aligned with opposing political factions, the Troupites and the Clarkites, parties bound by personal loyalty rather than ideological differences. The *Niles Register* remarked, "We do not know what they differ about—but they do *violently* differ." When the conflict came to a head in Milledgeville, friends urged Camp and Woolfolk to settle their differences by dueling. According to the *Augusta Chronicle*, when the two men faced off on that frosty morning before a crowd that included many prominent community members, "Gen. Woolfolk shot first and his ball passed through the flesh of Maj. C., an inch above the navel.... After Maj. C. received the wound, he shot Gen. Woolfolk. His ball passed through W. above the heart. W. walked seven steps toward the crowd of spectators and said, 'He has killed me.' The blood gushed out of his mouth; he viewed it attentively, laid himself upon the ground and expired immediately, without having again spoken." A few days later, the *Enquirer* deplored the "barbarous custom" of such affairs of "honor," but such personal quarrels remained common.[12]

A year and a half later, Camp, a Clarkite, died at the hands of John Milton, another promising young lawyer who had political aspirations and was aligned with the Troupites. On June 29, 1833, the *Democrat* printed an anonymous letter attacking Milton. Assuming that Camp was the author, Milton counterattacked in the July 6 *Enquirer*, assailing the author as "a base coward and worthless scoundrel" who "has been publicly denied the privileges of respectable society in consequences of his moral depravity." Milton accused the writer of stealing and forgery, alluding to a charge against Camp in Madison, Georgia. Camp shot back on July 20, calling Milton "a mere grub worm of the dung hill" and charging that he had lured a married woman from his church to the river and he "attacked her in the open light of day." These were fighting words the men flung at each other. As Wyatt-Brown explains, a man without honor had no reputation. Whereas a modern man might say, "I am honest," an antebellum southern man would have said, "I wish to be regarded as honest." In the prevailing climate, such attacks on a man's honor could only be avenged through violence.[13]

Camp and Milton subsequently armed themselves and exchanged insults on the streets, and on Sunday afternoon, August 11, Milton told a friend that things might reach a crisis point during the coming week. The following morning, Milton was on Broad Street when he saw Camp approaching the courthouse. Milton stepped into a store to retrieve a double-barreled shotgun he had hidden behind the door and then discharged the first barrel into Camp's chest. The blast spun Camp around, and Milton loosed the second barrel into his foe's back, killing him. The judge; Milton's defense attorneys, including Seaborn Jones; and most of the jury were fellow Troupites, and they accepted his plea of self-defense since, according to Milton, Camp had threatened "to shoot him in the street." Most Columbusites saw the killing "as a legitimate act of a man defending his name and family honor against the threats of a proven enemy." Despite his acquittal on the murder charges, the incident tarnished Milton's reputation and prevented him from finding local political success. He moved to Mobile in 1835 and to Florida a decade later, winning the state's governorship in 1861.[14]

Violence escalated during acquisition of Alabama's rich Creek territory. The 1825 Treaty of Indian Springs forced Georgia Creeks into Black Belt agricultural land between Columbus and Montgomery. Congress passed the 1830 Indian Removal Act authorizing the president to remove all eastern Indians to lands west of the Mississippi River. In May 1831, more than 120 Columbus residents, including Jones, de Graffenreid, Lewis, Bates, and Milton, signed a letter imploring Andrew Jackson to remove the Creeks. Negotiated in March 1832, the Treaty of Cusseta did not require the Creeks' removal but was intended to make their land available to white settlement. Ten days after the Creeks signed the treaty, Jones and his friend, Judge Eli Shorter, led a group of wealthy men in forming the Columbus Land Company, which sought to scoop up thousands of acres cheaply to sell at sizable profit. By the following year, the company had used fraud and intimidation to acquire property rights from between three and four thousand Creeks. In June 1832, local entrepreneur

Daniel McDougald and Robert Collins from Macon paid $35,000 for the one square mile directly across the Chattahoochee from Columbus that the treaty had awarded to a mixed-blood man, Benjamin Marshall. They intended to sell lots in a town created on the falls "for milling and manufacturing purposes." The town first became Girard and eventually Phenix City, Alabama.[15]

In 1835, Creek warriors raided farms on both sides of the Chattahoochee, leading the *Enquirer*'s editor to cry, "It is high time these blood thirsty beings should be hunted up and made to suffer for their crimes." In February, young men from the town's leading families formed the Columbus Guards to provide protection. Creek violence continued to escalate through early 1836, sending refugees pouring into town. In late January 1836, a local militia leader reported to Governor William Schley that Columbus was in a state of "great alarm and agitation" and "in a very *defenseless situation*." He requested "a force of well organized cavalry." At the same time, a federal investigation into land speculation fraud intensified, potentially implicating Columbus's elite businessmen. One official believed that the speculators who controlled Columbus were using the threat of Indian depredations to divert attention from the looming scandal: "The people of Columbus have resorted to their old tricks of getting up town meetings and calling for troops to save them from the Creek Indians. This farce is too contemptible to excite other feelings. The investigation of frauds in Indian reservations is the cause of real alarm."[16]

On May 5, 1836, Indians killed Russell County settler William B. Flournoy, causing widespread panic. The *Enquirer* screamed, "CREEK WAR AND MASSACRE" and claimed that fifteen hundred Creek warriors were "scouring the country in all directions..., indiscriminately butchering our neighbors, men women, and children." Terror rose to a fever pitch on May 13, when Creeks attacked the stage from Montgomery, killing the passengers. Two days later, three hundred Creeks invaded Georgia, burning plantations along the river, including that of Paddy Carr, a Creek who had assisted the speculators. Columbus's militia leaders enrolled every eligible man. Mayor John Fontaine, a partner in the Land Company, pleaded with Schley to send state troops after "friendly Indian" spies reported the Creeks had "three thousand men under arms" near Columbus, "secreting themselves in Swamps & thickets" in preparation for bursting out to "burn & massacre." Shorter, another speculator who stood to lose a fortune, falsely claimed in a letter to the U.S. secretary of war that the great majority of Creeks were hostile. Maj. John H. Howard, a Land Company speculator, reported to Schley that an all-

Paddy Carr, a Creek Indian friendly to Columbus whites.
From Thomas L. McKenney and James Hall, *History of the Indian Tribes of North America* (Philadelphia: Biddle, 1838).

volunteer effort would fail in the "general war" that was coming. On May 19, Schley responded with militias from twenty-eight Georgia counties. Gen. Winfield Scott arrived on May 30 to take command of fourteen companies of U.S. troops sent to Fort Mitchell.[17]

By the end of June, troops including Creek allies such as Carr and one hundred of his followers squashed resistance, ending the war near Columbus. Hundreds gathered in Girard to witness the November 1836 hanging of six Creeks convicted of murdering the stage passengers in May. The men smeared their faces with soot and sang their death songs before stoically "taking the fearful leap." Though their courage drew some sympathy from onlookers, the *Columbus Herald* saw justice done: "Blood for blood, life for life is the golden maxim; the wail of the widow and the cry of the orphan, sued for revenge in tones of thunder." Though fewer than twenty-five hundred Creeks had fought in the war, the federal government quickly removed fourteen thousand Creeks to bring "permanent peace and tranquility" to the Chattahoochee Valley. Even Carr, who had helped whites fight the Creek rebels, was removed. Chained together by their wrists, thousands died on the Creek Trail of Tears to Oklahoma.[18]

Creek removal was a prelude to the coming fight over slavery, raising questions about state versus federal power. In 1832, Columbus residents were split in the debate over nullification, the argument that a state has the right to nullify within its borders a federal law seen as contrary to its interests. The elites on both sides of the question sent out the faithful in carriages to collect "floaters"—men who were not members of either faction but who were open to bribes—and take them to a hotel, where they were plied with food and whiskey and prevented from leaving. The next morning, the two factions marched their "penned" voters to the polls and, in the absence of secret ballots, watched to see that they voted correctly. Columbus's upper classes used such tactics to control elections for decades, eliminating unfriendly candidates and discouraging true citizen participation.[19]

Enquirer editor Mirabeau Lamar, an ardent advocate of nullification, made two unsuccessful runs for Congress on that platform before departing for Texas in 1835 and eventually becoming the Lone Star Republic's second president. Jones, Shorter, and Howard also strongly supported nullification. The Mexican War exacerbated the slavery issue, with antislavery forces in Congress determined to block the institution from new U.S. territories. Support for state's rights superseding federal power subsequently grew in Columbus, and Howard explained advocates' position in the *Enquirer* in 1849: "The question of slavery or no slavery is really the only one before the American people." Enshrined in the Constitution, it nevertheless was subject to "deadly assault" by "a formidable party of abolitionists composed of the great mass of the people of the North." Howard saw civil war as a viable option, calling for "freemen to vindicate your rights, [to] meet the enemy at the threshold." The fight "will no longer be postponed—the cup cannot pass." By the 1850s, most of Howard's fellow townspeople embraced this view.[20]

The Creek War, a tragedy for the Indians, was an economic boon for Columbus. Government contracts and the presence of thousands of soldiers benefited local businesses. By 1837 the population of Columbus was about 4,100 people, 38 percent of them of African descent. The war and Indian removal ended the investigation into land fraud and opened the way for development. Typical of the upper class seeking greater fortune was John Banks, who moved to Muscogee County in February 1836 with his wife, Sarah, and their twelve children. He bought 265 acres in the wealthy Wynnton suburb east of the city and built his home, the Cedars, at the end of long drive lined with red cedars. He also purchased plantations, including Paddy Carr's, in Alabama, Georgia, and Mississippi, and worked about two hundred slaves on his roughly 10,000 acres. Banks quickly became entwined in the city's economic life.[21]

With the Creek War looming, the state legislature amended the charter to make the town a city, with a mayor and aldermen. Columbus became a regional trade center and transportation hub as cotton poured in from new farms and plantations. The Federal Road and St. Marys Road, also called the Old Salt Trail, enabled wagon and stage traffic, though most early visitors complained about the difficulty of travel on rutted and muddy roads. Stagecoaches usually carried nine passengers on three seats, with the middle one reserved for ladies, and could average four or five miles per hour. The rolling of the coach provoked motion sickness in some passengers, and at times, the driver would yell for the passengers to lean right or left to keep the coach from tipping over. By the 1840s, three stages traveled between Columbus and Montgomery, including the People's Line, operated by Randolph Mott and John Mustian. Rather than drive each other into bankruptcy, the three enterprises formed a cartel and agreed to a fare of ten dollars for the ninety-mile trip.[22]

Bridging the river was essential to trade. In 1831, Jones and S. M. Ingersoll, a Russell County planter, entrepreneur, and member of the Land Company, partnered to operate a ferry a mile downriver from Columbus. It could not handle the growing volume of wagon trade, so in 1832, the city council hired John Godwin of South Carolina to construct a covered bridge. Godwin brought with him Horace King, a slave with whom Godwin had a relationship more akin to a partnership. Godwin allowed King to buy his freedom in 1846, and he subsequently became a master builder renowned across the Lower South. Using mostly slave labor, Godwin completed the Columbus bridge (located at present-day Dillingham Street) in a year and a half, earning praise from the *Enquirer* for the gleaming white structure, "unequaled by any similar work in the South, [that] adds to the artificial scenery of the place, while it facilitates the communication with the western country." The bridge was destroyed in March 1841 when two days of rain swelled the river until it lifted one end of the bridge off its pier and swept it downstream. The *Enquirer* re-

View of Godwin and King's 1832 bridge to Girard from the Columbus steamboat wharf. Francis De LaPorte, *Pont de Columbus* (detail), ca. 1838, hand-tinted lithograph, 8 × 9 inches. From the Collection of the Columbus Museum, Georgia; Museum purchase, G.1983.75.

ported, "Never was there a more majestic sight seen, than the departure of that noble bridge, on its remarkable voyage. Its course was uninterrupted as we learn, until it reached Col. Woolfolk's plantation, eight miles below, where it took up new moorings, in the centre of a large cotton field." The members of the city council hired Godwin to rebuild, and he and King completed the new bridge in just over a year, priming Columbus's business district for growth. Jones and Banks put up commercial buildings on Broad and rented them to merchants and professionals. Eli Shorter chose Broad for his mansion, with terraced gardens stepping down to the river. An 1856 referendum approved an additional bridge upriver at present-day Fourteenth Street. Not built by King, this bridge was shoddily constructed, and a flood washed it away in February 1862. The city council wisely hired King to rebuild it.[23]

Steamboat traffic was crucial to Columbus's growth as a trading center. By 1835, six steamboats regularly connected the city with Apalachicola, hauling agricultural products—mainly cotton—downriver and returning with manufactured and dry goods, groceries, and even oysters. Larger boats carried passengers in relative luxury. As historian John Lupold wryly notes, "In the days when a stagecoach represented the only alternative, steamboat passage meant a great deal more comfort as long as the boiler did not explode." An 1834 account in the *Enquirer* detailed the bustling wharf below the new bridge: "Bales of cotton have rolled down one street, whilst up another, sacks of Salt and Coffee, hogsheads of Sugar, barrels of strong drink, and boxes of all manner of merchandise have moved to their place of deposit on every known and conceivable vehicle, from the strongest road waggon burdened with its thousands to the humble wheelbarrow, ratling under the weight of a solitary flour barrel. Every body and every thing seemed at times to be moving to and from the boat landing."[24]

The river was also essential for burgeoning industry. Jones first tapped its potential in 1828 at City Mills, a gristmill located north of the town limits that had a wooden dam across the shoals to funnel the current to turn the grinding stones. The enterprise was an immediate success, since farmers were eager to sell their corn and a community with few provisions was eager to buy. Through the nineteenth century, the value of ground corn and flour was second only to textiles. In May 1833, Muscogee County's first textile mill, the Columbus Factory, advertised for labor among "families who have several active hands between the ages of 12 and 24." The factory provoked optimism about the river's potential power, leading "A Friend to Manufacturers" to predict "a great source of wealth looming up to the people of this section" and to urge citizens "to go and behold what nature has done." In 1849, Julius Clapp gained control of the mill, which thereafter became associated with his name. Clapp's Factory sat about four miles north of the city near present-day Oliver Dam. Set among the trees above the rushing river, the mill workers' village surrounded the factory.[25]

Economic development demanded an effective system of banking and credit. In February 1829, the *Enquirer* observed, "Few of our citizens having the necessary cash or credit, they are often reduced to deplorable straits." The Bank of Columbus went into operation in the spring of 1832 under President Seaborn Jones. Three other banks formed within the ensuing five years, with Jones, his fellow Land Company partners, and other speculators serving as the directors and presidents. However, the banks lacked sound financial footing, and the cozy relationship among officers and stockholders allowed questionable bookkeeping. Columbusites joked that wheelbarrows were important banking equipment, because once the gold and silver currency in one bank was counted, it was wheeled over to another to include in that institution's asset report to the state.[26]

An 1837 national financial panic fueled by land speculation and erratic bank practices did not spare Columbus, and a six-year depression followed. Most banks suspended specie payments from 1837 to 1842, and businessmen could not repay their debts. Lawyer and planter Hines Holt declared, "The few who have any credit can only return it by not attempting to use it." His friends were "used up," and although "they may recover... for my life I can't see how." After the "unparalleled fall" in cotton prices, Jones pled for state aid to relieve "the unexampled distress existing among mercantile Men, and which ere long must extend itself to all classes of the community, unless some adequate relief is afforded." Because the Columbus banks had violated Georgia law by not redeeming notes in specie, the state placed them in receivership in August 1841, and all of them eventually failed. As the currency and credit crisis deepened, the economy stagnated. A young man working for the Insurance Bank wrote in June 1841, "Our town is so dull there has not been a man murdered from I know not when—all we have to do is set on a box at a store door, whittle a chip and abuse the U.S. Bank and other monsters." Facing bankruptcy in 1843, the city borrowed $30,000 from banker John G. Winter. A grateful citizenry elected him to the mayor's office the next year.[27]

Columbus's city council tried to spark growth by developing the riverfront and in October 1841 sought "proposals for erecting a dam across the Chattahoochee." On December 22, the council sold the even-numbered lots and water lot 1, the first one upriver, to Josephus Echols and his partner, John Howard, a Land Company member, a Creek War hero, and the brother-in-law of Seaborn Jones. Howard and Echols agreed to erect a "well-constructed" dam and raceway to draw sufficient power at low water for all downriver lots and to "keep the dam and race forever in good repair." They would start building by June 30, 1842; have power available for machinery on water lot 1 by October 1, 1844; and finish the project by June 30, 1847. In 1843, Howard convinced the council to sell him and his partner the remaining lots for $5,000, provoking strenuous objections from the *Enquirer*: "What possible motive could have induced the city authorities to transfer for a pitiful consideration, this valuable portion of the city property, unless it be that the majority of our Aldermen... are in daily expectation of the earth's dissolution." Lupold argues that the city's decision to privatize the waterfront crippled the river's future potential, since at around the time Howard and Echols gained Columbus's water lots, Augusta spent $100,000 to finance a seven-mile power canal for its mills. In 1844, Howard spent $8,000 to build a dam partway across the river, diverting water into a two-block raceway, thereby meeting his minimum commitment to the council.[28]

In early 1845, Howard and Echols's Coweta Falls Factory on water lot 1 began turning out yarn and fabrics from eleven hundred spindles and twenty looms. Despite citizen opposition, the men convinced the council to release them from their pledge to extend the raceway downriver, unrealistically promising the present two-block canal would power two hundred thousand spindles. Officials granted Howard and Echols absolute ownership of the water lots so that they could be sold, still requiring the two men to forever maintain the dam and raceway. Howard then bought out Echols's interest, created the Water Lots Company, and sold three-quarters of his interest to wealthy Middle Georgia planter Farish Carter, his nephew John Baird, and a Columbus entrepreneur. With cotton prices low and the local economy on the upswing, Carter and Baird started building their own five-story mill on water lot 1. The structure was topped by a belfry with the "Goddess of Yarn" holding a lightning rod, signifying "go it like lightning."[29]

Three years later, other local investors opened the six-story brick Howard Factory just downriver, with 5,000 spindles, 103 looms, and 100 workers, two-thirds of them women. By 1849, Clapp's Factory employed 80 operatives spinning 1,000 pounds of cotton thread and yarn daily. In 1846, William Brooks and John Winter built the Variety Works on an island on the raceway's western side. The factory's 100 hands operated a sawmill; turned out wooden buckets, tubs, sashes, and furniture; and produced thread on 3,000 spindles. South of the Howard Factory, Winter built the seven-story Palace Grist Mills, which opened in 1849 and began producing between eighty and one hundred barrels of flour per day—so much that a wooden barrel shortage resulted. Winter then revolutionized how people bought flour by selling it in cloth sacks that held a quarter or an eighth of a barrel. The same year, Winter also opened the three-story Rock Island Paper Mill on a four-acre island north of Columbus in what became the Bibb Mill Pond. The factory employed nine children and fourteen men to make printing, letter, and wrapping paper.[30]

Other industries opened away from the river, relying on steam rather than waterpower. The E. T. Taylor gin company opened a three-story factory in 1848, with forty workers producing fifty cotton gins a week. The city's several small iron foundries included one operated by William R. Brown started in 1849 that became the Columbus Iron Works in 1853. Six workers, including two Negroes, turned out steamboat parts, factory machinery, steam engines, railings, and cast-iron stoves. In the late 1850s, many smaller businesses helped create a diverse economic base, including leather products, shoes, ready-made clothing, candy, ink, and at least one whiskey distillery. Jewish attorney Raphael Moses, who came to town in 1848 from Apalachicola to join "the strongest bar in Georgia," was also an agricultural entrepreneur. In 1851, he began commercial shipping of peaches and plums from his Esquiline estate south of Columbus. With New York his major market, Moses was earning $75,000 annually from his one-hundred-acre orchard by 1860.[31]

Though Columbus's economy was somewhat diversified, its foundation was cotton, "the great staple that sets all the springs of trade in motion," as the *Enquirer* declared in 1841. "The planter is decidedly the greatest personage in all creation." Nearly all of Columbus's wealthy businessmen owned plantations in addition to other concerns. In 1850, Columbus warehouses received 17,741 cotton bales, 1,000 more than Montgomery and slightly fewer than Macon. On the eve of the Civil War, Columbus's four warehouses stored more than 122,000 bales. Local mills used about 3 percent of the crop, with the remainder sold at world markets such as Liverpool. Cotton factors and commission merchants, including aristocrats such as John Fontaine, graded, stored, and marketed the crop. Moreover, they provided credit to cotton farmers until they sold their crops. The factors' and merchants' capital greased the local economy, with investments in steamboats, railroads, factories, banks, and wholesale goods.[32]

The most important industry in Columbus's history arrived with William H. Young, who became the dominant local businessman of his generation. Young was attracted by Columbus's "immense water power, easily to be controlled, and a country well-adapted by soil and climate to produce cotton in perfection," which he believed resulted in an ideal location for "a great manufacturing city." Young bought water lots 2 and 3 near the head of the raceway and in 1850 built the five-story brick Eagle Mill. The enterprise was immediately profitable, paying annual dividends of up to 25 percent. Columbus finally had the entrepreneurial leadership it needed. Almost two decades after his death, a 1911 biographer asserted that "credit is due W. H. Young more than any other man for the development of this great [textile] industry in the South."[33]

Soon after the Eagle began operations, however, the river wreaked havoc on waterfront industry. A spring 1851 flood damaged the raceway wall, leaving an inadequate flow in the raceway. Baird blamed Howard's poor construction, but Howard turned his back on the Water Lots Com-

Eagle Manufacturing promotion, 1851.
Library of Congress.

pany. Another flood eighteen months later caused the raceway's east wall to collapse, shutting down the factories and throwing between four hundred and five hundred operatives out of work for four months. High water then blew out the dam in March 1853, suspending operations for two more months. Frederick Law Olmsted, later the foremost landscape architect of his generation, visited Columbus during the work stoppage and described the factory workers as mainly "'cracker girls' (poor whites from the country), who earn, in good times, by piece-work, from $8 to $12 a month." With the factories closed, Olmsted found "the labourers... in such a condition that... great numbers of them are at once reduced to a state of destitution, and are dependent upon credit or charity for their daily food."[34]

John Banks bought the bankrupt Howard Factory in 1853 for $3 and assumed its $40,000 debt, but it never prospered. Banks later deemed its purchase "a most ruinous step.... Have never made anything by it, but a loser generally." Young acquired the Howard Factory in 1860 for only $25,000, consolidating it with his Eagle Mill next door to create the second-largest textile mill in Georgia, with five hundred operatives producing twine, thread, rope, and a variety of fabrics. Young also diversified his interests, founding the Georgia Home Insurance Company in 1859 and building a fireproof three-story white iron building on Broad Street not only to serve as the company's headquarters but also to house his Bank of Columbus. The bank had originated as the mill's savings department three years earlier, when a woman operative's dress became snagged in a machine and the superintendent who freed her with his knife cut through sixty dollars in greenbacks sewn into the dress for safekeeping. The savings department paid 6 percent on deposits and soon grew into a sound bank, operating conservatively and never suspending specie payments.[35]

Winter suffered serious reversals after pulling Columbus from the brink of bankruptcy in 1843. In 1851, he sold his interest in the Variety Works. His Bank of St. Marys suspended specie payment in 1852, and the Georgia Supreme Court subsequently found that Winter and his family had fraudulently borrowed funds from the bank without security and had allowed stockholders to withdraw funds. The court ruled that Winter's other property could be attached to cover his Bank of St. Marys debts. Winter then sold Palace Mills to Randolph Mott and John Mustian, operators of the successful Peoples Stage Company, with Mott taking sole ownership by 1860. The factory prospered under Mott's guidance, setting "the price of corn and meal, and flour most inexorably," for an area of "perhaps five or ten thousand square miles." When Winter's Rock Island Paper Mill defaulted in 1855, Mott bought it for half its original value. In addition, he invested in real estate, agricultural land, and cotton warehouses, amassing a personal fortune. In 1858, after his "fine residence" uptown burned, Mott bought a riverside mansion built by land speculator and former mayor James Calhoun as well as four city lots between Bay Avenue and Broad Street, which became known for generations as Mott's Green and featured beautifully terraced gardens sweeping down to the river.[36]

Though John Howard did little to make the industrial waterfront successful, he won a lawsuit that greatly helped Columbus. When Howard and Echols built the dam across the shoals in 1845, its pooled water limited the operation of S. M. Ingersoll's gristmill upriver on the Alabama side. Ingersoll sued, claiming that water from the dam encroached on Alabama's border. The legal question was whether the boundary between the two states was the Chattahoochee's low-water or high-water mark, and in 1851 the U.S. Supreme Court ruled that the true boundary was the high-water mark, dealing a blow to Alabama and preventing Girard from developing water-powered industries that would compete with those in Columbus.[37]

With steamboat trade flourishing, Columbus leaders were reluctant to embrace Georgia's mid-1840s railroad boom. The *Columbus Times* described the railroad as an "iron boa" that would "eat up the wagon trade, and break down the business of the town." But officials could also see that if the railroad bypassed Columbus, the city would become an isolated backwater: "Either Eufaula or Macon becomes the grocery mart and depot, and the commerce that might have added thrift and wealth to this city, will be borne by us ... on the wings of steam." The state legislature granted the Muscogee Railroad a charter in December 1845, but construction did not commence until 1851. The Muscogee Railroad began carrying passengers to Upatoi on January 1, 1852, and to Butler on March 15, 1853, leaving a ten-mile stagecoach journey to connect to the railroad to Savannah.[38]

On May 20, 1853, the first nonstop train from Savannah arrived in Columbus after a thirteen-hour trip. Local businessmen hosted a "sumptuous dinner," with champagne corks falling "like a hail storm." The mayor closed the dinner by pouring water from the Atlantic into a container of Chattahoochee River water "in typical wedlock." Montgomery built a spur line from Opelika to Columbus in 1855. Contemptuously called "the elbow" by Columbusites, it remained for many years the only route to Atlanta. Despite fears that the railroad would cause Columbus to lose trade, the city benefited, with cotton receipts more than doubling between 1852 and 1859. More reliable than the Chattahoochee's unpredictable water levels, the railroads helped Columbus's exports. As businessman Paris Tillinghast wrote in 1853, "The river here is navigable, but boats doing very little. Most of the cotton, goes off now to Savannah direct, by the Rail Road." However, the railroads disadvantaged merchants by increasing the costs of importing groceries, clothing, and furniture and consequently raised prices for consumers.[39]

Columbus's initial municipal water system, created in 1839, featured rainwater cisterns with steam-powered pumps. In March 1842, however, when Columbus suffered its first major fire, the pumps provided insufficient pressure and volume, and the small volunteer fire department could not stop the blaze. Soon after concerned citizens funded the first fire engine in January 1843, the legislature formalized volunteers into the Hook and Ladder Company. The city council organized a company of Negro firefighters in 1854, giving them an old fire engine and $200 for equipment and paying each man 50¢ for fighting a fire. Nonetheless, terrible fires in 1845, 1846, and 1859 destroyed parts of the business district and elite neighborhoods.[40]

Columbus also needed reliable drinking water. The city first contracted with Seaborn Jones to run springwater from his property near the current Columbus Country Club through log pipes to Twelfth Street and Broadway. The spring produced two hundred thousand gallons per day, enough for the city's needs, but the inefficient wooden pipes allowed only fifteen thousand gallons to reach downtown. The *Times* spluttered in 1852, "We do not know of a community that is so poorly supplied with this first necessity for health, comfort, and cleanliness (water) as Columbus. There are many families in the city which have no regular and certain sources from which to derive their daily supplies of the precious element, and whose servants are actually obliged, at every turn of the water-bucket, to go forth on a foraging expedition to find it." The city dumped its residential and industrial waste into the river, and by 1846 it had become turbid and unsuitable for drinking. According to visiting English geologist Charles Lyell, "The clearing away of the woods...has caused the soil, previously level and unbroken, to be cut by torrents, so that deep gulleys may every where be seen; and I am assured that a large proportion of the fish, formerly so abundant in the Chatahoochie, have been stifled by the mud." Another sixty years passed before citizens could stand to drink river water, and a century elapsed before they took steps to clean it up.[41]

In 1852, after the *Enquirer* wondered why Columbus lacked gaslights, like its rival Montgomery, the city council appropriated $10,000 for stock in the Columbus Gas Light Company, a subsidiary of a New Jersey corporation. Headed by John Forsyth, son of a former Georgia governor, the company established a plant on the river north of the lower bridge to distill gas from wood. The city installed gaslights along downtown streets. Commercial enterprises embraced the new technology first, with upper-class residences not far behind.[42]

With the economy improving, middle- and upper-class residents were ready to support educational and cultural pursuits. However, the city had no public schools until after the Civil War; instead, middle- and upper-class children attended small private academies, mostly gender-segregated. John Banks sold ten acres for Wynnton Academy, chartered in 1837 and filled in no small part by his twelve children. Tuition in the academies ranged from $7 to $38.50 per twenty-week session. A Scottish Presbyterian minister visiting Columbus in 1844 found only about 150 pupils enrolled in a town of 5,000, "indicating a very small amount of education in progress amongst the young." By 1860 attendance was better, with 2,170 students from a population of about 9,600.[43]

The two black churches offered rudimentary education for free black children, most of whom also worked. One freedman testified before a congressional committee in 1883 that since Georgia law prohibited the education of slaves, "if a man had a slave and taught him to read he was sent to the penitentiary...; they had to keep us in gross darkness to demonstrate that we were their slaves." However, local historian Alphonso Biggs recalled in 1982 that a blacksmith on his enslaved great-grandmother's plantation ran a secret school at night. But even the white pupils' education was often of poor quality. Yale graduate Cyprian Willcox, who taught seven students at the East Common Academy, probably had high qualifications compared to other local teachers, but he was discouraged by his students' poor performance and quit after just six months, glad to be free of "urchins with a perennial flow at the nose." He huffed, "How sharper than a serpent's tooth it is to teach a Georgia school!"[44]

Early residents were more enthusiastic about theater, a pastime encouraged by the *Enquirer*: "Give to mankind innocent amusement, and they will be far less likely to seek for guilty pleasures." Construction began on the city's largest performance space, Temperance Hall, on December 22, 1849, and its grand opening occurred thirteen months later. Though the new hall had poor acoustics and a ceiling too low for some productions, it remained the city's most important meeting place for twenty years. Theater audiences in Columbus cut across class lines, from planters and merchants to middle-class clerks and mechanics to white and black laborers. Social rank determined seating, with box seats about one dollar and those in the pit fifty cents. "Colored persons" in segregated galleries paid between twenty-five and fifty cents. The Booth brothers performed at Temperance Hall in several of Shakespeare's plays—Edwin in the roles of Hamlet and Iago in December 1859, visiting Raphael Moses at Esquiline during the run. Edwin's younger brother, billed as John Wilkes, appeared as Romeo the next fall before an admiring audience that included many "debutantes." On October 12, 1860, during a rehearsal at Cook's Hotel (later the Rankin), a pistol accidentally discharged into John Wilkes Booth's thigh. Booth, laid up for ten days in Columbus, left on October 23 for Montgomery and his date with destiny four and a half years later.[45]

Despite such cultural opportunities, antebellum Columbus wore only a thin veneer of "civilization." Cyprian Willcox identified Girard, the former Sodom, as "the Sanctum-Sanctorum of villains": "If a fight occurs, and the one kills his fellow-combatant, he flies for the bridge and is safe. If a man shoots down his fellow-man in cold blood even, he crosses the Bridge and laughs in the face of Justice." Serious crime in Columbus rose by 70 percent between its founding and 1860, with more than 40 percent of felony indictments involving violence. During the 1850s, newspapers constantly printed reports of shootings, stabbings, and beatings in hotels, at polling places, and on the city streets. Alcohol fueled much of the violence. A British visitor observed in 1839 that "all classes" consumed "peach-brandy, whiskey, rum, and other ardent spirits" in "considerable" volume. In 1860, Columbus had fourteen saloons as well as fourteen other establishments that sold spirits to the city's roughly twenty-five hundred adult men. Irish native Laurence O'Keeffe noted that punishment for various offenses was meted out not according to the crime but depending on one's social standing. If a man killed someone and claimed self-defense, he was not outcast, "particularly if he is wealthy and punctual in paying up his debts." Thus, when Insurance Bank president Daniel McDougald shot his former Land Company partner, Burton Hepburn, when he entered the bank's Directors Room on January 5, 1843, the incident was ruled "justifiable homicide." With no witnesses, McDougald claimed self-defense, and the *Enquirer* declared, "There is no doubt that Gen. McDougald was expecting a similar attack by Hepburn at the time he fired."[46]

From the city's beginnings, slavery formed Columbus's foundation. The men at the 1828 auction brought slaves with them, and in 1830, more than 35 percent of the population was black. In 1860, 40 percent of white families owned slaves, most with six or fewer. Slaves built everything in Columbus—private residences, commercial structures and factories, streets, railroads, and dams. Many were employed in industry as skilled workers who competed with free white artisans. Slaves often grew gardens and kept profits from produce sales. The city streets bustled with vendors who rang bells and hawked vegetables and fruits, and as O'Keeffe observed, "industrious negroes" could "save one hundred dollars in this way in one year." Many masters hired out their slaves, sometimes allowing them to keep a portion of their earnings. But slaves who hired their time often tried to escape. Black workers on riverboats spread information helpful to slaves, much as railroad porters did later. The newspapers were full of ads for runaways warning that they might be mistaken for whites, betraying fears of racial mixing. An 1859 ad solicited help in finding a "White Negro Boy!"—the blue-eyed, straight-haired, and light-skinned Dave, who could "pass for a poor white boy."[47]

Masters sought to preserve the profitability of their chattel and thus were cautious about administering harsh punishments, but physical control nevertheless constituted an essential element of slavery, and owners had nearly absolute authority. Narratives from former slaves recorded during the 1930s included descriptions of severe treatment. Columbus-area freedman W. B. Allen remembered that his master caught a runaway and hung him by his thumbs, with his toes just touching the floor, to administer a beating. Carrie Davis recounted a master who had "regular days to whup all de slaves with strops" that had holes to raise big blisters. The master then cut open the blisters and washed them with saltwater. According to Allen, the infractions for which a slave would be whipped included leaving home without a pass, "sassing" a white person, and loitering during work. One punishment, "Rolling Jim," was delivered with the slave stretched out on his stomach on a log, his feet and hands tied to pegs driven into the log. The master or overseer would then whip the slave with a rawhide strap that cut the flesh or beat him with a paddle that raised blisters. For most slaves, the most potent control was the threat of sale and consequent separation from their families, a threat that was effective: as Davis remembered, "Bless yo' soul, us niggers'd go to work, too." Slaves were frequently sold, and about half were separated from spouses or parents. Selling children away from their mothers at about age ten was common. A British observer lamented, "Such separations as these are quite common, and appear to be no more thought of, by those who enforce them, than the separation of a calf from its brute parent, or a colt from its dam."[48]

Slaves often attended their masters' churches, with segregated seating, sometimes in balconies, unless an overflow of white congregants occurred and the slaves were pushed out entirely. A Baptist publication asserted that "sound religious instruction" for slaves was "the most *efficient police.*" The churches did not tolerate antislavery sentiment. After

Blind Tom Wiggins in London, 1866. Adolph Naudine, carte-de-visite. From the Collection of the Columbus Museum, Georgia; Museum purchase made possible by Daniel P. and Kathelen V. Amos, Julie and Mizell Alexander, Friends of the Museum, and Gift Exchange of Jim and Marge Krum, G.2015.14.5.

the American Baptists split over slavery in 1845, the Columbus church joined the Southern Baptist Convention formed in Augusta. The next year, Columbus Baptists created a Publication Society to censor "works issuing from Europe and the Northern States [that] contain sentiments which are objectionable to the feelings and dangerous to the peace of Southern Churches." The Methodists also divided over slavery, leading to the formation of the Methodist Episcopal Church, South in 1845. Northern-born Daniel Curry, the minister at St. Luke, did not support the split, though the lay members did. He either resigned or was fired and soon became an outspoken abolitionist and critic of the South. He would not be the last minister to be run out of Columbus over race.[49]

Ironically, Columbus's most famous native son in the nineteenth century was a slave, "Blind Tom," who today would be identified as an autistic musical genius. Thomas Wiggins was born on May 25, 1849, on a Muscogee County farm. Eight months later, newspaper editor James Bethune purchased the blind infant, his parents, and two of his sisters. When Tom was four, the family discovered that he could reproduce perfectly any musical piece he heard played on the piano. "Tom the Blind Musician" performed at age eight at Temperance Hall, the beginning of a lifetime of exploitation by white managers. An international sensation, he became the first black musician to perform at the White House when he appeared there in 1859. During the Civil War, Bethune's son, John, took Tom on tour to raise money for the Confederacy. His October 1862 performance at Temperance Hall raised $400 to help "our suffering soldiers."[50]

After emancipation, Bethune had Wiggins declared mentally incompetent and continued to control him. They toured nonstop across Europe and the United States for the next fifteen years, earning the modern equivalent of $5 million to support Bethune's extravagant lifestyle. Victorian audiences, including Mark Twain, loved Wiggins, who played classical pieces as well as music that imitated trains and industrial sounds, rainstorms, and even warfare—his most famous piece was "The Battle of Manassas." Wiggins died of a stroke in 1905; was buried in Brooklyn, New York; and then may have been reinterred on Warm Springs Road in Columbus in 1949, though a debate continues about Wiggins's true resting place. In 2008, he was enshrined in the Columbus Walk of Fame in the historically black neighborhood now called the Liberty District.[51]

Columbus became a major slave-trading center, with three auction houses by 1860 and a fourth market on the Alabama end of the lower bridge. By July 1858, Allen C. McGehee and Samuel J. Hatcher had become Columbus's biggest-volume slave dealers. In 1860, they advertised for sale a "large and well selected stock of **Men, Women, Boys, and Girls,** including Field Hands, House Servants, Mechanics, & c." From April 1858 through April 1860, they sold 465 slaves. Sometimes they sold mothers and children together, but only one transaction in those two years kept a father with his family. Women and children for household labor accounted for almost 70 percent of Hatcher and McGehee's sales. Children were often sold by the pound or by height. Buyers were interested in a young person's physical ability and how soon girls might bear children.[52]

The 1860 census listed 28 Columbus men who owned 20 or more slaves, led by John Woolfolk with 180 and Hines Holt with 118. However, the census figures were self-reported and inaccurate—John Banks, for example, was listed as having no slaves but actually owned about 200, though not all were in Muscogee County. Slave traders were not considered disreputable but were esteemed in the city's elite society. McGehee and Hatcher were Bank of Columbus directors. McGehee and Randolph Mott were involved with the *Wanderer*, which in 1859 became the last ship to bring Africans to Georgia. Though the U.S. Constitution had outlawed the African slave trade half a century earlier, McGehee endorsed a plan put forth by C. A. L. Lamar of Savannah to import African slaves. The men were ardent believers in state's rights and considered Georgia no longer governed by U.S. law. Mott purchased at least one of the Africans who arrived aboard the *Wanderer*. Federal authorities indicted Lamar, McGehee, Mott, and others involved in the scheme, but a sympathetic Savannah jury found them not guilty. Mott's African slave remained in his household even after emancipation.[53]

Support for state's rights grew through the 1850s. At Temperance Hall in late May 1853, John Howard, Seaborn Jones, Henry L. Benning, Martin J. Crawford, and others called for the formation of a southern sectional party. Most saw the move as a prelude to secession. Hines Holt and James Johnson rallied local Unionists. Attorneys Benning and Crawford emerged as leading disunionists. In 1849, Benning had written to a friend, "The only safety of the South from abolition universal is to be found in an *early* dissolution of the union." Benning twice ran unsuccessfully for the legislature before winning election to the Georgia Supreme Court in 1853, becoming the state's youngest justice at age thirty-nine. Crawford, an extreme proponent of state's rights, was elected to Congress in 1854 and five years later declared that it was "folly" to speak of settling the slavery issue and "madness" to consider compromise. In the 1860 election, the state's-righters, led by Jones, Howard, Benning, and Crawford, supported John C. Breckinridge, the pro-slavery Southern Democratic candidate. Holt and Johnson stumped for Constitutional Union candidate John Bell, who advocated compromise to keep the country together. All parties canvassed the streets on election eve to collect floaters and pen them in the hotels. The free flow of liquor and bribes prompted the *Sun* editor to jeer, "Oh, the glorious privilege of the unrestricted right of suffrage and other inestimable blessings of a Christian country!" The

Muscogee County tally was close—769 votes for Breckinridge, 767 for Bell, and 160 for Northern Democratic candidate Stephen A. Douglas, meaning that Unionist candidates won the majority of the votes. But as John Banks glumly wrote in his diary, the "Black Republican" Abraham Lincoln had won the presidency.[54]

When the news of South Carolina's secession arrived on December 23, Columbus celebrated. Militia companies organized, with most prominent young men joining the Columbus Guards or the Southern Guards. The *Times* editor, a fervent secessionist, accused unionist John Winter of encouraging workers to oppose disunion "because secession would produce war, that *'poor men'* will *have to fight* for the slaves of rich men; that they will have no interest in the fight!" Winter, a slaveholder, denied the charge, the first of many defenses he would make for his Unionism. On January 2, 1861, a cold rainy day, Georgia selected delegates for a secession convention. About 200 fewer people voted in Columbus than had turned out in November, perhaps a result of the weather or of a fatalistic sense that secessionists would win. They did, by a tally of 944–459, replicating the 2–1 margin found in every major Georgia city. Benning served on the committee drawing up the ordinance of secession and especially feared a coming racial apocalypse: abolition, he warned, "will excite an intense hatred between the whites on one side, and the slaves and the North on the other. Very soon a war between the whites and the blacks will spontaneously break out . . . a war of extermination." On January 19 the delegates overwhelmingly approved immediate secession.[55]

Columbus celebrated the news with torchlight and militia parades, cannon firings, and speeches. A minority despaired at the Union's dissolution. One man darkened his windows and paced across his parlor, predicting, "Poor fools, they may ring their bells now, but they will wring their hands—yes, and their hearts, too, before they are done with it!" Prior to the convention, the newspapers had split over secession, with the *Times* in favor, the *Enquirer* against, and the two editors of the *Sun* divided; now, however, they united in support. When the news of Fort Sumter's fall in April 1861 arrived by telegraph, Banks noted in his diary that "the people are rejoicing, the bells ringing, cannons firing, drums beating." He admitted "anxiety" about the war, and his foreboding was well founded—the war would cost Banks four of his sons. Columbus volunteers rushed to support the Confederate army. New York native William H. Young, who nonetheless backed the Confederacy, gave $65,000 to outfit an artillery battery. Joe Clark, free black barber and Creek War veteran, asked for permission to raise a company of free blacks. Georgia was not ready to arm black soldiers, but the *Enquirer* praised his patriotism. Columbus women led drives to sell war bonds, sewed and knitted, and collected brass for cannons.[56]

Some citizens, however, resisted the war fever. Winter was also a New Yorker, but citizens questioned his loyalty and feared his clout. A Columbus resident complained to President Jefferson Davis, "The Yankees of this place hold the controlling power." In a February 1861 letter, Winter called secession "a diabolical heresy" and claimed that others in Columbus shared his view, though he dared not express opinions publicly "for this climate is dangerous & I might not be permitted to live." Pressured to clarify his position after the fall of Fort Sumter, Winter explained in a letter to the *Sun* that he had always felt "an ardent veneration" for the Union, "the most precious of all earthly blessings which had ever been vouchsafed to man." But although he had resisted its dissolution, he now believed the Confederacy to be a legitimate government and would obey its laws. At the same time, however, he declared, "When my happiness shall be promoted by a change in residence, I shall *remove*, but *leave no sting behind*." He soon made good on his word, fleeing Columbus.[57]

Winter and other Union supporters who left the city would not be much missed. The white population supported the Confederacy and rabidly united against any threat to slavery. As one Columbus physician explained, "Our slave labor is the source of all our wealth and prosperity; from this we enjoy all the necessaries and luxuries of life, and it is the basis of the most desirable social and political system the world has ever seen." Four years of bloody war would shake those foundations.[58]

CHAPTER 2

The "Last Battle" and "Black Reconstruction"

The Civil War and Its Aftermath

Absalom H. Chappell feared the consequences of the South's secession. A former member of Congress and author of *Miscellanies of Georgia*, his descendants included one of Columbus's most progressive mayors and a succeeding generation of public servants. In December 1860, he wrote to his wife, Rebecca, sister of Mirabeau Lamar, "The perfect stillness of things is like that which prevails in nature just before a mighty earthquake. Never did a mighty empire yet fall to pieces without dreadful convulsions and are we the better than all former peoples that the Almighty should make an exception in our favor? I guess not and this far I see but slight signs of wise forecast on the part of those who have raised the whirlwind and who are taking the lead in ruling the storm." Chappell accurately predicted the "dreadful convulsions" ahead for Columbus. But in December 1860, few shared his forebodings.[1]

The Civil War brought Columbus growth and prosperity unimaginable to the most enthusiastic antebellum boosters. The city, unlike many in the Confederacy, did not suffer food shortages or invasion until the war's end. Perhaps not surprisingly, the elite prospered disproportionately. The city suffered divisions between Confederates and Unionists, the wealthy and the working classes, and ultimately between loyalists to the southern cause and those disaffected with the war. The Battle of Columbus destroyed most industry, but the economy rebounded quickly. Though the federal government granted enslaved Africans their freedom, resurgent white power and violence during Reconstruction constrained their political participation and social mobility.

In 1860, Muscogee was Georgia's third-most-populous county, distinctive because of its industry. Sixteen manufacturing concerns produced almost $1.5 million in goods, the highest per-factory output of any Georgia county and tenth overall in the South. The war boosted industrial production and attracted entrepreneurs who manufactured tents, socks, caps, buttons, paper, guns, gun carriages, belts, and fifes and drums. Merchants used Broad Street stores as factories, with production expanding to the East Commons. The Confederate government authorized local merchant F. W. Dillard to construct a Quartermaster Depot, and it trailed only Richmond in war materiel produced, including uniforms, shoes, wagons, cartridge boxes, harness, and saddles. Most of Dillard's five hundred workers were black. In January 1863, the city council granted permission to house the workers on the East Commons, beginning the neighborhood today called the Liberty District. The Columbus Iron Works began producing cannons in the summer of 1861. Women donated brass lamps, candlesticks, and andirons, which were cast into more than eighty six-pounders, including the Ladies Defender, which was captured by Federal troops at Shiloh and returned to Columbus by the War Department in 1903, and the Red Jacket, which was fired at Jefferson Davis's inauguration. In the absence of public entertainment during the war, large crowds gathered outside the rolling mill each night to watch red-hot scraps of iron put through the rollers. In June 1862, the Confederacy leased the Iron Works and sent Maj. James Warner to operate it as the CS Naval Iron Works. It eventually constructed two ironclads and one wooden gunboat, but they never saw action.[2]

The most important industries were the four textile mills, especially Young's Eagle Manufacturing. Wartime demand increased its production threefold, with the Confederate government purchasing two-thirds of that output. Huge profits allowed the Eagle to distribute $30,000 among its twenty stockholders every six months, making it "the most profitable stock in the Confederacy." Unlike most southern mills, the Eagle did not focus on profiteering. It voluntarily sold its products to the Confederacy at less than half the market price and charged civilians the same low prices until 1863, when the Confederacy contracted for all the factory's output. The Eagle also engendered goodwill by buying $1,000 in Confederate bonds and giving $100 for soldiers' families each month. Early in 1864, the mill built Columbus's first free public school for poor children, prompting the *Times* to declare that poor children "who hitherto have been neglected and permitted to run wild, can now be brought within the pale of civilization, and led on the useful virtuous and honorable paths of

View of Columbus from Girard. *Harper's Weekly*, September 19, 1868.
Hargrett Rare Book and Manuscript Libraries/University of Georgia Libraries.

human existence." A mill worker at the Eagle testified to a Senate committee in the 1880s that "before and during the war those who worked in factories were looked down upon. The people then would think you were worse than a nigger if you worked in a factory." However, the standard of living for the lower class rose somewhat during the war, as labor shortages forced the Eagle to raise wages by 300 percent by 1862.³

Most residents were loyal to the Confederacy in the war's first two years. By 1862, Columbus had sent more than twelve hundred men in eighteen companies into Confederate service. At least fourteen members of Columbus's Jewish community fought, among them Raphael Moses's three sons. Moses himself was too old to fight but became commissary for Georgia, working to feed and supply soldiers, and later filled the same post for Gen. James Longstreet in the Army of Northern Virginia. Moses's nephew spent $10,000 organizing a company of 120. At the breakfast table on Saturday, April 20, 1861, Moses's son, Albert, learned that his company, the City Light Guards, would depart that afternoon. At the depot, the soldiers were met by "an immense concourse of citizens, assembled to bid us 'God Speed.'" The crowd included his sisters and cousins, who had walked several miles into town to see him off because they could not ride on the Sabbath.[4]

On May 21, 1861, members of the Baptist church formed the Ladies' Soldier's Friend Society to supply men at the front. In a typical month in 1861, they raised $1,542 and furnished 2,403 articles of clothing to thirteen companies. Each day, the society provided between one hundred and three hundred meals to passing soldiers. Women working outside their traditional domestic roles provoked criticism. A Columbus man complained about women traveling alone on railroads "where they have no business." In addition, when walking, they held up their dresses "to an exceedingly great height" that was "perfectly disgusting" and had started to shingle their hair in a "disrespectable city cut." Moreover, "some of the ladies, now that there are so few men in the country, are becoming *too familiar* with the few remaining." Despite such opposition, women continued to contribute to the war effort.[5]

Columbus residents also organized for home defense. A February 1862 mass meeting of citizens at Temperance Hall approved the formation of a Committee of Public Safety. Newspaper editorials declared it "inconceivable that we can be beaten" and called on citizens to practice "patience, self-denial, and perseverance" to resist becoming "vassals of a degraded and fanatical population." Reality began to set in by 1863 as the Union blockade caused scarcity, battlefield casualty lists grew, and the Confederacy conscripted soldiers. Although local historical memory tends to present Columbus as unified in its support of the Confederacy, a strong minority supported the Union. Early in the war, Winter listed fifty-seven Columbus men—most of them, like Winter, northern-born—as staunch Unionists. Many were small craftsmen who resented facing competition from skilled slaves. One of Winter's close associates, Virginia-born Randolph Mott, opposed secession but supported slavery and never impeded the Confederate effort. His son served as Gen. Henry Benning's adjutant and his mills supplied Confederate troops as well as civilians. He served on the Committee for Public Safety, probably in part to protect his interests.[6]

Confederate loyalists tolerated little dissent. Judge Alfred Iverson headed the Vigilance Committee, which was formed in August 1861 and held "loyalty hearings" aimed at northern-born citizens. Writing to the *Columbus Sun*, Winter complained that his conflicts with the Vigilance Committee made his children "sick with apprehension" for his safety. He soon fled Columbus, spending much of the war in England and the rest of his life in New York, where he died in 1871. His body was returned for burial in Linwood Cemetery. A former resident said that pressure from the Vigilance Committee drove him to the friendlier environs of Louisville, Kentucky. In the spring of 1861, the committee condemned a traveling theater troupe of young men for not fighting, only to learn that they were furloughed soldiers raising funds for their regiments. In July 1862, a Jewish merchant was arrested for buying cotton with counterfeit Confederate money and was discovered to have $18,000 in counterfeit bills. Confederate patriots questioned his loyalty, suspecting that he was using the counterfeit money to undermine the economy. A majority of the Vigilance Committee resigned when Iverson defended the merchant, and the controversy soon forced Iverson out and led to the committee's disbanding.⁷

Columbus—or at least its wealthy inhabitants—never suffered serious shortages. The *Sun*'s editor declared in the summer of 1863, "There is perhaps no city in the Confederacy that has felt less the deprivations and inconveniences of war." The Union blockade caused some scarcity for all, but the main reasons for growing shortages were speculation, profiteering, and inflation. In March 1863, the Columbus Relief Association wrote to the Confederate secretary of war that "heartless extortionists" were "advancing the prices of all provisions to such rates as to place them beyond the reach of the laboring class and the families of absent soldiers." Confederate currency lost value as wages grew only fourfold but food prices soared by thirty times or more and the costs of rent, clothing, and equipment rose as well. A mechanic complained that although his family ate only bacon, cornmeal, and syrup for a month and he had sold his bed to pay rent, he was $164 in debt. Middle-class families felt deprivation. A minister's daughter wrote gloomily, "Yesterday was my birth day. I did not have any party becaus times are to hard." Her gifts were a squash, a cantaloupe, and a watermelon. The wealthy also complained about rising prices. Laura Beecher Comer, a cousin of Harriet Beecher Stowe, had married a local planter and lived in a big house in the Rose Hill suburb. She was outraged that oysters were $1.25 a dozen and kid gloves $4.00 per pair. But she never went hungry, as wagonloads of produce, chickens, pork, and eggs arrived from the family's Russell County plantation.⁸

By 1863, Columbus had become a refugee center. Gen. William T. Sherman's 1864 campaign pushed wounded soldiers into makeshift hospitals established in what had formerly been Columbus's stores, saloons, churches, and courthouse. The quality of medical care was poor. Doctors knew nothing of sterilization, and treatments were primitive. A physician in nearby Crawford, Alabama, earned a jug of whiskey by "nocking out two front teeth with a hammer & nail." A scarcity of medicines, especially chloroform, morphine, and quinine, meant that home remedies sometimes were used. A cure-all tonic of vinegar and molasses fermented with warm water and nails or iron filings was supposedly so effective that "no second dose was ever needed.... It was enough to show the patient the bottle."[9]

Scarcity and inflation helped the upper class prosper, as businessmen secured lucrative contracts with the state or the Confederacy and many planters continued to grow cotton despite government pleas for food. Cotton prices increased from a dime per pound before the war to one dollar per pound by 1864. Georgia outlawed planting more than three acres of cotton per slave, but planters did as they pleased. In 1862, a local Committee of Public Safety censured Stewart County planter and Confederate secretary of state Robert Toombs for growing hundreds of acres of cotton, prompting him to roar back, "My property, as long as I live, shall never be subject to the orders of those cowardly miscreants, the Committees of Public Safety.... You may rob me in my absence, but you cannot intimidate me." Planters refused to accept low prices offered by the Confederacy and smuggled thousands of bales through the naval blockade or shipped it directly to the North. As it became clear that the Confederacy was doomed, industrialists converted their Confederate bonds into gold and cotton. In January 1865, a buyer reported to industrialist George Parker Swift, who founded Muscogee Mills a year later, on the "demand for specie Exchange as well as Cotton" and promised to ship a new silk dress for Swift's wife, Cornelia, the next day. At the war's end, many elites, including Swift, William H. Young (Eagle Mill), George Waldo Woodruff (Empire Mills), J. P. Illges (Goldens' Foundry, Muscogee Manufacturing, Swift Spinning), Randolph Mott (Palace Mills), John Fontaine (cotton commission merchant and warehousing), and the Straus family (New York's Macy's Department Store) used profits from cotton or other assets hidden from the Confederacy to build postwar fortunes. A few of the wealthy, such as Martin Crawford, condemned planters' profiteering, convinced that "our people are not prepared to pay the purchase price of freedom if planters demand that a poor government ... shall pay them 2 or 3 cts a pound more for their cotton than the markets afford." Col. James Bethune, guardian of Blind Tom Wiggins, declared that upper-class greed was the Yankees' most powerful weapon, especially when contrasted with the hardships of soldiers and their families.[10]

By 1863, common citizens expressed their outrage. The *Columbus Enquirer* attacked speculators, claiming that profiting from the war would forever stain men's honor: "It will pass for robbery of the country at large, of the families of soldiers, of the poor." Anger boiled in letters to the newspapers: "That is right. pile up wealth—no matter whether the bread be drawn from the mouth of the soldier's orphan or the one-armed, one-limbed hero who walks hungry in your streets—take every dollar you can, pay out as little as possible, deprive noble warriors of every comfort and luxury, increase in every way the necesaries of life, make everybody but yourself and nonproducers bear the taxes of war." The condition of women proved a lightning rod for protests. Under the headline "Sympathizer of the Poor," the *Enquirer* printed a letter demanding, "Ye men who take these enormous contracts—pocketing your thousands, while the industrious work woman receives her paltry pittance, for the real labor, ... have ye no hearts? Have ye any shame? Oh, I blush for the land of my birth and for the Southern Confederacy." Ten days later, another writer sneered, "Only think of it. A sleek speculator growing rich by the labor of the poor half-famished needle-woman, who gave up her husband a sacrifice on the altar of our country! ... A Man that will deliberately rob the widow and orphan of their daily bread, that he may add to his opulence. A Man who professes not only to be a patriot but also a Christian. ... How dare such a monster look his fellow man in the face without cowering in very shame?" On April 11, 1863, sixty-five women stormed down Broad Street "to raid the stores of speculators." Armed and shouting curses, they "commenced to helping themselves to whatever they wanted" in a dry goods store. The police broke up the riot, and the *Sun* dismissed the women as vagrants, prostitutes, and thieves. Most observers were more sympathetic, however. One Harris County man opined that the riot "is no more than I expected. ... What will become of the women and children with the food situation?" Seven months later a group of Columbus women warned Governor Joseph Brown that if they got no relief, they again would seize food.[11]

That fall, discontent spilled into politics. The wealthy establishment was shocked when the Mechanic's and Workingmen's Ticket candidates for the October 7 election "prevailed by a very large majority." The *Enquirer* editor criticized workers: "Nothing can be more mischievous in any society than antagonistic organizations of the classes. Such divisions are more bitter in their alienations... and far more apt to produce hurtful collisions." The *Enquirer* and *Sun* proposed reinstating property requirements for voting and holding office, prompting one mechanic to reply that "our class should awake to a sense of their danger." General disaffection with the war spread by 1864, when a Harris County woman urged her brother to desert because "there is so much rascality carried on in this Confearcy." The *Enquirer* reported a "Strange Spectacle" when a young man was "marched through our streets in female apparel, accompanied by a guard." The man had fled to avoid conscription and was arrested in Albany, where he apparently was living as a woman. Flags flown along Broad Street were removed in February 1864 because "the hoisting of flags has played out." The fall of Atlanta provoked open criticism of the Confederate government, with the *Sun* citing "the most reprehensible incompetency on the part of those who mismanaged the affair." By the spring of 1864, merchants refused to accept Confederate currency. Raphael Moses came home in May of that year to gather food for soldiers, believing that "if I could go back to Georgia and speak to the people who had sons, brothers, relatives, and friends suffering for food... I could get supplies." He was therefore stunned when only thirty people attended the Temperance Hall meeting: "I thanked them for their presence and stated when I last spoke in this hall it was to urge the people of Columbus to send their sons and brothers to confront the hazards of war to redress their Country's wrongs; the house was full from Pit to Gallery with Patriotic Citizens ready for the sacrifices asked. Now I come directly from those near and dear to the people here to appeal to them for bread for the starving army, and I am confronted by empty benches!"[12]

Escalating casualties decimated a future generation of leaders. One of Moses's sons, Albert Luria, died at the 1862 Battle of Seven Pines. Gettysburg took banker/planter Paul J. Semmes as well as Seaborn Jones's only son, John. Peyton Colquitt, the son and brother of congressmen, fell at Chickamauga in September 1863. John Banks suffered even worse losses. One of his sons committed suicide in Wynnton in 1862, and three others were killed during the final months of the 1864 Atlanta Campaign, prompting a friend to offer condolences on their "glorious" deaths: "They have saved their honor, gained immortality,... lived for duty—they died at their post.... Compare the cold clay of your sons with the living clay of some skulken from duty! Which is really the living—which the dead?" Such thoughts may have been cold comfort to Banks, whose mind "became clouded" after the war ended.[13]

The war provided a little breathing room for blacks, both free and slave. Many worked in war industries and moved into jobs vacated by white soldiers, working as draymen and teamsters and even clerks and bookkeepers. The *Sun* blasted black labor early in the war, but in the spring of 1864 called it "laudable." Not all black labor was voluntary, however; Confederate authorities impressed hundreds of slaves to build fortifications and repair railroads. With Sherman closing in on Atlanta in June 1864, Confederate Gen. Joseph Johnston ordered "immediate impressment of every able-bodied negro. . . . Each negro will bring with him a blanket, and either an axe, shovel, or pick, and sufficient cooking utensils." Three hundred black laborers were dispatched from Temperance Hall as their wives and sweethearts wept. To answer abolitionist propaganda, the newspapers praised black laborers as "happy and contented."[14]

The loss of control over slaves worried local whites. In September 1864, Columbus's mayor ordered citizens to stop "servants" from having parties. The city council passed an ordinance targeting Negro street peddlers and shopkeepers. Many slaves with absentee owners hired themselves out or ran away. In April 1862, one valley slaveholder found his runaway slave working in a Columbus mechanical shop. A Muscogee county master wrote to Governor Brown complaining that seeing "two or three [slaves] in one whiskey shop" was common. An Atlanta refugee disgustedly wrote to her daughter that the Negroes "generally think them selves free and are eating accordingly." Masters clamped down, though not always with the desired effect. On February 22, 1865, an angry slaveholder struck his slave with the butt of his shotgun. The blow discharged the gun, killing the master. Many slaves understood that change was near. Mary Gladdy of Columbus remembered "the whisperings of the slaves—their talking about the possibility of freedom." People gathered two or three nights a week for secret meetings at which they "would sing, pray, and relate experiences all night long. Their great soul-hungering desire was freedom."[15]

Industrial production eventually made Columbus a Union target. In mid-April 1865, Brig. Gen. James H. Wilson's four-thousand-man cavalry bore down on the city. After three years of sporadic work, Columbus's defenses were only partially completed—two miles of trenches and gun emplacements along a ridge above the Chattahoochee on the Alabama side. The city's fighting men were mostly away on other fronts, so the mayor required all men capable of bearing arms to report for duty. Not all were willing to fight. At least three men were shot for refusing, thus demoralizing others drafted into service. Untrained and inexperienced, "superannuated men and schoolboys" primarily manned the defenses, with 150 convalescing veterans and a few state militiamen stiffening the lines. Between two thousand and three thousand men awaited the attack. On Easter Sunday, April 16, many attended Trinity Episcopal's sunrise service, conducted by Confederate chaplain Charles Quintard, who noted, "All hearts were filled with forebodings of what was to come. The enemy was close at hand." At 2:00 p.m., Wilson's advance troops surprised slaves digging entrenchments on Crawford Road in West Girard. A Union soldier could see "men, women and children in Columbus rushing to and fro ... pointing their spyglasses toward us. ... As soon as we came into view and they saw us on those hills, the bells were set ringing, whistles from factories shrieked their loudest and warning salutes were fired to summon the people to arms." About 8:30, the Federals launched a rare night attack on the semicircle of Confederate defenses. After two hours of "confused firing in the dark," the Tenth Missouri poured through the line. The Federals rushed for the covered upper bridge, illuminated only by buildings in Girard the Confederates had set afire to light the battlefield. Local residents remembered the spectacle as "a sheet of flame on the Chattahoochee." Rumors spread among the city's defenders that the Federals had superior numbers and already held the bridge, the only avenue of escape. Confederates broke and ran, mingling with Federals and entering a "melee at the bridge." Confederate defenders on the Georgia side could not fire for fear of hitting their own men. As the *Enquirer* later described the scene, "Horsemen and footmen, artillery wagons and ambulances were crowded and jammed together in the narrow avenue, which was 'dark as Egypt.' ... How it was that many were not crushed to death in the tumultuous transit of the Chattahoochee seems incomprehensible."[16]

Panic gripped Columbus. One witness reported, "At one place the women and children were running through the streets like people deranged, and the men, with mules and wagons, driving in every direction." Hundreds of defenders ran across the northern railroad bridge to escape capture. Porter Ingram, a volunteer in the battle, ran safely home, hid-

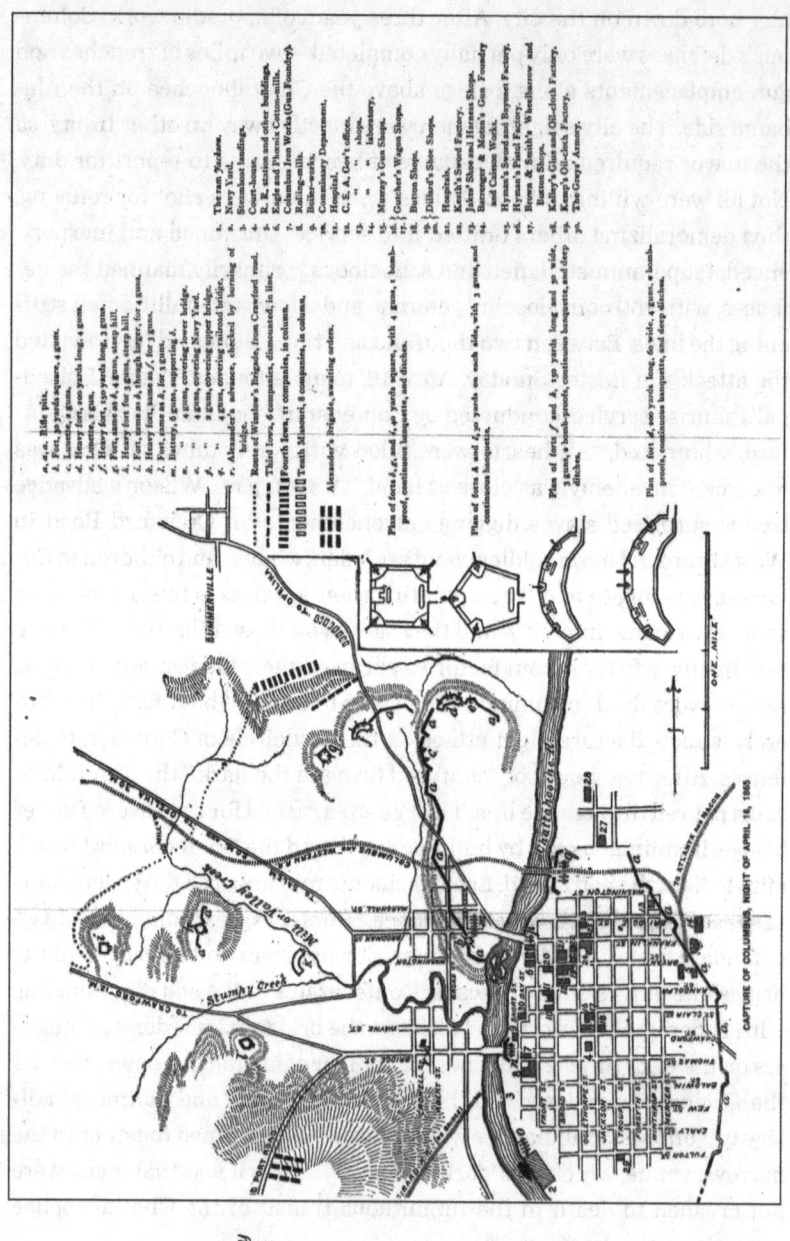

Map of the Battle of Columbus. From William Forse Scott, *The Story of a Cavalry Regiment* (New York: Putnam's, 1893).

ing his gun in the thick shrubbery in front of his neighbor's house. The neighbor, J. Rhodes Browne, Eagle Mill superintendent, supported the Confederacy when he saw war as inevitable, but when he learned that Federal troops had taken the town, he "threw his commission and sword into the well." The Federals quickly ended the fighting, taking about fifteen hundred prisoners. The Union forces reported five dead and thirty wounded and only nine Confederate dead, though the total may have been higher. Wilson crossed the Chattahoochee shortly after 11:00 and spent the night with Unionist Randolph Mott, who boasted that his riverfront house was the only Georgia property not to secede. Local lore says he flew the American flag on the cupola of his house throughout the war, but Wilson later wrote that the flag was inside "the dome" of the house.[17]

The next day, Wilson ordered destruction of all property "that could be made useful for further continuance of the Rebellion." His men burned bridges, textile mills, factories, and all cotton warehouses except Mott's. When Browne learned that the Eagle Mill was to be burned, he asked for leniency. A half-sympathetic officer promised that Browne could try to put out the fire, and the mill would not again be torched, but as Browne later lamented, "the firing was too well done." Federals also lit the ironclad *Jackson* and set it adrift; Confederates had already burned the gunboat *Chattahoochee* to keep it out of enemy hands. Union soldiers wrecked the presses of the secessionist *Sun* and *Times* but not those of the formerly Unionist *Enquirer*. At Wilson's order, U.S. forces allowed Woodruff's Empire Mill and Mott's Palace Mill to keep operating to provide meal for the citizenry. Soldiers burned ardent secessionist Seaborn Jones's City Mills.[18]

Soldiers opened stores along Broad, and citizens joined in the plunder. One local aristocrat characterized the mob as out-of-control "rabble." Two days after the battle, one Union officer described the "thousands of almost pauper citizens and negroes, whose rapacity ... was seemingly insatiable." According to an Ohio cavalryman, "Soldiers are going for the substantials, women for apparel, and the niggers for anything red. There is evident demoralization among the females. They frantically join and jostle in the chaos, and seem crazy for plunder. There are well-dressed ladies in the throng." The train of free blacks and escaped slaves following Wilson's army helped clean out the stores in a single morning, aided by local blacks who rejoiced at the sound of Union cannons. When slaves on Rhodus Walton's plantation heard the battle begin, "they cried joyfully, 'It ain't gonna be long now.'" When W. B. Allen's master told him to pray that God would stop Wilson, the slave refused, saying "flat-footedly that... I not only wanted to be free, but that I wanted to see all the Negroes freed!" Allen declared that God had sent the Yankees as a scourge against the slaveholders.[19]

Nevertheless, Union forces' destruction has been exaggerated. Although an 1898 United Daughters of the Confederacy publication reported that the city had been "sacked and burned," the reality was quite different. Throughout the campaign, Wilson issued strict orders, read daily to his men, that forbade burning, pillaging, and destroying private property. In his memoir Wilson claimed to have been "anxious that the burning warehouses should not set fire to private property and saw that every precaution was taken to keep the fire under control." Still, looting and impressment of livestock and foodstuffs occurred. Federals took hams, sugar, flour, meal, and silver from John Banks's house. One soldier, seeing the family's wealth, marveled, "Just look how many things you Southerners have[.] What did you want to fight for[?]" But had there been wholesale burning of the city, Columbus would not have so many antebellum houses. Convalescing soldier James Howard and a Confederate nurse observed that the Union troops did little damage to nonmilitary private property. Several private dwellings burned, including shanties along today's Dillingham Street and the Albright house at Ninth Street and Front Avenue, but they may accidentally have caught fire when the Iron Works burned. Confederates under Nathan Bedford Forrest's command entered Columbus after the Union troops departed and burned Mott's cotton warehouse. The other two private dwellings burned belonged to men on Winter's list of Unionists.[20] It is unlikely that Federals burned Union sympathizers' homes; the mob may have torched those houses to take revenge on men considered traitors to the cause.

Still, local citizens felt that the apocalypse had come. Thousands of workers were destitute, with the poor collecting burned ears of corn from warehouses. Some soldiers tried to relieve the suffering. A Missouri cavalryman commandeered sacks of meal for poor women and children. After a local woman fed a detachment of Federals, they threw a sack onto her porch, calling, "Sissy, you want some flour?" The family was thrilled—flour cost $400 a barrel. Freedmen flooded into town from the countryside. Wilson ordered forty-five hundred Confederate uniforms, fifty-nine hundred yards of gray flannel, and eighty-eight hundred pairs of army shoes to be issued to his troops and Negro followers. Gen. Benjamin Grierson, passing through after the battle, described "armed marauders, composed mostly of deserters from the late rebel armies," terrorizing residents. Union soldiers provided some security for wealthier homes. Quintard learned on April 17 of "infamous outrages committed in the presence of ladies" in his neighborhood and stormed into town to complain to Gen. Edward McCook, who paced angrily and declared, "If you could identify these men who have committed this outrage, I would hang them in a minute." He ordered a guard for the neighborhood.[21]

The loss of slaves dealt an economic blow to elites. Banks wrote in May 1865, "I owned about two hundred negroes, in which my property mostly consisted. This leaves me poor." He seemed amazed that his slaves did not choose to stay, recording in July, "Celia, who has cooked for me for more than forty years, left me.... George, my body servant has left me. All the negroes about the yard are gone." At the Federals' approach to Rose Hill, Comer wrote that "servant men left frightened with the mules & have not since then been seen." Forty-six of Moses's forty-seven slaves left: Old London, however, stayed until Moses died. A Union general observed, "The wealthy classes are still very bitter... and clutch onto slavery with a lingering hope to save at least a relic of their favorite yet barbarous institution for the future." George Brooks's owner sold him in the fall of 1865, months after war ended, and he learned of his freedom only when his new owner was arrested. Some whites felt relief at the end of slavery: declared Comer, "Slavery is extinct & I am glad of it.... I am glad for the sake of the white race they are free! By their being freed—I am free also."[22]

The Columbus Historical Society fought for two decades in the early twentieth century to commemorate the Battle of Columbus as the last battle of the Civil War. At the society's inaugural meeting in 1915, Charles Jewett Swift declared, "On Sunday night, 16th of April, 1865, the life of the Confederacy went out, and... faded into 'the infinite azure of the past.'" The society's secretary, Alva C. Smith, exchanged letters with Gen. Wilson, securing his endorsement of Columbus as the final battle, and during the 1930s, Smith aggressively pressured the U.S. government for official recognition, pleading with the Army War College, the War Department, the Department of the Interior, and Georgia's senators and representatives to fund a monument in Columbus. A 1938 compromise resulted in a granite marker at the Fourteenth Street Bridge to memorialize the fighting men on both sides but did not gain Columbus the recognition Smith sought. In 1953, the Georgia Historical Commission placed a marker on what is now Veterans Parkway reading, "The last important land battle of the War between the States was fought here on April 16, 1865."[23]

However, Columbus was not the site of the last battle. According to a forty-five-page document the U.S. Department of the Interior sent to the Columbus Historical Society in the 1930s, the fighting at Columbus constituted not a "battle" but merely an "action." The report listed thirty-one military encounters that occurred after the fighting in Columbus and concluded that to concur with "the statement that the battle of Columbus was the last one of the Civil War, would not only be taking a position inviting much controversy, but one very difficult, if not impossible, to maintain by actual evidence."[24]

Columbus's memory of Reconstruction justified a difficult past, painting a lurid picture of "Negro domination" and "Black Reconstruction." Nancy Telfair's 1929 history claims that a "horde of Carpetbaggers, ... whose sole aim was to profit from the ruined country," descended on the city, as "strutting darkies with Federal power on their side, held sway." Moreover, "'scalawags,' low class white Southerners, [were] hand in glove with their Yankee conquerors in stirring up racial hatred." Etta Blanchard Worsley's 1951 *Columbus on the Chattahoochee* similarly argues that Negroes were confused by "bad men, the carpetbaggers from the North ... and the scalawags at home, the turncoats of the lower class, stirring up racial hatred while in search of public offices." Into the 1960s, Columbus schoolchildren internalized the evils of "Black Reconstruction" from textbooks that blamed Republicans for "forc[ing] the Negro domination of the South."[25]

Federal troops occupied Columbus from May 1865 until July 1868 but were generally welcomed to the city as residents feared anarchy and lawlessness. For their part, white occupying troops engendered goodwill by enforcing white Columbus's racial expectations. Beginning in September 1865, soldiers arrested "idle negroes," forcing them to work. Black citizens "with no visible means of support" went into a "chain gang." Civil and military authorities agreed that "no idlers, who can only exist by pilfering and robbery, [would] be allowed to remain in the city, unless they are forced to earn their own bread." The following December, when fears of a freedmen's "Christmas insurrection" swirled across the South, the Union commander allowed local whites to organize two militias of ex-Confederates commanded by former Confederate officers Henry L. Benning and Martin J. Crawford. No insurrection occurred, and the city remained quiet over the holidays. In April 1868, with the occupation nearing its end, the city council thanked the commanding federal officer for his "uniform kindness and courtesy in cooperating with city authorities whenever called upon."[26]

Most former slaves struggled to find adequate food and shelter. The Freedmen's Bureau helped, but its resources were limited. It distributed fewer than one hundred coats and pairs of brogans in Muscogee County in 1867 and did little to resolve complaints about unpaid wages or crop shares. Newspapers complained that too many idle Negroes on the streets of Columbus "loaf, starve, and steal," and soldiers repeatedly aided city authorities in clearing freedmen from East Commons shanties. The *Sun* offered paternalistic sympathy, noting that the freedman was "not responsible for the new career that has been thrust upon him" and concluding that the Negro race will vanish "before the superior genius and prowess of the Anglo-Saxon," just as the "untutored red man" had. Moses eschewed black workers in his fruit orchards, writing to a labor recruiter, "I am satisfied... that one good Scotch laborer will do more work, and do it better, than two of our former slaves or three of the present freedmen."[27]

African Americans nevertheless created vibrant communities and institutions during Reconstruction. Horace King prospered and by 1867 had become an independent contractor with his own black crew, supplying brick, stone, timber, and sawn lumber for construction projects across the Deep South. Columbus's more prosperous African Americans held a Cotillion Party in Temperance Hall in the winter of 1866. Black fraternal organizations such as the Prince Hall Masons, the Chattahoochee Lodge Odd Fellows, and the Broadwell Lodge Free and Accepted Masons provided for members' illnesses and burial as white insurance agencies refused service to colored citizens. The East Commons neighborhood now known as the Liberty District thrived. St. James African Methodist Episcopal Church, organized in 1863, spent $20,000 to construct a grand sanctuary in 1876 and added a Gothic spire and twin turrets a decade later. In August 1865, black congregants left the white-dominated Baptist church and formed the First African Baptist Church, building its sanctuary in 1915. Though most former slaves worked as manual or domestic laborers, African Americans comprised nearly 20 percent of Columbus's retailers and tradespeople in 1873.[28]

Perhaps black citizens' greatest accomplishment was their schools. In January 1866, New England missionary teachers arrived in Columbus to educate black citizens. Though students paid no tuition, seventy-one black parents pledged financial support in November 1866.

Churches and benevolent organizations raised funds for four schoolhouses for about six hundred students, though the facilities were less than adequate. Republican Randolph Mott persuaded the city council to grant two acres of land in the city's northeast corner for a school for ex-slaves. Financed with about $6,500 in federal funds, the missionaries named the two-story wooden school for Massachusetts governor William Claflin. The structure was "by far the finest for school purposes... in this city." The brightest students were identified as future teachers. William Spencer, who went on to become a force for African American education in the coming decades, was schooled at Claflin and eventually taught an "ABC class" there. Columbus whites initially saw black education as positive, but white supremacy soon reigned. As tensions grew, newspapers accused northern teachers of stirring up hatred against white southerners. Elite private schools provided the only education for whites, raising fears that Negro children would surpass their white contemporaries. Public school advocates did not want poor white children "squeezed out." On November 19, 1866, city council member John McIlhenny offered a resolution establishing a white public school system. Under federal pressure in March 1871, the council appropriated $750 to create four three-month colored schools, the first of which opened in Temperance Hall in July 1872. Unlike other southern cities during Reconstruction, Columbus's school board hired black teachers, finding that "the colored people have a strong prejudice in favor of their own color." Officials also found it easier to control black teachers.[29]

From the beginning, black schools were inequitably funded, with white schools receiving three to four times as much support. Though African Americans paid city taxes, those proceeds went to white schools. Black schools were sustained by African Americans' small property taxes; grants from the Peabody Fund, established in 1867 to improve education in the South; and sparse allocations from the state school fund. Pay for black teachers amounted to about half of what white teachers received. In contrast to African American enthusiasm for education, many whites were apathetic. Despite equal numbers of school-age black and white children, African American attendance was higher through the 1880s. Warned the *Enquirer* in 1873, "There can be no doubt that a race among us is making rapid strides towards education, and if the white people would maintain their supremacy, *they must become educated.*"[30]

Lawlessness remained a problem during Reconstruction, with U.S. and former Confederate soldiers prominent among the offenders. Newspapers regularly reported drunkenness and disorder. In October 1865 twenty men in gray and blue uniforms appeared at a white man's home in East Wynnton and "hung him four times from a tree, each time until he was insensible, in order to exhort from him where his money was." They ultimately took his guns as well as $220 in gold and nearly $1,000 in currency. In the tense days before Christmas 1865, locals downtown heard a riot on what is now First Avenue and feared that a freedmen's insurrection had begun: the commotion turned out to be drunken whites tearing down fences, yelling obscenities, and throwing bricks while they caroused. Tensions escalated in early February 1866 when a company of African American troops arrived. Aristocratic former Confederate Cooper Lindsay shot a black soldier who had supposedly jostled Lindsay. The white lieutenant arrested Lindsay, but a mob of a thousand whites forced his release. With the mob threatening to attack the Negro soldiers, white officers ordered them to return to their barracks, but gunfire from both sides filled the afternoon. Unreconstructed rebel Robert Howard later remembered, "But for the pleading of many older and influential citizens of the city, the entire garrison would have been annihilated that night." Near dusk, a random shot struck the leg of Maj. James Warner, the former head of the Confederate Naval Iron Works, as he was passing by; infection set in, and he died a few days later. The *Enquirer* deplored the violence, but blamed it on the federal officers' "inability to control the men under their command." Columbus's most prominent Republicans, including Mott and James Johnson, met with military officials to demand black troops' removal, and the garrison left on February 23, ending the three-week "Negro domination" of Columbus.[31]

Black Reconstruction was equally ineffectual on the political level. Most of the few Republicans who held local office in the immediate postwar years were homegrown white men such as Mott. He supported the moderate agenda, often allying with conservative Georgia Democrats. Two local black ministers held political posts: Van Jones served as a delegate to the 1867 Constitutional Convention, while Abram Smith won election to the General Assembly in April 1868 but served only until September, when moderate Republicans joined white Democrats to expel all Negro legislators. Gen. John Pope, Georgia's supervisor under the

March 1867 Reconstruction Act, mandated that each state senatorial district have a three-man federal voter registration board that included at least one black member, meaning that the Muscogee County's district would have had at least one black registrar. Beyond those posts, however, Columbus-area African Americans held no offices during Reconstruction.[32]

Organized white resistance tamped down black and Republican political aspirations, as Telfair describes: "By intimidation and a thousand and one kinds of indirect influence, the negro was made to feel that his sphere was the field, not politics, and that polling places were not healthy resorts for black men." Georgia's 1868 poll tax effectively disfranchised blacks, and the number of registered black voters plummeted. Violent intimidation forced African Americans into their "sphere." The Reconstruction Act placed Georgia and the other southern states under military rule, requiring that they adopt new constitutions and ratify the Fourteenth Amendment, which granted citizenship rights to the former slaves, to regain entry into the Union. Outnumbered at the polls, most Columbus whites boycotted the November 1867 election for delegates to the constitutional convention. The convention, held in Atlanta in March 1868, was dominated by Radical Republicans and produced a constitution guaranteeing freedmen's rights, including suffrage, which provoked a power struggle in Columbus. The Radicals believed that Georgia should cooperate with the federal government and approve the new constitution, while Democrats pledged to fight "Carpetbaggers, Scalawags, and Negroes."[33]

Nathan Bedford Forrest, the former Confederate general who became the first Imperial Wizard of the Ku Klux Klan, came to Columbus on March 13. Soon thereafter, newspapers began printing vivid daily warnings to Scalawags, calling them traitors who sought "to secure the domination of the negro over the white man." The most hated local Scalawag was George W. Ashburn, a North Carolina native who had lived in Georgia for three decades and in Columbus at least since 1856. After fighting in the Union army, Ashburn returned to Columbus and chaired Georgia's 1867 Constitutional Convention, apparently hoping to win a seat in the state legislature in April 1868 and perhaps even aspiring to a post in the U.S. Senate. The *Sun*'s editor nicknamed him Stinkee but also feared and grudgingly admired him. Just before the Constitutional Convention, the paper declared that Ashburn "is today the ablest, most adroit and influential man, black or white, in the radical ranks in Georgia. Resolute in purpose, unscrupulous as to means, and sustained by the

The murder of George W. Ashburn. From "The Ku Klux Klan at Work—the Assassination of the Hon. G. W. Ashburn, in Columbus, Georgia," *Frank Leslie's Illustrated*, Apr. 25, 1868.

chief managers in Washington, he is bound to be the leader in [the] convention.... To those who doubt the ability of 'Stinkee,'... we would say that he has ruled the niggers and white men of his party in this section alike with a rod of iron."[34]

Anxieties grew as the April 20 constitutional referendum approached. At Temperance Hall on March 30, Ashburn attended a Republican rally featuring the fiery black Radical Henry McNeal Turner. Just after midnight, masked men broke into Ashburn's room and killed him in a hail of gunfire. The white leader of the local Union League and two "notorious" women—a white seventeen-year-old and a mulatto in whose name the house had been rented—witnessed the murder and identified the killers as prominent young white men. However, a coroner's jury concluded the next day that Ashburn had been killed "by persons unknown." The newspaper refused to print the names of those accused, asserting, "That respectable white men should as a body plan murder was incredible, and the suggestion was cast aside as unworthy of credence for a second."[35]

Gen. George Meade, Georgia's second military commander, sent an army captain to investigate. Local authorities would not cooperate, so Meade suspended Columbus's civil government and appointed Mott mayor pro tem. On April 6, military authorities began arresting suspects—young men from Columbus's finest families active in the local Democratic Party. Twelve were ultimately charged with the assassination. Their incarceration and trial before a military commission at Fort McPherson electrified Georgia's conservative Democrats. Ladies from Columbus and Atlanta brought the men "delicacies," then returned home to spread stories of the abuse of the "Columbus prisoners." The military trial began on June 29 and ended abruptly on July 22. A day earlier, Radical Republicans had used the trial to force moderate Republicans and Democrats to approve the Fourteenth Amendment, prompting Meade to suspend the trial on the grounds of "the probable immediate admission of the state of Georgia [to the Union] and consequent cessation of military authority." He returned the prisoners to Columbus, where they were hailed as heroes. City authorities promptly dropped the case.[36]

Ashburn's assassination had a chilling effect on Columbus Republicans. Many of his white Radical colleagues fled town. Politically active African Americans went underground. As one local Republican wrote to the *New York Tribune*, "Union men all over the city now feel their lives are at every moment in danger. They do not know at what hour they may be massacred in their bed." Conservatives used intimidation, fraud, and violence to regain control in the November 1868 presidential election. The Klan and other groups terrorized black and white Republicans across Southwest Georgia. The most deadly encounter was September's Camilla Massacre, where whites fired into a political rally and killed at least nine blacks. The Freedmen's Bureau reported that between January 1 and November 15, 1868, the Columbus district saw twenty-five murders and assaults on freedmen. With no secret ballot, African Americans bold enough to vote for Republican Ulysses S. Grant risked assault. Those who voted for Democratic candidate Horatio Seymour, however, "would be assured of work."[37]

The November 1868 election provoked significant conflict. By the beginning of the month, 3,757 whites and 5,258 blacks had registered to vote in Muscogee County, and on Election Day, many freedmen came into town to vote. According to the *Columbus Enquirer*, they freely crossed the bridge from Alabama, resulting in "good reason to believe that many Negroes voted in both states." Moreover, the paper asserted, because hated Republican governor Rufus Bullock had ordered each courthouse to have multiple ballot boxes, blacks could "vote under different names at two or three of the boxes in the same locality." An agent for the Freedmen's Bureau reported that although Bullock had suspended collection of the poll tax, black voters were rejected for nonpayment. Democrats recruited minors, repeaters, and Alabamians to stuff ballot boxes, easily carrying the day, and as wealthy businessman Lambert Spencer wrote after the city elections the next spring, "we are at last to be relieved of the Scalawag [Mott].... The Radicals did not show fight at all. Negro vote rather small." In 1870 and 1872, a few black candidates ran for local offices, but none finished higher than third place. By 1875, white Democrats firmly controlled the black vote, leading the *Enquirer* to declare, "The negroes made a good deal of money in the election yesterday. They sold themselves cheaply."[38]

Whites used the historical memory of Ashburn's murder and the Columbus prisoners' trial to justify their actions during and after Reconstruction. The day after Ashburn's murder, the *Columbus Sun* described him as "ignorant, energetic, vain, unscrupulous, cruel, malignant, and vindictive." He had been "corrupted by a life of crime" and had become "the most dangerous man to the peace and good order of society it has ever been our misfortune to meet." The article constituted the opening volley in a campaign to demonize Ashburn that came to include a fusillade of rumors about his character and cause of death. He was living in "a colored bawdy house" and had supposedly had a falling out with his fellow Radicals that, the newspaper insinuated, had led them to kill him. Nearly every local account characterized Ashburn as the "lowest sort of white man." Writing more than sixty years later, Telfair declared that the "better class of people" had decided that he constituted "a public nuisance and menace" who "must be gotten out of town," and she defended the Klan as having organized "to take charge of such legally protected scoundrels as Ashburn." Such rationalizations of white terrorism continued for many more years: in the 1940s, Georgia Supreme Court justice Sterling Price Gilbert of Columbus saw the Klan as akin to the World War II "'underground,'... working to restore order and protection."[39]

But of course, conservatives' real objection to Ashburn was his advocacy of African American rights, and other sources paint a different picture of the man. Methodist bishop J. H. Caldwell of LaGrange, a fellow Scalawag and Radical Republican, who knew Ashburn for years before the war, served with him in the 1867 Constitutional Convention, and was in Columbus the night of his death, described him as "among the very few men in Georgia who openly resisted the secession mania all through the war." Caldwell called Ashburn "a very clever, kind man, and I never heard anything against his character personally." Ashburn had been staying in the brothel only because he was refused a room at the local hotel, and Caldwell denied that his friend had had any altercation with other Radicals: Ashburn was "a martyr to liberty," killed by the Ku Klux Klan. Ashburn, like other Republican and Democratic politicians of his day, likely was power-hungry and willing to let ends justify means, but Caldwell's description shows a man of strong moral convictions driven by an antiplanter class consciousness. When Georgia seceded, Ashburn organized a company of southerners to fight for the Union, a move guaranteed to make him an outcast among his neighbors. In letters to the local newspapers, he urged all to "stand firm... until the hydra-headed monster, *slave aristocracy*, shall not only be slain but buried." British journalist David Rose's description of him as a "principled would-be statesman" goes too far, but so do the portrayals of him as an adulterous, manipulative, dangerous opportunist. To local apologists, Ashburn had to be vilified to justify the subsequent oppression of African Americans. The reality of Columbus's Reconstruction was that military rule was short and mostly cordial for local whites, who only briefly lost control of city government. Local historians perpetuated myths of Black Reconstruction to justify the subsequent racial order, portraying white supremacy as a rescue from anarchy and the domination of corrupt Carpetbaggers, manipulative Scalawags, and ignorant Negroes.[40]

In its first edition published after the Battle of Columbus, the *Sun* mourned a "dirty" city where "empty shelves were the chief commodity." It predicted an upturn "as soon as the river rises," but economic recovery was already under way. The Columbus Iron Works was back in business by the beginning of June 1865, casting kettles, household goods, and machinery parts. Broad Street business returned at around the same time. The Eagle Drug Store owners, including John Pemberton, who went on to invent Coca-Cola, appealed for the return of furniture, equipment, and formula books taken by looters. The *Sun* reported in October, "Never has the business of Columbus been more active.... Never were the prospects of the city more bright and hopeful. Do not listen to the croakers. There's a better day coming, and what we daily see—the numerous wagons in the streets, the absence of idle negroes and the general life and industry in every department of trade are not illusions, but facts—the beginning of a happy and permanent prosperity."[41]

Owning most of the waterfront, the Eagle Mill had waterpower, an ample labor supply, market demand, and capital. It and other businesses put unemployed locals to work cleaning burned brick. Former soldier James Howard earned forty cents per thousand at the Lowell warehouse: though he said he "wore the ends of my fingers off," he was grateful for the work. Mill superintendent J. Rhodes Browne took the loyalty oath in November 1865, ready to resume operations, but William H. Young refused to rehire him and named G. Gunby Jordan as the new manager. Browne then sued for lost wages and won, becoming an implacable foe of the company. With Young still in charge, the mill's stockholders reorganized as the Eagle & Phenix and in 1866–1867 rebuilt Mill No. 1 on the old foundation. The new five-story facility was larger than the old Eagle and Howard mills combined. Clapp's Factory rebuilt and ran twenty-five hundred spindles by 1867. In 1866, Massachusetts native and longtime Georgia resident George Parker Swift built Muscogee Mills on the Carter Factory site on water lot 1, and business picked up quickly. Swift's partner, Louis Hamburger, lining up customers in New York in 1866, reported on a species of reverse Carpetbaggers: "Trade here is very brisk, the whole City is full of Southerners."[42]

In the immediate postwar period, Columbus developed two dynasties, one centered on Young, Jordan, and W. C. Bradley, the other on Swift and Browne. They and their allies ran banks, railroads, and industries but, with the exception of Jordan, rarely mixed businesses. The rivalry extended into politics. Young's faction controlled local politics, and those on the outside saw the powerful Eagle & Phenix as their primary enemy, with Raphael Moses leading the fight against Young's "grasping monopoly." When Young's 1878 congressional candidate launched an anti-Semitic attack, Moses responded, "I feel it an honor to be of a race whom persecution can not crush, whom prejudice has in vain endeavored to subdue." In 1877, the city council passed an ordinance requiring men who did not own property to pay a two-dollar poll tax, prompting the *Enquirer* to declare such "a capital against labor fight" "unfair, unjust, and oppressive." By the editor's calculations, at least eight hundred of the city's one thousand voters were "small merchants, clerks, mechanics, and laboring men" without real estate—"the real tax payers" who rented stores and houses from the wealthy. The state also disfranchised black voters by instituting a cumulative poll tax that required payment of all previous years' levies before a ballot could be cast. The strategy was effective: in 1880, only eighty-seven of Columbus's voting-age African American men, most of them skilled workers, were registered to vote, and the number fell to eighty-three a decade later. And according to African American Columbus blacksmith Robert W. Williams, even when colored men voted, their ballots were "nailed to the bottom of the ballot-box, and they have never been drawn out in this county." Over that same period, the number of white voters nearly doubled to around nine hundred. Candidates still "penned" their supporters, plying them with whiskey the night before and marching them to the polls on election morning while women remained locked inside their houses. Blacks, too, avoided appearing in public. Williams said that African Americans thought it best to stay away from whites at election time because "there's death in the pot then."[43]

Columbus's postwar business elite became increasingly diverse. For example, whereas 80 percent had been native southerners in 1850, just two-thirds were southern-born thirty years later. By the early 1870s, Columbus boasted six cotton mills, eight iron foundries, an agricultural implements factory, a cotton gin manufacturer, a brewery, three carriage manufacturers, twenty-four shoe and boot makers, and four furniture works. The city embraced the postwar railroad craze, with five routes proposed. But the 1873 national financial panic led to a six-year depression, reversing much of Columbus's economic diversification. Construction at the local end of three railroads never began, and the other two went into receivership, leaving Macon the only significant city to which Columbus had a direct connection, a crippling weakness. Many small businesses closed or left. Investors ditched plans for at least three new textile mills, and the remaining mills cut hours and wages by 10 percent. During the 1870s, the value of local manufacturing, excluding textiles, declined by 20 percent and total number of manufacturing establishments fell from 108 to 64.[44]

Textiles boomed, however, expanding 339 percent from 1870 to 1880. The Eagle & Phenix added a huge third mill in 1878 and for a time ranked as the largest textile factory in the South. The scale of the construction amazed the community, leading brick masons working on the edifice to post a sign that read, "300 feet long. Please don't ask any more questions." Young gave engineer John Hill a free hand, and the Illinois native devised new machinery, installed electric lights a year after their invention, and developed one of the first automatic sprinkler systems in the country. In 1882, he designed and erected a stone dam that stood for 130 years. By

1880 the Eagle & Phenix's annual output was worth $1.5 million, 80 percent of all textiles produced in Muscogee County. It employed 63 percent of the town's industrial workers and controlled 95 percent of the waterpower. In 1880, Muscogee Manufacturing expanded with Mill No. 2, which historian John Lupold describes as "one of the finest examples of New South industrial architecture. The keystones over its windows bore letters proudly spelling out the name of the company." In 1885, Swift installed the first local arc light dynamo. When the switch was flipped, hundreds thronged Broad Street to see the new lights. In 1887, Muscogee Manufacturing built a third mill. In 1882, Swift's son, William, started a small weaving operation in Temperance Hall; the next year, it became Swift Manufacturing and moved to present Sixth Avenue on the East Commons. By 1899, seven cotton mills ran nearly one hundred thousand spindles. The mills' success reflected national trends toward consolidation into large economic units and regional specialization. But as Young declared in 1883, the rest of the state and country considered Columbus "outside of civilization," so "we have to take care of ourselves." Young's waterfront domination stifled industrial development, resulting in inefficient use of the river. The city's isolation in extreme western Georgia with poor rail connections made outside capitalists reluctant to invest. The mills remained locally owned until after World War II, and no new mills were built in the textile-saturated city. Nevertheless, most of Columbus remained content to ride the wave of textile prosperity and did not see the dark clouds looming on the horizon.[45]

CHAPTER 3

"Plethoric, Laborious, Well-Fed, Jolly, and Complacent"

Politics and Economics, 1880–1920

Columbus writhed in the throes of economic depression by the late nineteenth century. Though the city had quickly rebounded after the Civil War, economic downturns and lack of unified political leadership led to an unhealthy dependence on textiles. The community was divided, with members of the various factions hurling charges of corruption and municipal mismanagement at each other. Tension between workers and millowners mounted. The river stank with human and industrial waste, and factory smokestacks spewed toxins. Still, boosters published hyperbolic propaganda to attract business. An 1892 book declared the view of the Chattahoochee from Phenix City's hills "as sublime and imposing in its grandeur as the Yosemite valley" and offered a dubious take on air pollution: "The smoke-stacks of industry rising at countless points, form a forest of progress, while the clouds of smoke vomited from their untiring throats bathe the city in vapory folds, and seem climbing one on top of the other to kiss the 'God of Day.'" Odder still, the "native Columbusonian... is always florid, plethoric, laborious, well-fed, jolly, and complacent. He works like a drayhorse in daylight and is a profound sleeper at night—open, loquacious, liberal, he patronizes church festivals, and while yet a beau, congregates in scores at club dances. He is... a deuced clever fellow [who] takes great interest in politics, but never allows public matters to interfere with business."[1]

Residents were hardly liberal in the modern sense, as the local response to Union veteran Alfred R. Calhoun's 1873 purchase of the *Columbus Enquirer* demonstrated. Although the Philadelphian sought to help Columbus improve, one of his first editorials provoked anger by criticizing women for "wearing New York or Paris fashions when they should be wearing cloth from Columbus's own mills." He crossed the Rubicon nine months later expressing his "unspeakable contempt" for southerners' ongoing refusal to celebrate Independence Day in the wake of the Confederacy's losses at Vicksburg and Gettysburg on July 4, 1863. Calhoun unloaded on a local man who blamed the South's problems on the North's oppression, declaring that southerners bore responsibility for their present sad state: the South has "fed on delusions" and "is a century behind the North." In Calhoun's view, the South's ills resulted from "too much talk about the balderdash and buncombe of 'Southern chivalry,' and too few schools, too few well-cultivated farms, and too few good roads." Facing numerous death threats and other forms of abuse, Calhoun fled to Philadelphia, predicting that "the South will be the tattered, cotton-stuffed footstool of the civilized world" as long as it rejected viewpoints different from "the sons of Southern chivalry." The incident would not constitute the last time Columbus rejected outside efforts to promote change.[2]

By 1888, the savings bank that William H. Young had started for his workers thirty-two years earlier had more than $1.2 million in deposits. The war had killed the Bank of Columbus, but new banks subsequently formed. In 1871, *Enquirer* publisher William Salisbury formed the Merchants and Mechanics Bank. J. Rhodes Browne, a former Eagle Mill superintendent and president of the Georgia Home Insurance Company, organized the First National Bank in 1876. Gunby Jordan established the Third National Bank in 1888 and renamed the Eagle & Phenix bank the Columbus Savings Bank in 1889. Under the guidance of W. C. Bradley, the city's leading entrepreneur in the first half of the twentieth century, these two institutions merged into Columbus Bank and Trust in 1930. Thomas E. Blanchard, who made a fortune in dry goods, steamboats, and cotton factoring, founded the Fourth National Bank in 1892 and served as its president for three decades, until Trust Company Bank of Atlanta absorbed it in the 1930s. It eventually became SunTrust Bank.[3]

Improved access to capital helped industry and retail establishments. Though smaller iron foundries died in the 1870s depression, the Columbus Iron Works prospered, becoming the largest in the state. With W. Riley Brown as president and George Golden as superintendent, the foundry turned out stoves, kettles, sawmills, cotton gin parts, and steam engines. Although a local myth claims incorrectly that the Iron Works manufactured the first commercial ice machine, its Stratton absorption ice machine was probably the most successful such machine in the late nineteenth century, setting "a standard of excellence." A 1902 fire destroyed the Iron Works, and its new owners failed to keep up with technological advances. After Golden's death in 1880, his sons, Porter and Theodore, formed Golden Brothers foundry on Sixth Avenue. In 1899 local entrepreneur A. Illges became a major stockholder in the reorganized Goldens' Foundry, and he served as its president until his death in 1915. Innovations based on Theodore Golden's patents helped it thrive.[4]

Two gristmills operated profitably in the late nineteenth century. Empire Mills at present Ninth Street and Front Avenue survived the war, and Connecticut native and longtime local merchant George W. Woodruff bought the mill in 1865, soon dominating the local market. It was the city's largest gristmill through the 1880s. Woodruff retired in 1904, and A. Illges bought the majority of its stock. The mill operated into the 1930s. After Seaborn Jones's death in 1864, African American contractor Horace King, "with the excellence that always characterizes his work," rebuilt City Mills, Columbus's oldest business, in 1869. George Pearce worked at the mill for years before buying it in 1885. In 1890, he built a modern flour mill beside King's corn mill. Illges became its major stockholder as well. The new mill never flourished because it could not compete with mass-produced Midwest flour flooding the country. City Mills focused on cornmeal, grits, and animal feeds, with moderate success. In March 1872, Randolph Mott's Palace Mills burned, leading embittered Confederates to rejoice at the former Unionist's misfortune. Mott did not rebuild, selling the property to the Eagle & Phenix, which consolidated its hold on all water lots except no. 1.[5]

After the panic of 1873, Columbus continued to suffer from its lack of rail connections. Prominent businessmen tried to build lines north to Atlanta, south to Mobile and Florida, and west to Mississippi, but none had any success. Gunby Jordan stepped into the breech. His brother later said that he "wanted a railroad and he built it. As a matter of fact, he built two railroads"—the Midland and Gulf Railroad, which sought to connect Columbus to Atlanta beginning in 1881, and the Columbus and Florida Railway (later the Columbus Southern), which opened in 1887 and ran through Valdosta into Florida. But the Midland and Gulf never got closer to Atlanta than McDonough and went bankrupt in 1895, while the Columbus Southern built only eighty-eight miles of track, reaching Albany, and was bought by the Seaboard Air Line in 1897. Columbus remained isolated in far western Georgia.[6]

Though railroads were the wave of the future, local leaders still focused on river trade. The late nineteenth century was the heyday of steamboating on the Chattahoochee, with the amount of cotton passing through the city via the river doubling to 20 percent of the total bales warehoused in Columbus by the early 1880s. The *Enquirer-Sun* editor started what became a long-running fight with Atlanta, claiming that the booming metropolis sucked in too much of the river, wasting seven million gallons of water a day and leaving boats unable to "come within many miles of Columbus" and the textile mills without power. The end of riverboating came quickly. The People's Line and Central Line went out of business in 1899, and the remaining steamboat companies merged into a monopoly controlled by W. C. Bradley of the Merchants and Planters line. By 1914, railroads carried 90 percent of the cotton that passed through Columbus. Trucks and improved roads also took trade from the river. Bradley donated his three remaining steamboats to the chamber of commerce in 1918, but during high water in 1923, they broke loose from the city wharf, drifted downriver, and sank.[7]

Broad Street remained the city's main commercial artery, with wagons, buggies, horses, and mules kicking up dust as businessmen, laborers, and consumers bustled on wooden sidewalks. By the turn of the twentieth century, Columbus boasted 622 retail businesses with more than $9 million in annual trade, most of it in groceries. The largest wholesale grocer was Bradley and Carter. W. C. Bradley had come from his native Russell County to Columbus in 1882 to clerk for a cotton factor. Two years later, he and his brother-in-law, Samuel A. Carter, bought the business. Bradley married the daughter of a steamship mogul in 1887, bought out his partner in 1895, and formed the W. C. Bradley Company. Bradley became one of the city's leading entrepreneurs, and the company engaged in a variety of interests: wholesale groceries for cotton planters; "Chattahoochee Guano"—high-grade fertilizer manufactured from seabirds' excrement mixed with phosphorous; and cotton warehouses that lined Front Avenue.[8]

The drug business also accounted for a fair share of Columbus commerce. By the 1890s, two wholesale and eighteen retail drug firms pulled in $682,000 a year. A. M. Brannon founded his drugstore on Broad in 1859, and the family ran the business for eighty-five years. John Pemberton served as an associate there for a time. Future mayor H. C. Smith opened his first pharmacy in 1907 and eventually operated six drugstores in Columbus and Phenix City. Dry goods were the second largest mercantile category. Irish native Joseph Kyle opened a dry goods store on Broad in 1838, with his nephew, James P. Kyle, joining the business after the war. By the late 1800s, J. Kyle's had become a dry goods wholesaler, with its own brand of pants and jackets, Ironclad. The Kyles invested their wealth in textiles, banks, railroads, and real estate. Columbus native J. Albert Kirven opened Kirven's, another icon, on Broad Street in 1876. The establishment moved near the corner of Broad and Twelfth Streets eight years later and subsequently expanded until it occupied four floors and half the block between Broad and First Avenue. Kirven added departments for ready-to-wear clothing and hats and in 1890 hired the city's first female sales clerks. The self-proclaimed Emporium of Fashion, Kirven's promised "the Highest Quality, the Most Select Stock, and Always the Lowest Prices." Opening in 1884, Chancellor's men's clothing store on Broad was more upscale, offering "high class merchant tailoring" for "prudent men." Chancellor's remained in the family's hands until the first decade of the twenty-first century and by 2019 was the only historic retail business still on Broadway.[9]

Most of Columbus's prewar Jewish merchants left the city by 1870. Thomasville and Talbotton attempted to expel Jewish merchants during the Civil War, so the Straus family of Talbotton, the county's only Jews, came to Columbus in 1863. They moved to Philadelphia in 1865 and from there to New York, where they acquired Macy's Department Store. Anti-Semitism apparently was not the primary factor in their departure. The *Columbus Enquirer* expressed no overt anti-Semitism in the postwar years and in December 1865 reprinted a Chicago article praising Jews as "the moral and intellectual and artistic teachers of the world." When Jewish women held an 1886 fair to raise funds for a new temple, the *Enquirer-Sun* urged citizens to attend. When the fair opened, the mayor described the Jewish community as ever ready to help its neighbors and asked the public to respond "with open-handed liberality" in supporting "an ornament" to Columbus. Raphael Moses never mentioned open discrimination in his autobiography and had no shortage of legal clients. Rebecca Dessau kept her millinery shop on Broad until 1875, when she moved it next to her home in Rose Hill. The Reconstruction-era Ku Klux Klan, unlike its early twentieth century descendant, did not harass Jewish merchants: as historian Stephen Whitfield asks, "Who else would have sold Klansmen their denim, their shoes, and even their sheets?" Howard Rabinowitz argues that the late nineteenth-century South was among the nation's least anti-Semitic regions, at least outwardly accepting all white southern men as equals. Perhaps that explains the influx of Jewish peddlers and merchants to Columbus by the 1880s.[10]

Most prewar merchants were assimilated Germanic Jews, who continued to account for a good portion of postwar Columbus merchants even as Eastern European anti-Semitism in the late nineteenth century pushed between forty and fifty Russian and Polish Jewish families to Columbus by the 1880s. The newcomers settled on both sides of Fourth Avenue between Eighth and Ninth Streets. Those who did not speak English or lacked formal education often started as peddlers, carrying goods to the countryside on their backs or in mule-drawn wagons and selling their merchandise to black and white farm families. Most were Orthodox and faced difficulties in keeping kosher. One peddler lived on hard-boiled eggs, homemade pumpernickel bread, and coffee, refusing farm wives' biscuits because they contained lard. Many Christians made fun of the unassimilated Ashkenazi peddlers, with young boys hollering epithets and throwing rocks. The two Jewish factions stayed within their own communities, worshipping separately and avoiding intermarriage and interaction.[11]

At the turn of the twentieth century, at least fifteen Jewish merchants in Columbus operated dry goods stores, with others in groceries, hardware, jewelry, and livestock. Netherlands-born Moses Simon arrived in Columbus by 1870 and by 1886 owned a general merchandise store in what is now the Liberty District. Jewish merchants commonly acted as middlemen, serving African American customers unwelcome at other white-owned stores. Despite the religious and cultural differences between Christians and Jews, skin color brought Jews some fundamental privileges, but they also had to walk a fine line in obeying Jim Crow system rules. Still, Jewish merchants often earned a reputation for treating African Americans with more respect than other whites did, possibly because of their shared experiences with discrimination. Jewish merchants were often the only ones willing to extend credit to African Americans. In addition to following the racial caste system, Jewish stores had to open on Saturdays, though many closed for religious holidays. Moses Simons's eldest son, Max, opened M. Simons & Co. Grocers on Broad Street in 1889, moving in 1894 into larger quarters at the northwest corner of Broad and Eleventh Street and adding a saloon. When Max Simons died at age forty in 1907, the *Enquirer-Sun* called him an "esteemed citizen" of the city, and Rhodes Browne, who was elected mayor later that year, was an honorary pallbearer. Max's fourteen-year-old son, Sidney, left school to provide for the family, and by the 1920s, he had become a wealthy business owner.[12]

David Rothschild started a wholesale dry goods company on Broad in 1886, sending his salesmen into the countryside in horse-drawn wagons. By the 1940s, the company specialized in custom upholstery and drapery fabrics, and 133 years after its founding, the company was still headquartered in downtown Columbus. Solomon Loeb arrived in Columbus from Bavaria in 1869 to join his brother-in-law in a dry goods store that evolved into a wholesale grocery and liquor business. After his partner died, it became the Sol Loeb Wholesale Grocery Company, and in 1944, it moved into a large warehouse at the corner of Ninth Street and Front Avenue that his descendants operated for decades. In 2001, it was renovated to house the Columbus Visitors Bureau. Simon Schwob, a tailor from Alsace, came to Columbus in 1911 and the next year opened the Standard Tailoring Company, which sold twenty-nine suits on its first Saturday in business. Schwob operated from several locations on Broadway until establishing the Schwobilt factory, home office, and retail store in the 900 block. By 1950, the company produced four thousand suits each week and boasted, "Schwobilt Suits the South." Simon and his wife, Ruth, contributed millions for the Schwob Library and Schwob School of Music at Columbus State University. Lithuanians Max and Frank Cohn landed in Columbus soon after the turn of the century, with Max opening a clothing store, and Frank starting a scrap metal business. They brought their brother, Sam, to Columbus in 1906, and he established a profitable horse- and mule-trading business, with a brick stable at Front Avenue and Eleventh Street. Cohn sold livestock to wealthy plantation owners as well as to black and white sharecroppers, often carrying poor farmers' debts for years. His son, Aaron, later served forty-six years as a Muscogee County juvenile court judge, where he was known for having a soft spot for those in need.[13]

African Americans were fairly well represented in Columbus commerce. By 1878, about 6 percent of black citizens were self-employed craftsmen or skilled laborers, including brick masons, carpenters, plasterers, blacksmiths, painters, cabinet makers, harness makers, and draymen. African American businessmen owned saloons, barbershops, funeral parlors, and grocery stores catering to the colored population. One young black grocer grossed about $8,000 annually as of 1883. John Lunsford was an engineer at the Dudley Lumber Company. Brick mason Alex Toles built the First African Baptist Church in 1916 and directed his own mortuary. In 1917, another mortician, John Sconiers, opened the first black-owned bank, the Laborers' Savings and Loan, at Ninth Street and Fifth Avenue in the future Liberty District. The bank building also housed professional offices and an auditorium. Amos Sherald opened a barbershop in 1898, eventually operating with six barbers, a manicurist, and a shoe shine stand. Claiming to be the city's oldest black business, the shop was still offering haircuts in 2019. The *American Missionary* reported in 1889 that Columbus had "the only colored daily paper printed in America...a four column folio, neat in make-up and well-edited." Twenty-one entrepreneurs formed the Colored Men's Business Association in January 1886. By 1900, 62 of Columbus's 358 businessmen and women were African Americans, including 11 barbers, 14 shoemakers, 5 grocers, a dentist and a physician, 2 dressmakers, a restaurant owner, and 10 midwives and nurses. Turn-of-the-century Columbus also supported six Chinese laundries, and according to one elite woman, the Chinese "wore long pigtails and did the most beautiful work."[14]

Columbus's population grew robustly through the late nineteenth century, from 7,401 in 1870 to 17,614 in 1900. The Board of Trade was founded in 1882 with Gunby Jordan as president. Six hotels operated at the turn of the century, with four offering budget accommodations. The elegant Rankin House dated from the early 1860s, but on a January 1879 night, a spectacular fire left just its brick walls standing. The eighteen-degree weather froze the firemen's hands to the hoses as well as the water in the steam-powered pumpers. Colored firemen "did valuable service" with an old hand-pumper, but the fire burned out of control. The structure was rebuilt in 1880 and remained a popular downtown hotel in 1900. The three-and-a-half-story antebellum Perry House on Thirteenth Street was renovated in 1889 and boasted electric lights, what may have been the city's first elevator, and a rotunda billed as the coolest midsummer location in town. Nevertheless, J. Ralston Cargill, president of the Board of Trade, began soliciting funds for a modern hotel on Twelfth Street, near the downtown business district and on the streetcar line to the train depot. Cargill hoped that the hotel would draw northern and western tourists on their way to winter in Florida. Named for its booster, the Ralston Hotel was finished in 1914 with one hundred rooms on nine floors, making it the tallest building in the city. Expansions in 1919 and 1940 added two hundred rooms, and the hotel ballroom became *the* place for formal dinners and dances. The downtown power brokers, calling themselves Knights of the Round Table, daily gathered for lunch, "a forum for the exchange of diverse points of view...with a happy absence of restraint of expression." In the 1970s, the deteriorating hotel was refurbished and transformed into senior citizen housing.[15]

Columbus remained a hard-drinking town, with twenty-six saloons and five liquor wholesalers in 1900. An 1892 promotional publication gave a nod to the growing temperance movement, asserting the paradox that liquor is both "a destroyer of mankind" and "abreast of the vanguard of progress." Liquor fueled violence against African Americans during and after Reconstruction as well as white-on-white conflict. On December 26, 1874, two brothers from Cusseta, "boystering bullies, local terrors, and habitual pistol-toters [and] hard drinkers, ... 'powerful ugly fellows to rile,'" got drunk and killed marshal Matt Murphy. Quickly captured, one of the murderers died of his wounds, while the other was hanged soon thereafter. Six months later, Columbus's police captain and two officers engaged in a shootout on Broad Street that killed a local businessman. All had been drinking at the Sans Souci. In October 1896, an *Enquirer-Sun* headline screamed, "Crime Runs Riot in Columbus." A shoemaker and his son, nursing a grudge against the police, began drinking one morning and at 2:00 in the afternoon emerged from a saloon to kill two police officers on patrol. The father barricaded himself in his Sixteenth Street house, which the police soon surrounded. They handed weapons to anyone in the sizable crowd of onlookers who wanted to help "capture" the murderer. In the ensuing gun battle, two more officers were wounded, one fatally. The police finally rushed the house, broke down the door, and killed the "sin-hardened and drink-crazed" man. The son was captured and hanged.[16]

In May 1920, after Prohibition had gone into effect, a black bootlegger killed two policemen, prompting a countywide search by hundreds of armed citizens. All African Americans were suspect, and whites forcibly entered houses, crushing "minor" resistance from residents who did not understand "the gravity of the situation." Vigilantes fired thirty-five shots at a Girard house falsely rumored to harbor the fugitive. A posse returning from Waverly Hall ordered an unfamiliar Negro in a buggy to stop. Terrified, he whipped his horse in an attempt to flee, but the vigilantes shot it. The innocent man escaped into the woods just as a car crashed into the buggy. Despite bloodhounds and a cash reward, the bootlegger escaped, but was killed riding a freight train in Oklahoma in September. In addition to such spectacular incidents, high levels of drunkenness and violence persisted well into the twentieth century. In 1912, drunkenness was a factor in 70 percent of all arrests. Crime festered inside the dark covered bridges over the Chattahoochee, "the paths for many children of both sexes as well as women with and without escort." The police diligently patrolled the river, arresting twenty-five people for skinny-dipping in 1898.[17]

Violence also occurred without lubrication. In April 1878, a disgruntled reader sued *Enquirer-Sun* editor William E. Salisbury for libel in a Russell County court. Ten minutes after receiving one cent in damages, the plaintiff fatally shot Salisbury in the back while he waited for a train. An Alabama jury found the man not guilty, despite eyewitnesses and ballistic evidence. Dueling reemerged as the aristocrat's violence of choice in 1889. B. T. Hatcher, the major stockholder in Gunby Jordan's Midland Railroad, publicly charged Jordan with manipulating the stock to his advantage, causing huge losses to other investors. Jordan strongly objected to this slur on his "honor as a gentleman" and demanded that Hatcher withdraw his charge. They exchanged "fighting words" until Jordan challenged Hatcher to a duel. Because Hatcher was partially deaf and might not hear the command to fire guns, his second proposed "bowie knives with ten-inch blades to be used in a ten-foot ring." Jordan's second declared fighting with knives to be "barbarous." Local businessmen led by John F. Flournoy mediated, and Georgia senator Hoke Smith finally rode into town to persuade Jordan to withdraw "his card" and Hatcher his "offensive language," defusing the conflict.[18]

The most "thrilling" violence occurred before a thousand racetrack spectators during the 1890 Chattahoochee Valley Exposition. Prominent businessmen and grandsons of early entrepreneur John Howard, Robert and Richard Howard, and their brother-in-law, James Bickerstaff, ambushed T. C. Dawson as he finished driving in a harness race. Near the judges' stand, Robert Howard stabbed Dawson in the left shoulder, severing an artery. When the injured man fled onto the racetrack, the assailants opened fire with pistols. Dawson returned fire, and the shooting continued for two minutes, in full view of the crowd. Spectators first thought they were witnessing a Wild West show, but when Dawson fell, "his life blood... fast ebbing away," pandemonium erupted. After the three men were arrested for murder, their supporters issued a plea to withhold judgment on the grounds that the shooting was "a serious and private family matter." The defendants claimed to have acted in self-defense, but testimony at their arraignment revealed that the Howards had purchased two pistols and an eight-inch Bowie knife two days before the incident. Despite Robert Howard's dramatic plea that "if anyone had to be incarcerated, let it be him," the grand jury charged the three with murder, and they were held without bail until a habeas corpus ruling released Richard Howard and Bickerstaff. Robert Howard remained in jail for a year, awaiting trial.[19]

The sensational trial stretched over ten days in November 1891. Prosecutors presented compelling evidence of a "bloody conspiracy" to kill Dawson, while the defense retorted that the killing had been justified: Dawson had seduced the Howards' younger sister, Ruth, in the winter of 1889, "injuring" her mind. When the family learned that she was pregnant, Richard Howard forced Dawson to marry her. The baby died soon after birth, and while Dawson claimed that Ruth had "done away with it," the Howards thought that Dawson was responsible. Dawson abandoned Ruth, and Richard brought his ruined sister to Columbus. Robert Howard passionately defended their actions in court, decrying the man who had "foully desecrated... and wantanly ruined my helpless weak-minded sister and ruthlessly robbed her of that precious jewel, dearer and more precious by far than life itself." Ruth, "the perfect type of pure, noble womanhood, the fairest, sweetest lily of the field," was defenseless before the seducer. And, Howard charged, Dawson had previously seduced another "pure, virtuous orphan girl." Demonstrating the oratory that later made him a renowned Confederate Memorial Day speaker, Robert Howard thundered, "When I stood with beared breast, in front of Atlanta,... and 10,000 other dead, dying, and wounded Confederates lay bleeding upon the field, and Sherman, with 100,000 men and 300 cannons, was thundering at her gates... was Dawson there, discharging his duty to his oppressed country?" No, Howard answered: he was home seducing innocent young women. After a day and a half of deliberation, the jury found the Howards and Bickerstaff not guilty, a verdict that reflected not only their social status but also notions of honor that could justify even premeditated murder.[20]

Progressive national political, economic, and social ideas had made their way to Columbus by the 1890s. Southern progressives yearned for orderly and cohesive communities based on white bourgeois ideals—"a single, economically-interested, ethically shaped, middle-class attitude toward life." Aiming for efficiency, Columbus changed street names to numbers in 1885. The legislature approved a new city charter in 1890, mandating nonpartisan elections and giving the mayor and city council power to extend the city limits. The city's first expansion had occurred three years earlier, when voters approved the annexation of Rose Hill (despite that community's resistance) and the Northern Liberties. City leaders wanted to sidestep such "unremitting opposition" in the future. The charter granted the council power to regulate liquor sales, to prohibit "lewd or disorderly houses" and gambling, and to compel smallpox inoculations. It gave aldermen authority to run the public schools, including levying taxes for education. The council named a sanitary inspector for the city's meat and produce market, located on the median of First Avenue between Tenth and Eleventh Streets. The county and city erected a new courthouse/city hall in 1896 in a parklike setting facing Tenth Street. Despite such improvements, businessmen in 1897 revolted against political corruption. Stoked by *Enquirer-Sun* editorials decrying tax increases during the 1893 depression, entrepreneurs tried unsuccessfully to draft Gunby Jordan for mayor and held mass meetings to solicit a slate of candidates. On November 25, before two hundred "prominent citizens and taxpayers," Albert Kirven charged that "about 400 purchasable voters... absolutely ruled" Columbus. Most of the votes procured through penning were white, but white middle-class voters soon blamed "ignorant, debauched, purchasable negro[es]" for the corruption. Within days, reformers offered a slate of "progressive" candidates headed by Lucius H. Chappell, a successful real estate and insurance businessman. He pledged "to every citizen of Columbus, white and black, rich and poor... an honest, clean, impartial, and progressive city government." He promised a balanced budget with lower taxes, economic growth, quality education, clean water, and relief for the sick and destitute. Chappell's ticket also advocated an all-white Democratic primary. Black leaders fought for their voting rights, but after an "intense and heated" campaign, progressives swept into office in May 1898, and the Democratic executive committee approved the white primary soon thereafter. The number of African Americans registered to vote continued to decline, falling to seventy-seven in 1898 and seventy in 1910 even though Columbus's population topped thirty-six thousand, nearly half of them African Americans.[21]

Chappell served a dozen years as mayor, seeking professionalization and efficiency within city departments and ushering in modern Columbus. He and the aldermen reorganized the volunteer fire department and made it full-time. On a windy day in April 1912, Columbus's worst fire swept up Fifth Avenue, destroying forty-two houses, including that of Mayor Rhodes Browne. The firemen performed bravely, but the inadequate water supply and antiquated equipment hampered their efforts.

L. H. Chappell, ca. 1915. Columbus State University Archives, Columbus State University, Columbus, Georgia.

Water for fires was still collected in cisterns in basements of Broad Street stores. The city soon purchased its first motorized equipment, an expenditure rejected as too costly just eighteen months before the fire. In addition, the council outlawed wood-shingled roofs downtown. Chappell also restructured the police department, emphasizing merit and professional behavior. In 1906, the city built a four-story crenellated brick fire and police headquarters on First Avenue, facing the courthouse.[22]

Public health was a major concern. When Chappell took office, Columbus had more than twenty-four hundred outhouses, and the city's only sewer was the Canal, which ran into Weracoba Creek and was often blocked by dead animals and garbage. The city council required permits for residential sanitation, but only seventy-six toilets and forty-four bathtubs had been installed by 1900. The superintendent of public works predicted a "calamity" if the city failed to install sanitary sewers, but voters nevertheless rejected a bond initiative in 1901. Reformers finally succeeded the following year. Keeping the city streets clean constituted another monumental task. More than four hundred cows and five hundred horses lived on private lots in the city at the turn of the twentieth century, and in 1890, the sanitation inspector reported,

> During the past twelve months there has been hauled from the streets and alleys over fifteen thousand loads of garbage and trash, forty-eight dead horses and mules, twenty-six cows, two hundred and eighty-seven dogs, over four hundred cats, nearly two thousand chickens, ten goats, three hundred and twenty rats, eight white rabbits, eleven ducks, seven turkeys, two peafowls, one opossum, one thousand five hundred barrels of oyster shells, one hundred twenty barrels night soil [human feces], one carload of condemned Kansas City beef and thirty barrels rotten Irish potatoes.

The aldermen outlawed free-range livestock and flocks of geese in the streets. The filth caused illness, but the city still had only a rudimentary medical system at the turn of the twentieth century. Anyone who could afford a doctor likely received treatment at home. Doctors operated on kitchen tables and delivered babies in bedrooms. Children who visited the office of city physician Frank Schley might be enticed to cooperate by being given a pigeon from a coop in the office window. The patient would be told that if he behaved, he could take the bird home. Having fulfilled his end of the bargain, he would go home with his prize, only to discover when he released it that it was a homing pigeon—it would fly back to the doctor's office. Columbus had built its first hospital, the Pest House, on the South Commons around 1836 to quarantine patients with infectious diseases. By the 1890s, the facility was in rat-infested disrepair, and in 1895, the city built a three-story wooden Queen Anne–style hospital near Linwood Cemetery. Despite the new hospital's electric lights, hot and cold running water, and "every modern convenience," rapid advances in medicine immediately rendered it obsolete. In 1915, the city built a modern four-story brick hospital on the highest point in Rose Hill, the precursor to what is now Midtown Medical Center. It had wards for Negroes and criminals in the basement and state-of-the-art operating rooms on the top floor, so modern that residents rode up in the elevator (an attraction in itself) and gawked.[23]

Chappell also modernized Columbus's infrastructure. Rain turned the dirt streets into quagmires, and to gain public support for paving, the superintendent of public works posted "No Fishing" signs at the potholes on Broad. Chappell and his progressive team tackled the problem scientifically, hiring a city engineer to plan the work. The wide streets were too expensive to pave, so on Broad Street and First and Fifth Avenues, the engineer used vitrified brick to pave two roadways divided by a Bermuda grass median. On either side were grassy sidewalks edged with granite curbing. The other avenues had curbed roadways down the center, with fifty-foot "parks" on either side. Backed by women's clubs, Chappell endorsed the "City Beautiful" concept popular with urban progressives nationwide. Proponents believed that beautifying the city inspired moral and civic virtue in urban dwellers, building pride and a sense of community. Columbus planted ten thousand trees—two lines down the middle of the median, and one on each side of the street—to "provide insulation from the filth and germs of the street and from the noise of the street and the heat." Loretto Chappell, the mayor's daughter, recalled standing at Tenth Street and seeing a canopy of green stretching all the way to North Highlands.[24]

The old wooden river bridges needed replacing. A 1901 bond referendum for a steel bridge at Fourteenth Street received overwhelming support, with only ten voters dissenting. Four months later, a flood washed out the old Horace King bridge there, and a steel bridge with plank flooring was ready by August 1903. It featured pedestrian walkways outside traffic lanes and trolley lines down the center. A sign read, "$5 fine for going faster than a walk. Pedestrians and vehicles." King's other Reconstruction-era bridge, at Dillingham Street "survived for years and years beyond its natural life." After another bond issue, engineer B. H. Hardaway in 1910 was the only bidder on the first concrete bridge to be built across the Chattahoochee, which opened to traffic in November 1912.[25]

New streets literally paved the way for automobiles. Driven by a young salesman for Octagon Soap, the first "self-propelled carriage," a steam locomobile, arrived in Columbus on August 13, 1900. By fall, stores advertised "automobile coats" to wear while driving. Leon Camp was the first resident with a horseless carriage. On August 23, 1901, Camp amazed observers by driving up Wynn's Hill at twenty-five miles per hour. He declared that his locomobile could travel easily over any road surface and that "no sand bed or grade can stop it." However, Camp became the first charged with reckless driving when he got stuck in a sandy spot at Twelfth and Broad. At full throttle, he lost control, lurched onto the sidewalk, pinned a screaming pedestrian against a building, and broke a shop window. His case was thrown out because the city council had never passed a law to prohibit reckless driving, an oversight the councillors quickly rectified. Leon Camp and his brother, Wilson, sold automobiles from their bicycle shop on Broad, with customers choosing cars from a catalog. By 1904, the Columbus Driving Association built a racetrack to host competitions for bicycles, motorcycles, and automobiles, noting, "There will also be horse racing." Noisy automobiles spooked horses, sometimes with tragic results. On April 5, 1903, a woman was driving her grandson in a carriage on Broad Street when a steam-driven car terrified the horse, and it stampeded south. As some men at the Rankin House tried to head it off, the horse swerved, flinging the buggy into a trolley pole and throwing the woman and child onto the brick pavement. The boy died the next day.[26]

Automobiles remained beyond the means of most residents, who walked or took streetcars. In 1866, the city had granted the Columbus Railroad Company the right to use any or all streets, but the company made no progress until 1883, when it reorganized and began to lay track. John F. Flournoy became the company's president in 1887 and oversaw streetcar operation for decades. The route followed Fourth Street to Broad, then Fourteenth Street and Second Avenue to Twenty-Second Street in Rose Hill. Coming back down Rose Hill, the conductor unhitched the mule while the driver used the brake to ease the car down the grade. In 1888, the company added donkey steam engines to pull some cars. The "dummy" steam line ran to Wynnton, East Highlands, and along the industrial waterfront. The coke-burning engine was contained in a wooden boxcar to avoid frightening horses. In 1890, the noisy, dirty, and dangerous lines were electrified.[27]

That same year, Rhodes Browne opened a rival line, the North Highlands Electric Railroad Company. Competition was so intense that fistfights broke out between employees of the two companies. In 1894, Flournoy purchased the North Highlands line, promising that "the lion and the lamb will now lie down together." He issued stock and used the proceeds to build a brick transfer station at Twelfth and Broad and a car barn beside company stables at Second Avenue and Eighteenth Street, next to City Mills. Track mileage increased from three in 1895 to fifteen in 1897 and more than twenty-four in 1908. In 1902, the owner of the Racine Hotel negotiated for new track to be laid down Thirteenth Street, in front of the hotel, rather than on Twelfth. When told that he would have to pay for the track, the owner refused, saying that he would get autos and omnibuses to carry guests to the train station, to which the railroad company manager scoffed, "I do not take much stock in them." For a nickel's fare, people found cheap entertainment riding streetcars at six miles per hour "around the belt," the seven-mile loop to East Highlands. The transportation could be hazardous. An elderly gentleman smoking on the car's platform suffered a skull fracture when he was thrown from the trolley as it veered around a sharp curve. The railroad company constantly faced suits for injury, though compensation reflected the realities of Jim Crow: a white man who broke his arm in a fall got $132, while the mother of an African American girl struck and killed received $25.[28]

The streetcar was fundamental to Flournoy's primary business: real estate development. He and his lifelong friend, Louis F. Garrard, formed the Muscogee Real Estate Company in 1887, the same year Flournoy took over the railroad. The following year, Muscogee Real Estate developed the fifty-six-block East Highlands neighborhood, Columbus's first streetcar suburb. Flournoy enticed lower-middle-class families to buy houses in a neighborhood undisturbed by "the rattle of heavy dray or steady tramp of weary workers," "where there is no question as to who your next door neighbor will be." Suburbanization was a national trend. By the late nineteenth century, many residents not unreasonably viewed cities as dirty, unhealthy, and dangerous and chose to segregate by class in socially homogeneous bucolic settings along streetcar lines that offered easy access to workplaces. Flournoy's advertising promised escape from "the heat, dust, and smoke of the city" and pledged pure water when downtown had no reliable supply; however, he also claimed falsely that there were no mosquitoes and guaranteed that "none but the best and most desirable of residents are ever invited to locate." A major selling point was forty-five-acre Wildwood Park, a "beautiful Eden" on the development's east side. Muscogee Real Estate used mule teams to scrape out a lake filled by Weracoba Creek, building up islands connected by "Chinese hump-back bridges." It leased the park to the Columbus Railroad for one dollar a year. The streetcar from downtown circled the park, the farthest point on the belt line, returning along Eighteenth Street, past Linwood Cemetery. The 1890s depression slowed sales in East Highlands, and decades passed before the neighborhood was filled, but Flournoy remained undeterred, developing suburbs for a wealthier clientele: Hilton and Wildwood Avenues and later Peacock Woods, Wynnton Place, and Wildwood Circle. He also built the Empire Building downtown at Twelfth Street and First Avenue.[29]

Flournoy had competitors as the city expanded. From 1890 to 1920, Columbus's population nearly doubled, topping thirty-one thousand, with most of East Highlands annexed in 1915 and 1920. In 1892, Grigsby

E. Thomas, son of a prominent judge, divided the family's fifteen acres in Rose Hill into forty-five lots and sold them for a total of $15,000, increasing the land's value by 300 percent. Jordan formed a real estate company in 1904 and in 1910 included Thomas's properties in Waverly Terrace, a twenty-five-acre subdivision bounded by Hamilton Road, Twenty-Seventh Street, Twelfth Avenue, and Thirtieth Street. The streetcar suburb attracted professionals, skilled tradesmen, and small business owners who built homes reflecting diverse architectural styles, including Spanish Mission, Craftsman, and Georgian Revival. The Jordan Company touted Waverly Terrace as Columbus's "first planned suburb," although East Highlands was developed a decade earlier. The Jordan Company also developed commercial real estate, erecting the Exchange Building at First Avenue and Thirteenth Street in 1912 and the Waverly Hotel across the street a couple of years later.[30]

The Columbus Telephone Exchange opened with two operators in the Iron Bank on April 21, 1880, four years after Alexander Graham Bell had made his famous call to his assistant. Most of Columbus's first thirty-two subscribers were businesses, though Jordan had a home phone. The Eagle & Phenix had numbers 1 and 2 on the exchange. Subscribers made six hundred calls on the first day—an average of forty-six per hour and nineteen per subscriber. The *Columbus Enquirer-Sun* noted that a "considerable amount of goods... were sold over the wires." Wealthier citizens and nearly all businesses soon had telephones.[31]

Modern communication, streetcars, industry, business, and housing created a critical need for electricity. The city began to electrify streetlights in 1887, using power from Muscogee Manufacturing's dynamo, but the textile mill produced insufficient excess power to meet growing demand. George Pearce at City Mills shored up its old dam and in 1885 signed a fifty-year lease to sell his excess power to the railroad company power station next door, the city's first centrally generating electrical plant. However, the river's unreliable flow meant that the plant often failed to meet the demands of streetcars and business and residential customers. In 1897, Jordan and investors from the Bibb Manufacturing Company in Macon bought water rights on both riverbanks at Lover's Leap in North Highlands. They formed the Columbus Power Company and hired Hardaway to build a masonry dam, which was completed in 1901. At the North Highlands dam, the Bibb Company built a textile mill powered by a rope drive from turbines at the dam's base. The smaller Columbus Manufacturing Company, fifteen hundred feet south of the Bibb Mill, also ran on the dam's hydroelectric power. Frederick B. Gordon organized the company in 1899, with Bradley and Browne among its directors. Columbus Power Company and the railroad company informally agreed that the former would provide industrial electricity and the latter would power residences and businesses. Jordan characterized the local players as "amateurs" whose companies could not meet growing demand. River flow too high or low caused streetcars to operate "at a walk" and lights to dim. The North Highlands dam promised reliability but did not deliver.[32]

Into this arena strode Savannah's George Johnson Baldwin, who went on to dominate Columbus's utilities for nearly two decades. The Harvard-educated Baldwin was the regional representative for Stone and Webster, a Boston engineering consulting firm that by 1902 controlled twenty-four municipal street railway and electrical lighting companies worth $60 million. In an age of monopoly and cutthroat capitalism, he was master of both. An original investor in Flournoy's Muscogee Real Estate Company, Baldwin knew the city's economic prospects and wanted a hydroelectric monopoly—"the best method for turning this power [of the Chattahoochee] into money." In a "strictly confidential" letter written in late 1899, he suggested collusion between the railroad company and the power company, but the power company directors wanted to divide the business, preferring not "to drift into any" needless competition. Baldwin purchased the railroad company in June 1901 and the gaslight company in 1902. He formed a holding company, Coweta Power Company, and secretly sent Flournoy up the river to buy riparian rights for a dam. By 1903, Baldwin owned fifteen miles upriver from the North Highlands dam, with a fall of 161 feet and potential 12,000 horsepower. Rumors swirled that Coweta Power would build an impoundment dam at the old Clapp's Factory site and a second dam at Mulberry Shoals.[33]

The power situation became critical when the new Bibb dam suffered major breaks in a January 1902 flood. The Columbus Power Company immediately built a coffer dam at North Highlands and got Bibb Mill and Columbus Manufacturing operating by mid-April, though the dam was not fully repaired for eleven months. The railroad company alone lacked the capacity to meet the city's electrical needs. For future power, Baldwin reached an agreement with Columbus Power to build an impoundment dam at the old Clapp's Factory site (currently the site of

Oliver Dam). When Hardaway asked for Columbus Power's recommendation to build the new dam, the director wrote to Baldwin that the engineer's work on the Bibb dam was "very unsatisfactory," and Baldwin declined to hire him, antagonizing Hardaway. In 1903, Baldwin consolidated Stone and Webster's local holdings into the Columbus Electric Company, which controlled the railroad company, Coweta Power, and the gaslight company. Correctly fearing that Baldwin sought a monopoly on the city's electrical production, Mayor Chappell considered building a municipal power plant and sought confidential estimates from two Atlanta companies. But Baldwin was too clever: he had already arranged for both companies to stay out of the Columbus market, received copies of all their correspondence with Chappell, and coached the companies so that their estimates were too high. Baldwin also bought off council members and the *Ledger* editor by offering them reduced electrical rates. Baldwin flattered Chappell to his face, writing to him after his 1903 reelection that "the recent progressive movement in Columbus has been very largely due to your personal efforts and administration." Privately, however, Baldwin dismissed "his highness" the mayor as ineffectual and easily manipulated.[34]

After an analysis of costs and benefits, Stone and Webster decided against building the impoundment dam, infuriating Columbus Power but delighting the City Mills owners, who feared that the dam would reduce the flow of water they needed to generate electricity. Power in Columbus was "exceedingly bad," resulting in a December 1904 gathering of all "riparian interests"—the Eagle & Phenix, City Mills, Muscogee Mills, Columbus Power, and Columbus Electric. The wealthy businessmen agreed to fight Atlanta's use of river water but did not resolve the power issues. The *Ledger* complained that "capitalists" had bought up the riverbanks but sat on the hydropower. The Bibb Mill directors wanted to double its size and agreed in 1906 to merge Columbus Power with Columbus Electric under the Columbus Power name and to raise $1 million in capital. Jordan endorsed the merger, declaring, "With Boston brains backed by ample Boston capital our future is assured." After seven years of effort, Baldwin had his monopoly. But unfortunately for him, opposition was growing.[35]

In the 1906 municipal elections, a "Citizens' Ticket" urged the overthrow of "high salaried office holders and politicians banded together for ... the secret domination of the affairs of Columbus regardless of the will of the people." Baldwin acknowledged that citizens saw Columbus Power as an evil monopoly, musing, "It is of course evident that where we have such complete control of the life blood of any community as we have in Columbus, this control must be exercised with the very wisest discretion and the utmost moderation. The bigger the weight you put on the safety valve the greater the explosion when it comes." Adding to Baldwin's woes, Hardaway reemerged in 1909 to take his revenge. He had slipped beneath Baldwin's formidable intelligence-gathering network, formed a group of investors that included Baldwin's supposed allies at City Mills, and bought property to build a dam on the Chattahoochee in Harris County. Alarmed, Stone and Webster advised blocking construction or "trad[ing] them out of field" because the dam would lead to "sharp competition with no profit to any one." Baldwin reached an agreement with all parties to join in building one very large dam at Stone and Webster's Goat Rock property, seventeen miles above Columbus. Hardaway got the construction contract, $120,000 in cash and stock, and probably satisfaction at the unusual opportunity to best Baldwin. On December 19, 1912, two special trains carried a thousand people to watch as Mayor Chappell flipped a switch to transmit power and baptize a goat with Chattahoochee water. The dam's additional power led the chamber of commerce to call Columbus the Electric City. In the next five years, however, Stone and Webster shifted to selling electricity northward to Newnan and points in between. Despite the Board of Trade's breathless predictions that the river above the city would become "a staircase of dams" lined with industry, the increased electricity did not bring new industry to Columbus, which was saturated with textiles. In 1922, the railroad company and Columbus Power merged to form the Columbus Electric and Power Company, which, in turn, merged with Georgia Power in 1929. The acquisition included streetcars; buses, which had begun to replace streetcars in 1925; and the gaslight company. Streetcar operation ended in Columbus on August 5, 1934. Georgia Power continued to operate the gaslight company until 1948, when federal regulation required it to sell the utility back to the citizens. After reorganization, it operated as the Gas Light Company of Columbus.[36]

Around 1902, Baldwin turned his eye to Columbus's water supply. The city's water situation had improved little since 1860. In the mid-1880s, Columbus installed twenty-five fire hydrants with water pumped from the river by the Eagle & Phenix, but as a public official remarked, "The waterworks is continuing to supply an excellent brand of MUD through its hydrants." In 1894, the Water Works Committee reported that only a quarter of Columbus's twenty thousand residents got city water. The Chattahoochee offered unlimited quantity but with "extreme muddiness and a known contamination"—the raw sewage that Atlanta dumped into the river. The committee recommended that the city construct a reservoir atop Factory Hill, above the Clapp's Factory site. Twenty feet deep and four hundred feet in diameter, the reservoir would be filled from a 580-million-gallon storage facility on Roaring Branch Creek, and gravity would bring the water to the city. By the time the city decided to act, however, Baldwin owned the proposed site.[37]

In 1902, Chappell asked whether Baldwin was "really for the City." Baldwin was for Baldwin and played the mayor like a fish on a line. For a decade, he dangled the possibility that the city could purchase Factory Hill. Though a 1904 headline had declared that "People Will Never Accept River Water," the water commission finally resolved in 1912 to draw the city's water from the Chattahoochee. On October 18, 1913, 94 percent of Columbus's thirsty voters approved $450,000 in bonds to build a municipal waterworks. In 1914, the city purchased Baldwin's seven Factory Hill acres for $10,500. Two years later, Columbus completed a pump station that sent 5 million gallons daily to a storage reservoir, a filter plant producing 6 million potable gallons a day, and a hilltop reservoir that could hold 2.5 million gallons of clean water. Water flowed through a twenty-four-inch cast-iron pipe down Third Avenue and through sixty miles of iron mains to consumers. In 1919, the water board purchased a chlorine gas machine, and a century later, chlorine remains the principal water disinfectant.[38]

In addition to crafting a modern infrastructure, Chappell created a partnership with the U.S. Army that greatly benefited the city. After the Spanish-American War began in April 1898, Chappell lobbied the War Department for a brigade of thirty-five hundred soldiers to train at Camp Conrad, between First Avenue and Hamilton Road in North Highlands. Three regiments arrived in November 1898, boosting business downtown. Gen. James H. Wilson, whose Union troops had burned local industry at the Civil War's end, came out of retirement and made a troop inspection in Columbus in December. The newspaper reported that he "was received in a pleasant and friendly manner," but one unreconstructed rebel remarked "with vehemence" that he would like to shoot "the damn Yankee" on sight, and "if he had a dog who licked his blood, he would shoot the dog, and if a buzzard came and picked the dog's bones, he would shoot the buzzard." The Columbus Guards trained but were not deployed because the war ended quickly, and Camp Conrad closed in February 1899.³⁹

A decade and a half later, when World War I heated up in Europe, the Guards trained in Macon and deployed from there. Columbus women formed the state's first Red Cross chapter in January 1916. They gathered in the Ralston Hotel lobby to make items to send to Europe, including seven thousand surgical dressings, knitted socks, sweaters, and helmets. Food was rationed, so schools and families raised conservation gardens. The Conservation Kitchen on Twelfth Street, between Front and Broad, taught women to can and preserve produce. Women in the Motor Corps learned to drive tractors and trucks and to repair vehicles as well as to provide transportation and ambulance services for local troops. In their blue uniforms with matching veils, the members of the Canteen Corps, led by the mayor's wife, Cynthia Chappell, offered refreshments to soldiers at the train station. On one occasion, a soldier asked her young son, Bentley, whether he knew any girls in Columbus. The boy obligingly provided the names and address of his sisters, but it turned out that they were off-limits. Other girls, however, were available. The presence of soldiers led to an influx of prostitution, which became so prevalent that police and public health authorities segregated the women in a special district. At the army's request, the chamber of commerce paid for a venereal disease clinic in the city hospital basement.⁴⁰

Nevertheless, Mayor Chappell sought to bring a permanent army training camp to Columbus. When news leaked that the Infantry School of Arms was looking for a new home, Jordan Company engineer John A. Betjeman went to Washington and successfully negotiated the school's move to Columbus in August 1918. Named for Civil War general Henry L. Benning, the camp was initially located on Macon Road, near what is now the site of the public library. In October, Benning's daughter, Anna Caroline, by then an elderly woman, led a parade to open the camp, riding in a car bearing an American flag. Historian Louise DuBose remembered her unreconstructed Confederate grandmother, a longtime friend of Benning's, shaking her fist and shouting, "I'm ashamed of you—riding down Broad Street behind that old rag!"⁴¹

Less than a month later, it had become apparent that the camp was too small and too close to town. In early November 1918, the army brushed aside opposition and used purchases and condemnation proceedings to acquire the old Cusseta Plantation, which had formerly belonged to John Woolfolk. Construction began for a camp that could house ten thousand enlisted men and four thousand officers. After

World War I ended on November 11, the army ordered Camp Benning closed; however, the officer in charge used ambiguous language in his orders about "salvaging" existing structures to continue building. Some residents sought to derail the continued construction, believing that so many soldiers would threaten community morals and sending telegrams bearing messages such as "Save our homes, our churches, and our schools." But in the midst of an agricultural depression and a boll weevil infestation, many landowners were eager to sell, and Betjeman and the chamber of commerce mounted a lobbying juggernaut focused on the economic benefits. When powerful Georgia senator Hoke Smith threw his support behind the effort, the newly renamed Infantry School received permanent funding in June 1920. Two years later, the secretary of war christened the post Fort Benning.⁴²

Though World War I highlighted the need for a stable workforce, managing labor had been a focus of white business owners since the Civil War. One method was the convict lease system. In December 1866, the Georgia General Assembly approved "farming out" convicts to the highest bidder. Whites soon realized that they could use petty criminal statutes to control the former slaves, creating a large pool of leasable convicts. Early in 1875, Columbus entrepreneur John Howard leased a group of convicts at twenty dollars each annually, but the state canceled the contract when he did not properly care for the prisoners. Conditions for leased convicts were horrific. The Columbus newspaper expressed outrage at the beating death of a young white convict in 1881, though the prison population by then was overwhelmingly black. Testimony before a legislative committee in 1908 revealed that J. T. Fletcher and John P. Illges's Muscogee Brick Company attached spikes to convicts' ankles to prevent escape. Companies leasing prisoners used rolling penitentiaries, cages about the size of half a boxcar, that followed construction and railroad camps. The city of Columbus ordered three of the "portable bastiles" to roll inmates over county roads. Unbearably hot in the summer, each cage held about twenty-four prisoners. In 1905, Muscogee County's convict camp had thirty-eight prisoners who repaired eighty-five miles of roads.⁴³

Gunby Jordan's Midland Railroad depended on convict labor, and an 1886 report noted that "a large convict force are now busy grading the Columbus end of the line." On August 26, 1887, a physician reported that

Muscogee County convict road crew, ca. 1910. Columbus State University Archives, Columbus State University, Columbus, Georgia.

on a recent visit to the Midland camp, he found evidence that one man had been "very severely whipped... the skin had been denuded from both buttock[s]" and "contusion or bruising beneath the skin was very severe." The camp boss had whipped the man with a wet strap rubbed in sand, deliberately seeking to peel off skin. The boss was fired, but in 1888, Jordan contracted with the Chattahoochee Brick Company, Georgia's largest and most notoriously abusive convict leaser. Moreover, Jordan's railroad stopped at the Georgia line because convicts could not work out of state. Georgia outlawed the convict lease system in 1908 but quickly passed a law allowing counties to use convicts for public labor. In 1914, Muscogee County worked 125 convicts an average of nine hours a day, and three years later, an engineering journal reported that convicts "have built practically every paved mile of road in the state," providing labor worth $5 million annually.[44]

African Americans labored at jobs that were difficult and poorly paid. A local minister reported in 1883 that most black women worked as cooks, laundresses, and domestic servants, earning between five and six dollars per month. Unskilled male workers earned $1 to $1.50 per day.

The steamboat lines employed many black stevedores to push barrels down the steep riverbank, spinning them to a stop and guiding them as though the barrel "knew [the stevedore's] wishes." These laborers also tumbled four-hundred-pound cotton bales down the bank, "bouncing like a ball." Injuries such as smashed hands and severed fingers were common, and bouncing bales sometimes knocked men unconscious. White attitudes toward black labor ranged from contempt to paternalism. Thomas Jefferson Bates, son of antebellum contractor Asa Bates and also a contractor, declared that African Americans were incapable of thinking for themselves and had "an imitative character." He believed they were not suitable for factory work. Columbus Manufacturing president Frederick B. Gordon allowed that further industrial training would be required before black laborers could be used in the textile mills. During this period, no African Americans operated machinery inside the mills.[45]

Most white laborers worked in factories, especially in textiles. In 1883, Columbus manufacturing establishments employed 2,231 men, 1,408 women, and 557 children—18 percent of the total population of the city and its suburbs. Women and children accounted for more than 65 percent of textile labor. The Eagle & Phenix employed three-quarters of the area labor force in 1880. These white workers endured only slightly better conditions than their black counterparts. Temperatures in the mills soared to 120 degrees in August, with no air-conditioning, and workers lacked filters to prevent them from breathing in cotton lint or hearing protection to mitigate the din of the machinery. Wages ranged from 25 cents a day for children to $1.50 for skilled and experienced workers. Mill operatives worked twelve-hour shifts five days a week, with a half day on Saturday. One factory owner admitted that twelve-hour workdays were unhealthy and that many laborers "appear to be 'worked out,' as mules sometimes are." As labor agitation grew at the century's end, Jordan advocated importing immigrant workers, though William H. Young preferred native southerners. He brought in fifty English weavers in 1870 but soon fired them, finding them "a turbulent set, and very troublesome," believing they "had a right to dictate to us." Mills occasionally offered benefits to placate workers. The Eagle & Phenix took workers by train to Fort Mitchell each summer for a picnic and by 1901 provided a library, gymnasium, eight-hundred-seat auditorium, night school, and music course. As the number of mill workers doubled from 1870 to 1880, operators began to fear labor unrest and sought to

William H. Young, ca. 1889.
From *Biographical Souvenir of the States of Georgia and Florida* (Chicago: Battey, 1889).

G. Gunby Jordan, ca. 1880.
From the collection of Katherine Jordan Waddell.

combat the problem in part by providing some housing for workers as a means of isolating them. The Eagle & Phenix, for example, offered two-room houses across the river in what became Phenix City.[46]

Led by the Eagle & Phenix, textiles dominated the Columbus area's economy by the century's end. The company's hydropower monopoly discouraged new investment in the 1880s, when other southern textile centers boomed. During the 1890 recession, depositors in the Eagle & Phenix's savings department withdrew funds, so the company issued its first bonds. A group of Atlanta investors gained control, forcing Young to resign. The depression deepened, and in 1896 the new directors cut weavers' wages. They walked out at noon on March 28, setting in motion Columbus's first organized strike. The directors shut out all seventeen hundred operatives on March 31, and the mill remained closed until May 11, when most of the workers returned—including weavers at the lowered wage. Nevertheless, the mill declared bankruptcy on June 14, with Jordan named receiver. In June 1898, he and a group of other investors bought the Eagle & Phenix and sent in men with sledgehammers to smash obsolete machinery. Jordan modernized the factory with two powerhouses and electric generators and remained president until 1914.[47]

The Eagle & Phenix's revival spurred textile growth, with six new mills, most notably the Bibb Manufacturing Company, locating north and east of Columbus by 1910. Jordan was among the initial investors in the Bibb mill, advising the Macon company to locate outside the city to avoid high taxes and distractions such as "street parades, accessibility of the directors to interruptions from promoters, begging committees, people who desired to consult on many possible and impossible affairs, and the demoralization natural to incidents occurring in a city." With growing labor unrest, he advocated the creation of a rural mill village under the company's control. Large-scale textile production continued to dominate Columbus's economy, and textiles accounted for 60 percent of total goods produced in Columbus by 1930.[48]

Despite the hopes of Jordan and the Bibb Mill directors, the mill's location did not immunize it from labor agitation. Led by Prince Greene, Weavers Union No. 111 organized on April 18, 1896, during the Eagle & Phenix lockout, becoming the first southern chapter of the National Union of Textile Workers. Under his leadership, Columbus became a major organizing center. Greene served as the union's national president from 1897 to 1900 and was among the organizers of the southern region of the American Federation of Labor (AFL). The textile workers' local joined the AFL's United Textile Workers of America in 1901. Two years later, Columbus's skilled trade unions united in a conservative Central Federation of Labor whose constitution promoted skilled workers' unification, higher wages, moral and material advancement, and heightened political awareness. Business leaders sought to suppress what they perceived as labor radicalism. Jordan served with Andrew Carnegie and AFL president Samuel Gompers on the executive committee of the National Civic Federation, which promoted harmony between management and labor. The management of both the Eagle & Phenix and the Bibb Mill formed workingmen's social clubs to develop "the moral and mental elevation of members." The mills also hired conservative Baptist and Methodist ministers who preached hard work, loyalty, and obedience. Despite the walkouts that occurred, the Board of Trade assured potential industrialists in 1913, "In Columbus, strikes are almost an unknown quantity."[49]

Other enterprises sought to prevent unions from taking hold during this era. In 1901, Baldwin and Flournoy fired any streetcar employee who tried to organize, but on July 30, the operators struck, demanding a wage hike, a twelve-hour day with an hour for lunch, and recognition of their union. Flournoy ranted to Baldwin, "This is a free country.... So far as allowing a UNION of any kind to dictate its terms to the railroad Company... I am absolutely opposed to it." Though he immediately dismissed anyone associated with the strike and hired scabs to operate the streetcars, Flournoy agreed to rehire the fired workers three days later and gave a twelve-cent-per-hour raise to conductors and motormen. He refused to recognize any union, however. Exactly two years later, when the still-fledgling union attempted another strike, Baldwin and Flournoy placed a mole in the organization and again fired anyone associated with it. In addition, they created a blacklist of union sympathizers to share with other employers, and placated the remaining workers by setting up a "benefit association" that offered sick leave and hosted a midnight oyster feast for white employees at the Rankin House as well as a separate "bountiful supper" for the fifty colored employees. Baldwin used the same strong-arm tactics again the next year when gaslight workers threatened to strike, discharging the leader "inside of two hours, and the other men having lost their spokesman made no stand." Unskilled workers had even less chance of withstanding owners. When a group of Negro laborers at the Eagle & Phenix "refused to do some certain work assigned to them," the manager fired them and "filled their places before they had scarcely left the yard."[50]

The most intense labor-management conflict arose during World War I. The federal War Industries Board and War Labor Board allowed workers more leverage in expressing grievances to management and promised a living wage. Organized labor claimed its right to collective bargaining, while owners sought to ban closed-shop unions and eliminate bargaining. W. C. Bradley of the Eagle & Phenix and Bibb Mills refused to hire union workers and declared that he "would discharge every official of the Union found on his plant, or anyone, man or woman, who was active for the Union." Instead, he and other managers endorsed "welfare capitalism," where owners rather than unions or government addressed worker grievances. Management encouraged teenagers to begin work at the mills as soon as possible, so mill workers tended to be young and their earnings peaked before they turned thirty. In 1920, 40 percent of Columbus's mill workers were between ages sixteen and twenty-four, with 29 percent aged between twenty-four and thirty-five. Only 15 percent were older than forty-five. Younger workers were less likely to be union activists; moreover, torn between the cultural norm of individuality and the need for a union's collective action, Columbus workers had no real class consciousness or ideological cohesion. That

Labor rally in North Highlands, 1919. Columbus State University Archives, Columbus State University, Columbus, Georgia.

lack, coupled with management's unwavering resistance to organized labor, doomed unionization.[51]

Renegade organizer John A. Callan began agitating in Columbus in April 1917. Rejecting local traditions of labor-management cooperation, his hyperbolic rhetoric alienated conservative trade union leaders and terrified owners. Callan recruited hundreds into the United Textile Workers of America (UTWA), though joining cost them their jobs. The owners conspired to frame him, planting in his rented room explosives, illegal liquor, and diagrams of factories with German instructions to "destroy the mill with dynamite or fire, make haste and flee." Jailed under the 1917 Espionage Act after grand jury testimony by George Parker Swift of Muscogee Mills and other textile officials, Callan lost credibility. The UTWA sent John Thomas of Philadelphia to replace Callan, and textile operatives formed Local 1124 on April 1, 1918. Mills announced a 3.5 percent raise to placate workers, at the same time threatening termination for anyone who joined a union. In protest, four hundred operatives walked out at the Eagle & Phenix the next day. Bradley retaliated by firing seven hundred union members though he offered to allow them to "return to work when they agree not to organize in bodies against the mills." The next day, five hundred Swift Spinning operatives walked out when management locked out union members, attracting hundreds of supporters as they paraded to Union Hall on Eleventh Street. On August

W. C. Bradley, ca. 1929. From Nancy Telfair, *A History of Columbus, Georgia* (Columbus: Historical Publishing, 1929).

Frederick B. Gordon and ladies at the Columbus Country Club, 1923. Library of Congress.

14, North Highlands strikers attacked a nonstriking worker; when his wife came to his aid, she was beaten, requiring hospitalization. Sheriff Jesse Beard then cited "rioting," prompting the governor to declare martial law on August 15.[52]

On August 16, Swift Spinning got an injunction to prevent Thomas from engaging in further organizing activity. Two days later, the mills signed a full-page letter "To the Law-Abiding Citizens of Columbus, Georgia," alleging that all trouble came from outside agitators: "evil and vicious strangers..., irresponsible men who have no interest in our community." Owners claimed that workers were well paid and content and accused Thomas of organizing the city's Negro workers. Speaking to the Southern Textile Association, Gordon declared the industrial South "will never...allow itself to be bound hand and foot...by that THING that seeks to stab in the heart that inherent right of selective employment.... That unholy, foreign-born, un-American, socialistic, despotic THING known as LABOR UNIONISM." However, after the National War Labor Board sent a mediator to Columbus, owners raised wages by 25 percent and conceded that during the war, workers had the right to organize. Five thousand workers gathered at the Meritas mill baseball field on August 20 and in a spirit of "patriotism" unanimously agreed to return to work and pledged not to strike or actively organize for the war's duration.[53]

The peace was short lived. After World War I ended, workers expected the federal government to protect their gains. The War Labor Board had established an eight-hour day, equal pay for women, time-and-a-half overtime pay, and the right to organize. Yet factory owners believed that they were no longer bound by these concessions and cut wages and outlawed unions. Beginning with Seattle's general strike in January 1919, disaffection spread, with four million workers walking off their jobs across the country. The Columbus millowners angered operatives by manipulating and strictly adhering to the bonus system, under which workers received 30–50 percent of their base pay for producing a set amount of goods and working a full week. Owners cut the workers no slack. For example, when a Swift union member died on a Friday evening and thus did not complete her full work week, the company deducted the bonus from her final check. Another father lost his bonus when he missed work to attend his child's funeral. An eighteen-year-old boy was docked after he was absent from work for mandatory draft registration. Supported by the UTWA, workers demanded an eight-hour day and forty-eight-hour week. On February 3, more than seven thousand

Columbus workers, along with their counterparts across the nation, worked eight hours of an eleven-hour shift and then walked out. When they returned to work the following day, owners paid their wages and fired them. Every mill in the city locked out workers. One owner charged the union with disrupting the "one great happy family within the mills." Thomas retorted that the owners "might have been happy, but God and ourselves alone know how little happiness we have had."[54]

The strike dragged on for ten weeks, though the initial enthusiasm began to crumble within two. Owners continued to refuse to make concessions, citing the plummeting postwar demand for textiles and the consequent need to keep costs at rock bottom. By February 23, Meritas, the Eagle & Phenix, and Swift Manufacturing resumed operations using nonstriking and scab labor. Many elite citizens feared violence. A local Woman's Christian Temperance Union state officer wrote, "I feel we are walking on gunpowder on account of the antagonism between these factory folks and negroes.... They say the whites have made dreadful threats if a negro dares to take factory work.... If it were not for the short supply of whiskey we would be in awful trouble before this." The owners twice had Thomas arrested and hired thugs they labeled deputies to patrol the picket lines. These men, along with those from the sheriff's office and police department, beat the strikers. To protect workers, the UTWA withdrew the picket lines on April 4, abandoning the strike.[55]

Over the next six weeks, Thomas continued organizing and considered resuming the strike. On May 21, he led a nighttime rally at the northeast corner of Thirty-Second Street and Second Avenue, opposite the Bibb Mill and near Swift Spinning. A group of nonunion men taunted Thomas, beating on tin washtubs to drown him out. A bottle struck a union man, knocking him to the ground, and he responded with a stream of invective. Dared to repeat his "blasphemy," he did so "with added vigor, using a more complete description of his assailant." The company men then sprayed an estimated seventy-five bullets into the crowd, killing a World War I veteran and union member and wounding six. A bullet that "ranged down almost the length" of his spine crippled a twelve-year-old bystander. After several minutes of "wholesale shooting," a millhand under owners' orders cut electricity at the Bibb Mill's powerhouse, plunging the panicked crowd into darkness as the shooters escaped. A reporter described it as "the nearest thing to a battle here in years." A grand jury indicted three men on charges of murder—a worker and a foreman at the Bibb mill and the Bibb City police chief. At their trial, they were defended by prominent local attorneys, who called witnesses—all on the company payroll—who insisted that the men had not fired, and they were acquitted. Gompers unsuccessfully called on Georgia's governor to investigate. At its national convention in June, the AFL unanimously adopted a resolution condemning the "cold blooded" shooting by "officials and hirelings" of the mills. But such protests fell on deaf ears, and the violent repression solidified capital's victory over labor. A 1921 strike for a 30 percent wage increase failed, with Bradley arguing that the workers should be grateful that he kept the mill open since the best interests of stockholders "would have been to sell out every bale of cotton we had and close." The owners eliminated the worker bonus, cut wages, and fired strikers. The strike collapsed, killing Columbus's unions for the next decade.[56]

By 1920, Columbus boasted a modern infrastructure, and suburbs to the north and east, with Fort Benning poised to expand south. City government had become more progressive. Its economy relied too heavily on textiles, but the captains of industry refused to diversify, confident that they could control workers via a combination of paternalistic benevolence and violent intractability. Their defeat of unionization rested on three assertions proclaimed in August 1918: outside agitators were responsible for the conflict; workers were content; and unions would destroy the community's way of life. The owners employed this conservative template against unionization in the 1930s and 1940s. By the 1950s and 1960s, it underlay white opposition to civil rights.

CHAPTER 4

Lynching, Industrial Education, Babe Ruth, and Christian Communism

Social Change at the Turn of the Twentieth Century

Despite advancements under Mayor Lucius H. Chappell, Columbus remained a small southern town, a place "where few people had ever been far afield in their travels or their thoughts," as one woman remembered. Entertainments were "slow but sure": steamboat trips down the river, band concerts on the courthouse green, church on Sunday. By the late 1800s, members of the upper class began to illuminate their houses with electric incandescent lights. People and animals lived in symbiosis. Residents kept chickens, pigs, and milk cows in their yards, with wealthier families hiring black men and women to drive the cows to the Commons during the day and back home for evening milking. Individuals and businesses used horses and mules for transportation and as draft animals. A 1908 newspaper article described an incident involving a downtown grocery company's mule that had been bitten by a rabid dog, revealing much about life in turn-of-the-century Columbus:

> About 12:15 o'clock the mule was noticed by the negro driver, who was also bitten by the mad dog at the same time the mule was, to be biting viciously at the bit and Mr. Thompson, employed in the grocery, went out to where it was and saw at once that the animal was suffering from what appeared to be hydrophobia. Immediately steps were made to tie its feet.... The mule made a dash to the corner of Broadway and being unable to run fell on the sidewalk in front of the company's store.... Two police officers came up, and they decided that the mule had better be killed at once. Officer Oliver fired three shots into it from a forty-four caliber revolver. The affected animal died in a few minutes.
>
> It will be remembered that this was the mule which was bitten on the nose about a month ago by a mad dog which made its escape across the lower bridge into Alabama, and was last seen several miles in the coun-

Mule wagon with Negro driver and Shriners, Cargill Grocery Company, ca. 1910. Columbus State University Archives, Columbus State University, Columbus, Georgia.

try. Nothing has since been heard of the dog.... The [mule] was a valuable one, being worth fully $250.

The negro who was bitten at the time by the dog has since been treated at the Pasteur Institute in Atlanta and is now engaged in his usual duties, and feels no effects from the bite.

The story is notable in that it highlights the valuable mule, then provides information about the dog, and discusses the "negro driver" only as an afterthought. Despite the town's embrace of the progressive reform movements sweeping the country, race relations reached their lowest point in American history, with African Americans fighting an uphill battle for education, equal treatment, dignity, and even their lives.[1]

Segregation hardened by the 1890s, with whites especially fearing the rising black middle class and determined to maintain social control. Residential segregation in Columbus restricted African Americans to neighborhoods in the East Commons and the Bottoms—low land along Weracoba Creek, just down the hill from Wynnton—where black domestics and yardmen were within hailing distance of their wealthy employers. Many African Americans fought back against other denials of the rights guaranteed in the Fourteenth and Fifteenth Amendments. In 1883, a colored porter at a local auction house asked for social equality and cited the unfairness of paying the same train fare as a white man but receiving poor accommodations. And in 1898, the president of the Georgia Industrial College for Colored Youth asked for black representation on juries, equal seating on trains and streetcars, and the right to cast a ballot free of intimidation and to have it counted.[2]

Georgia institutionalized de facto segregation in 1891 when the legislature mandated separate railroad coaches for black and white travelers. Subsequent Jim Crow laws included an 1895 measure that required racial separation "as much as practical" on trolleys. In 1900, Rose Hill residents attended mass meetings to demand streetcars for whites only, with businessman and noted orator Robert Howard inflaming the crowd with talk of lynching. Alarmed at the potential costs of barring black patrons from whites-only streetcars, Columbus Railroad president John Flournoy persuaded the city council to give conductors the power to seat Negroes in the rear. Utility magnate George Johnson Baldwin fumed against streetcar segregation laws, noting that they provoked black boycotts resulting in company losses. Indeed, African Americans did not quietly acquiesce. In August 1900, a black woman sat in the middle of a car and refused to move. She was fined two dollars.[3]

By 1900, white southerners accepted violence and lynching as methods of social control. As noted author Richard Wright acknowledged, the threat of lynching was an "effective control of my behavior, . . . something whose horror and blood might descend upon me at any moment, [and] I was compelled to give my entire imagination over to it." From 1880 to 1930, Georgia trailed only Mississippi in the number of lynchings, with almost five hundred taking place and at least four of them in Columbus. On June 1, 1896, dozens of men burst into the courtroom where African American Jesse Slayton was on trial for the rape of a pregnant white woman, looped a noose around his neck, and dragged him onto Broad Street, where they fired "hundreds of shots" into him, hauled his body up into a tree in the median, and poured more bullets into it. "Drunk with fury," the mob rushed back to the jail and seized Will Miles, who was awaiting trial for another rape, hanged him from the same tree, and riddled his body with bullets. Leaders of the vigilantes pinned signs to both bodies: "All Cases of This Kind Shall Be Treated Likewise." The same afternoon, a grand jury ruled that Slaton and Miles had come "to their deaths by strangulation and gun shot wounds at the hands of parties unknown," and the next day's *Columbus Enquirer-Sun* declared that the "unwritten law of the South" was death to rapists.[4]

On June 10, 1900, "unknown" men lynched Simon Adams, who had been caught in the bedroom of some young girls. Muscogee County bailiff A. B. Land was supposed to take Adams to jail but instead left the main road and entered the woods, moving toward the Chattahoochee, where Land claimed that six or eight armed men had seized Adams and killed him. His body was never found, and Land most likely had a hand in the murder. In this case and many others, local law enforcement facilitated lynchings.[5]

Columbus's last confirmed lynching victim was T. Z. McElhaney, a black fourteen-year-old who accidentally shot a white boy, twelve-year-old Cedron Land, a cousin of A. B. Land. McElhaney was tried and convicted of involuntary manslaughter after a jury deliberated for just an hour, and on August 13, 1912, Judge Price Gilbert sentenced the boy to three years of hard labor. Members of the Land family found the sentence too lenient. They seized the boy from the courthouse and dragged him to Tenth Street and Second Avenue. There, at gunpoint, the mob hijacked a streetcar, forced the operator to drive to the city limits, and yanked the boy off the car. With McElhaney "pleading and screaming for mercy," the men pulled out pistols and shot him numerous times, leaving his lifeless body facedown in a shallow ditch beside the streetcar line until almost midnight, when undertaker Alex Toles fetched the body.[6]

Public opinion favored a "thorough investigation" of the lynching. The Federation of Women's Clubs and church leaders signed a "solemn protest" of horror at "the brutality of mob violence." A grand jury indicted A. B. Land; Cedron's father, W. L. Land; Cedron's uncle, R. E. L. Land; and mill worker Lee Lynn for murder. No white man in Georgia had ever been convicted of first-degree murder of an African American, and the jury found McElhaney's killers not guilty in under a half hour. The incident provoked the departure from Columbus of all African Americans who could afford to flee. Two years later, the murder conviction of Leo Frank, a white Jewish man, roused more opposition. Despaired Nathan Straus, who had spent much of his childhood in Columbus before moving to New York and becoming one of the owners of Macy's Department Store, "I must own that just at present I am thoroughly discouraged about Georgia.... I am trying to forget my connection with the State where my brothers and myself were educated and spent our early life." Frank's 1915 lynching could only have deepened

Straus's despair. In 1919, when the Georgia legislature considered an antilynching law, the *Enquirer-Sun* endorsed the measure, declaring, "Lynching in this state and throughout the country must stop." Nevertheless, the legislation failed, and segregation continued in Columbus neighborhoods, businesses, churches, and schools for more than a half century.⁷

Columbus, Georgia, and the rest of the South provided children with a dismal public education in the late nineteenth century. Funding for Columbus's schools averaged less than a dollar a day per student, about 40 percent of national per pupil expenditures, with children in the colored schools getting about half that. A white teacher earned about $475 annually, nearly twice the colored teacher's salary of about $250. The city's school year lasted eight months, while that in Muscogee County was only five. Black schools offered an education up to eighth grade, while white schools went one year longer, and about half of all children did not attend public school at all. Many whites believed that education made African Americans unfit for labor, but city superintendent George Dews did not share that view, believing that education increased everyone's "capacity to contend with the difficulties of life." Black parents agreed. In May 1882, 160 African Americans successfully petitioned the Columbus School Board to add ninth grade at colored schools, with the additional year funded by student tuition. Columbus thus became one of only four Georgia cities to offer nine grades for black students. African Americans then asked for a night school and Latin, Greek, geometry, and bookkeeping, but the board refused. William H. Spencer became principal of the city's colored schools in 1885 and soon offended board members by requesting athletic equipment and facilities. They responded by warning Spencer "that going to school was a matter of grace and not of right."⁸

By the 1890s, high schools became a priority for both whites and blacks. Though high school studies had been offered to white students since 1868, attendance and support had been spotty. In 1884, Dews backed an African American petition to add a "collegiate department" funded by blacks themselves, but the board took no action. White supremacy would not allow black schools to offer any course that was not available for whites. In response to lobbying by middle-class white parents, a high school opened in 1898 in a new brick building at Fourth Avenue and Eleventh Street. The board nevertheless continued to deny requests from "leading colored citizens" for a high school, again at their own expense. Middle-class black parents sent their children to high school departments at universities in Tuskegee, Alabama, and Albany, Fort Valley, and Atlanta, Georgia.[9]

Influenced by the national progressive movement, leaders transformed Columbus schools between 1899 and 1908. Across the South, education expanded to all classes, but wealthy white children received schooling different from poor black and white students. Led by superintendent Carleton B. Gibson, Columbus's public schools incorporated innovations inspired by Columbia Teachers College in New York City and John Dewey's Laboratory School at the University of Chicago, including kindergarten, special classes for working-class white children, and industrial education. Gibson was a typical southern progressive, endorsing white superiority and distrusting working-class whites and blacks but also believing that education could elevate children on the margins of society: the boys who dropped out of grammar school for mill work, the little "dinner toters" who carried their parents' lunches to the factories, the poor black children of manual and domestic laborers. He argued that schools should not lower their standards but should instead target "the ones whose home training is dangerously defective, even vicious. These are the ones that the public schools ought to save and turn into good citizens for the state—not the ones who will make good citizens anyway." Philanthropy was an important factor. Contributions from local industrialists, notably board of education member G. Gunby Jordan, were supplemented by support from Columbus native George Foster Peabody, a New York investment banker with a special interest in education, and the Rosenwald Fund, established by Sears, Roebuck president Julius Rosenwald for "the well being of mankind." These organizations trained teachers to offer special programs, outfitted laboratories and workshops, and purchased machinery and equipment. Philanthropy came at a price, as donors expected school programs and curricula to fit their ideologies.[10]

By 1895, charitable groups sponsored classes for poor children too young to work in the mills, and within three years, prominent citizens joined the crusade for public kindergarten. Some industrialists, led by Frederick Gordon of Columbus Manufacturing, saw child labor as beneficial, since children were "better employed in some industry than learning the first lessons of a vagrant's life," but the progressive impulse

The Eagle & Phenix's image of child labor, ca. 1890. Columbus State University Archives, Columbus State University, Columbus, Georgia.

An operative from Columbus Manufacturing, 1913. Lewis Hine photograph, Library of Congress.

sweeping the country countered Gordon's views. Jordan established a kindergarten for children of Eagle & Phenix workers in 1903, and the Columbus school system followed in 1905. Gibson and the school board first focused on the nearly seven hundred children who brought hot lunches to mill operatives. Gibson proposed the creation of a Primary Industrial School to meet their needs. He sent a list of $989.20 in vocational equipment to Peabody and received a check for $1000. In May 1901, Jordan explained Columbus's "peculiar necessity" for industrial education: "Nature intended" Columbus be a "beehive of industry," meaning that residents therefore "should fit our own school children for taking positions, and especially responsible ones" in hometown factories. The school would supply skilled workers for mills.[11]

The Primary Industrial School had a rocky September 1902 opening. In August, the three teachers had visited every home in the mill districts, encouraging parents to send children to school, but only about sixty children and parents attended opening day. One barrier may have been class bias: the *Columbus Enquirer-Sun* described the children as "very dirty, very disrespectful, and amazingly ill-mannered." The "kindly" teachers overlooked "finger smudges" on furniture, rude remarks, "expectoration on rugs and walls, and divers other evidences of absolute lack of breeding." But by the second semester, 150 children enrolled, and by 1906, that number had more than doubled to 343. Classes met from 7:30 to 10:30 a.m. and 1:00 to 4:00 p.m. so that children could bring dinners to their parents in the mills. Boys took carpentry, while girls learned cooking, sewing, laundry, and housekeeping. All took gardening, pottery, basketry, weaving, and art. Students learned traditional subjects—reading, writing, spelling, arithmetic, and history—through the vocational curriculum, without textbooks. Students repaired and painted the building and planted flower and vegetable gardens. The non-dinner-toting girls prepared lunch daily in a dining room, with the meal served on a white tablecloth the girls had also laundered. In addition, they sewed their aprons, carpenters' aprons for the boys, table linens, and cushions. Boys constructed coal bins, looms, and bookshelves.[12]

In addition to teaching manual skills, the school encouraged "moral uplift," instilling middle-class values. Teachers lived at the school, which was promoted as a model middle-class home, "orderly, tasteful, attractive in every detail." The goal of imbuing the students with "the home-ideal" seemed successful, and visitors noted the children's cleanliness and proper dress. By 1907, the school offered a day nursery for children under five. The Primary Industrial School was so successful by 1904 that, with Peabody's help, the board purchased and renovated a mansion in North Highlands, adding a playground and swimming pool, not only "a valuable means of education in cleanliness" but also open at all hours to neighborhood residents. The board renamed the facility the North Highlands School in 1912 and the McIlhenny School three years later, adding a new emphasis on academics. In 1913, city superintendent Roland Daniel, comparing it to other city elementary schools, emphasized its "severer adherence to the 'three R's.'" Nevertheless, the school did not alter children's destinies as mill operatives: "Not more than 1 per cent finish this school and pursue their studies further."[13]

For those who did go beyond primary education, in 1906 Columbus established a Secondary Industrial School—the first public vocational high school in the United States. Jordan donated 2.5 acres in Waverly Terrace and $5,500, with additional thousands in the coming years. Exemplifying self-interested philanthropy, the school made the Jordan Company's Waverly Terrace development more valuable, and Jordan's manufacturing enterprises benefited from skilled workers the school turned out. The Columbus Power Company provided free electricity, training "every child...to use our product," thus creating consumers accustomed to electric power and gas stoves who would demand those conveniences at home and in factories. As Baldwin concluded, "There is no way we can advertise our products more thoroughly." Jordan laid the new school's cornerstone in November 1906, calling it the "capstone of the system." Boys took either Mechanical Arts (carpentry, metal foundry work, machine work) or Textile Arts (carding, spinning, weaving, dyeing, designing). Home Economics was required for all girls. Each also chose Industrial Sewing (dressmaking, millinery, machine sewing), Textile Arts, or Office Help (stenography, bookkeeping, typing, filing). The academic subjects were English, mathematics, science, and history, all of them geared toward practical applications. Students attended from 8:00 to 4:00 six days each week for eleven months and finished in three years. They then served a two-month apprenticeship before graduating.[14]

The Beaux Arts–style school opened on December 10, 1906, with twenty-nine students. Daniel eliminated Saturday schooling in 1910 and in 1911 cut the school year to ten months. Though enrollment jumped 40 percent, it remained low, fluctuating between 146 and 225 from 1911 to 1916. The first graduating class of nine students "astonished" observers with their skills, cutting and sewing a dress onstage from fabric woven that day in the textile department. In 1914, the board of education changed the name to Columbus Industrial High School, and in 1930, it had 701 students and 25 teachers. In 1937, it moved into a new building and took on a new name: Jordan Vocational High School, after its benefactor. The former high school building became Columbus Junior High School.[15]

Columbus schools were organized by social class and racial hierarchy, with Negro education the lowest priority. Columbus joined systems across the South in implementing Negro industrial education based on Booker T. Washington's model at Tuskegee. As with working-class whites, the approach subordinated African Americans to their prescribed place in society. In 1898, Gibson told the board that Columbus schools were not serving Negro students' best interests by "attempting to give them a literary education"; such subjects rendered them unfit for the service jobs that were "the nature, the most congenial, and the most remunerative" for African Americans. Spencer, who spent half a century in charge of Columbus's black schools, heartily endorsed the Tuskegee model and cultivated a relationship with the board that enabled him to marshal privately donated materials and labor from Peabody and other sources. He wielded nearly absolute power. When he died in 1925, the board praised his "appreciation of the proper relations that should exist in this community between the races." The vocational curriculum required boys to learn carpentry and blacksmithing for one hour daily, to prepare Negroes "for the lines of industrial work open to them." No machinery training was available. Girls took sewing, cooking, laundering, and housekeeping, including "sweeping, house cleaning, scouring, care of the dining room, and table service," providing the skills needed for service in white homes. In 1907, mill president Frederick Gordon chuckled over a prominent African American minister's protests against his daughters washing dishes and cleaning floors, "but his objections were quietly and firmly over-ruled, and his high-toned daughters soon took the scrubbing brush and on their knees in the good old way cleaned the kitchen floors and washed the dishes and utensils of the school kitchen." Not only were the schools producing good help for whites, Gordon asserted, they kept the "less bright, slower, more plodding" black children from becoming "idlers and young criminals."[16]

By 1913, 85 percent of Columbus's school-age children attended, resulting in an illiteracy rate of only 2.8 percent, better than most other Georgia cities. Teacher qualifications improved, especially after state-level reforms in 1911. Low pay led to the departure of many teachers during the World War I economic boom, and at the end of the conflict, white teacher salaries averaged about $900, though black teacher incomes had not budged. Student health became a priority. Parent-teacher associations sought a free health clinic, dental services, and student medical inspections. When inspections began in 1914, the dreadful health of the poorer children became apparent, with more than half found to have "physical defects." Diphtheria outbreaks shut down schools in 1916, 1917, and 1918, as the overcrowded and unsanitary buildings proved to be incubators for disease. The 1918–1919 influenza pandemic closed schools for weeks, and many teachers and students succumbed to the virus. The board continued to monitor student health, but as with schooling, a family's social standing was the most important factor in its children's well-being.[17]

By the late nineteenth century, urban dwellers' work schedules permitted more leisure time. In 1884, the city gained an afternoon newspaper, the *Columbus Ledger*. The Columbus Public Library, which had opened in the Webster Building in 1880, moved to the new high school building in 1898. In 1907, the library remained in the school system but found a home for the next forty years amid the huge oaks on Mott's Green thanks to a $30,000 grant from Andrew Carnegie. Crowds flocked to the library's opening, and nearly five hundred children attended the first Children's Hour storytelling, a tradition generations of youngsters cherished. In 1915, Loretto Chappell, the mayor's daughter, was hired as an assistant librarian, and she went on to serve as the library's public face for half a century. But the library was for whites only; African Americans did not have a public library until the 1950s.[18]

All social classes enjoyed attending performances by traveling theatrical shows and circuses. On February 21, 1871, with seating for more than a thousand, the Springer Opera House opened with a "Grand Amateur Contest" to benefit Trinity Episcopal. A reviewer praised the Springer's acoustics but wryly noted of one singer, "This lady roams at will amid the labyrinth of sound." The Springer remained Columbus's only public hall until the 1950s, elegant with marble floors and painted frescoes. It offered diverse entertainment: minstrel shows, plays, vaudeville, lectures, and concerts. John Philip Sousa conducted a 1906 concert. Among the prominent political figures who spoke from its stage were Booker T. Washington, Eugene V. Debs, William Jennings Bryan, and Franklin Delano Roosevelt when he was stumping for Democratic candidate Al Smith in 1928. Around 1910, Roy E. Martin projected Columbus's first moving picture in an open field in North Highlands. In 1912, he purchased the city's first movie house, the Bonita, a nickelodeon that had opened on Broad two years earlier. By the early 1920s, Martin owned ten "high class" theaters, one each in North Highlands and in Phenix City and several downtown, including the Liberty, off Eighth Street, which catered to Negroes. In 1927, he opened Rose Hill's spectacular Royal Theatre, the largest movie house in Georgia, with seating for twenty-seven hundred.[19]

Buffalo Bill Cody brought his Wild West show to the South Commons in 1895, a nighttime performance illuminated by powerful electric lights, an attraction in itself when few homes had lighting. Circuses evoked great excitement, with dozens setting up on the East or South Commons. Most paraded from the train depot through downtown to drum up interest. On November 22, 1915, a Con T. Kennedy circus train from Atlanta to Phenix City derailed in a fiery crash north of Columbus. According to the circus press agent, "Flames were billowing thirty feet high. Injured people were screaming and shrieking—a lot of them were trapped under the wreckage and couldn't get out." At least twelve died and dozens were injured, with all of them brought to Columbus. Three burned beyond recognition were buried in Riverdale Cemetery, where survivors erected a monument in the shape of a circus tent. For years, circuses traveling to Columbus held memorial services at the grave. Reflecting New South boosterism, a craze for fairs and expositions swept the southern states in the late nineteenth century. Columbus held its first ten-day exposition in the fall of 1888, touting local industry and agriculture. The exposition was open only to whites except on Colored People's Day, a tradition that continued into the 1960s, by which time the exposition had long since morphed into the Chattahoochee Valley Fair, which remained popular into the 1990s.[20]

As leisure time grew, so did interest in sports. In the early 1870s, Frederick Reich created Villa Reich, which occupied a block on lower Front Avenue and featured a grand dance pavilion, a stage, and gardens. In 1881, Columbus joined nearly every other city in forming an exclusive athletic club. Patterned after the German *Turnverein* (gymnasts' clubs), it emphasized gymnastics, with its rings, trapezes, and other equipment in the Villa Reich's dance hall. The Columbus Cycle Club also met at the Villa Reich, and a second athletic club for younger men, the Queen City Club, formed in 1896. After the deaths of the Reichs, the dance hall became a roller-skating rink, providing a venue for one of the few sports in which women participated. Some men nevertheless objected to even that activity. Future railroad mogul Samuel Spencer told his fiancée, Louisa Benning, that she should never compete for the prizes at the roller rink: "I dread publicity for you beyond anything. A newspaper paragraph on you would be a most severe blow to me." Sports highlighted patriarchal gender roles that defined men as active and women as passive. The competitiveness, physical violence, and emphasis on winning essential to sports were masculine ideals, excluding women from widespread participation.[21]

The Young Men's Christian Association (YMCA) assumed that supervised athletics promoted morals and communal values lost in city life. Peabody and his two brothers offered $35,000 to build a white YMCA in Columbus if a local association bought the land and invested at least $10,000 in a trust fund. He made a similar offer to African Americans, though for only $15,000. Both communities responded enthusiastically, and the white Y, constructed of marble, opened on Tenth Street on December 2, 1903, with Peabody in attendance. The three-story brick African American Y located on Ninth Street at Sixth Avenue opened October 9, 1907, with a keynote address by Booker T. Washington. In the aftermath of the 1906 Atlanta race riot, Peabody hoped that the presence of the Negro Y would promote racial harmony and prevent such a "breakout" in Columbus. Initially, however, the Y instead provoked dissension. Working-class African Americans refused to use it because they felt that "only a certain class is welcome." The colored Y's white board believed its secretary pushed "this everlasting race question" to the forefront and withheld funds to bring him into line. The Y nevertheless attracted thousands of black men and boys during its first year, and it ultimately became a community institution.[22]

Columbus's sports scene long predated the founding of the YMCAs, however. In August 1867, the *Columbus Enquirer* reported on a baseball game between the Empire and Excelsior Clubs at the racetrack, and three years later, the Columbus Independents played for a prize awarded to the "best base ballists" but lost 70–12 to a team from Montgomery. Local African American teams included the Metropolitan Club, the Mutuals, and the Girard Blackfeet. In 1888, Columbus Railroad Company president John F. Flournoy and others bought a franchise in the Southern League, winning the pennant that year. Flournoy likely hoped that people would ride the streetcar to Wildwood Park to watch, but he lost a large amount of money and quit. Columbus did not field a professional team again until 1896. In 1908, Theodore Golden of Goldens' Foundry raised $10,000 for a team in the Southern League the next year. The team was named the Electrics after the Electric City but became known locally as the Foxes after their charismatic manager, Jim Fox, who was also the team's hard-hitting first baseman. The Foxes won pennants in 1910, 1911, and 1917 and led the league in attendance until World War I, when the league folded.[23]

The Cincinnati Reds became the first Major League team to visit Columbus in March 1899, when they arrived for a week of spring training at Wildwood Park. They returned in the spring of 1912, prompting the *Enquirer* editor to quip, "When the Georgia sun gets through with the Cincinnati baseball players, they will be entitled to their sobriquet, 'The Reds.'" In March 1913, the St. Louis Cardinals trained at Driving Park, the racetrack on the South Commons. The Pittsburgh Pirates arrived in the spring of 1917, and the Boston Braves followed in March 1919 and 1920, bringing their catcher, Hank Gowdy, MVP of the 1914 World Series and a World War I hero. In 1925, Fort Benning named its new baseball diamond Hank Gowdy Field. On April 2, 1924, the reigning world champion New York Yankees and their star player, Babe Ruth, played an exhibition game at Driving Park. The Rotary Club hosted a pregame father-son luncheon at which Ruth spoke "on the development of the body as well as the mind"; the game itself was "listless," with Ruth walking three times and striking out once.[24]

The Foxes formed again in 1926 in the South Atlantic League, with controversy over where they would play. The Baseball Association rejected Driving Park and persuaded the city to put a baseball stadium in Golden Park, a 125-acre recreation area on the South Commons named for Theodore Golden, the chair of the city's recreation board. Workers completed the stadium in less than two weeks, in time for the Foxes' season opener. The grandstand held a thousand spectators, with the bleachers holding an additional fifteen hundred, including three hundred seats in the Negro section, which had a separate entrance on Fourth Street. Golden regularly attended the games, winning admirers by handing out chewing gum to children. After his death, Golden's family estimated that he had given away $40,000 worth of Juicy Fruit gum. On April 24, 1929, the Negro National League's Birmingham Black Barons, led by legendary pitcher Satchel Paige, played Fort Benning's Twenty-Fourth Infantry team, before a mostly African American crowd. The Foxes entertained local fans until the Great Depression killed the league in 1932. Four years later, the Redbirds, a farm team for the St. Louis Cardinals, took up residence in Golden Park, winning five pennants over two decades. Among the players who worked their way to the Majors via Columbus were future Hall of Famers Enos Slaughter (who played for the Redbirds in 1936 and 1937) and Bob Gibson (who appeared in ten games in 1957), while notables including Dizzy Dean, Leo Durocher, and Pepper Martin played in Columbus when general manager Branch Rickey brought the Big Leaguers to town for exhibitions.[25]

The rise of college football also dates to the late nineteenth century. Teams at both Auburn Polytechnic Institute and the University of Georgia played their first intercollegiate games in 1892, with the two squads facing off against each other at Atlanta's Piedmont Park on February 20 to begin what is now known as the Deep South's Oldest Rivalry. Columbus divided its loyalties between the two teams and lured them to play at Driving Park in 1916 with the help of pledges from alumni and businessmen. A dedicated football stadium was constructed on the South Commons, with women's clubs raising funds for a Grand Entrance to honor World War I veterans. The stadium hosted its first games in the fall of 1925, with the Auburn–Georgia contest played there until 1958, when the huge social event finally outgrew the venue. Fans circulated among open houses and parties, with such festivities often overshadowing the game. An Auburn professor once left his school's $7,000 share of the gate atop a piano after attending a raucous party at Judge Frank Foley's house; the Judge, a Georgia fan, nevertheless returned the cash. Since 1935, Tuskegee and Morehouse Universities have played each year at Memorial Stadium, and by the early 2000s, the weekend of the game featured RV camping, tailgating, a golf tournament, a dinner dance, a parade, and private parties, while the contest itself raised about $50,000 annually for scholarships.[26]

One offshoot of the turn-of-the-century sports boom was the growth of public parks, which were seen as benefiting members of the working classes who otherwise lacked access to lawns and gardens. Parks were often built in conjunction with public libraries, as at Mott's Green, and were linked to educational, recreational, and music programs. The goal of a sound mind in a healthy body also resulted in the addition of physical education to school curricula. Columbus High School fielded boys football and baseball teams by 1900. The high school also formed a Girls Athletic Association that included nearly every female student and organized a basketball team and later added volleyball and tennis. Edwina Wood, an early advocate for kindergarten in Columbus, fervently supported organized play for children and in 1921 persuaded the city council to put all parks and playgrounds under city control. On August 1, an amendment to the charter created the Recreation Department. The

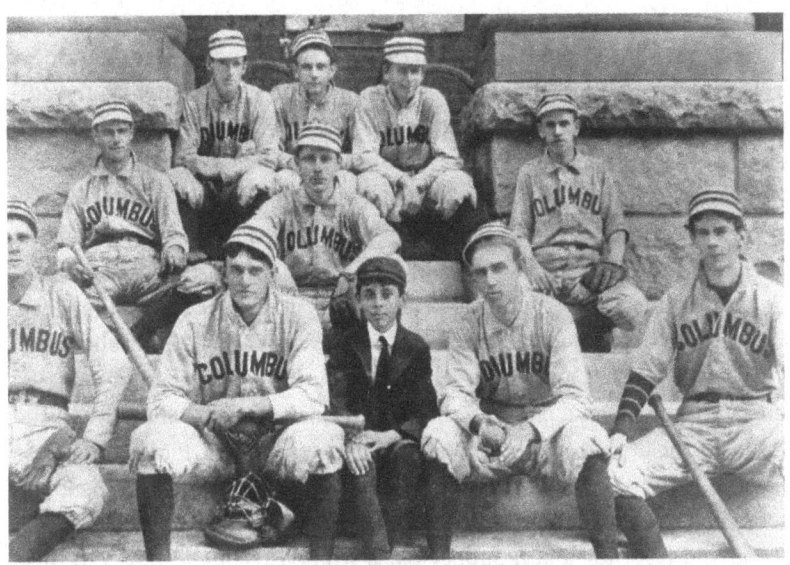

A baseball team on the courthouse steps and the Columbus High School girls basketball team, ca. 1910. Columbus State University Archives, Columbus State University, Columbus, Georgia.

same year, Wood became the first woman appointed to the school board; three years later, she was named to the new Recreation Board, where she helped to inaugurate city-sponsored summer programs at white and colored playgrounds, boys and girls clubs, Little League baseball, and band concerts. Wood became the Recreation Department director in 1932.[27]

The most popular parks were located outside the city. In 1892, Rhodes Browne created the whites-only North Highlands Park at the end of his streetcar line. Flournoy bought Browne's company in 1894 and added a dance pavilion, a tower with panoramic view, and boat rides on the Marie Springs pond. North of Lovers' Leap was "the gleaming Chattahoochee, curving in and out among the emerald islands and churning its waters into white mists and snowy foam as it dashes between and around the gigantic rocks that vainly impeded its onward rush." Park attendance declined after the Bibb Mill opened, and then an April 1908 tornado demolished the dance pavilion. As the city considered buying the lovely woodland tract for a park, upper-class women tried and failed to raise funds to keep it a park for whites, and a residential development company acquired the property.[28]

For African Americans, the railroad company located Lincoln Park at the end of the Rose Hill line. Between 1896 and 1908, the Jim Crow park hosted camp meetings, labor rallies, and "excursions" that required special trains to accommodate the throngs. White Rose Hill residents resented having trolleys filled with black revelers pass through their neighborhood and started referring to the green space as "Lynching Park" to discourage African American attendance. In April 1908, when the park's pavilion was demolished, the *Columbus Enquirer-Sun* lamented, "Any negro institution, solely for negroes, without the aid and influence of white people, is among the things that are impossible."[29]

Between roughly 1890 and 1920, middle- and working-class whites found their recreation at Wildwood Park, developed by Flournoy at the boundary of East Highlands. The name came from the Columbus birthplace of popular southern novelist Augusta Evans Wilson, author of *St. Elmo*. People flocked to the thirty-six-acre park to swim, fish, and boat on the lake, which featured arched bridges connecting three islands. In addition, visitors could dance in the pavilion, stroll the wooded paths, and see alligators, rabbits, and peacocks at a small zoo. The railroad company offered the park as an alternative to out-of-town summer vacations, with dances five evenings a week, a bowling alley, croquet, and lawn tennis. In 1902, six thousand people, a third of the city's population, rode streetcars to the Easter egg hunt held at Wildwood. The men in charge of starting the hunt were unable to hold back the crush of children eager to begin finding the "twelve hundred brilliantly dyed eggs." On May Day and Labor Day, mills and factories closed and workers and their families gathered at the park for pie-eating competitions, greased pig chases, and sack races. The post–World War I influenza epidemic discouraged such gatherings and killed the amusement park. In September 1920, Flournoy Realty announced plans to divide the park into residential lots, but in 1922, in response to requests from park patrons, the city purchased the property for recreational purposes. The Recreation Department filled in the lake to create playgrounds, ball fields, a track, and a miniature golf course. White residents continued to enjoy the park for decades.[30]

Wealthy families had their own diversions. They might bring children to the Wildwood Easter egg hunt, but most of their events were exclusive. An elite woman who grew up in Rose Hill's Redd mansion remembered that her aunt would ride sidesaddle through acres of violets on moonlit nights. For modesty, she sewed buckshot into the hem of her skirt to hold it down. Riverboat excursions were popular in the 1880s and 1890s. African American deckhands entertained passengers with secular and gospel songs, after which they "clear[ed] up the voice" by sharing liquor from "an alligator-brand oyster can." In 1920 Gunby Jordan II and ten of his friends organized the exclusive Big Eddy Club located where Standing Boy Creek emptied into the Chattahoochee River. Though it was intended to allow men to gather for fish fries and barbecues, affluent ladies were holding luncheons there by 1921. Columbus's famous Country Captain chicken dish made its first appearance at a Big Eddy Club dinner.[31]

Wealthy businessmen formed the Muscogee Club around 1890 in Eli Shorter's antebellum mansion on Broad. A gathering place for local and out-of-town businessmen and for dinners, dances, and oyster roasts, the club held members to high standards of behavior, prohibiting gambling, sleeping on couches, and dogs. The upper-class golf and tennis craze sparked interest in a private country club, leading Lloyd Bowers to build a small golf links in the orchard beside his Wynnton home, the Elms, with tomato cans serving as the holes. The men wanted a more formal course, so in 1909, two hundred members formed the Country Club of Columbus, constructing a golf course and tennis courts on sixty acres of the Wildwood estate's pasture but restricting membership to white Christian men. In July 1919, the original "rustic-style" clubhouse burned so intensely that golf balls exploded, sounding like gunfire. Though the cause of the blaze was never determined, it coincided with the acquittal of one of the suspects in a mass shooting at a Bibb City labor rally; the shooting had been orchestrated by the millowners, all of whom were club members. The club rebuilt a two-story Mediterranean-style clubhouse, which opened on June 1, 1920. Barred from Country Club membership, Columbus's Jews formed their own exclusive clubs. The city's earlier-arriving and more assimilated Germanic Jews had founded Columbus Concordia in 1870 to ease the "monotonous evenings and Sundays in this city"; in 1909, the organization became the Harmony Club. And in 1907, Eastern European Jews chartered the Standard Club, "an organization for recreation, pleasure, social, and literary entertainment of its members."[32]

Men's secret societies were popular at the turn of the century. The Improved Order of the Red Men, the Knights of Pythias, and the Odd Fellows were the largest Christian white groups, with B'nai B'rith for Jewish men. In 1903, the five-hundred-member Masons built a four-story temple at Twelfth Street and First Avenue, with retail space on the first floor, offices on the second and third, and Masons and other orders sharing the fourth. Most of these groups were fraternal organizations, sponsoring dances and dinners, though some also provided death benefits. In the old Trinity Episcopal building on First Avenue, the Eagle & Phenix had a club for operatives that featured a gym, bowling alley, and library and hosted concerts and lectures aimed at "the uplifting of its industrial population." African American fraternal organizations such as the Prince Hall Masons and the colored Odd Fellows and Knights of Pythias as well as the smaller Brothers and Sisters of Benevolence also aspired to uplift their members. The societies worked primarily to aid ill or aged members and to provide death benefits, a critical need since most African Americans lacked the opportunity or the means to buy insurance. The Brothers and Sisters of Benevolence, for example, provided "aid and comfort to its members wherever found in a state of hopelessness or infirmity." The Children of Mount Tabor provided cash for doctors' visits and paid for funerals of members' children. These groups also helped assimilate black members into the white social order. For example, Georgia's International Benevolent Society, headquartered in a two-story brick building at First Avenue and Tenth Street, promoted sanitary conditions in homes, schools, and churches and counseled African Americans to live more like whites. In 1919, the society's president urged African Americans' "good behavior everywhere and at all times"—coded language for accommodating whites.[33]

Male secret societies had women's auxiliaries, such as the Pocahontas Tribe of the Red Men, the Order of Calanthe for colored Knights of Pythias, and the Order of the Eastern Star for black and white Masons. Upper-class Christian women were active in the Daughters of the American Revolution, the United Daughters of the Confederacy, and the King's Daughters, "a sisterhood for the performance of kindly deeds." The Century Club, founded around 1909, accepted both Christian and Jewish women. The women's clubs differed from most men's societies in their emphasis on educational or civic betterment. Founded in 1912, the Federation of Women's Clubs immediately denounced lynching after T. Z. McElhaney's murder. The club also sponsored Chautauqua lectures and health conferences for new mothers and pushed city beautification and cleanup. The Federation of Colored Women's Clubs solicited donations from the Southern Railroad, the City of Columbus, and George Foster Peabody for a playground and athletic fields. The white federation's most lasting contributions occurred in the area of public health, as the group established free medical and dental clinics for poor children, campaigned for the creation of the city's health department, and certified sanitary conditions for "pure milk." Soon after the beginning of World War I, the federation launched a campaign to eliminate Columbus's vice district. Crusading on behalf of public morality, members wanted the city to be "clean, not only for our boys in Khaki, but also for our sons and brothers [and to] cleanse the city of vice." Such efforts had less success than the federation's other endeavors.[34]

The urge for perfectibility motivated the creation of the Christian Commonwealth, a short-lived utopian community in Columbus. The late nineteenth-century social Christianity movement focused on transforming society rather than saving individuals. The Christian socialists foresaw "a society founded on good will and mutuality" where "the whole world [was] a neighborhood and every man a neighbor." The same utopian impulse spawned the 1894 single-tax community in Fairhope, Alabama, and the 1899 Ruskin Commonwealth in Ware County, Georgia. In November 1896, the Christian Commonwealth Colony purchased the 931-acre Dozier plantation near Upatoi to raise fruits and vegetables for market. The colonists were middle-class farmers, mechanics, ministers, doctors, and teachers from California, Massachusetts, Nebraska, Washington, and Florida, and they shared the belief that society's wrongs could be righted through unselfish socialism. Each pledged "to love my neighbor as myself"; to provide labor, income, and property for all who needed it; and to "withdraw myself from the selfish competitive strife and devote myself to the cooperative life and labor." By late 1898, eighty-five colonists had constructed a sawmill, barns, a blacksmith shop, and a schoolhouse. The colony sold tomatoes, cabbage, potatoes, plums, blackberries, and watermelons. Members bought five-dollar secondhand looms to make Turkish towels, but the quality was so poor that they did not sell, and the mill closed in May 1899. The only financial success was a printing business. The colonists used a forty-six-dollar used press to turn out pamphlets, small books, and custom print jobs. From February 1898 until July 1901, the colony's journal, the *Social Gospel*, reached a circulation of two thousand, with readers in every state and seventeen foreign countries. Columbus generally viewed the colony favorably, with the *Enquirer-Sun* approving the new arrivals as "strict church and temperance people." Their communal setup was acceptable because the colonists were not "calamity howlers" but industrious, white, and monogamous members of the middle class.[35]

Utopia did not arrive, however. Living on a vegetarian diet of cowpeas, sweet potatoes, sorghum, and peanut butter, colony leaders concluded that "our bill of fare was far below health requirements." The old plantation house, three existing tenant shacks, and rough-sawn barracks were also inadequate. Dissension surfaced when twenty-seven colonists left in May 1899 and petitioned the superior court for the value of their labor beyond room and board, though they had relinquished any claim to wages. The court ruled that the plaintiffs were not entitled to any payments. A week later, locals were titillated when one of the litigants published a book on free love. As spicy gossip spread, the colony's support dried up, and the situation grew dire when nine colonists contracted typhoid from tainted creek water. By the spring of 1900, only about thirty colonists remained, and in June, the Christian Commonwealth entered voluntary receivership. W. T. Harvey and Company purchased the land at a November auction, and by October 1903, the utopian experiment had been erased and replaced by a sawmill and cotton gin.[36]

Local reforms were controversial, but none raised a ruckus like woman suffrage. Most nineteenth-century Americans accepted the notion that woman's sphere was the home while man's was the public arena. "Piety, purity, submissiveness, and domesticity" characterized a "true" woman. Any woman who stepped outside her "natural" place was "a mental hermaphrodite" who challenged civilization's foundation. Columbus's Helen Augusta Howard personified that challenge. Despite her impeccable Old Columbus lineage as a granddaughter of entrepreneur John Howard, grandniece of Seaborn Jones, and cousin of novelist Augusta Evans Wilson, Augusta Howard embraced feminism—as well as atheism, vegetarianism, and spiritualism. In addition, she occasionally wore trousers and never married, clearly marking her as an "unnatural" woman. In 1890, at age twenty-five, she founded the Georgia Woman Suffrage Association. Howard said she was motivated by her mother's "taxation without representation" after her father's death in 1867. A few Columbus men supported suffrage, including Gunby Jordan, who stated, "Woman as a taxpayer should have her full share of the selection of the gatherer of these funds, and in saying what disposition should be made of them." Howard described the virulent opponents of woman suffrage as "of the most malignant and underhand sort, scrupling not at insult, lying, and slander, in hope of intimidating the few advocates of equal rights." Augusta's older brothers, businessmen Richard and Robert Howard, sought to stifle Augusta but initially had no success. In 1894, she convinced the National American Woman Suffrage Association to hold its next annual convention in Atlanta, the first time the organization met outside Washington, D.C. Howard predicted that the convention would fill the Atlanta Opera House, and indeed, the February 1895 convention was a rousing success. The association's president, Susan B. Anthony, noted that the Opera House was "packed to suffocation" and that hundreds had been turned away. At Atlanta University and Bethel Church, Anthony "talked to 1000 or more" African Americans, "some *whiter* than me—Still doomed to go with the blackest." The *Enquirer-Sun* sniped, "Atlanta is now in her element and happy. She is entertaining the charmed circle of worshippers of the most interesting modern fad, the woman suffragists, with the venerable and esteemed Col. Susan B. Anthony at the head."[37]

After the convention, Augusta and her sisters hosted Anthony at Sherwood Hall, the family's mansion located outside Columbus on Talbotton Road. Anthony found that the fireplaces in the "old slaveholder's mansion" barely "touched the frigid air of the rooms," but her reception was warm: "The hearts of the Howards are great and gave us a cordial welcome." Nevertheless, she noted, "over this dear conscientious family hangs a heavy cloud," and "a sadness reigns over the house." Howard's brothers likely were scandalized that the sisters had invited a Yankee advocate of gender and racial equality into their home and furious that they had paid the convention's costs out of the men's pockets—the Howard women had no incomes. "Monomaniacs in manifesting opposition and dislike for woman suffrage," the brothers redoubled their efforts to constrain Augusta, and she resigned as president of the Georgia Woman Suffrage Association late in 1895, never again playing a major role.[38]

On May 20, 1920, after Gunby Jordan had built Jordan Mills and an adjacent village on the western edge of the Sherwood Hall property, Augusta heard someone up in a huge magnolia tree in her yard and fired a pistol twice into the tree as a warning, hitting an eight-year-old boy in the abdomen. The boy screamed, and Augusta helped him descend, lectured him about property rights, and sent him away. A passerby found him crawling down Talbotton Road and took him to the hospital, where for three weeks he hovered between life and death. Augusta was arrested and jailed until it was clear that the boy would live, when she was released on bond.[39]

The grand jury charged Howard with intent to murder. At her trial's opening, she demanded a jury of her "peers," meaning women, likely irritating everyone involved. The trial was a sensation, with a packed courtroom and newspapers printing breathless summaries. Augusta delivered a three-hour speech, rambling on, evoking class principles, noting her lofty lineage, and generally displaying paranoia. She referred to her "practical outlawry" and claimed that twenty-five years of persecution had forced her to become a "hermit." She asserted that because "one's house is one's castle," the "boy's blood is not on my hands but on the hands of his parents who failed to train him properly." She went on so long that wrist pain forced the court reporter to stop transcribing her words. A jury of white men convicted her of unlawful shooting, and the judge sentenced her to between one and two years in prison. Howard unsuccessfully appealed all the way to the Georgia Supreme Court. Horrified at the scandal, her brother, Richard, asked the governor for clemency on the grounds that she was mentally unbalanced. Augusta vigorously objected, but Richard supported his claim with letters from prominent Columbus citizens such as W. C. Bradley, John F. Flournoy, and L. H. Chappell—most of whom did not know Augusta. Letters from personal acquaintances stressed her culture, lineage, intelligence, and humanity. More impressed by Richard's allies, the trial judge recommended a pardon, "convinced that she did not possess a normal mind."

Augusta Howard's headstone in Linwood Cemetery.
Photo by Virginia E. Causey.

The prison board concurred, declaring her "mentally unsound and suffer[ing] from delusions." On December 2, 1921, the governor pardoned Augusta. She subsequently moved to New York, where, according to family legend, Richard had exiled her. She died in 1934 and was buried in Columbus's Linwood Cemetery, where by far the largest word on her grave marker is "Martyred!" Such was the fate of an independent woman in the early twentieth-century South.[40]

Though the center of Georgia's suffrage struggle thereafter shifted to Atlanta, Columbus remained a hotbed in a largely cold state. Thanks in part to Jordan's support, many of the city's elite women and men advocated suffrage by 1912. In May 1914, the Equal Suffrage League held Columbus's first women's rights parade, featuring automobiles with yellow ribbons proclaiming "Votes for Women." The league held card parties, tea dances, and suffrage schools; circulated petitions; and sold baked goods in the City Market. Beginning on February 16, 1914, the *Ledger* ran a pro-suffrage column, "Equal Franchise," and on June 28 of that year, it published a special edition on suffrage with articles by women leaders as well as by Jordan and Frank J. Dudley. The national and state United

Daughters of the Confederacy opposed voting rights for women, instead advocating that they wield power as wives and mothers "against universal suffrage, believing in white supremacy and states rights." Yet Anna Caroline Benning, charter member and president of the Lizzie Rutherford chapter of the Daughters for forty years, was a founder and officer in the Equal Suffrage League. Her support may have been a reaction to the men in her family: A drunk cousin shot the Russell County sheriff. Another cousin embezzled money and gambled it away—three times. And her brother-in-law, Reese Crawford, also drank and gambled. Never married and largely dependent on such men, Anna Caroline not surprisingly saw a need to be active in organizations that empowered women.[41]

Opposition to suffrage was more typical among Georgians, however. Ministers called it "an attack on the home" that would "lead to the conditions that destroyed Sodom and Gomorrah." Described by the *Enquirer-Sun* as a "womanly woman," Augusta Evans Wilson predicted that the day that suffrage passed "will be the blackest in the annals of this country and will ring the death knell of modern civilization, national prosperity, social morality, and domestic happiness." White women feared Negro domination if black women voted, resulting in loss of control over black servants and disorder in the household. Middle-class men and women feared that the votes of working-class women without genteel moral character might erode the social order. Nevertheless, after vigorous campaigning by national suffrage organizations during World War I, the *Enquirer-Sun* admitted, "The women of this country have done a most noble work: they are still doing it and will continue to do it. This very fact is going to give them such a hold upon the consideration of the men of the country that the latter will not think of withholding from them the ballot when the time comes."[42]

Congress passed the Nineteenth Amendment on June 4, 1919, and sent it to state legislatures for ratification. On July 24, Georgia became the first state to reject it, prompting an approving editorial in the *Enquirer-Sun*: "No mother can give attention to [politics] without neglecting her home affairs, and she is the proper person—the person intended by our Maker—to take care of the home." The *Ledger*, in contrast, blasted the legislators as "mossbacks" determined to "advertise to the world that we are a backward and a slow-minded people." Two days after Tennessee's August 26 ratification put the amendment into effect, the Muscogee County Equal Franchise League asked churches, factories, and railroads to sound bells and whistles at noon to salute women's right to vote. But the city was quiet, leading League president Anna Griffin to claim that the suffragists were treated like "snakes in Ireland." And still Georgia's women could not vote: the registration deadline for the 1920 elections had already passed. The Equal Suffrage League morphed into the League of Women Voters and continued to apply pressure, and on January 18, 1921, the county tax collector's office finally began accepting registrations from women. The League requested that each woman who registered pick up a sticker for her window: "A Woman in This House Has Registered to Vote Thereby Assuming the Responsibilities of Citizenship."[43]

By 1920, education, sports, leisure activities, entertainment, and reform movements had made Columbus bigger, more modern, and more cosmopolitan than ever before. Over the ensuing decade, the color line hardened. In addition, elevated by the franchise, women contributed to a major political reorganization. As in other cities across the South, Columbus's explosive growth sparked optimism that the Electric City would take its place as a regional leader.

CHAPTER 5

The Klan and Coca-Cola

The Roaring Twenties

As the states debated whether to ratify the Nineteenth Amendment and give women the right to vote, the editor of the *Columbus Enquirer-Sun* crankily surveyed the landscape that he feared lay ahead: "The modern dress, the modern dance, the modern music, and modern manners are symptoms that indicate somehow in this age we have lost our bearings, and the old values of life, once so brightly prized have been forgotten. There is a danger of a lessening, if not a loss, of the old time reverence for womanhood. Real men may look [at women wearing more revealing clothing], they may smile, but secretly they scorn." He was not alone in his desire to preserve "old values." Across the nation, the 1920s saw conflict between modernists and traditionalists that sometimes turned violent, but those who sought to resist change were fighting a losing battle. As one journalist wrote of his travels through the South, "Down in Dixie they tell you, and always with cheerful pride, that the South is the new frontier. There is a thrill in the air; big tomorrows seem to be coming around the corner.... Everywhere are new roads, new automobiles, new hot dog stands, tea shops, movie palaces, radio stores, real estate subdivisions, tourist campgrounds." Columbus experienced all of these things, and they brought political reorganization and economic growth.[1]

Obsession with efficiency dominated American culture in the 1920s. Henry Ford applied efficiency expert Frederick W. Taylor's ideas to mass-produce automobiles, and the concept spread to government. As early as 1913, Columbus progressives pushed to replace the city's sixteen aldermen and mayor with a commission government, an approach pioneered by Galveston, Texas, in 1901 that subsequently spread. Voters elected commissioners at-large, with each one responsible for a specific aspect of municipal business, (for example, public works, recreation, finance, or public safety) and the group as a whole passing appropriations and ordinances. The commissioners chose one member to serve as mayor and to preside at meetings and ceremonies and hired a professional city manager to serve as the top administrator. The commission thus blended the legislative and executive functions, creating a system that supporters touted as streamlined and efficient, reflecting a businesslike approach to government in which ward politicians had less opportunity to muddy the waters. Critics feared that the city manager would be a dictator unanswerable to voters and that at-large commissioners would reduce personal representation. Though Columbus is often touted as among the first southern cities to adopt the commission form of government, the opposite is actually true: by 1914, about four hundred cities across the nation, including most Alabama municipalities, had commission governments. Though both Columbus's newspapers and its chamber of commerce campaigned for the idea, with headlines trumpeting "The Sentiment for Commission Government Almost Unanimous," Columbus citizens twice failed to approve the new government. Not until September 1921, when 82 percent of newly enfranchised women, voting in a separate booth newly lit with electricity, backed the measure, did the city adopt a commission government.[2]

The top vote-getter in the November 1921 general election, Homer Dimon became Columbus's mayor, a position he held for eleven years. His election set the informal precedent that the person who won the most votes would become mayor. League of Women Voters president Anna Griffin won a commission seat, becoming the first woman elected to public office, although her tenure was brief. In a 1922 case that divided the city, Griffin served as a character witness for the county police chief after he shot an accused bootlegger in the back. When she ran for reelection the following year, she lost soundly to a man. Seventy percent of women supported Griffin, while 70 percent of men, who turned out in much larger numbers, opposed her. A half century passed before another woman was elected to the Columbus city government. The career of the first woman legislator from Columbus was similarly brief. Love Tolbert won a seat in the General Assembly in a 1933 special election but came in a distant last behind three male candidates in her 1934 reelection bid, and four decades elapsed before another woman won election to the legislature. When Tolbert was named national Mother of the Year in 1954, the *Columbus Ledger* made no mention of her brief political career.³

In early 1922, the commission hired Pennsylvanian Gordon Hinkle as the first city manager, resurrecting fears of a dictatorship. After threats from a local organization, the Alaga Club, three white men beat Hinkle on April 21, leading the *Enquirer-Sun*'s liberal new editor, Julian Harris, son of noted journalist and author Joel Chandler Harris, to denounce the "cowardly" attack. Harris had previously sparred with the Alaga Club, otherwise known as the Ku Klux Klan. The local chapter solicited "native born" members who believed in the "tenets of the Christian religion," "White Supremacy," the "Sovereignty of our States Rights," and the "limitation of foreign immigration." With approximately five hundred members, the Columbus group had its headquarters above the police station, and in early 1921, the police chief had called the Klan "a blessing to any community." Despite threats and sabotage, Harris had launched a crusade against the Klan, and on September 23, 1921, 5,000 residents watched as 125 hooded Klansmen paraded through Columbus and Phenix City, deliberately marching past the *Enquirer-Sun* offices. Harris and city editor Cliff Tucker had pretended to recognize participants and take names.⁴

The day after the beating, Hinkle and Mayor Dimon received letters demanding that they resign and that Hinkle leave town within forty-eight hours. "And remember," Dimon's letter threatened, "you SHALL not bring a Yankee as manager over our city." If the mayor failed to fire Hinkle, the authors would "kill you and sink you in the depths of the river where no man talks." Dimon shrugged off the threat, but a month later a bomb shattered the front of his Third Avenue home as he and his family slept. Four days later, Hinkle and his family returned to Pennsylvania. Harris blasted the Klan, publishing members' names and denouncing them as "grafters, black-mailers, spy-chiefs, seducers." His relentless attacks led commissioners to fire the police chief on Christmas Eve 1922. After policemen were implicated in another bomb plot, the new police chief weeded out known Klansmen. A week later, the head of the Georgia Klan ordered the Columbus chapter to disband. Membership in the Columbus chapter declined, and it quietly dissolved early in 1926. Also that year, the *Enquirer-Sun* won a Pulitzer Prize for its anti-Klan campaign.⁵

The commission replaced Hinkle with a civil engineer with impeccable Columbus credentials: Henry Benning Crawford, son of Gen. Henry Benning's daughter, Augusta, and Congressman Martin Crawford's son, Reese. Crawford left the job after five months, but his replacement was another good southerner, Walter Richards, son-in-law of millowner Frederick Gordon. Despite the opposition, the transition to the commission form of government indeed improved the city's efficiency and economic health. The city's $45,000 debt in 1922 had become a surplus within twelve months. Columbus's population grew almost 30 percent in the 1920s, topping forty-three thousand, mainly as a result of the 1925 annexation of Wynnton. The growth brought a renewed focus on the idea of city planning, which had largely been neglected since Columbus's early days. The commission created a Planning Board and in 1924 hired national expert John Nolen to produce the first of many improvement plans. The city ignored most of Nolen's suggestions, however, including the creation of a civic plaza near Twelfth Street and Third Avenue that would include the city hall, an auditorium, a library, and a museum; the removal of railroad tracks and rail yards within the city; and the addition of green space to counter Columbus's "industrial character." The council did build the recommended commercial aviation field. Worried that incoming planes would not be able to find the airfield south of Riverdale Cemetery, the local Ford dealer painted "Columbus, Georgia" and a directional arrow on top of his building. The Southern Air Express Company inaugurated passenger flights in June 1929, with Columbus serving as an intermediate stop between Atlanta and Montgomery.[6]

The commission also embraced Nolen's ideas for improving transportation. At the time of his report, about 25 percent of the city's seventy-four miles of roads had a hard surface, but by decade's end, most streets downtown and in suburban white neighborhoods were paved, as were sixty-seven miles of county road. In 1927, Broad Street became Broadway, and variously named streets were consolidated into Linwood Boulevard and Buena Vista Road. The commission approved two major bridge projects. In July 1920 a U.S. Army truck had nearly fallen through rotten flooring on the steel Fourteenth Street bridge; exactly two years later, hundreds gathered to hear L. H. Chappell open its replacement, a concrete bridge constructed by the Hardaway Company. In addition, an 1,888-foot concrete viaduct on Thirteenth Street completed in 1925 bypassed the rail yards on Sixth Avenue, channeling traffic over the tracks from downtown to Wynnton. Enthusiastic boosters called the structure the longest in the South.[7]

The viaduct opened a convenient route to the eastern suburbs, spurring the construction of at least thirty subdivisions north and east of the city. The Jordan Company targeted upper-class residents with Green Island Hills, a development on rolling, forested land along the river adjoining Gunby Jordan's Green Island Ranch where, the company promised, "The ogre of city taxes never intrudes," "Mosquitoes have no abiding place," and "Altitude insures ozone—Ozone guarantees health." The affluent began moving in soon thereafter, and the first house was finished in 1926. With installment purchasing gaining popularity, the Jordan Company became the first in the area to open a financing department: "We furnish the Lot, the Plans, and the Money."[8]

By the 1920s, most people in Columbus had stopped thinking of the Chattahoochee River as an economic conduit, but city boosters sought to revive river trade. In 1925, the chamber of commerce successfully lobbied Congress to construct locks and dams on the Chattahoochee, a deeper navigation channel to Apalachicola, and an intracoastal waterway from there to New Orleans. In 1928, Columbus partnered with downriver municipalities to create the Chattahoochee Valley and Gulf Association, which promoted regional development through transportation "by rail, water, highways, and airways." The 1929 stock market crash brought an end to congressional appropriations, however, and no significant river improvements occurred for three decades.[9]

Further discouraging interest in the river, Columbus experienced its worst flood in history in March 1929. The wet winter caused streams to overflow, and high water in the Chattahoochee shut down the riverfront mills. In early March, as the muddy river continued to rise, gawkers thronged the Dillingham and Fourteenth Street bridges. By the middle of the month, torrential rains drove the river to a record high-water mark of 13 feet above flood stage—53.3 feet at the Dillingham Street bridge, almost enough to reach the tops of its arches. The city's south end flooded, with water coming halfway up Golden Park's fences. Bay Street and Front Avenue were under several feet of water. The Central of Georgia Railway weighed down a trestle with a string of boxcars. The gaslight plant and the Columbus Power Company on the riverbank flooded. Homeowners fired up old wood, coal, and oil stoves, while the *Enquirer* "with great difficulty" used acetylene torches and steam boilers to operate press equipment. Property damage was extensive, especially to industry and warehouses along the river. Low-lying Phenix City was even harder hit, with twelve hundred people left destitute.[10]

Downtown Columbus's economy remained brisk during the 1920s, with a few national chain stores, including Kress, Woolworth, A&P, and Piggly Wiggly, pushing their way into the local market. As installment buying increased in popularity, Columbus stores such as H. Rothschild furniture began offering "terms for convenient payment." Textile mills still dominated, with Muscogee Manufacturing, Columbus Manufacturing, Swift, and the Bibb expanding their plants. The combined mills produced $400,000 worth of products daily, with other manufacturing adding another $100,000. By 1929, the mills' combined annual payrolls approached $23 million. The chamber of commerce identified Columbus as the second-largest cotton manufacturer in the South, central to a "great cotton-growing region," though a boll weevil infestation significantly reduced yields. The Lummus Cotton Gin Company had moved to Columbus in 1898, begun overseas sales in 1907, and incorporated in 1910. During the 1920s, it expanded its plant to produce textile machinery as well as gins, becoming an industry leader in making equipment for new synthetic fibers. W. C. Bradley expanded his cotton warehouses along the river, and the Bradley Company's fertilizer business boomed as well. In 1925, Bradley brought the dilapidated Iron Works to life as a division of the Bradley Company. After an immediate expansion, the foundry began selling cast-iron stoves and continued marketing ice machines, commercial refrigerators, and agricultural implements. By 1929, the Columbus area had five brick and tile plants, the largest of which was Bickerstaff on the Alabama side of the river.[11]

Columbus also diversified during the 1920s. Sidney Simons, son of grocer and saloonkeeper Max Simons, had started the Southland Pecan Company just before World War I, selling two barrels of shelled pecans during his first year in business. By 1921, however, the company was shipping pecans all over the United States and Canada. Five years later, Southland had become the world's largest pecan factor, shipping twelve million pounds to confectionaries, bakers, and grocers around the world and mailing more packages from Columbus than any other institution. But Southland was dwarfed by Tom's Peanuts, founded by Tom Huston, the son of a Texas peanut farmer, who began selling roasted peanuts from a shotgun house on Thirty-Second Street in 1925. Although Huston patented an effective peanut sheller as well as roasting methods, his real genius was marketing. Rather than parcel out portions from a big can, as was the custom, he invented the "long tall sanitary bag," a serving in a glassine packet with an iconic red triangular logo. Houston displayed his nickel packets of peanuts by cash registers at the point of sale. In addition, he perfected a distribution network of independent salesmen who bought trucks, vending machines, and products from Tom's. By 1928, Huston's company had four hundred employees and was operating out of a forty-five-thousand-square-foot Tenth Avenue plant, and in 1929, the company recorded $2.5 million in sales. George Washington Carver at Tuskegee Institute served as a consultant to Huston for a decade, helping to improve the company's products, but declining a position with Huston's enterprise in favor of assisting African American students and farmers.[12]

Huston fell as quickly as he rose. In 1928, he became obsessed with marketing frozen peaches, borrowed 15 percent of his net worth using stock as collateral, and built a "quick-freeze plant" at Montezuma, in the heart of Georgia's peach country. But railroads did not yet have freezer cars and grocery stores lacked freezer cases. When the market crashed in 1929, the value of stock in his company plummeted from twenty dollars a share to two dollars. In 1931, the banks foreclosed, and the board of directors of the peanut company forced Huston out. Embittered, he left Columbus, returning only after his death in 1972, when his body was buried in Linwood Cemetery. The company retained his name, appointed former city manager Walter Richards as president, and prospered after the Great Depression, becoming one of Columbus's major industries.[13]

In 1907, streetcar company president George Baldwin received a request from a vendor to serve his product at Wildwood Park. Baldwin rejected the application, replying that such "people who are doing as much to debase the youth of this State ought to be prevented from doing it." His manager agreed that the product was not "the right kind of stuff for an amusement park, although 'dope' fiends expect to be able to procure it there." The "dope" was Coca-Cola.[14]

Columbus and Coca-Cola have a long and rich relationship. John Pemberton, who developed the Coke formula, moved to Columbus in 1855 to establish retail and wholesale drug companies selling patent medicines, perfumes, hair restorers, oils, paints, and other concoctions from his laboratory. He marketed wines not only for drinking but also as medicinal tonics. Pemberton enlisted in the Confederate army in 1862 but resigned on October 12 on the grounds that "I am now suffering and have been for a long time with chronic disease of the stomach ... which renders me unfit for military duty." Pemberton still hoped to serve the Confederacy as "a Chemist and Pharmaceutical Druggist," and he formed a home guard unit that helped to defend Columbus on April 16, 1865. During the fighting, he was shot and slashed with a saber, giving rise to a neo-Confederate claim that his war wounds led to an addiction to morphine. More likely, Pemberton had initially taken laudanum (a tincture of opium to which he would have had easy access as a pharmacist) years prior to the war to ease his relentless stomach pain but switched to morphine, a superior pain medication, after it became commercially available by the mid-1850s and the hypodermic needle was perfected in 1853. Records show that two Crawford, Alabama, physicians administered copious amounts of morphine to patients just before the war, so a wholesale supplier such as Pemberton would have had plenty on hand.[15]

After the war, Pemberton and a partner invested $20,000 in the Eagle Drug and Chemical House, and his ads list dozens of products. Among the drugstore's popular items were the alcoholic drinks available: brandy and bourbon punches, mint julep, and St. Domingo wine. Pemberton used his "new and elegant Apparatus" to deliver "pure cold soda water" mixed with fruit syrups, creating a sensation. Nevertheless, despite the range of his offerings, Pemberton was a talented chemist but a poor businessman, and he did not prosper. Early in 1870, he left his Columbus partnership and moved to booming Atlanta, where he perfected the Coca-Cola formula in 1886.[16]

Myths swirl around the early years of Coca-Cola. One story holds that Pemberton invented the formula in a brass kettle in his Columbus backyard. His wife's grandniece claimed in 1992 that Pemberton developed the formula in Columbus, but that story is highly unlikely, and he certainly did not do so in his yard since he had a sophisticated lab in which to work. In 1884, Pemberton developed "French Wine of Coca," a patent medicine combining red wine, coca extract, and caffeine from kola nuts that was patterned on a popular European tonic, Vin Mariani. Cocaine had emerged in the late 1870s as a possible treatment for alcoholism and morphine addiction, and Pemberton learned of coca's potential in Atlanta. His French Wine of Coca, probably inspired by his own addiction, sold robustly, but Atlanta approved Prohibition in 1885, leaving Pemberton scrambling to create a "temperance drink." After a winter and spring of experimentation, Pemberton settled on a formula that his partner named Coca-Cola. It was an instant success, dispensed from fountains as a tonic and as a refreshing nonalcoholic drink. But Pemberton did not benefit from its popularity. Nearly bankrupt and ill with stomach cancer, he sold his rights in 1887 for about $1,200, died in 1888, and was buried in Linwood Cemetery. Atlanta druggist Asa Candler, who owned the formula and the right to distribute the syrup, essentially gave away the bottling rights, and in 1902, Columbus Roberts began building a fortune with his Columbus-based Coca-Cola Bottling Company, advertising the drink as a "temperance beverage." Still, textile workers for decades called the mill's snack cart selling Coke the dope wagon, and that reputation kept the beverage out of Wildwood Park for a few more years.[17]

Columbus's most important connection to Coca-Cola was W. C. Bradley. In 1919, with national Prohibition set to take effect on the following January 1, he and Columbus native Ernest Woodruff bought Coke from Candler for $25 million. During a post–World War I sugar crisis, local lore holds that Bradley personally borrowed $4 million to save the company. Ernest's son, Robert Winship Woodruff, became the Coca-Cola Company's president in 1923 and led it to international renown. Bradley chaired the board of directors for more than twenty-five years. His son-in-law, D. Abbott Turner, had an even longer tenure on the board, serving from 1923 to 1980, and Bradley's grandson, Bill Turner, was a board member from 1980 to 1996. Bradley and the Turners were known as humble and practical. After Abbott Turner's driver complained about taking him to board meetings in his run-down green Ford LTD, Turner gave the man a blank check and he returned with a Cadillac Seville, which became Turner's "going-to-the-Coke-meeting car." The investment in Coke stock paid dividends for the community. By the beginning of the twenty-first century, one 1919 Coke share had split into 4,608 shares worth $7 million. At Abbott Turner's death in 1982, his children merged the Bradley Foundation, created in 1943, with the Turner Foundation, begun in 1961, and by 2019, the Bradley-Turner Foundation had invested more than $270 million in education, cultural institutions, and community projects. When an interviewer asked Turner what W. C. Bradley considered his most important contribution to Columbus, Turner unhesitatingly replied, "Coke."[18]

RC Cola was also born in Columbus. In 1905, after a conflict with Coke bottler Columbus Roberts over the payment of a commission for sales of the beverage, pharmacist Claud Hatcher set up a lab in the basement of his family's wholesale grocery to experiment with carbonated drinks. Hatcher developed a cherry cola, Chero-Cola, in 1907 and incorporated his company in 1912. The following year, he erected Columbus's first giant electric sign on a Broad Street building, with crowds gathering to watch as a thousand incandescent lights depicted a bottle of Chero-Cola pouring into a glass and foaming over "in a very realistic manner." During the sugar crisis that bedeviled Coke, Hatcher built an expensive refinery in his Tenth Avenue factory, loading the corporation with debt, but in 1924 it introduced Nehi fruit-flavored soft drinks, and sales took off. In 1928, the company changed its name to Nehi Corporation. Hatcher's sudden death in 1933 struck a blow to the company, but it rebounded the next year with Royal Crown Cola, called RC from the start. RC sponsored a popular national radio show, *Ripley's Believe It or Not*, and featured celebrities such as Joan Crawford, Shirley Temple, Lucille Ball, Ronald Reagan, and John Glenn in blind taste tests against Coke and Pepsi, which RC invariably won.[19]

Hatcher and RC have been responsible for numerous business innovations. For example, Hatcher introduced the idea of corporate naming rights in Columbus in 1914, when the chamber of commerce was seeking funding to construct a new hotel: Hatcher offered to provide the money if the new hotel was called the Cherocola. The chamber split about whether to accept the offer, with some members suggesting that they take it and tell the public that "Cherocola" was a female Cherokee and others finding the idea of naming the hotel for a soft drink crass. The chamber ultimately rejected the offer, but Hatcher's proposal led other donors to step up and fund what became the Ralston Hotel. RC also sold the first fruit-flavored soft drinks, produced the first cola in a can, and developed the first diet soft drink. In the 1990s, *Beverage World* magazine observed, "Historically, the single most creative company in the soft drink industry is the Royal Crown Cola Company." But one misjudgment had long-lasting effects for the company. When Pepsi-Cola was in financial straits early in the Great Depression, Hatcher turned down the opportunity to buy the Pepsi name for a mere $12,000.[20]

By 1930, Fort Benning had become a beautiful and architecturally harmonious campus centered on the Main Post Cantonment, and much of the $8 million that the federal government spent on construction of the base had landed in the pockets of Columbus contractors and workers. African

American troops provided much of the construction labor, with the first black soldiers coming in 1920 and the Twenty-Fourth Infantry, the regiment most associated with Benning, arriving in 1922. Commanded by white officers whom the National Association for the Advancement of Colored People (NAACP) called "racist" and "hostile," African American soldiers served as night watchmen, stable hands, janitors, drivers, and maintenance workers and performed manual labor that included logging, maintaining roads, hauling concrete, and building facilities. Base facilities were segregated: for example, white personnel could watch sound movies in the Main Theater, but black troops could see only silent films at the Twenty-Fourth Infantry Service Club. In 1933, after the NAACP filed a complaint with the secretary of war, the army gave sound projectors to the Service Club and built a theater for black soldiers. In addition, the post commander barred African American troops from certain Columbus neighborhoods and censored mail to prevent soldiers from spreading the details of discrimination at the camp.[21]

Despite such limitations, African American soldiers became part of Columbus's civilian life. Members of the Twenty-Fourth Infantry participated in local sports, including boxing, football, and baseball. The regiment's band played public concerts, commonly performing one night for black patrons and the next for whites, and marched in parades and played at football games. Locals marveled at the musicians' skill: in 1943, a white band director wrote that "the band 'goes to town' on a simple ground bass theme ... with simply fantastic variations over it, with the solo trumpet or a sax or perhaps a trombone taking the lead. The orgiastic fervor aroused by the winning team and the 'hot' band approaches the class of a religious experience for the participants." But the director also described the men of the Twenty-Fourth as illiterate, of low intelligence, unhygienic, and morally "primitive." Nevertheless, he believed that they had glimpsed a better life and that "their children will be the living proof to us that our work was not in vain."[22]

Many famous or soon-to-be-famous visited Benning. For five months in 1926, Maj. Dwight D. Eisenhower served as the Twenty-Fourth Infantry's executive officer, a posting white officers considered the equivalent of "the Infantry's Siberia." In the 1930s, Infantry School assistant commander George C. Marshall led the "Benning Revolution," stressing rapid deployment of tanks and airplanes and gathering a coterie of bright young officers that included Joseph Stilwell as chief of tactics and Omar Bradley as head of weapons. Though many Columbus citizens sought to prevent their daughters from fraternizing with enlisted men, officers socialized with members of the city's middle- and upper-class families. Marshall, for example, met an attractive widow at a dinner party and married her two years later, and Stilwell's son, also an officer, married a Columbus woman. Such unions earned Columbus the nickname the Mother-in-Law of the Army.[23]

In 1921, the board of education recommended building a new high school to replace overcrowded Columbus High. Three years later, the Rose Hill company offered fifteen acres of free land, while Flournoy Realty proposed a site overlooking Wildwood Park that would cost the city $65,000. The populist *Ledger* framed the situation as pitting the blue bloods around the park against the common folk even though supporters of the Rose Hill site included such elites as Richard Howard, L. H. Chappell, and John P. Illges. The issue was put up for popular vote, and on December 13, more than 60 percent of voters selected the Wildwood site. The school was completed in 1925 at a cost of $400,000. Ten of the nineteen faculty members had college degrees. Paul "Pop" Austin came in 1929 to teach physics and biology and coach various sports. Athletics were a big draw. His baseball practice diamonds were located in a mushy area of the park that until recently had been the lake. The school also had a forty-by-seventy-foot gym, the Cracker Box, that could house two hundred basketball spectators.[24]

But like its predecessor, the new school permitted only white students to enroll. Although Columbus's African Americans had been campaigning for a high school for more than a quarter century, the city offered its black students only nine grades. Moreover, Negro education remained mostly vocational, with girls washing white students' uniforms and boys required to take brick masonry and blacksmithing. Middle-class black parents began demanding an emphasis on academics: as community leader Roscoe Chester remembered, "Diplomas [for black students] were passports to nowhere... but they did open many doors—stable doors, barn doors, a few chauffeur-driven car doors, and a whole lot of kitchen doors." Nevertheless, many of the African American children who attended school in the 1920s became the first literate members of their families, thus opening up the world to their community. Historian John Henrik Clarke, for example, taught Sunday School when he was ten and read the Bible to elderly women in his Liberty District neighborhood. In 1924 Dr. Manley Taylor, the city physician for black schools, petitioned unsuccessfully for the addition of the tenth and eleventh grades. Arriving in Columbus in 1920, Alabama native Dr. Thomas Brewer spent the next three decades working on behalf of racial justice. He organized the Columbus Colored Civic Club in 1924 and subsequently requested the creation of a colored school board to oversee the black schools; once again, however, the board declined to create one. The idea of a high school for African American students did not begin to gain traction until 1927, when a delegation of black ministers appealed to "our friends, honorable, fair-minded, and liberal souled white citizens"—and pledged $2,000. The board spent two years pondering the idea of adding two grades before convincing voters to fund a Negro high school.[25]

The board named the school after William H. Spencer, the longtime superintendent of the city's colored schools who had recently died. He might not have been the choice of many members of the black community who resented his accommodationist stance toward white leaders. According to local historian Alfonso Biggs, Spencer had told superintendent Roland Daniel that black students did not need a high school, and the board minutes from 1920 to 1925 indicate that Spencer never requested school improvements. Spencer's daughter recalled that black parents complained to the board that he "wasn't capable of taking charge of a school." Chester claimed that Spencer segregated students by skin color into what Clarke called the light brigade and the dark brigade. Chester and Clarke were in the "dark brigade," with middle-class "little pretty girls and little fancy boys" in the other. Still, the high school named for Spencer had a tremendous effect, offering, as Chester acknowledged, "a chance for a better life." George Foster Peabody, the Rosenwald Fund, and Jordan contributed toward the school's construction. In line with the benefactors' philosophy, Spencer stressed vocational education, but many students went on to college. Of the thirty-seven young men and women who graduated from Spencer in 1934, sixteen earned undergraduate degrees and eight did postgraduate work, not only at local colleges but also at Harvard, New York University, Kent State, and the University of Pittsburgh. From its opening in 1930, Spencer was a source of pride for the black community.[26]

By the 1920s, Columbus's African American community had a substantial middle class that comprised 18 percent of the city's professionals and included entrepreneurs, ministers, and doctors as well as nurses and teachers, the only professions open to African American women. Because they served a black clientele, these professionals were somewhat insulated from the Jim Crow system's controls. The most prominent member of the city's African American medical community, Dr. Edwin Turner, completed a postgraduate course at Harvard University, impressing even the white community. In 1922, black physicians gained access to treat African American patients in the basement of the City Hospital. Barred from membership in Columbus's white medical society until 1952, African American doctors formed the Colored Medical Association. Dr. Brewer worked for improvements in public health, family welfare, and juvenile justice, becoming the city's leading voice for civil rights. In 1929, he and others formed the Social-Civic-25 Club, the nucleus for political organization.[27]

Today's Liberty District was a bustling African American neighborhood and commercial center in the 1920s. Anchored by the First African Baptist, Friendship Baptist, and St. James African Methodist Episcopal Churches; the Fifth Avenue School; and the colored YMCA, the densely populated thirty-block area included Sconiers Funeral Home, Laborers' Savings and Loan, a dry cleaner, a billiard parlor, a stable, a barbershop, three benevolent societies, six restaurants, and seven groceries (two of them white owned). Most residents were working class, but professionals also lived there. Turner and Atlanta's Episcopal bishop founded St. Christopher Episcopal Church in 1916. The most impressive commercial structure was the three-story Pierce Building on Ninth Street at Fifth Avenue, which came to be called the Magic Corner. Lizzie Pierce Lunsford and her husband, Watson Lunsford, ran a grocery store in the Bottoms, an African American neighborhood along low-lying Weracoba Creek, just north of the Liberty District. Lizzie Lunsford and her brother, Richard Pierce, a pharmacist, financed the Pierce Building, and the first and second floors housed his Ninth Street Drug Store as well as other professional offices and the Elks Club. On the third floor, the Pierce Auditorium hosted meetings, dances, and other entertainment. Columbus had no hotels accommodating black visitors, so many traveling men stayed at the YMCA, while Lizzie Lunsford often opened her spacious Lawyers Lane home to middle-class visitors. In the late 1920s, Joseph Clarke, a mail carrier and active Republican who later became an assistant postmaster general, started an African American weekly, the *Columbus Times*, with its offices located in the Sconiers Building, across from the Pierce Building.[28]

In 1928, the *Columbus Enquirer-Sun* asserted, "Splendid relations have always existed between the races here, where the negro is treated as a citizen, knows his place and fills it well." But outside of their own community, African Americans' "place" in Columbus was quite constrained. Although Clarke's paper praised the "harmonious relations between the white and colored races," that harmony required African Americans to accept Jim Crow and avoid challenging the status quo. Most women worked in domestic service. John Henrik Clarke's mother, for example, washed for poor white families, collecting their laundry in a red wagon with Clarke sitting on top and earning three dollars per week for her efforts. Clerks in white-owned stores addressed African American shoppers by their first names, denying them the respect accorded by courtesy titles such as "Mr." and "Mrs.," though African Americans were expected to use such titles for whites. Any black man who dared to walk into Wheat's Drug Store on Broadway without removing his hat would have it knocked to the floor by the white owner. On one occasion, when Primus King, who worked as a chauffeur for a white family, told his female employer that a Negro woman was at the front door to sell vegetables, the employer's husband cursed him for bringing a colored woman into his wife's presence. In response, King, who in the 1940s challenged Georgia's white primary, declared that he treated *all* ladies with courtesy and then quit his job. Years later, he mused, "I'm a man that loved my people, black folks, and couldn't say that about them white people."[29]

The center for African American entertainment was the Liberty Theatre, which Roy Martin opened in 1924 on Eighth Avenue between Eighth and Ninth Streets. The largest movie house in Columbus at the time, it also staged live performances. It was a stop on the Chitlin' Circuit, a white-owned entertainment network established in 1909. Its formal name was the Theater Owners' Booking Association (TOBA): performers said that the acronym stood for "Tough on Black Asses" because of the low pay, primitive backstage accommodations, and punishing schedules. Many of the greatest African American musicians of the 1920s and 1930s graced the Liberty's stage, among them Bessie Smith, Ella Fitzgerald, Ethel Waters, Lena Horne, Fats Waller, Louis Armstrong, Bill "Bojangles" Robinson, and the big bands of Duke Ellington, Cab Calloway, and Fletcher Henderson.[30]

Columbus's best-known performer, Ma Rainey, was born Gertrude Pridgett in 1886 and first appeared with a Bunch of Blackberries at the Springer Opera House when she was fourteen. She began traveling in vaudeville tent shows the next year and in 1904 married comedic singer

Ma Rainey and the Wildcats, 1924–1925. Gelatin silver print.
From the Collection of the Columbus Museum, Georgia; Museum purchase, 2002.27.

William "Pa" Rainey and began touring with the Rabbit Foot Minstrels, one of the most popular black shows. In 1915, the Raineys billed themselves as the Assassinators of the Blues, reflecting her powerful, aggressive style. Everything about Ma Rainey's performance was larger than life. Not a classically beautiful woman, she accentuated her full figure with sequined gowns, headdresses, and what became her signature gold coin necklace. She wore a diamond tiara and carried an ostrich plume fan. Although one of Rainey's musicians found her "ugly," he added that "she had such a lovely disposition, you know, and personality, you forget all about it. She commence to lookin' good to you." Paramount Records tagged her "Real pig-meat!," a description of a sexy person of either gender.[31]

In 1923, when she signed with Paramount, Rainey became one of the first black women recorded, producing "race records" and billed as Mother of the Blues. Rainey wrote many songs, the best known of which is probably "See See Rider," based on a traditional blues song. She recorded it in 1924, backed by Louis Armstrong on cornet and Fletcher Henderson on piano. It has since been recorded by more than a hundred other musicians, including Leadbelly, Elvis, the Grateful Dead, and Cher. Rainey's songs played on the theme of the sexually aggressive woman rather than on women as victims as in much of the period's music. In

"Shave 'Em Dry," Rainey sang blithely about an affair with a married man. In "Barrel House Blues," she demanded equal-opportunity carousing:

> Papa likes his sherry, mama likes her port
> Papa likes to shimmy, mama likes to sport
> Papa likes his bourbon, mama likes her gin
> Papa likes his outside women, mama likes her outside men.

Rainey was bisexual and recorded several explicitly lesbian songs, such as "Prove It on Me Blues," in which she sings of reveling with friends: "They must've been women, 'cause I don't like no men." Several of her songs dealt with male homosexuality, including "Sissy Blues," in which she lost her husband to another man.[32]

Rainey was a pivotal figure in moving the blues from rural areas to the cities. She personified country blues, and her recordings introduced this rougher down-home style to nonsouthern audiences. For a 1925 Chicago concert, "audiences lined up from the box-office to the streetcar tracks." Rainey's appeal, as Georgia poet Sterling Brown noted, lay in the fact that her songs "went straight to the heart," offering tales of "heart break, promiscuity, drinking binges, the odyssey of travel, the workplace and the prison road gang, magic and superstition—in short, the southern landscape of African-Americans in the Post-Reconstruction era." Her performances were electrifying. According to Thomas Dorsey, her act opened with her inside a giant Victrola as "the band picked up the 'Moonshine Blues.' Ma would sing a few bars inside the Victrola. Then she would open the door and step out into the spotlight with her glittering gown that weighed twenty pounds and wearing a necklace of five, ten and twenty dollar gold pieces. The house went wild.... Ma had the audience in the palm of her hand." Dorsey added, "When she started singing, the gold in her teeth would sparkle. She was in the spotlight. She possessed listeners; they swayed, they rocked, they moaned and groaned, as they felt the blues with her."[33]

The TOBA and record industry collapsed with the stock market, and Rainey's opulent standard of living declined. She retired in 1935, returning to Columbus, where she lived with her brother, a deacon of the Friendship Baptist Church, and sang in its choir. She owned and managed two movie theaters, one in Columbus and one in Rome, Georgia. Rainey died of heart disease on December 22, 1939, at the age of fifty-three, and was buried in Porterdale Cemetery. Despite her pioneering status, financial success, and influence on countless musicians, Columbus has never fully embraced Rainey, in part because of her race and gender—a black woman marginalized by the dominant culture. But African Americans were also slow to recognize her greatness. Rainey's articulation of sexual freedom and rejection of monogamy threatened religious doctrines, with churchgoing African Americans dismissing the blues as "the devil's music."[34]

Rainey was inducted into the Blues Hall of Fame in 1983, the Rock and Roll Hall of Fame in 1990, and the Georgia Music Hall of Fame in 1992, and she was named a Georgia Woman of Achievement in 1993. The following year, the U.S. Postal Service issued a stamp in her honor. But her hometown nearly let her house fall down. The once-vibrant neighborhood along Fifth and Sixth Avenues had declined by the 1970s, with the Liberty Theatre closing in 1973, a victim of desegregation and the demolition of its surrounding neighborhood. Spencer High School's alumnae society, the Golden Owlettes, saved Rainey's house by having it placed on the National Register of Historic Places in 1984 and campaigning for its renovation. In 1991, the city bought her home for $5,000, but with the roof collapsing, the cost for stabilization was $90,000. Most white members of the city council saw no value in spending money in a derelict neighborhood, but Mayor Frank Martin cast the tiebreaking vote to approve the funds. In 2004, Congressman Sanford Bishop arranged a $149,000 Save America's Treasures grant, which the city agreed to match. After the $300,000 renovation, the Ma Rainey House Blues Museum opened to the public in 2006.[35]

Another notable cultural figure from this era whose roots lay in Columbus was artist Alma Thomas. Her mother, Amelia Cantey Thomas, was a daughter of former slave Winter Cantey (sometimes spelled Canty), patriarch of one of the city's most prominent black families, and Alma's cousin, Inez Canty, served as secretary to W. E. B. Du Bois, typing the manuscript of *The Souls of Black Folk* on the Thomases' front porch in Rose Hill. In the 1910s, with Columbus's black population terrified by the outbreak of racial violence in the area, Alma's parents fled to Washington, D.C., with their four daughters. Alma went on to become a highly acclaimed artist and was the first African American woman to have a solo exhibition at New York's Whitney Museum of American Art (1972) and to have her work included in the White House's permanent collection (2009).[36]

One block north of the Liberty Theatre stands the Columbus Stockade. Italianate in style, it may have been built as early as 1859, but the corbeled brick resembling fancywork on other downtown buildings dated to about 1870. It closed in 1972 and might have been razed if not for an iconic country song, "The Columbus Stockade Blues." Local musicians Jimmie Tarlton and Tom Darby had recorded the song in Atlanta for Columbia in 1927, and it became one of the record label's biggest hits, selling two hundred thousand copies that year and a million within a short time. The song put Columbus, Georgia, on the map and became an immediate country standard, with at least a dozen different recordings released by the 1950s. A local columnist noted in the late 1960s that the Stockade "is easily the most renowned of our local tourist attractions, with the possible exception of Ft. Benning."[37]

Born in 1892 in South Carolina, Tarlton had taken up the guitar at ten. Influenced by African American bluesmen, he was coaxing wails and moans from his guitar bottleneck style by age twelve and soon substituted a knife for the bottleneck. In 1922, he met popular Hawaiian guitarist Frank Ferera, who showed Tarlton a slide steel bar. This Hawaiian influence is evident in some of Tarlton's melodic changes and unusual open guitar tunings. In Columbus around 1925, Tarlton met Darby, who also played blues-inflected guitar. The owner of White Music Company offered to take Tarlton and Darby to Atlanta to audition for Columbia. After their first session, Columbia signed them to record again in November 1927, when they recorded "Columbus Stockade Blues"—and made a decision they long regretted. When Columbia offered a contract, they accepted a flat payment of seventy-five dollars rather than royalties. When the record became a smash hit, each man blamed the other. Had they taken royalties, they would have received payments for the rest of their lives; instead, they sank into obscurity and poverty.[38]

Darby and Tarlton recorded more than sixty songs by the early 1930s and toured with top old-time acts. Fame brought their only mention in the Columbus newspapers—a live appearance on the *Chancellor's Hour* on WRBL radio in December 1928. The Great Depression crushed Darby and Tarlton's recording career just as it had Ma Rainey's, and the duo's rough improvisational bluesy style soon began to sound archaic, unsuited to the slick, close country harmonies gaining popularity on radio. Darby returned to Columbus, performing locally with his Georgia Wildcats band. Tarlton and his wife wandered the South before drifting back to Phenix City. Estranged from Darby, he played commercials for the Goo Goo Drive-In Restaurant on local radio in the late 1930s and performed

Darby and Tarlton, ca. 1930.
Internet Archive.

his last professional gig for nearly two decades in 1945. In 1963, in the midst of the folk revival, an old-time record collector from Roanoke, Alabama, ran an ad seeking Darby's whereabouts: the musician responded and helped the collector locate Tarlton. Although they had not spoken for twenty years, the two reunited that June to perform at the dedication of the new Weracoba Park band shell. It was their final performance together, and Darby died in 1971. Rediscovered by a new generation of fans, Tarlton made a comeback, playing for a week at the Ash Grove folk club in Los Angeles and earning a rave review from the *Los Angeles Times*: "His music came from a private world and was like nothing anyone had ever heard before. It was the unique style of a grandfather who can only express his wisdom through music." He appeared at the Chicago and Newport Folk Festivals. Tarlton supposedly met both Joan Baez, who he thought had a beautiful voice, and Bob Dylan, who "couldn't sing a lick."[39]

Tarlton subsequently returned to obscurity, living with his wife in poverty in a Riverview Apartment. After his death on November 29, 1979, his grave in Riverdale Cemetery had no headstone until local musicians raised money and finally erected a marker in 1999. Buried a few hundred feet away, Darby had a headstone, but it did not mention the song that made Columbus famous. In the mid-1970s, the Columbus Chamber of Commerce used "Columbus Stockade Blues" to promote the city. The Stockade itself was listed on the National Register of Historic Places in 1980, and a historic marker placed there in 1985 honors the song.⁴⁰

In 1930, Columbus's city manager estimated that the city's population had doubled since 1900. To meet the growing demand for modern entertainment, William "Radio Bill" Lewis and Monte Moore established WRBL radio in 1928 at the new Royal Theatre. The station's call letters supposedly came from Radio Bill Lewis's initials. The station had several owners until James W. Woodruff, grandson of George Waldo Woodruff of Empire Mills, bought it in 1931. Under the Woodruffs' control, the station blossomed. Etta Blanchard Worsley led those interested in highbrow culture in organizing the Three Arts League in 1927, bringing together eleven women's clubs to showcase music, drama, and dance. Bolstered by financial pledges from one hundred "public-spirited citizens," the first four programs in Columbus High School's auditorium featured two singers from New York City's Metropolitan Opera, a play by the New York Theatre Guild, and journalist Lowell Thomas's famous lecture on Lawrence of Arabia. The programs moved to the Springer Opera House for the 1928–1929 season. Even during the depression's worst years, the league held onto about six hundred members, and as the economic picture brightened, the league grew even larger.⁴¹

In April 1928, the city hosted a gigantic centennial celebration centered on Confederate Memorial Day. The Centennial Committee mailed fifteen thousand invitations that proclaimed, "In 1828—a trading post, established by the State of Georgia on the frontier of a growing commonwealth. In 1928—one of the South's leading industrial cities!" Restaurants offered special menus, and merchants illustrated local history in store windows. Kirven's Department Store attracted thousands with displays of a spinning wheel and vintage dresses, antique toys, needlework, quilts, and jewelry. Fort Benning kicked off the three-day festival, drawing twenty-five thousand spectators to a mock artillery and aircraft battle. In the evening, a cast of three thousand presented a pageant in Memorial Stadium. Miriam Howard, sister of Augusta, worked with Loretto Chappell on the historical research. Descendants of many early notables portrayed their ancestors in a pageant that traced Columbus's history from Creek settlement and "the barbarism of the Indians" to the present, including its rise from the Civil War's ashes as "a city of new life, hopes, ambitions, purposes and achievements." The industrial portion, labeled "March of Progress," started with cotton and moved through iron foundries, lumber, and brick before presenting a "carnival" of industries, including Columbus Power Company, Chero-Cola/Nehi, and local merchants. The final segment focused on the "Greater Gifts" of religion and education, with portrayals of Truth, Benevolence, Faith, Hope, Charity, Intelligence, Order, Leadership, Sportsmanship, Art, Music, Dance, and Drama before the "Hallelujah Chorus" introduced a grand finale with odes to Prosperity, Joy, Peace, Happiness, and Patriotism. The entire cast took the stage at the end as "Stars and Stripes Forever" played. Nearly ten thousand spectators attended the pageant's two performances.[42]

The following day, Confederate Memorial Day, featured more somber commemorations that followed the traditional format of morning church services and an afternoon parade down Broadway to the Confederate monument, where Fort Benning troops fired a salute. The procession returned up Broadway to the Springer Opera House for a speech evoking Lost Cause themes: defending the constitutionality of secession and rejecting southern responsibility for slavery. The parade ended at Linwood Cemetery where Confederate graves were decorated. Frivolity returned on the final day of the festival, as thirty thousand spectators witnessed a downtown parade featuring four thousand soldiers, artillery, tanks, eight bands, twenty floats with beauty queens and maids, and many civic floats and decorated automobiles. The parade concluded at Memorial Stadium, where Gunby Jordan spoke before Miss Columbus's coronation as Centennial Queen with county queens as her maids. The parade regrouped at 8:15 in the evening, again passed through downtown, and culminated in a street dance on Broadway for common folks and a queen's ball at the Country Club. The centennial marked the last celebration Columbusites experienced for more than a decade, as the stock market crash, the depression, and war brought on a dark time for the city, the country, and much of the world.[43]

The City Market's grand reopening, 1921. Columbus State University Archives, Columbus State University, Columbus, Georgia.

A controversy that opened the 1920s should have been a cautionary lesson. Responding to requests from business owners along First Avenue in May 1920, the mayor and city council voted to demolish the historic City Market, which had operated on the avenue's median since 1867. White farmers sold vegetables, fruits, and freshly slaughtered beef and pork. Black women toted baskets of produce from the country on Saturday mornings, while black men sold venison, doves, and other game. At the end of the day, African Americans gathered at Kinfolks Corner—Front Avenue and Tenth Street—to catch rides home. By 1920, however, businessmen claimed that the market was an eyesore that exacerbated traffic congestion downtown, while the mayor labeled it a revenue drain with few vendors or shoppers. Newly empowered with the vote, the elite members of the Federation of Women's Clubs rallied, arguing that the market was a landmark that should be saved. The women won the first round, with the council rescinding its removal and appropriating $2,000 for renovation if the women cleaned up the market and made it profitable.[44]

The market held a spectacular grand reopening in April 1921. A Fort Benning band led hundreds of children down Broad Street, with many of them dressed as flowers or "realistic carrots, beets, radishes, and eggplants." Girls in rosy "Grecian drapery" performed a maypole dance, and hundreds of people browsed the market. But business declined within a few months, prompting First Avenue store owners again to petition for the market's demolition. In response, committee chair Henrietta Blanchard pleaded, "It would be a crime to do away with the quaint old building." The commissioners turned a deaf ear, with the women complaining that they had been treated like "a class of children at school." The city tore down half the building in July 1923 for parking and demolished the rest a year later. Over the next forty years, one local landmark after another succumbed to parking lots and shopping centers, until the children and grandchildren of the 1920s clubwomen jammed their feet in the doors closing on Columbus's architectural heritage and said, "No more."[45]

CHAPTER 6

Columbus in the 1930s and 1940s

Depression and World War

The Great Depression brought deprivation, dislocation, and labor unrest to Columbus. Textiles still dominated the city's economy, but wages were too low to boost prosperity. The city manager wrote of the industry, "I feel like a woman with fifteen children. I love those that I have, but I wouldn't give a thin dime for another one." The mills, particularly the Bibb, sought to quash support for unionism not only with paternalistic programs aimed at worker welfare and improved company housing but also with violence and intimidation. The New Deal and construction at Fort Benning in the 1930s helped keep Columbus afloat, and the base's massive wartime mobilization provided the engine for the city's subsequent recovery and prosperity. World War II ushered in other changes both positive and negative: two of Columbus's most famous denizens, screenwriter Nunnally Johnson and author Carson McCullers, rose to prominence during this era, but the city also struggled with vice, inadequate infrastructure, and changing racial and gender expectations.[1]

The Great Depression did not hit Columbus as hard as many other cities. It missed no public payrolls, met all bond payments, and amassed no floating debt. But as the crisis worsened, tax revenues plummeted. Despite protests by the Central Labor Union, with tax returns down 10 percent, the city cut workers' wages in January 1932 and reduced operating expenses by a third. At year's end, anticipating more revenue declines, the city again lowered wages. By 1934, teachers had endured salary reductions of 18 percent and found themselves with as many as fifty students in a classroom. The board of education dismissed married women in order to give single women jobs. In 1930, the principal of St. Elmo Elementary taught forty children four days a week. Most schools had no food service, so he borrowed thirty dollars from the parent-teacher association to start a lunchroom, charging twenty-five cents per meal. At Pou Street School, a neighborhood woman fed black children vegetable soup and a muffin for two cents. Many students could not pay book fees, and the board eliminated music and art instruction for four years. Despite the cutbacks, however, students celebrated Georgia's 1933 bicentennial: twelve thousand spectators filled Memorial Stadium on May 19 for thirteen historical skits presented by white children, while colored students held a separate parade and pageant the next day. Columbus's longest-serving educator, eighty-nine-year-old Fornie Holmes, retired in September 1934, having taught since the public schools' inception in 1867.[2]

Many residents had large gardens and kept milk cows and chickens, while farmers from the countryside hawked produce and meat from mule-drawn wagons and pickup trucks. But as the depression deepened, starvation and homelessness threatened scores of families. The city initially provided relief through direct appropriations and the Family Welfare Bureau, whose employee salaries and office rent were paid by the city and county commissions, though relief depended on private philanthropy. The city physician and public health nurse referred cases to the bureau, who helped the needy find employment, "correct[ed] marital troubles," and furnished food, fuel, and clothing. By 1930, however, the scope of the problem had grown beyond what the bureau could handle, and the director called the situation "desperate." Three years later, the city spent $50,000 on relief programs, including more than $16,000 in direct aid. In 1935, the Family Welfare Bureau had to drop "a number of worthy families" and deny new applicants as public support and donations dwindled. And as things worsened, many families received only about a dime's worth of daily aid the following year, meaning that they no longer had adequate food.[3]

Churchwomen set up a soup kitchen for underprivileged children at North Highlands School, and the Social-Civic-25 Club served soup to the black community at the Ninth Street YMCA. In Boogerville, a white working-class neighborhood bordering East Highland and Linwood Cemetery, residents could get credit at Cain's Grocery. The Bloody Bucket, the local bar where the mob allegedly ran illegal moonshine, also provided credit. But local efforts could not keep up with the demand. Federal and state Social Security programs began to provide direct relief in 1936. Like many New Deal programs, Social Security disproportionately helped whites: two-thirds of Georgia's black workers were employed in agriculture or domestic service, both of which were excluded. In August 1937, the state welfare department established the Muscogee County Department of Public Welfare, and a month later, the county and city assumed the department's administrative costs.[4]

Passage of the 1937 U.S. Housing Act sought to promote urban "slum clearance," which primarily targeted working-class neighborhoods. In response, the city created the Columbus Housing Authority in May 1938. Theo McGee, who chaired the Family Welfare Bureau's advisory board, first headed a committee that proposed the city seek a $225 million federal loan for public housing and then became chief of the Housing Authority, which would administer the funds. The first two projects were Peabody Apartments (named for George Foster Peabody) on the city's north side, with 510 units for whites, and Booker T. Washington Apartments across from the South Commons with nearly 400 units for African Americans: both received their first residents in 1940. Begun in 1940, the Housing Authority's third project, Newton D. Baker Village, on the edge of Fort Benning, provided much-needed housing for military personnel as war escalated in Europe and the base expanded. Baker Village's 612 units were located in brick buildings that went up quickly but nevertheless won praise in national architectural publications for their superior quality. The first inhabitants were a master sergeant and his family who took up residence in January 1941. In 1940, fewer than half of Georgia homes had electricity, only a quarter had refrigerators, and even fewer had electric stoves, so many of the so-called slum-dwellers displaced by the Housing Authority were eager to move into the modern apartments.[5]

The presence of Fort Benning and other federal programs helped to insulate Columbus residents from some of the suffering of the Great Depression and brought the city significant public improvements. "Thanks to Fort Benning," the city manager announced, Columbus had fewer unemployed and got less direct relief than any other city in Georgia. Still, the city sought its share of federal funds. In 1932 Congress appropriated $410,000 for a federal building at Second Avenue and Twelfth Street to house the post office and federal courts. In 1934, the New Deal's Federal Emergency Relief and Civil Works Administrations provided partial funding for four new classrooms at North Highlands School, a new fire department headquarters, and renovations of the police department and jail. Under the Works Progress Administration, the government paid construction workers and furnished between 25 to 50 percent of the materials for infrastructure projects. In sewing rooms, hundreds of women made thousands of garments for the needy. Women canned "immense amounts" of beef from Dust Bowl states for charitable distribution. The Public Works Administration pumped in hundreds of thousands of dollars to build the new Industrial High School, completed in 1937 and named for Gunby Jordan. In 1938, Columbus voters approved a bond issue to secure federal funds for a public swimming pool, a hospital, school improvements, thirty-five miles of sewers, and twenty miles of paved streets.[6]

Two other New Deal programs put youth to work. Open only to young men whose families were receiving public assistance, the Civilian Conservation Corps (CCC) provided jobs in forestry, erosion control, and construction, paying each enrollee thirty dollars per month, of which twenty-five dollars went to his family. The CCC followed a military organizational style, with companies of men living in four camps in Muscogee County, with the one at Fort Benning housing black enrollees, who were limited to 10 percent of the total. White southern officers supervised black corpsmen, who remained in their home state. Despite the program's discrimination, some African Americans benefited from the wages sent to their families and from CCC job training and education. Young women and younger men received help through the National Youth Administration (NYA), which paid them while they attended school or college in return for community service. The NYA paid African American and white students the same rate, but job training and community service reflected white attitudes. While whites helped on archaeological digs or worked in city or New Deal agency offices, black youth did manual labor for the recreation department or served lunch in schools. NYA instruction for African Americans sought to provide "well-trained colored help." Girls learned "cooking, house-cleaning, serving, washing, sewing, child care and personal hygiene," while boys learned to be porters and valets. Again, despite the discrimination, black students benefited because the program provided them with funds that enabled them to pursue their true interests.[7]

The New Deal program most reviled by African Americans was the 1933 National Recovery Administration (NRA), which for the first time set minimum wages and maximum working hours. As with Social Security, agriculture and domestic service were excluded, and in some cases, the NRA codes permitted the minority of Georgia's African Americans who were covered to receive lower wages than their white counterparts.

Employers who thought that the mandated pay rates for African Americans were too high replaced black workers with whites or simply ignored the codes: declared one Georgia businessman, "I will shut down my business before I will pay a nigger a white man's wages." In addition, many small businesses, particularly those owned by blacks, could not pay the mandated higher wages and folded. In Columbus, the NRA cost African Americans more jobs than in any similar-sized southern city, leading them to call the program the Negro Removal Act.[8]

For white textile operatives, however, the NRA had an overall positive effect. Prior to the program's creation, southern millhands had earned one-third as much as their New England counterparts, and southern millowners were determined to preserve that differential. But the NRA set a minimum wage for textiles of twelve dollars for a workweek of no more than forty hours. In addition, the program abolished child labor and guaranteed workers the right to join a union and collectively bargain. In July 1933, the number of hours Bibb Mill operatives were required to work each week dropped from more than sixty to forty, and some workers saw their pay double. These new standards meant that factories would need to produce more goods per worker to maintain profitability. The "stretch-out," which required workers to operate larger numbers of machines, had been introduced in the 1920s, but operatives thought that the NRA's rules would end it. Instead, stretch-outs increased, prompting millhands across the South to write to President Franklin Delano Roosevelt to complain. "A committee of half starved human beings, looking to you for help," alleged that the Eagle & Phenix was ignoring the New Deal mandates and that the only changes were "to increase the work and cut the force." Another Eagle & Phenix worker charged that his wife had been fired for refusing to take on four looms and called mill president W. C. Bradley "the hardest piece of humanity on earth." A widow with four children, including one with tuberculosis, pleaded for help after the Bibb fired her for attending a union meeting.[9]

After the strikes of 1919–1921, the Bibb Mill had generally used paternalistic corporate welfare to pacify workers. The mill was in a picturesque, company-owned incorporated village on the Chattahoochee just north of Columbus. Until 1939, the mill superintendent served as both mayor and town judge. The mill owned workers' houses and the school and provided day care for younger children. The Bibb donated land and built the Hamp Stevens Methodist church and staffed a free clinic with two full-time nurses. It hired an athletic director for recreation programs, including basketball in Comer auditorium's gymnasium, swimming in the natatorium, baseball and softball teams, a bowling league, and tennis courts. It sponsored men's, women's, boys', and girls' clubs and sent them on trips as far away as Washington, D.C. In return, the Bibb expected worker loyalty and conformity to standards of conduct—and no unions. The penalty for misbehavior in or out of the mill, including chronic drunkenness or rowdiness, was loss of the offender's job and that of his or her spouse as well as expulsion from company housing. Although the company president, William D. Anderson, acknowledged that workers had the right to join a union, he declared that doing so was unnecessary. Millhands understood that "unions were a taboo subject... and just the mention of the word resulted in firing and subsequent expulsion from the town." W. C. Bradley at the Eagle & Phenix also sought to cultivate a reputation for generosity and thus prevent workers from seeking to organize. According to his son-in-law, D. Abbott Turner, Bradley doled out cash to those in need, with people gathering at the gate in front of his home every night for food and money. Though the mill struggled financially, Turner said, "We didn't feel like we ought to [close it] because we were all in the same box."[10]

Nevertheless, worker discontent grew. Beginning in April 1934, Columbus mills reduced operations 25 percent, with some going to a four-day work week and the Bibb dropping to a three-day week. Workers could not feed their families even as Anderson insisted that a family of four could live comfortably on $1.86 per week—$1.36 if they eschewed "luxuries" such as coffee, sugar, and meat. In his view, anyone who complained about the stretch-out was a slacker. Many struggling operatives joined the United Textile Workers, and beginning on March 28, 1934, Columbus-area mills experienced a series of wildcat strikes over "the work load, wages and distribution of work." On June 4, "melees" led to the arrest of fourteen picketers—mainly strikers retaliating against scabs. On June 22, the Eagle & Phenix settled its strike and agreed not to fire striking workers. When the workers returned, however, they found new hires doing their jobs: returnees who complained to the general manager were fired. Twenty-five hundred angry millhands gathered and threatened to resume the strike, and over the next six weeks, strikers shut down more local mills.[11]

The spark that ignited a general labor uprising in Columbus flared on August 10, 1934, after Georgia Webbing and Tape management announced that it would break the strike and resume operations. When the first shift ended at 2:00, six nonstrikers tried to drive a car through the picket line. The picketers stopped them and a passenger fired a pistol into the crowd, killing Reuben Sanders, a Swift Manufacturing union member. Thousands of workers viewed Sanders's body the next day at the Central Textile Hall. The funeral procession to Riverdale Cemetery included more than 600 automobiles and 450 men on foot. As tension grew, the local union head admitted that he could not "hold these workers in line." On August 15, after fruitless appeals to federal authorities detailing the "discrimination, coercion, intimidation, and discharge of workers who joined organization[s] of their own choosing," four thousand Eagle & Phenix operatives agreed to strike. Twenty-two hundred workers formed picket lines the next day, and by afternoon, the mill was at a standstill. With similar wildcat strikes across the South, on August 13 the United Textile Workers called for a nationwide general strike immediately after Labor Day. A festive mood pervaded Columbus on the holiday, as thousands watched a parade down Broadway, listened to speeches by labor leaders, participated in and watched athletic events, and danced at the fairgrounds.[12]

The following day, September 4, brought a somber mood. More than 370,000 textile workers across the nation joined the strike, the largest labor protest in U.S. history. Columbus's mills came to a standstill, with about 95 percent of the area's 12,000 textile operatives striking. For the next twelve days, a truce held, and the workers' spirits rose with news of strike successes across the nation. Governor Eugene Talmadge was in the midst of a reelection campaign, with the primary set for September 12. Portraying himself as "a friend of labor," he pledged not to send troops in to break any strike, telling Columbus workers on September 6, "You folks just keep cool and calm and I feel there will be no disturbances." But the outlook in Georgia began to darken, even as national union leaders and Roosevelt pursued conciliation. Cotton manufacturers across the South refused to make concessions, choosing instead to guard mills with machine guns and bayonets, and after winning the primary with strong textile worker support, Talmadge called out the entire thirty-seven-hundred-man Georgia National Guard to "protect the right of those who wish to work." The Bibb broke the strike, opening on September 17 under the protection of two hundred National Guardsmen, including a machine-gun company with twelve guns on mill roofs, under orders "to use such force as may be necessary" to keep the mill open and to prevent unauthorized gatherings of more than three people. Management brought in strikebreakers from Lower Alabama by train. Soldiers patrolled North Highlands, and on September 19, Guardsmen arrested two men and placed them in the Bibb City jail—a "sweatbox... an awful place"—for trying to gather together strikers. Talmadge infamously housed other arrested strikers incommunicado at Atlanta's Fort McPherson. In Columbus, National Guardsmen took some strikers off picket lines and trucked them to a holding facility in Newnan.[13]

On September 22, the United Textile Workers terminated the strike after FDR asked workers to return to their jobs. The president expressed "the sincere hope... that textile manufacturers will take back employees without discrimination." At mass meetings the following day, Columbus mill operatives expressed confidence in Roosevelt and agreed to return to work, approving a telegram thanking the president for recognizing low wages and denouncing stretch-outs. FDR said he counted on a "spirit of cooperation and fair play" on both sides. Instead, Talmadge declared martial law in Columbus and Bibb City. All local mills opened on September 24 under the protection of two additional Guard companies. Owners continued to freely discriminate against union activists, as the federal boards established after the strike remained as impotent as their predecessors. The Bibb fired every union officer and picketer. Muscogee Manufacturing laid off six hundred union members, and a total of up to thirty-five hundred striking local textile workers—nearly a third of the prestrike workforce—were not rehired. Many found themselves blacklisted throughout the industry.[14]

In May 1935, the U.S. Supreme Court declared the NRA codes unconstitutional, but on July 5, Congress passed the National Labor Relations Act (also known as the Wagner Act), which guaranteed workers the right to organize and bargain collectively. Three years later, the Fair Labor Standards Act permanently established minimum wages and maximum hours. The General Textile Strike had elicited a high price from mill workers—thousands fired and blacklisted, fourteen dead, including Reuben Sanders—but child labor remained illegal, and by 1936 operatives worked fewer hours for higher wages. Federal legislation closed the wage gap between North and South, boosting southern operatives' compensation and laying a foundation for a uniform national labor market in textiles. In November 1936, local mills announced that workers' total wages would increase from $200,000 to $700,000 annually.[15]

Rarely mentioned in history books, the General Strike has an odd historical legacy. Though the tens of thousands of southern textile workers who participated in the strike have frequently been stereotyped as hostile to labor organization, the aftermath in Columbus contradicts this view. During the 1930s and 1940s, five unions represented hundreds of operatives at ten local mills. On September 1, 1934, a year after the strike, Swift Spinning employees organized. In April 1936, unions formed the Columbus Textile Council to represent workers in Columbus and Phenix City, and a resolution to form cooperatives called clothing and food retailers "profiteers" living like "parasites upon profits gleaned from the necessary purchases of the workers." More strikes shut down southern mills in 1935 than in any other year since 1921, and the number of strikes grew through 1938. In April 1935, Meritas Mill workers walked out when the company cut wages and attempted a stretch-out. Amid rumors of another strike, Meritas closed in September, though the official reason was "slack orders." Bibb Manufacturing bought Meritas in 1937 and renamed it the Anderson Mill.[16]

An internecine fight between the American Federation of Labor and the Congress of Industrial Organizations (CIO) in the late 1930s spilled into Columbus mills. In 1938, local unions affiliated with the more radical CIO-sponsored Textile Workers Organizing Committee (TWOC). After a petition from the TWOC, the National Labor Relations Board (NLRB) ordered the Eagle & Phenix to allow operatives to vote on whether they wanted the committee to represent them. The first election was a landslide against the union, but the TWOC charged mill overseers with intimidation and coercion. The NLRB agreed that management had engaged in "unfair labor practices" and ordered a second election. In the April 1939 balloting, workers again rejected the union but by a much narrower margin—23 of 1,481 votes. The local textile industry remained unorganized through World War II, and the CIO made one more push for unionization after the war.[17]

WRBL radio continued to provide Columbus residents with a diversion from economic depression and labor woes, bringing news, music, drama, and sports into homes. In 1937, James W. Woodruff Jr. moved the station from the Royal Theatre to the former Woodruff mansion at 1420 Second Avenue and broadcast Columbus Little Theatre plays, live Royal Theatre vaudeville, and local musical performers. That year, WRBL began airing the games of the Columbus Redbirds, a St. Louis Cardinals farm team. The station affiliated with CBS in 1939, gaining access to syndicated news and programming. A second Columbus station, WDAK, an ABC affiliate, took to the airwaves in 1942. WRBL-FM started broadcasting in 1946. In those last years before television, the radio lineup featured news, sports, comedy, drama, and music, with such popular offerings as *Hit Parade, Hedda Hopper's Hollywood, Dick Tracy*, the Duke Ellington Orchestra, college football games, and news with Edward R. Murrow. George Gingell became WRBL's program manager in 1948 as well as the beloved Voice of the Bulldogs announcing University of Georgia football. Rozell Fabiani began her career at WRBL in 1949 and went on to become a longtime local television host. In the 1930s, the Springer Theatre hosted Little Theatre productions and occasional boxing matches but mostly showed first-run films, including Laurence Olivier in *Wuthering Heights* (advertised in the *Columbus Enquirer* in 1945 as *Withering Heights*). The Three Arts League continued to bring highbrow artists to town, presenting four concerts a year and moving from Columbus High to the larger Jordan Vocational High auditorium in 1940. During the war, the League offered hundreds of free tickets to servicemen, and by 1946, membership had grown to 1,153.[18]

In 1938, the editor of the *Columbus Ledger-Enquirer*, Nelson Shipp, tried to enlist novelist Margaret Mitchell's support for a "white-columned mansion" to serve as a city museum and tribute to her. Mitchell tactfully refused, citing *Gone with the Wind* passages in which Tara was described not as a mansion but as a plain upcountry house. She did, however, support the idea of a museum: "When I look back to my childhood and remember the many relics of War days which surrounded me... I wring my hands in regret." The idea moved forward a few years later, when influential members of Columbus's elite became involved. In 1941, local artist Edward Swift Shorter led a group that received a charter for the Columbus Museum of Arts and Crafts. Shorter was well positioned to galvanize interest among wealthy supporters. Grandson of textile magnate George Parker Swift and first cousin of Judge Eli Shorter, an infamous Indian land speculator, Edward Shorter had one-man shows in New York, Washington, and Atlanta during the 1920s. One of his paintings, *Between Courses*, a study of "his negro butler," was among forty American works exhibited at the 1939 New York World's Fair. After a major donation from Georgia Collier Comer of Savannah, local supporters elected Shorter to serve as president of the museum association. The group considered locating the museum at Weracoba Park and in the historic St. Elmo mansion, but the Japanese attack on Pearl Harbor shelved museum plans until after the war.[19]

The R. W. Page Corporation, owner of the *Ledger*, bought the struggling *Enquirer-Sun* in 1930, renamed it the *Enquirer*, and consolidated the management of the two newspapers, with the *Enquirer* publishing in the morning, the *Ledger* in the afternoon, and a joint *Ledger-Enquirer* Sunday edition. In April 1931, the Page Corporation opened a Mediterranean-style corporate headquarters for both newspapers at Twelfth Street and Front Avenue. The people of Columbus, like their counterparts elsewhere, were fascinated with flight, and the airfield south of Riverdale Cemetery hosted Sunday barnstorming shows. An elderly woman four decades later recalled one Sunday when a plane "fell in the cemetery and burned up, and I never did forgive myself" for missing it. The marathon dancing fad reached Columbus in 1932. The dances offered cash prizes for participants, provided grandstand seating for spectators, and featured comedians, bands, and vocalists. Dances were segregated, but white spectators often had reserved sections at the Negro dances. The dances became increasingly rowdy, leading to growing public opposition and occasional police raids, and the fad died out by 1935. In 1930, the Lions Club raised funds to build a nine-hole municipal golf course on the South Commons. The city hired Nolan Murrah as the resident golf pro. In 1935 Murrah and his brother, Edward, used Federal Emergency Relief Administration laborers to expand the course to eighteen holes. In May 1941, after a federal "security agent" criticized the Columbus recreation department's lack of adult leadership and programs, Paul B. "Pop" Austin, successful Columbus High coach, became the city's director of athletics, remaining with the Parks and Recreation Department until 1968. The department expanded playgrounds, league play, community centers, and swimming pools, though for whites only. The Ninth Street YMCA had a pool for African Americans, but it was condemned in 1943 and required more than a year of repair. In 1944, more than one million soldiers and residents enjoyed Columbus's recreational facilities.[20]

Columbus's two best-known writers had love-hate relationships with their hometown, moving away but frequently returning to visit. Nunnally Johnson was born in 1897 to metalworker and railroad superintendent James Nunnally Johnson and Johnnie Pearl Johnson, who helped to found the local parent-teacher association in 1905 and served on the school board for twenty years beginning in 1922. Johnson grew up downtown; attended public schools; spent time at the marble YMCA near his house, which he called "his social club"; and graduated from Columbus High in 1915. After working briefly as a reporter for the *Enquirer-Sun*, Johnson moved to Savannah and then New York, where he became reporter for the *New York Tribune* and the *New York Post*. In 1925, he sold his first short story, the start of a brief but successful career in fiction that included fifty-two short stories that appeared in the *Saturday Evening Post* and satirized life in New York and Columbus (which he called Riverside).[21]

When work grew scarce during the Great Depression, Johnson borrowed train fare and headed to Hollywood in 1932. Over the next three decades, he became Hollywood's most highly paid screenwriter, logging seventy credits, including *The Grapes of Wrath, The Three Faces of Eve, How to Marry a Millionaire*, and *The Man in the Gray Flannel Suit*. In 1938, Johnnie Pearl Johnson wrote to her son, "The news of your new contract is wonderful. However, I believe it would be wiser for me not to mention this new increase to anyone else in Columbus. You may remember that I wrote you once of the strange look that came into Professor Kendrick's face when I told him at a Parent-Teacher meeting that you were getting six hundred dollars a week as a writer. It was even worse when I told your aunts, May and Minnie, that you had been raised to two thousand dollars a week.... They thought I was telling them fibs." Johnson's screenplay for Erskine Caldwell's novel *Tobacco Road*, a tale of depraved Georgia sharecroppers, resulted in an oft-repeated and perhaps apocryphal anecdote that caused much resentment in his hometown: when a wealthy Georgia woman scolded Johnson for casting such a negative light on his native state, he replied, "Why, madam, where I come from, we look on that crowd as the country club set." Famous for his caustic wit, he did not suffer fools and loved to puncture Hollywood pomposity. One critic observed that Johnson's humor was "a civilized man's way of speaking his mind without pestering or bludgeoning you." Johnson visited Columbus regularly until his parents died around 1950. In 1941, Columbus High's journalism society, Quill and Scroll, named itself in his honor.[22]

Born Lula Carson Smith in Columbus in 1917, Carson McCullers grew up there until she left for New York City at age seventeen. In 1949, when one of her New York friends wondered about her frequent sojourns in her native city, McCullers explained, "I must go home periodi-

Nunnally Johnson at home in Columbus with his father, James Nunnally Johnson, and his mother, Johnnie Pearl Johnson, ca. 1945. Columbus State University Archives, Columbus State University, Columbus, Georgia.

cally to renew my sense of horror." A Southern Gothic writer, McCullers explored themes of love and loneliness, isolation and despair. Like Johnson, McCullers spent her early years downtown, but her family moved to affluent Wynnton in the mid-1920s after the viaduct opened. Her Columbus High classmates thought her eccentric: her clothes, hair, interests, and behavior did not fit the dainty femininity expected of wealthier Columbus girls, and her family did not attend church, a pillar of Columbus society. After contracting rheumatic fever at age fifteen, McCullers was never again physically strong, and at age twenty-four, she began to suffer debilitating strokes. Her physical limitations may explain her sympathy for characters with deformities and disabilities, such as deaf-mute John Singer in her acclaimed first novel, *The Heart Is a Lonely Hunter* (1940). Over the next three and a half decades, she published several additional novels as well as short stories and plays before succumbing to another stroke in 1967. Though critics generally loved her work, many Columbus residents resented what they saw as attacks on their city. *Reflections in a Golden Eye* (1941) depicted sexual deviance, repressed homosexuality, and voyeurism on a southern U.S. Army base. When the story appeared in *Harper's Magazine*, the *Columbus Enquirer*'s woman's editor huffed, "All [the characters] are neurotics; that, we believe, is a polite term for it." She apologized to the army, claiming that the people in the novel "are figments of the young author's mind.... Certainly, [the story] could have been built around no living people the young author has known." Reviewing *The Ballad of the Sad Café* (1943), which centered on a love triangle involving a hunchbacked dwarf, an Amazon-like café owner, and a convict, another local admired McCullers's style but wished that she would write a novel with "normal" characters.[23]

Columbus provided both concrete and thematic context for McCullers's work. She drew not only on local settings but on locally inspired themes of gender, sexual identity, social class, and race. As protagonist Frankie Addams walked the main street in *The Member of the Wedding* (1946), she saw 1940s Columbus: "The same brick stores, about four blocks of them, the big white bank, and in the distance the many-windowed cotton mill. The wide street was divided by a narrow aisle of grass on either side of which the cars drove slowly in a browsing way." Early in *The Heart Is a Lonely Hunter*, McCullers described a town with "several blocks of two- and three-story shops and business offices. But the largest buildings in the town were the factories, which employed a large percentage of the population. These cotton mills were big and flourishing."[24]

McCullers's female characters suffocated in traditional roles: Mick Kelly in *The Heart Is a Lonely Hunter*, for example, was "defeated by society on all the main issues before she can even begin"; Amelia Hunter in *The Ballad of the Sad Café* suffered as an outcast as punishment for defying societal norms. McCullers would have known of the "martyred" Augusta Howard. Not only did Howard's obituary appear in the local paper a few months before McCullers left for New York, but her father, Lamar Smith, had written a 1921 letter to the governor in support of a pardon for Howard, "a person of keenest regard for integrity and justice." Howard was akin to Miss Amelia, living in dilapidated Sherwood Hall "let[ting] her hair grow ragged ... and the great muscles of her body [shrinking] until she was as thin as old maids are thin when they go crazy." As one McCullers scholar has commented, "To fail at what one's society expects of women in life is to end up alone, broken, crazy, and tragic."[25]

McCullers was "somewhat gender-ambiguous" growing up and was a bisexual adult. Writer Sarah Schulman has suggested that McCullers was transgender, "an identity that history had not yet discovered." Columbus intellectual Edwin Peacock, a gay man, was McCullers's "first adult friend," and she credited him with introducing her to the world of ideas. Open homosexuality was taboo, although closeted gay aristocratic men were tolerated, and people winked at "old maid schoolteachers," preferring to believe that they lived together out of financial necessity. As McCullers scholar Carlos Dews has noted, in the 1930s and 1940s South "the very idea of advocating for the rights of gay, lesbian, bisexual, or transgender individuals was untenable." Yet in her first novel, McCullers included an "ambi-sexual" character, Biff Brannon, who was impotent, wore perfume, and sewed curtains for his apartment. She shocked her hometown with the repressed homosexual army captain, Weldon Penderton, in *Reflections in a Golden Eye*. After its publication in February 1941, McCullers spent the winter with her family in Columbus and found herself at the center of "a furore" as people assumed that the book was based on Fort Benning, though it was not. She even received a Klan threat. Captain Penderton, perhaps speaking for McCullers, endorsed the notion that "it is morally honorable, for the square peg to keep scraping around the round hole rather than to discover and use the orthodox square that would fit it."[26]

Social class issues permeate McCullers's novels. In *The Heart Is a Lonely Hunter*, Mick attended the Industrial High School, not elite Columbus High. In the novel, McCullers recorded the squalor and hopelessness she had observed while walking through the mill neighborhoods as a young girl: "Most of the workers in town were very poor. Often in the faces along the streets there was the desperate look of hunger and of loneliness." That poverty was also evident in *The Member of the Wedding*, in which Frankie wandered "the gray crooked streets of the mill section, ... among the choking dust and sad gray rotten shacks" of Boogerville. In *The Heart Is a Lonely Hunter*, Jake Blount learned of an unsuccessful strike six years earlier—the Textile Strike of 1934—and railed, "The bastards who own these mills are millionaires. While the doffers and carders and all the people behind the machines who spin and weave the cloth can't hardly make enough to keep their guts quiet.... When you walk around the streets and ... see hungry worn-out people and ricket-legged young-uns, don't it make you mad?"[27]

Early in her life, McCullers found segregated drinking fountains puzzling, since black domestics cooked for whites and tended their intimate needs. She understood African Americans' second-class status and the racial codes that required even educated black professionals to avoid making eye contact with and to speak subserviently to whites, as is evident from the beating that Dr. Benedict Mady Copeland suffered in *The Heart Is a Lonely Hunter* when he failed to adhere to such codes. McCullers's empathy for African Americans drew admiration from both white and black critics. In his review of *The Heart Is a Lonely Hunter*, African American author Richard Wright marveled at "the astonishing humanity that enables a white writer, for the first time in Southern fiction, to handle Negro characters with as much ease and justice as those of her own race." Some black characters acquiesced to the caste system: Copeland's daughter, Portia, advised, "Best thing us can do is keep our mouth shut and wait." But the doctor sought to "uplift his people"—using the language commonly employed by black professionals in the first half of the twentieth century—and decried his people's oppression: "We have no representatives in government. We have no vote. In all of this great country we are the most oppressed of all people.... People of the Negro race, arise!... We must arise and be whole again! We must be free!" In *Clock without Hands* (1961), which was set in 1954, the year of *Brown v. Board of Education*, a white character, Jester Clane, declared to his racist grandfather, "I question the justice of white supremacy," while African American Sherman Pew demanded his civil rights: "I vibrate with every injustice that is done to my race." As with Richard Wright's *Black Boy*, Sherman "knew of every lynching, every violence that had happened in his time and before his time, and he felt every abuse in his own body."[28]

In 1948, when McCullers learned that Columbus's new public library would be segregated, she wrote to the *Ledger-Enquirer*, "Always it has been an intolerable shame to me to know that Negroes are not accorded the same intellectual privileges as white citizens." She asked that "all citizens regardless of race" be allowed access to great authors "to benefit by their wisdom, which is our dearest inheritance." The library ignored her. A decade later, when directors asked McCullers to deposit her manuscripts in the library's collection, she responded that she would do so only if the library was "truly a public one" and open to all citizens. The library declined, and so did she.[29]

The U.S. government ended its experiment with Prohibition in 1933, and Columbus followed suit a few years later, legalizing beer and wine sales in 1936 and liquor in 1938. The city had barred whiskey for more than two decades, and at least one local doctor believed that ending the "bone dry" ban would improve local health: "I defy any physician to prove that whiskey does not have good effect, with poor weak, emaciated consumptives, it mitigates the cough, cheers up the feelings and softens the path to the grave." Despite Prohibition, members of the upper class had always had access to liquor at private social clubs, but the tap now opened for everyone. Wholesaler Fate Leebern received his liquor license on March 29, 1938, and had whiskey delivered from Florida the next day. By 1940, thirty-six Columbus bars, clubs, and cafés sold beer and liquor. Ending Prohibition proved excellent for the city's economy, with thousands of thirsty soldiers pouring into Fort Benning as tensions rose in Europe and Asia.[30]

The army base's growth through the 1930s provided Columbus with a lifeline during the worst of the depression, as big privately funded construction projects came to a halt after the opening of the *Ledger-Enquirer* and Southern Bell buildings in 1931. Thousands of Federal Emergency Relief Administration, Civilian Conservation Corps, and Public Works Administration employees received jobs connected to projects at Fort Benning, where the number of personnel ballooned to one hundred thousand after World War II began in Europe in 1939. George S. Patton came to Benning with the Second Armored Division in 1940 and was named its commanding general in April 1941. A member of a wealthy California wine-growing family, Patton ensconced himself in local society, appearing with his wife, Bernice, at costume balls as Rhett and Scarlett and as King Arthur and Guinevere. On most Saturday nights, the Pattons dined at a popular local establishment, Spano's, where he usually spoke quietly through clenched teeth but occasionally became excited and yelled loud enough to be heard "three blocks away," as Sara Spano recalled. After publication of *The Heart Is a Lonely Hunter*, Patton attended a tea for McCullers given by George Parker Swift's granddaughter, Edith Kyle Harrison, in her antebellum mansion at Third Avenue and Twelfth Street. He shocked and thrilled the ladies present by shooting his pearl-handled pistols off the front porch. Harrison's nephew, Clason Kyle, who was eleven at the time, remembered a "sea of khaki" as soldiers hearing gunfire filled the yard. Another soldier stationed at Benning, Paul Tibbets, married Columbus native Lucy Frances Wingate in 1938. Lucy Tibbets remained with her two young sons in Columbus when her husband was stationed overseas later in the war, and after he piloted the plane that dropped the atomic bomb on Hiroshima, the press besieged her. She told Jesse Helms, at the time a naval recruiter stationed in Columbus who moonlighted as an *Enquirer* reporter and later a longtime senator from North Carolina, that the bomb's use was "wonderful," although she worried that "the Japs certainly would like to kill him now."[31]

World War II also brought thousands of African American soldiers to Fort Benning, where white officers ran the country's first colored Reception Center. Soldiers remained at the base for a few days while they underwent processing—tests, immunizations, uniforms, and duty assignment—and then were shipped out. Black troops served as cooks, laborers, mechanics, and draymen, but the army initially found them unfit for combat. Fort Benning's all-black 555th Parachute Infantry Battalion, the Triple Nickels, was activated in December 1943 but never saw combat. Instead, black paratroopers served courageously in the Pacific Northwest as firefighting "smoke jumpers."[32]

In keeping with the ideology evoked by their Confederate namesakes, Fort Benning and other U.S. Army installations across the South maintained policies that discriminated against African Americans. As one black officer asserted, "The Negro's first taste of warfare in World War II was on army posts right here in his own country." An African American colonel with the Twenty-Fourth Infantry at Benning in 1941 noted that "racial policies at the fort were certainly not going to build morale or patriotism in young Negro draftees." The base was segregated, with African Americans denied access to the Officers' Club and the main theater. White officers were frequently racist: as one African American sergeant later observed, "The Negro enlisted man was never allowed to forget he was a Negro" and was expected to stay in his place "both in and out of camp." Any Negro who displayed "intelligence [or] belligerency" or who "acted like a man" was labeled a "smart nigger" and found himself subject to punishment. On one occasion, a white military policeman shot a black enlisted man for talking back to a white telephone operator. In an instance of double jeopardy, soldiers in the Twenty-Fourth Infantry convicted of a crime in a Columbus court were subsequently court-martialed for the same offense. When city police beat and permanently disfigured a colored lieutenant, the army did nothing. Worst of all, Pvt. Felix Hall was lynched in February 1941. Hall disappeared on the afternoon of February 12 after walking through a white neighborhood on base, but apparently no one at Benning looked for him, and not until six weeks later did a platoon of engineers training in the nearby woods find Hall's decomposed body. His hands and feet had initially been bound, though Hall had worked his legs and one hand free before the noose around his neck suffocated him. A Benning physician initially ruled Hall's death a homicide, but base officials labeled it first a suicide and then a sex crime. In the face of pressure from the NAACP and other advocacy groups, the army and FBI investigated Hall's death, but no one was ever charged with Hall's murder. In 1942, however, African American leaders launched the "Double V" campaign, seeking victory against fascism abroad and against racism at home. Black publications drew parallels between Nazi ideology abroad and racism in the United States: the NAACP *Bulletin*, for example, charged Benning's military police force with using "concentration camp tactics" against Negro troops.[33]

The local community worked to help the soldiers at Fort Benning acclimate to the area. The Columbus Defense Service Committee, for example, disseminated information about transportation, housing, churches, recreation, and social activities. *Ledger-Enquirer* publisher Maynard Ashworth chaired a Defense Service committee that advocated the creation of a YMCA for Negro troops, an effort to which African American civilians eagerly contributed. In 1941, Lizzie Lunsford donated $15,000 to construct what became the world's first Negro Army-Navy Y. Located behind the Pierce Building, which Lunsford and her brother, Richard Pierce, had constructed in the 1920s, the Y opened with fanfare in July with E. E. Farley at the helm. It hosted dances, socials, and church activities and offered board games, ping-pong, and first aid classes. Its sixty-five dorm beds were not nearly enough to meet demand. A machine enabled soldiers to record messages on phonograph records that could be sent to loved ones. Fredye Marshall, a local radio and later TV personality, led group sing-alongs. The Negro Army-Navy Y, its white counterpart, and the Ninth Street YMCA also served as United Service Organization (USO) clubs, offering servicemen lounges, libraries, counseling, radio, arts and crafts, writing paper, package wrapping, and mailing. A. J. McClung, later a city politician, helped run the Negro USO at the Ninth Street Y. As racial conflict spread on army bases, Farley claimed that Columbus's recreational facilities and programs for colored troops contributed to "the comparative absence of racial strife" in the city.[34]

Lizzie Lunsford and her family were astute entrepreneurs who created numerous products and services for African American soldiers. Because bus service to Fort Benning ended early and white taxis refused to serve black customers, Lizzie's son, Walter, started the Red Bird Cab Company at the corner of Sixth Avenue and Eighth Street. Walter eventually formed two more taxi companies, employing one hundred drivers and becoming the city's largest African American employer. Behind the drugstore operated by his uncle, Richard Pierce, Walter established an amusement company that sold pinball machines and jukeboxes. Walter's wife, Sally, opened the Annex, a restaurant on Ninth Street. Walter wanted to sell beer there, but no African American could get a local

Lizzie Lunsford holding her granddaughter, Lula Lunsford, in front of her Lawyers Lane home, ca. 1950. From the Collection of Lula Lunsford Huff.

distributorship. To get around the problem, he used family connections in Chicago to obtain the only southern distributorship for Fox Deluxe Beer.[35]

When Congress standardized time zones across the country in 1918, two-thirds of Georgia was located in the Eastern Time Zone, but Atlanta and parts west were on Central Time. In March 1940, despite Columbus legislators' opposition, the General Assembly moved the entire state to Eastern Time. A few months later, to save energy, President Roosevelt put the country on "War Time" (now known as Daylight Saving Time). With locals grumbling about the shock to their body clocks, the *Enquirer* urged residents to buck up—beating Hitler would require sacrifices.[36]

More than six hundred thousand soldiers trained at Fort Benning during the war, and the influx of soldiers, families, and civilian workers overloaded the city's infrastructure. In 1941, the bus company built a new depot at Broadway and Ninth Street to handle increased traffic, and two years later, buses were carrying 1.5 million passengers more than 231,000 miles each month. The war accelerated construction of a four-lane "super highway" to Benning that had been under discussion since the 1930s. In August 1945, the city council named the route Victory Drive. Local leaders wanted to replace the city's old airfield by Riverdale Cemetery, but in mid-1943, with construction already underway on two runways at a North Columbus site, the War Production Board refused to provide $65,000 to fund a proposed three-story administration building because the airfield was not under military control. After Muscogee County attorney Bentley Chappell, son of former Columbus mayor L. H. Chappell, discovered that the board had no jurisdiction over buildings valued at $1,000 or less, the county built a small temporary building with donated labor and secondhand fixtures. On August 1, 1944, Eastern Air Line began twice-a-day service to Columbus from New York and Houston.[37]

Housing shortages spurred nearly continuous construction. Fort Benning built residential housing and barracks, including Sand Hill and Harmony Church, at a cost of more than $5 million. In 1940, private home construction reached the highest value and volume in more than a decade. The Jordan Company built numerous modest homes, developing the Summerfield subdivision between Columbus and Fort Benning with 150 small houses on lots measuring 50 by 150 feet. The company trotted out a new sales gimmick, "the talking house," with hidden speakers announcing the residences' features. According to company president Gunby Jordan II, the houses sold "like hotcakes." After Pearl Harbor, however, few building materials were available for private construction. Existing housing stock was sufficient for only 80 percent of city residents, and some families began boarding soldiers as a means of earning extra money. One Boogerville family that took in a soldier became terrified when they awoke to find him howling like a dog. Convinced that the soldier was possessed, the family evicted him, only later learning that he had epilepsy.[38]

Enrollment in white schools downtown dropped but soared nearer Fort Benning and the new housing developments. Classes commonly topped forty students in white schools and sixty in Negro schools. High school curricula shifted to war needs, with the new Jordan Vocational High School offering popular classes in aviation mechanics, welding, and electrical work, and soldiers attended night courses for high school equivalency. With male teachers leaving the schools to join the military, army wives often filled the vacancies, but staffing shortages persisted, even after teachers received a 10 percent pay raise in 1944. The war also opened doors for women to move into administrative positions in education. When the principal of Columbus High School joined the U.S. Navy in 1944, the board named assistant principal Annie V. Massey to serve as acting principal, making her the first woman to head a high school in Columbus. When the male principal returned, however, Massey had to give up the post, and five decades passed before another Columbus woman received that opportunity.[39]

World War II–related labor shortages also opened other jobs to members of previously excluded groups. In the first years of the conflict, women took new positions in the mills, but by 1943, textile manufacturers were complaining that "women just can't do all those jobs" and African Americans began moving into skilled positions. The first positions offered to black workers were difficult jobs that white operatives did not want, such as making tire cord. Skilled workers continued leaving the mills for better jobs in shipyards in Brunswick, Georgia; Mobile, Alabama; and Pascagoula, Mississippi. Textile executives tried to stem the tide by appealing to patriotism, claiming that "there are plenty of essential jobs for the people trained to do them right here in Columbus." In 1940, when W. C. Bradley learned that the U.S. Air Force was considering building a base near Columbus, he blocked the plan, fearing that the base would offer higher wages and force the textile mills to increase their pay rates, and the base located in Warner Robins, Georgia. Much of the mills' wartime production went to satisfy military needs, as soldiers used an average of two hundred pounds of cotton products a year. Textile mills made uniforms, rifle slings, gas masks, mosquito nets, parachute harnesses, and pontoons. The Bibb Mill added twenty-five hundred wide looms to make cotton duck for tents and tarps. The Lummus Cotton Gin Company retooled to manufacture artillery shells, ammunition, and ship parts. Goldens' Foundry made steam steering engines for Liberty cargo ships, winning an award for excellence in 1943.[40]

Soldiers' needs also fueled the city's snack food industry. By 1942, the Tom Huston Peanut Company had become one of the country's largest manufacturers of peanut snacks and one of Columbus's largest employers. Sugar rationing beginning in February 1942 boosted sales of peanuts, which were not rationed, and Tom's tripled its volume during the decade. Most soft drink companies suffered from sugar rationing, but Coca-Cola became a symbol of "almost religious significance to the American soldier." After Pearl Harbor, Coke president Robert Woodruff pledged, "We will see that every man in uniform gets a bottle of Coca-Cola for five cents, wherever he is and whatever it costs our company." Within months, Coke sales to soldiers were exempted from rationing, a loophole that included every retail business in Columbus. Similarly, Kinnett Dairies, which supplied ice cream to Fort Benning, was exempt from rationing. Nehi Corporation was less fortunate. Its RC Cola and other drinks earned decent profits in 1941–1943, but earnings dropped in 1944 and 1945 as a consequence of sugar shortages.[41]

Shortages of food products and other goods hit citizens hard as well. In addition to sugar, rationed items included flour, meat, shoes, and tires. Growing up in the Liberty District, Eddie Lindsey, later Muscogee County's first African American assistant school superintendent, remembered having to use cardboard to cover holes in his shoes, leaving his feet soaked on wet days. With meat scarce, Lindsey's father shot rabbits. People grew vegetables in what were known as Victory Gardens, with women learning canning and preservation techniques from classes offered by Georgia Power and high schools. Beginning in May 1942, gasoline rationing limited people to an average of between 2.5 and 5 gallons per week. People who needed their cars for jobs or other activities related to war production were allotted more gas, a situation that caused great embarrassment to Benjamin Hardaway, president of Hardaway Construction, when his wife took his business car to a club meeting and received a ticket for improper use of the vehicle. The newspaper reported the transgression, and as Hardaway's daughter remembered, "That never happened again, I can tell you!"[42]

On March 5, 1943, 135 members of the Women's Army Auxiliary Corps (later the Women's Army Corps) arrived at Fort Benning. The five detachments of women, including a colored unit, served as clerks, hospital technicians, librarians, cooks, photographers, and teletype operators. They rigged parachutes and flew with the men but never jumped. Many civilian women worked for the Red Cross. Sara Simons coordinated knitting and sewing at the Red Cross headquarters on Thirteenth Street.

Helen Lumpkin headed Volunteer Special Services and organized the blood bank, handling hundreds of donations at St. Luke Methodist. Women also served as nurses' aides and Grey Ladies at the Fort Benning Hospital. Black and white families frequently hosted soldiers for meals, particularly home-cooked Sunday dinners after church and holiday dinners. On one Mother's Day, Ralph Shipmen of Indiana was among the two dozen or so soldiers invited by Edith Kyle Crawford and her cousin, Edward Shorter, to dine at the Swift-Kyle mansion. According to Shipman,

> We had Coco Cola's before dinner. The dining room was filled with serving tables arranged with huge silver trays, one heaping with real southern fried chicken, another with roast lamb, crisp rice, with gravy for both, beets, green beans, loads of pickled peaches and a couple more relishes. The most heavenly beaten biscuits and pocket rolls you dreamed about! Tall glasses of iced tea.... We sat at small tables and were served a dessert there. I made a pig of myself on that—which was Marshmallow Charlotte, made with excellent Bourbon Whiskey, marshmallows, macaroons, and whipped cream—over which you put globs of homemade ice cream. Then individual chocolate and white cakes were passed.

Such Columbus hospitality must have eased the ache of being far from home.[43]

The 1940s also spawned honky-tonks, strip joints, tattoo parlors, and brothels, establishments that caused great concern among local leaders. In 1940, the venereal disease rate at Fort Benning was so high that the army threatened to bar soldiers from Columbus and Phenix City if it was not reduced. Police formed a "vice squad" to round up women "without visible means of livelihood" or "of questionable character." Within a day, police had arrested fifty women, beginning a five-year crusade against prostitutes. On July 11, 1941, Congress passed the May Act, which outlawed prostitution near military bases, leading Columbus-area authorities to fear federal involvement if they could not put an end to such activities. The U.S. Public Health service appointed a doctor to coordinate local efforts, and the army established "prophylactic stations" across the city and on base, seeking to reduce the forty thousand man-days lost to venereal disease at Fort Benning in 1941. The following May, the commanding general responsible for the southeastern states declared that prostitutes should be classed as "fifth columnists" and fought "with all the force at our command." He complained of lax enforcement of anti-prostitution laws around Benning, where prostitutes spread syphilis

V-E Day on Broadway in Columbus.
Columbus Ledger-Enquirer, May 8, 1945.

and gonorrhea, "the prime wasters of manpower, destroyers of the effectiveness of [the armed forces] and of the civilian forces engaged in the essential industries." Benning soon had a "venereal disease control officer" who compared prostitutes to "a horde of enemy agents spreading poison among our soldiers and civilians."[44]

Officials claimed that Negroes were responsible for 90 percent of all cases of sexually transmitted disease. The public health officer asked the city to take action against "at least half of Columbus' colored honkytonks." African American leaders requested "Negro auxiliary police," a Negro truant officer, and health education funds to stem vice and sexually transmitted diseases, but those requests were denied. In September 1944, a judge found two Negro teenagers guilty of public indecency after they were picked up wearing bathing suits on a public road. The girls, who claimed that they had been swimming in Bull Creek and were headed home, were found to be infected with venereal disease and were sentenced to a year at the state prison farm. After a public outcry over the lengthy sentences, six prominent attorneys, including Theo McGee, convinced the judge to set the punishment aside and turn the girls over for Health Department treatment. In 1945, the Muscogee County Commission criminalized failure to take treatment for sexually transmitted diseases, with repeat offenders sentenced to a year at the county work camp, though white offenders often got deferred sentences. Despite such efforts, venereal disease remained a problem in Columbus.[45]

Though textile operatives' wages rose 200 percent from 1937 to 1948, they remained the lowest-paid industrial workers, prompting the CIO to launch a 1946 unionization drive, Operation Dixie, that sought to consolidate labor's wartime gains. Arriving in Columbus in June, brash young Pittsburgh native George Johnston brimmed with confidence that he would bring textile bosses to their knees.[46]

Southern textile towns remained "dominated by an interlocking structure of factory owners, church officials, politicians, law enforcement officers, newspaper editors and others with little concern for the democratic and constitutional rights" of workers. Johnston found Columbus to be "a classic anti-union cotton mill town, with a history of violent opposition to unions." He believed that operatives were "emotional, violent, irresponsible," handicapped by "a marked degree of psychological insecurity," racism, and anti-Semitism. One worker claimed to have "nothing against the nigger. He has to buy his groceries in the same store as me and at the prices I pay. But I just don't want to mix and mingle with him." A particular thorn in the CIO's side was Evall G. "Parson Jack" Johnston, minister at Columbus's Independent Baptist Tabernacle. By the late 1930s, Parson Jack used his publication, *The Trumpet*, to rail against the CIO with articles such as "Communistic C.I.O. Would Place Negro Men Along Side of White Women in Cotton Mills in the Southern States." By the 1940s, he had achieved national renown as an antiunion and anti-Semitic white supremacist. The Bibb Mill and Swift Manufacturing bought full-page ads in *The Trumpet*: they and other local mills supported Johnston as a means of control over unions and Negroes. Johnston's publication appeared in workers' mailboxes whenever a union organizer came to town.[47]

Mills also continued to rely on paternalism to keep workers unorganized. "Substantial school buildings ... gymnasiums, natatoriums, clubrooms, and auditorium facilities, and handsome debt-free churches" reinforced the "values" of the "Bibb Family." Constructed in 1941, the company's Comer Auditorium featured a polished hardwood floor that not only served as a basketball court but also hosted entertainment, including Gene Autry and his cowboys and horses. Despite such amenities, the working conditions in the mills were still deplorable—filthy, deafening, and hot. The lint-filled air caused byssinosis, or "brown lung," an asthma-like condition. On winter mornings, workers would draw in deep cold breaths before facing eight hours of "mill air," high in humidity and the raw smell of cotton. Operatives walking into Bibb's weave room felt as though "you could not fall down, because the hot humid air would hold you up." Laborers returned from their shifts exhausted: according to George Johnston, one woman came home and fell asleep nursing her baby, awakening later to find the baby dead, smothered at her breast.[48]

Assigned to Swift Spinning, Johnston feared mill officials, who stood sharpening their knives while eyeing union men. On September 5, 1946, while Johnston and an organizer from Atlanta passed out leaflets, a worker slugged the Atlanta man. Told that organizing Bibb Mill was impossible, Johnston snuck into the village, knocked on a worker's door, and briefly talked with him. As soon as Johnston left, Bibb police told the worker that he would find his furniture out on the street if he ever again talked to an organizer. Johnston defiantly leafleted Bibb workers. A dozen men rushed out, slapped the leaflets to the ground, and threatened him with "grisly violence." When he complained to Columbus police, "dumbfounded, they referred us to the Bibb City police." But in Bibb City, he was "taken aback to find the police station located in the basement of the mill!" Not surprisingly, his complaint was ignored. After meeting with African American leaders just before Thanksgiving 1946, Johnston handed out pamphlets at Swift's back door, where black workers entered. A large white man came out, beat Johnston to a pulp, and threatened to kill him if he returned.[49]

In response, a majority of Swift workers joined the union. As Otis McIntyre, a weaver, stated, "I know that the union in the north is the only reason we ever get anything down here, and until we organize... and start to run things for us poor people, this country ain't never goin' to straighten up." The mill went on the offensive early in 1947, dismissing and blacklisting union members. After taking one sick day, McIntyre was fired for "excessive" absences, charged with misconduct so that he could not receive unemployment, and blacklisted. The National Labor Relations Board offered little help, and CIO leaders in Atlanta seemed indifferent, a situation that appalled Johnston. The organizer mourned "the badly damaged lives of my people" who "were unemployed and, as black listed cotton workers, unemployable, while I was still on salary. I had accomplished nothing. I had caused no little misery by asking them to demand their rights." Less than a year after his arrival, Johnston slunk back north, the union dead. Decades passed before labor organizers took another crack at Columbus's textile mills.[50]

After surviving the Great Depression, Columbus thrived during World War II. With a return to peacetime, most people believed that the future would be brighter. But white and African American residents had different visions for that future. While whites anticipated a resumption of the prewar social status quo, African Americans refused to return to the bad old days of second-class status. With fascism abroad defeated, they turned their attention to the second part of the Double V campaign, redoubling their efforts to overcome racism at home with a fight for equality that shook up the old order.

CHAPTER 7

Violence, Direct Action, Negotiation

The Struggle for Civil Rights, 1944–1975

Columbus's African Americans played a significant part in the post–World War II fight against racial discrimination. In 1946, a Columbus barber's lawsuit ended Georgia's Democratic white primary, opening the door for black voting and ushering in the modern civil rights movement. Dr. Thomas Brewer led the area's black community in its quest for civil rights, which included protests and boycotts that peacefully desegregated public facilities and Columbus College in the early 1960s. The issue of integrating the public school system was more divisive, however, as teachers were reassigned and students were bused based on racial quotas in the early 1970s. Accompanying such economic and political progress for Columbus's African Americans, racial tensions grew.

Brewer, a charismatic leader whom his followers called "Chief," had begun his civil rights activism before World War II, helping to charter a local chapter of the NAACP in 1939. During the 1930s and 1940s, he unsuccessfully requested funding from the city council for black police, recreation facilities, and public health services. In April 1944, the U.S. Supreme Court ruled in *Smith v. Allwright* that Texas's white primary was unconstitutional, prompting Georgia's black leaders to discuss the possibility of testing their state's primary. Primus King, a Columbus barber and pastor, volunteered to, as he put it, "put a bell around the cat's neck. The rats talked about" attempting to cast ballots, and "I told 'em, I said, 'I will.'" On July 4, he and two other Negroes "appeared at the polls before noon. They were not allowed to vote." According to King, police detectives grabbed him when he entered the courthouse and announced,

"Ain't no niggers votin' here today." King walked three blocks to attorney Oscar D. Smith's office to start the suit, which was financed by members of Columbus's black elite, including Brewer, E. E. Farley, and Lizzie Lunsford. King received a phone call from "an old cracker" who said, "'You must want to be put in the river.' I said: 'Well, they've put so many negroes in the river for nothin', I'm willin' to go in there for something!'" The Fifth Circuit Court of Appeals in Macon upheld King's claim, and on April 1, 1946, the U.S. Supreme Court declined to review the ruling, making the Georgia primary law unconstitutional.[1]

Increased African American activism triggered white fear. Moderates like Theo McGee urged acceptance of the court's ruling, but most whites supported the position taken by former governor and 1946 candidate to return to the office Eugene Talmadge. Standing on the steps of Columbus's courthouse, he acknowledged that "nigras" would vote in 1946 but promised the cheering crowd, "If I'm your governor, they won't vote in our white primary the next four years." By this time, the local Ku Klux Klan operated openly with Parson Jack Johnston as its leader, and he told a 1947 interviewer that if "the boys . . . can't keep niggers from votin' any other way, they'll have to use force." Klan activities continued in the Columbus area for the next two decades, with the newspaper publishing accounts of a 1947 meeting in the basement of Johnston's church, a 1949 rally at Golden Park, a 1958 cross-burning off Macon Road, a 1959 group stroll down Broadway, and a 1960 cross-burning outside an African American revival, with many other meetings and cross-burnings going unreported. The violence and intimidation had the intended effects: a 1956 Morehouse College survey found that Southwest Georgia officials had engaged in a "pattern of excluding Negroes as registrants and voters" through the "ever-present threat of racial violence."[2]

The Klan and white supremacists in the Columbus police department relentlessly pressured the black community. In 1948, just before Talmadge's son, Herman, was elected governor, an airplane dropped KKK leaflets over African American neighborhoods, warning residents not to vote. In February 1949, five Klansmen abducted three Spencer High students, drove them to Phenix City, interrogated them about their participation in an NAACP-sponsored Brotherhood Week, and then whipped them before releasing the boys in a hail of gunfire. On April 30, 1951, police roared into the Liberty District to stop a fight in a café; outraged, a black soldier threw a grenade under a police car, and the explosion caused minor injuries. The police retaliated with a "midnight orgy" of violence, invading Negro restaurants and bars and injuring at least one hundred people. African American leaders responded by renewing their demand for the hiring of black police officers. As one minister told the county commissioners, "We're almost afraid to call an officer, no matter what happens.... They don't come as peace officers. They come as slave drivers.... They've got to knock somebody down." When police again responded to a Liberty District disturbance on May 20, another grenade blasted their car. Five days later, police arrested eight soldiers in connection with the grenade attacks. On May 30, two soldiers were arrested for throwing bricks and bottles at a bus passing under the Thirteenth Street viaduct.[3]

Inequities persisted in many other areas of life as well. Lieutenant Stevens, the African American originator of the scrambled dog, a local tradition available at Dinglewood Pharmacy since the mid-1940s, earned $9.50 for a one-hundred-hour workweek. African Americans who wanted to eat his popular scrambled dog—a hot dog with chili and a variety of other toppings—had to stand at the restaurant's back door to place their orders, which were then handed to them to eat outside. Black customers could neither try on nor return clothes at downtown department stores, which also refused to employ African American sales clerks. Schools, cemeteries, parks, and public transportation were segregated. White and black witnesses testifying at the courthouse even were sworn in using different Bibles. When Albert Thompson, Columbus's first modern-day black legislator and judge, returned to the city after graduating from law school in 1950, he had difficulty finding the requisite three local attorneys to endorse his bar exam application. For his first decade in practice, Thompson saw no African Americans on juries.[4]

Exclusion from so much of white Columbus meant that black communities in the Bottoms and Liberty District became bustling residential and business centers. In 1949, 14 percent of the city's business operators and professionals were African American, down from 18 percent in the 1920s. Until passage of the 1964 Civil Rights Act, African American doctors could treat patients only in the hospital basement, and Columbus had no black surgeons until Delmar Edwards, the first black graduate of the University of Arkansas Medical School, opened an office downtown in 1964. Even then, he was denied admitting privileges at the hospital until "an uproar" forced officials to relent. During much of the 1940s and early 1950s, white leaders across the South grudgingly made improvements to African American facilities in hopes that making them more equal would persuade courts to allow segregation to continue. Many of Columbus's improvements came in response to requests from Brewer, whom African American activist and politician A. J. McClung said was feared by both blacks, "because they thought he was too militant on the race question," and whites, "because of what he tried to do for his people." In April 1948, Brewer requested the creation of a park with a swimming pool for African Americans, and Carver Park opened four years later. Similarly, Brewer's efforts resulted in the dedication of the Fourth Avenue Library in 1952. On January 1 of that year, four black police officers began patrolling the streets in African American Neighborhoods, though they were not allowed to arrest whites and one soon left for a job with the post office. Three others were fired in 1958 for what could have been a trumped-up charge, receiving stolen clothing from a downtown store.[5]

The U.S. Supreme Court's 1954 and 1955 *Brown v. Board of Education* decisions, however, sounded the death knell for "separate but equal" facilities. Whites refused to go down without a fight in what many perceived as the opening salvo in a war to destroy their way of life. Parson Jack formed the Christian Civic League, screamed about miscegenation in his *Georgia Tribune*, and called on "the best class of people" to join a local chapter of the White Citizens' Council, a white supremacist organization that appealed to middle-class businessmen. In November 1955, the Court outlawed segregation at public swimming pools and golf courses, leading Muscogee County to devise a plan to privately lease the all-white Flat Rock Park if blacks tried to integrate it. Though African Americans publicly declared that they did not seek "social equality" and merely wanted "the rights and privileges afforded all citizens by law" and the same amenities available to white taxpayers, discrimination continued: on January 4, 1956, four African American men were turned away from the city golf course when they attempted to play a round. Brewer's calls for integration of the schools and the golf course produced no results.[6]

In February 1956, Brewer's civil rights activism led to his death. He and Luico Flowers, the white man who operated a department store on the ground floor of the First Avenue building owned by Brewer that also housed his office, saw a white police officer break a nightstick over a black suspect's head. Flowers refused to join Brewer in filing a complaint about police brutality. Flowers claimed that Brewer, who was known to carry a pistol, had threatened him, and he consequently asked for police protection. On February 18, Brewer entered Flowers's store. At least one police officer was in the store, two others outside. Accounts of what exactly transpired differ, but after a series of gunshots, Brewer

Dr. Thomas H. Brewer, early 1950s. *Columbus Ledger-Enquirer.*

Primus King, 1977. *Columbus Ledger-Enquirer.*

had suffered seven bullet wounds and lay dead. Members of Columbus's African American community were stunned, while whites' reactions ranged from disbelief to approval. Flowers claimed self-defense despite the fact that Brewer's gun remained in his pocket, and a grand jury refused to indict Flowers. Almost a year later, Flowers was found near his store dead from gunshots to the head, a handkerchief in his mouth and two pistols by his side, both fired. His death was ruled a suicide, though the puzzle pieces did not fit. His clothes were ripped, his pockets turned out, and his head bruised. The pistols were wiped clean of fingerprints. A rumor swept the white community that one of the black police officers killed Flowers, and the Klan paraded down First Avenue in his commemoration. The black community, which believed Brewer was assassinated, contended the police later killed Flowers to cover up his role in the plot. Brewer's death attracted national attention, including an article on the front page of the *New York Times*. Brewer's obituary in the *Journal of the National Medical Association* asserted that he had been "quietly lynched." A week after Brewer's death, a local black leader told a *Pittsburgh Courier* correspondent, "The white folks are desperate, there is a definite move on to remove all Negro leadership, by hook or crook."[7]

Racial tensions continued to rise in Columbus. On December 21, 1957, a police officer arrested Clarence Pickett, a preacher and ad salesman for the *Columbus World*, and charged him with public intoxication. While in a jail cell, Pickett shouted and cursed the police, and an officer responded by beating Pickett senseless and telling him "You will be quiet—now, you son-of-a-bitch—now you will be quiet." Friends arranged Pickett's release the next day. In severe pain and unable to walk on his own, he was taken to the hospital, where a white doctor examined him, declared that "the trauma was not of a serious nature," gave him narcotic pain medicine, and sent him home. On December 23, Pickett died of what an autopsy determined was "shock and toxemia due to peritonitis, resulting from traumatic rupture of duodenum" due to a "massive blow to the abdomen." After Pickett's family and the black community protested, the officer was arrested on January 3, 1958. Like Brewer's murder two years earlier, the case received national publicity, with African American U.S. congressman Adam Clayton Powell of New York requesting that the FBI conduct an inquiry. But as in Brewer's case, an all-white jury refused to bring Pickett's murderer to justice.[8]

Just three days after the white officer's arrest for Pickett's beating, a bomb shattered four Negro homes on Fourth Avenue, in the same area where a cross had burned the preceding fall. The following July, when

Martin Luther King Jr. speaking at the Prince Hall Masonic Temple, July 1, 1958.
Columbus Ledger-Enquirer, July 2, 1958.

Martin Luther King Jr. planned to speak in Columbus, an anonymous caller to the *Ledger-Enquirer* "profanely" threatened to bomb the building where he was slated to speak. Police increased security while armed members of the black community stood guard on the building's roof, and King spoke without incident. At 12:30 that night, however, another bomb exploded at a black home. The police chief claimed that the attack appeared to be "an inside job" intended "to obtain publicity and sympathy for various colored organizations or groups making issues of the race difficulties."[9]

Recognizing that the climate in Columbus was such that whites could terrorize African Americans with impunity, black professionals—doctors, lawyers, teachers—fled the city, leaving a leadership vacuum. Those who left included Brewer's wife; his daughter and her physician husband; and physician F. V Miller and his wife, dentist Rosalie Miller, who subsequently settled in Seattle. When asked years later why they left, Rosalie Miller replied, "We left the home of the brave and went to the land of the free." Her husband said, "We believed in human dignity." By 1964, an NAACP organizer declared Columbus "the toughest town I had to deal with": "The blacks here didn't seem to want to do anything."[10] The campaign of intimidation and fear had taken its toll.

As in Atlanta, Charlotte, and Nashville, moderate and pragmatic wealthy white businessmen controlled Columbus. Most were not progressive on race issues but nonetheless wanted to avoid conflict that might cause economic damage to the city. A few qualified as liberals, at least in the context of the Deep South. Theo McGee, head of Columbus's Housing Authority and president of the Columbus–Phenix City Religious Council, the first local organization to bring together Protestants, Catholics, and Jews, embraced fair treatment of all people as a Christian principle. In 1951, McGee persuaded the *Columbus Ledger-Enquirer* to begin using courtesy titles—Mr. and Mrs.—for African Americans, as it did for whites. Members of the Jewish community, who had their own experiences with discrimination, also took racially liberal stances. When attorney Aaron Cohn, who went on to become a judge in the juvenile court, was first admitted to the bar after World War II, an opposing attorney told the judge, "All he knows is Jew Law." After participating in ecumenical services with Protestants and Catholics, Cohn became chief voter registrar for Muscogee County in 1960, and he used his position to have African Americans register white voters, and vice versa. With the backing of his congregation, Rabbi Alfred Goodman of Temple Israel was outspoken on racial equality and social justice, helping to create the Columbus Council on Human Relations, affiliated with the liberal Southern Regional Council.[11]

But McGee, Cohn, and Goodman were exceptions among Columbus's whites, most of whom rejected racial progressivism. In 1959, Robert B. McNeill followed in the footsteps of St. Luke Methodist's Daniel Curry, becoming the second Columbus minister dismissed because of his racial views. In the fall of 1952, McNeill had become the pastor at First Presbyterian Church, whose members included many Old Columbus elites who believed that God had ordained the separation of the races. Explained one church elder in 1958, "A whole lifetime of rearing has gone into certain fields of feeling, and we can't get over that in one year." As early as 1950, McNeill had predicted that segregation was on borrowed time and that the church would have to adjust, but his Columbus congregants had different, more conservative expectations, as he learned soon after arriving in the city when he was warned to stay away from race. Although he believed that standing on the moral high ground would win over his flock, McNeill's overt attention to racial issues ultimately proved to be his undoing. The day after Brewer's death, McNeill became the only white minister to speak out against the murder, asking in his sermon, "When we pray...do we consider the other men of the earth, diverse in color and in origin, as brothers, creatures of God, justly deserving our reverence for their personality?" He was "primarily concerned with the thousands of us who created the spiritual climate that made this act possible and with those who approve it." In a May 1957 *Look* magazine article, McNeill declared, "I shall never earn my own freedom until [Negroes] have realized theirs" and argued that white southerners who rejected this position were "not spiritually and intellectually free." Moreover, he indicted the supposedly moderate white majority: "There is little indignation expressed over the Klan or racial violence, just silence—cold, sweaty silence. The Klan is the impassioned tip of refined prejudice." McNeill stopped short of advocating integration or social equality, instead supporting "creative contact" between the races: mutual respect, dialogue, and representation "on city councils, grand juries, school boards, medical societies, ministerial associations, and other public agencies." Although McNeill's positions now seem uncontroversial, at the time they further inflamed the situation.[12]

McNeill subsequently found himself "strictly on the defensive." The community widely regarded *Look* as a "damnable, South-killing magazine," and no other Protestant ministers rose to McNeill's defense. Parson Jack attacked the *Look* article, labeling photos of black men embracing white women "creative contact." Though the majority of McNeill's congregants either supported him or remained undecided, the church elders split, with eight adamantly opposed to McNeill remaining in the pulpit and sixteen strongly supporting him. In March 1958, the head elder announced that he could not back the pastor because "Mr. McNeill appears so confident that the fault lies mainly with others, that I do not believe he will change." After extensive interviews, the regional Presbytery Judicial Commission concluded in November that it could not restore unity within the church and took control of its affairs.[13]

When McNeill's enemies began pressuring the commission chair, the pastor himself gave them ammunition. Early in 1959, the Columbus League of Women Voters sponsored a pair of forums on the *Brown* decision and invited liberal *Atlanta Constitution* editor Ralph McGill to speak in favor of school integration. The county commission initially agreed to allow McGill to give his talk at the superior courtroom but revoked permission in the face of public pressure. McNeill joined League leaders in supporting McGill, but the commissioners stood firm. The issue again brought national attention to Columbus, with newspapers calling the affair "a shocking disgrace" and asking, "Is Thinking, Even, Forbidden?" Locally, however, the reaction was far different: editorials on WRBL radio ridiculed "Rastus" (a racial slur) McGill and insisted that its "Big Johnnie Reb" poll showed strong support for segregated schools. McNeill's stance further lowered his enemies' estimation of him.[14]

On June 3, 1959, the chair of the Judicial Commission informed McNeill that he would be removed as pastor the next Sunday in "the interests of religion." Four days later, the chair read the decision to a shocked congregation at the conclusion of the pastor's sermon. The commission had based its decision on McNeill's "effort to relate the Gospel of Jesus Christ to the current racial problem in our Southland." McNeill gave the benediction and walked out. Women in the choir burst into tears. The former director of the chamber of commerce told the chair, "You and your commission have failed a Christian man and his family." That evening, despite his feelings of humiliation and numbness, McNeill returned to the pulpit to deliver one final sermon. He did not hold back, telling the congregation that southerners who claimed to embrace democracy yet supported racial segregation "have lost the capacity to reason logically.... No longer as consistent Christians can we retain our social pattern of life." He declared, "I can never again look upon any person as being inferior to me. Nor can I ever again require my conscience to consent to a system, legal or traditional, that enforces separation that is in effect subordination and which leads invariably to alienation." News outlets across the nation reported McNeill's ouster. Three days after his firing, McNeill suffered a major heart attack and was hospitalized for nearly four weeks. In August, he became associate pastor at a West Virginia church.[15]

It is likely that other factors played at least some role in McNeill's dismissal. One church elder accused the commission of acting because a few powerful members did not like McNeill, and indeed, even some church members who were sympathetic to his views found that he possessed an irritating, smug, and arrogant self-righteousness. At least a handful of congregants believed that he was too friendly with female church members; others perceived him as disorganized and unprofessional. Nonetheless, there is no question that his positions on racial matters—and his willingness to openly state those positions and criticize those who disagreed with them—lay at the heart of the church's decision.[16]

McNeill was one of several southern pastors whose moderate racial views cost them their pulpits in the mid-1950s. In fact, at a time when the issue of displaced persons (DPs) in the wake of World War II remained very much in the public consciousness, the phenomenon was common enough that the Southern Regional Council commented, "In the South we have a new class of DPs—displaced parsons." McNeill published a 1965 memoir, *God Wills Us Free: The Ordeal of a Southern Minister*, in which he offered only muted criticism of Columbus but nevertheless revealed the pain caused by his tenure there: "They could cut you to the heart without raising their voices."[17]

In the wake of the success of bus boycotts in Montgomery, Alabama, and elsewhere, Columbus activists turned their attention to the city's bus system. The local ordinance said drivers could "assign" seats, and "no passenger shall remain in any car, compartment, or seat other than that to which he has been assigned." Drivers had the power to eject uncooperative riders. On Christmas Eve 1956, four days after the U.S. Supreme Court upheld a lower court ruling requiring Montgomery's buses to integrate, police arrested a Negro soldier for sitting in the front of a Columbus bus. Five months later, another black soldier faced charges for violating the bus ordinance. On June 2, 1961, Freedom Riders passed through Columbus, with black and white students sitting together in the Greyhound terminal without incident. Shortly thereafter, the local Black Ministerial Alliance petitioned the city commission to integrate Columbus's buses, to no effect. Early in July, under federal pressure, the county commission desegregated the Columbus airport, where segregated waiting rooms had offended "colored" military officers from Latin American countries receiving training at Fort Benning. At around the same time, local activists renewed their assault on bus segregation. Columbus native Rudy Allen had been attending the American Baptist Seminary in Nashville, where he and classmates John Lewis and James Bevel had participated in the nonviolent sit-ins that eliminated segregation at lunch counters. Allen wanted "to get something started" in Columbus and requested help from students. A Student Non-Violent Coordinating Committee representative conducted a workshop at the Ninth Street

YMCA, but many young people objected to the idea that they would have to endure being spit on or slapped without retaliating, and the group shrank to about a half dozen.[18]

On July 17, representatives of the Non-Partisan Voters League again requested the integration of the buses. When the mayor brushed off the request, a League spokesman warned that a "group of impatient citizens" would be riding the buses that afternoon. One hour later, black students were sitting in the front of three city buses. Bunky McClung, whose father, A. J., directed the YMCA, opened a book to appear relaxed but was so nervous that she did not realize she was holding the book upside down. The bus driver ordered McClung and the three other activists to the back of the bus, but they did not respond. The driver called the police, and within minutes the four found themselves under arrest. Two other protesters on another bus were also arrested, but the police did not detain Allen and his partner on a third bus. At the old stockade, the police separated the arrested students, questioning them repeatedly on the assumption that they were "outside agitators." Albert Thompson, the only black attorney in town, bailed them out. The adult leaders, including Thompson, A. J. McClung, and NAACP president George Ford, wanted to sue to desegregate the bus line, but Allen believed a lawsuit would take too long. On August 4, he and the students again rode the buses. Police arrested all riders, charging them with disorderly conduct. After the students returned to college, Thompson and others negotiated with white power brokers in secret meetings at John Banks's antebellum home, the Cedars, which was owned by his great-grandson, Watkins Dimon. They convinced white leaders to bring bus segregation to a peaceful end. Not long thereafter, the KKK burned a cross in front of the Cedars.[19]

Desegregating most of the rest of Columbus, according to Allen, was "a piece of cake." The bus protest convinced moderate white leaders to cooperate to end segregation of public facilities. Through 1961 and 1962, civic leaders watched negative media coverage of the nearby Albany Movement as well as violence accompanying sit-ins and Freedom Rides in other cities and determined to avoid having such problems in Columbus. Members of the white business community may not have been interested primarily in social justice, but they were unquestionably committed to maintaining prosperity. In the mid-1950s, Kiralfy's had become one of the first stores to integrate its water fountains and restrooms, and by early 1962, WRBL reported that "white" and "colored" signs in other downtown stores had "quietly disappear[ed]" and that desegregation of water fountains and restrooms had happened "almost without notice."[20]

In mid-December 1961, after negotiations by "a group of responsible Columbus citizens, white and Negro," the chamber of commerce announced plans for lunch counter desegregation in early 1962. After careful planning, on January 24, 1962, five lunch counters downtown and two near Fort Benning served twenty-two Negro patrons "without incident." Plainclothes police at each location protected African Americans, a stark contrast to the police role in many other southern communities. Other downtown restaurants began serving African Americans over the next few months, although the iconic Kirven's department store and its tearoom remained a holdout. Allen and Robert Wright, a young black optometrist who was emerging as a political leader, met with Dupont Kirven Sr., who became so angry that Allen "thought he was going to have a heart attack." African Americans boycotted and picketed the store through the summer of 1962, but Kirven refused to serve black patrons. Ultimately, however, Kirven's capitulated, opening the tearoom in July 1964 on an integrated basis, and it and other stores soon hired African American sales clerks as well.[21]

In June 1963, a delegation including NAACP youth field secretary Bobby Hill, Ford, and five young African Americans unsuccessfully discussed integration with E. D. Martin, owner of four segregated Columbus theaters. The NAACP Youth Council pledged to "take to the streets, if necessary," and about 150 students rallied on behalf of desegregation. Older black leaders resisted open demonstrations, and once again, negotiations gained the objective. On September 4, 1963, the city commission appointed a committee of fifteen whites and ten African Americans to discuss racial issues and make recommendations. The committee moved too slowly for some people, and a black real estate agent resigned, noting, "All the Negroes seemed to have turned white." Still, on October 1, Columbus's theaters peacefully desegregated. A white pediatrician and his wife joined Rudy Allen and his wife at the Georgia Theatre, encountering no problems. The county also created a biracial advisory group after Wright petitioned for the integration of county parks, playgrounds, and swimming pools; the naming of Negroes to county boards; and the employment of African Americans in the county courthouse and as police officers. When one commissioner declared that he opposed the desegregation of parks because some African Americans were "radicals... and I don't think the county should furnish the battleground," Wright countered that blacks as well as whites paid taxes that provided for park maintenance and that "the wind of change is blowing over the country."[22]

Ford became the Columbus area's first black political candidate in almost a century when he ran for county commission in 1964. He lost but quickly became a Democratic establishment power broker. Reapportionment in 1960 had given Muscogee County an additional seat in the Georgia Legislature, and African American leaders convinced the Democratic Party to support a black candidate in 1966 even though the district was 70 percent white. Albert Thompson won, becoming the county's first black legislator since 1868. Although members of the white community may have found the pace of change dizzying, many African Americans were impatient. A 1963 editorial in the African American *Columbus News* decried the city's complacency: black citizens could ride buses, sit anywhere in bus and train stations, and eat in a few formerly all-white restaurants but remained barred from white parks, hotels, churches, and schools. At the same time, a young activist criticized black ministers who refused to allow their churches to be used for civil rights organization, charging that these men were too content with "their comfortable homes, their big cars, their big churches and fat salaries" to be concerned with "the welfare and freedom of their people." Perceived as tools of the white establishment, Thompson, Ford, and McClung faced similar criticisms from members of the African American community. After the YMCA's roof collapsed in a December 1963 snowstorm, some observers blamed McClung, the facility's director, for having neglected the black community's assets. In 1967, McClung was appointed as the first black member of the Public Safety Board, leading the *Columbus News* to accuse him of selling out the Negro community by engaging in "power seeking for an individual" rather than advancing the community as a whole. McClung's service on various boards added up "to nothing for the Negro community" still hampered by segregation, poverty, and a lack of job and recreational opportunities. The editorial condemned McClung as a yes-man who acquiesced to closing swimming pools rather than integrating them, to segregated parks, and a new segregated YMCA. Wright, a Republican, likened Ford to New York City's Tammany Hall political machine and claimed that "the black man is still on the auction block. He is being sold by his black brother in Columbus, Ga." White leaders, in contrast, perceived Thompson, McClung, and Ford as cooperative moderates. It is likely that both they and the younger activists who espoused direct action played important roles in achieving a relatively rapid and peaceful integration of Columbus's public facilities.[23]

George Ford (*left*), **Calvin Smyre** (*center*), and **A. J. McClung, ca. 1975.**
Columbus State University Archives, Columbus State University, Columbus, Georgia.

Albert Thompson, ca. 1980.
Columbus Ledger-Enquirer.

In October 1948, the Columbus Chamber of Commerce hired George J. Simons to create a comprehensive city plan, which called for consolidation of city and county schools as well as the construction of a new library and the establishment of a local museum and a community college. Appeals for school consolidation had first occurred four decades earlier, in 1909, and had recurred in 1920, but with Columbus's explosive postwar growth and the accompanying influx of children, city leaders warmed to the idea. In 1945, the board of education had hired a dynamic young superintendent, William Henry Shaw, who strongly advocated consolidation. In a May 1949 referendum that attracted very low turnout, voters approved the school merger, and consolidation occurred on January 1, 1950, with a fifteen-member school board appointed to oversee the new Muscogee County School District (MCSD). Though Shaw established a single salary schedule for black and white teachers, segregation continued and gaps persisted. The principal at African American Spencer High had a master's degree and an annual salary of $4,800, while the three white high school principals received $6,500 each. The board of education constructed new schools to accommodate enrollment growth as a consequence of the postwar influx of people and the baby boom, and the school board claimed early in 1951 that "no difference is recognized in the city and county schools or between colored and white schools." The black community disagreed. On February 12, 1951, Primus King and others from the Non-Partisan Voters League petitioned the board to end "gross discriminations" within the district on the grounds that they were "unfair, unjust, unchristian, unwholesome, and to a great extent illegal since they are based wholly on race." It asked for equalization of facilities, teaching materials, transportation, lunchrooms, gymnasiums, and teacher salaries. The editor of the *Columbus Enquirer* noted in response to the petition that multiple court decisions predicted "segregation's last defense is in the provision of 'separate, but equal' school facilities" and urged the board to use a recent $4.25 million school bond to equalize facilities. The board pumped in resources to accredit Spencer High School in 1951 and to build three Negro elementary schools in the early 1950s and Carver High School in 1954.[24]

The school board also put into effect Simons's recommendations regarding a library and a museum. With the Carnegie Library on Mott's Green having outgrown its space and in need of repairs, the city commission sold it to Muscogee Manufacturing in March 1947. A few months later, wealthy millowner W. C. Bradley died, and his daughter, Elizabeth Bradley Turner, and son-in-law, D. Abbott Turner, gave the city $125,000 to buy Bradley's Wynnton Road estate, stipulating that the property be used "for public, educational, library, recreational, or park purposes." The idea of building a library on the Bradley estate evoked public outcry from members of both the black and white communities. African Americans objected to upgrading the whites-only library when their community had no library at all, while whites, led by the League of Women Voters, argued that the location was too far from the city center. Various Bradley family interests—the Bradley Foundation, the Eagle & Phenix, Columbus Manufacturing, and Columbus Foundries—started a library fund, and Muscogee Mills donated $50,000. On December 9, 1947, the city commission unanimously approved the Bradley site, and the new library opened on October 31, 1950, at the foot of Wynn's Hill, on the Bradley property's western edge, with beautiful gardens and a humpbacked bridge over a pond.[25]

The end of World War II had caused Edward Shorter to revive his quest for the creation of a city museum, and the Turners proposed that it be housed in the Bradley mansion. It, too, would be open solely to whites. The city commission had no interest in a museum, but the board of education was enthusiastic, and the legislation that created the MCSD had authorized it to "construct, maintain, and operate public art galleries and art centers." A corporation, the Columbus Museum of Arts and Crafts, was created to oversee the new museum, and Shorter was named director. The agreement called for the board of education to pay the salaries of a curator, a secretary, and a janitor and to maintain the building and nine acres of gardens designed in the 1920s by the Frederick Law Olmsted landscape architecture firm, while the museum would be free to the public but would have to raise funds to acquire items for display. On March 29, 1953, the museum opened in the Bradley mansion, which had been remodeled to exhibit historical artifacts as well as fine art. The museum's board made cultural choices "on the basis of personal likes, dislikes, [and] gratifications," adding to the challenges of building a museum in what Shorter described as a small southern city "more or less confined in itself." Nevertheless, membership grew slowly but steadily, and in February 1963 a black-tie gala celebrated the opening of a new $200,000 wing funded entirely by donations. African Americans were admitted by 1964, although most visitors and benefactors remained middle- and upper-class whites. The museum added a children's science wing in 1967 and changed its name to the Columbus Museum of Arts and Sciences a decade later.[26]

The proposal to create a community college predated Simons's report by about half a decade. In 1943, Theo McGee, Walter Richards, and others had floated the idea as a way to develop middle-class skilled workers. By the end of the decade, business leaders had raised $92,000 and donated the money to the school board for the college. In January 1949, the board bought 115 acres on Warm Springs Road, and county commissioners added 38 adjacent acres. However, development stalled until February 1958, when Georgia's Junior College Act provided $300 per student if a college were operating by September. George C. Woodruff offered to allow the board to purchase the empty Shannon Hosiery Mill for $250,000 to use as a temporary site. The board accepted the offer and spent $100,000 to remodel the building into classrooms. On May 29, voters overwhelmingly approved a $6 million school bond, with $1 million earmarked for the new Columbus College. In July 1959, MCSD also funded two vocational junior colleges, and the General Assembly approved matching funds for technical schools the following year. The two junior colleges opened in 1961 as the Muscogee Area Vocational-Technical School and the Columbus Area Vocational-Technical College.[27]

In the summer of 1958, Dr. Thomas Y. Whitley became Columbus College's first president, retaining the post for more than two decades. He initially hired fourteen faculty and five administrators. Two hundred freshmen registered on September 22, with the first classes held in the renovated textile mill on September 29. The all-white student body chose the Rebel as the school's mascot, with Confederate "gold and grey" as the school colors. The masthead of the college newspaper, *The Saber*, featured Confederate battle flags. In January 1963, the permanent campus opened, with nearly eight hundred students in attendance. In April 1965, the Board of Regents approved Columbus College's transition to a four-year institution. In July 1966, the two technical schools merged to form the Columbus Area Vocational-Technical School (Columbus Tech). Undergirded by Whitley's philosophy that "the college and the community are one," Columbus College received strong local support and prospered. Businessman Simon Schwob, who died in 1954, and his widow, Ruth, were major benefactors, with Schwob's estate donating $100,000 to the college building program in 1962. The following year, the school named its library after Simon Schwob. Ruth Schwob also led a 1965–1966 fund-raising campaign that brought in $500,000 for a Fine Arts Hall, which was completed in 1969. D. Abbott Turner funded construction of the million-dollar Continuing Education building, which bore the name of his late wife, Elizabeth Bradley Turner. By 1967, enrollment had reached fifteen hundred, and the chamber of commerce enthusiastically predicted that it would triple over the next five to seven years.²⁸

Many of the South's flagship white universities, including those in Mississippi, Alabama, and Georgia, fought the idea of admitting African American students, refusing to do so until faced with court orders and in some cases the presence of federal troops. The January 1961 enrollment of Charlayne Hunter and Hamilton Holmes as the first African Americans at the University of Georgia provoked campus rioting. In contrast, and in keeping with the general approach to desegregation pursued by local leaders, Columbus College voluntarily admitted its first black student, bowing to the inevitable and seeking to avoid conflict. After hearing rumors in the summer of 1963 that black activists were planning a mass "protest registration" for the fall semester, Whitley accepted a highly qualified graduate of Spencer High School, John Townsend, whom Whitley later paternalistically characterized as a "very likeable low-key desirable type of black." Taking personal responsibility for making Townsend's matriculation "pleasurable," Whitley assured the young man "if you can let the little things bounce off, we'll handle the big things." Despite Whitley's vow, Townsend's reception on campus could hardly be described as "pleasurable," as white students greeted him with, "We're being integrated! Here comes a nigger!" and twice burned his locker during his first year at the school. In addition, classmates subjected Townsend to demeaning racial dialect, and he sat at the front of his classes so that he could not be accused of cheating. He also feared physical harm. The situation settled down in his sophomore year, when Townsend participated in student government and served as business manager for the literary magazine, and Townsend hoped that his presence had helped white students "think differently about my race." After receiving his associate's degree from the college, Townsend moved on to the University of Georgia, where he earned bachelor's and master's degrees and eventually a doctorate in educational administration. Columbus State University now recognizes Townsend with an annual award for community service that bears his name.²⁹

As the 1960s progressed and more African Americans enrolled, institutional racism became an issue at Columbus College. Black students objected to the band's practice of playing "Dixie" at basketball games, unsuccessfully requesting that the band director remove the song from the musicians' repertoire. At a basketball game in the fall of 1969, with racial tensions high, the pep band refused to play "Dixie." White students responded by unleashing a hail of coins, peanuts, and other debris, and the following January, the Student Government Association banned the song. Also in 1969, black students targeted the Rebel mascot for elimination. When the administration refused, the students appealed to the U.S. Civil Rights Commission, which sent an investigative team. Whitley recognized that the school stood to lose federal funds if the commission found a hostile racial atmosphere. After two student referendums overwhelmingly favored retaining the Rebel, Whitley, with the support of the Student Government Association, announced on February 27, 1970, that he was eliminating the mascot. Two months later, when the "bitterness and meetings and shouting" engendered by Whitley's decision had died down, students chose the Cougar as the school's new mascot.[30]

Despite these changes and the efforts of biracial organizations such as the Cosmopolitan Club, which formed in 1968 and sought to create an inclusive campus culture, racial problems continued to plague Columbus College. In 1970, Whitley fired three nontenured white faculty who were sympathetic to African American students and who opposed the war in Vietnam, later describing the faculty members as rabble-rousers from "liberal institutions of the North" who were passing black students even when their academic effort and ability did not warrant such grades. One of the professors, Howard Beeth, was the Cosmopolitan Club's sponsor and had encouraged members to engage in direct-action protests against discrimination in the Columbus community. After students picketed the local J. C. Penney for refusing to hire black sales clerks or managers, the retailer's national office instructed the local manager to meet student demands. The Cosmopolitan Club also took on the local United Way, which funded a variety of groups that included four segregated institutions. Club members picketed the United Way headquarters at Twelfth Street and Broadway, attracting the attention of the commanding general at Fort Benning, who threatened to halt the charity's campaign on the base. In response, three of the institutions began accepting black members, and the United Way stopped funding the one refusing change. But the United Way was dear to the hearts of many powerful local decision makers, and Whitley declared that because Beeth had "counseled deliberate disobedience," he had to go. The president's actions had a chilling effect on faculty speech and academic freedom, but it did not put an end to black students' activism. In *The Saber* in 1970 and again in 1974, African Americans demanded that the school add black administrators, increase the number of black faculty members and black student scholarships, and institute athletic competition with historically black colleges. Such calls went unheeded, though the administration did approve courses in African American history and literature. As of the mid-1970s, African Americans accounted for 30 percent of Columbus's population but only 14 percent of Columbus College students and just 2 of the school's 175 faculty members. Many black students described a campus culture where they felt either invisible or demeaned. At the time of Whitley's 1979 retirement, the school had never had a black administrator.[31]

A commuter school in a conservative community with close ties to the military, Columbus College largely escaped the Vietnam War–related turmoil so prevalent on other campuses during the late 1960s. *The Saber* acknowledged the antiwar movement in only two articles that appeared between 1966 and 1970. In 1966, the Student Government Association supported the statewide Affirmation: Vietnam movement, which proclaimed that "the majority of Georgia's youth ... endorse the U.S. commitment in Viet Nam." By the fall of 1969, however, opposition to the war had reached even Columbus, and a handful of students, faculty, and townsfolk created an off-campus group, Patriots for Peace, that participated in the national Moratorium to End the War in Vietnam. A communications professor arranged a formal debate between a student veteran who supported the war and one who opposed it. The debate was civil and well-reasoned, but the discussion period degenerated into a shouting match between pro-war students wearing red, white, and blue armbands and the vastly outnumbered moratorium supporters, who were decked out in black. A poll conducted the same year confirmed that a majority of students still supported the war.[32]

Like the antiwar movement, the nascent feminist movement attracted little attention at Columbus College. When the school opened in 1958, female students made up 39 percent of the student body, but only three faculty were women. In 1969, student Mary Jane Wadkins helped break an informal dress code by arranging with other female students to wear pants rather than skirts or dresses to class one day. Though Wadkins "was afraid the others would back out" and consequently "had a skirt and pantyhose rolled up in my purse," she was not alone, and despite some disapproving looks, the students were delighted that "we had won." Two years later, Wadkins became the school's first female history faculty member but found herself assigned to make coffee along with the secretaries. She informed the department head that she would make coffee only when other professors did. By her second year of teaching, Watkins had added a Women in American History course, and she started a child care center for faculty and students. Also in 1972, Whit-

Streakers running across the Columbus College campus, March 1974. Columbus State University Archives, Columbus State University, Columbus, Georgia.

ley appointed the Committee on the Status of Women, which found that women faculty with equal qualifications to men held lower academic ranks and were paid significantly less. The Miss Georgia Pageant had begun in Columbus in 1944, with the selection of Miss Columbus College a long-standing campus tradition by the 1970s. The first African American woman did not enter the contest until 1974, and she lost, prompting a black activist to allege that "racist contributors" prevented "black women from becoming campus queen" and to call for a boycott of all extracurricular activities. Fearing the eruption of a "racial volcano," Whitley "finagled a way" to end the campus pageant. [33]

The college was not immune to what some saw as a less weighty societal trend: streaking. In early March 1974, the streaking fad that had begun on college campuses the preceding January reached Columbus. Naked except for masks, streakers raced past the administration building in broad daylight as hundreds of spectators watched. As was true nationally, all of Columbus's streakers were white males (except for one Lady Godiva on a horse), perhaps as one contemporary analyst concluded, their public demonstrations attempting "re-territorialization" of the campus by white men under threat from African Americans and feminists. The public nakedness evoked a range of reactions. One student huffed, "Streaking... affects the faith of some, imposes on students, and disrupts classes." Others retained a sense of humor: when someone asked a genteel older librarian whether the streakers had been male or female, she replied, "I couldn't tell. They were wearing masks." Whitley took the fad in stride, commenting, "The sap rises in the spring and so do the saps."[34]

The desegregation of Columbus's public schools proved far more difficult than integrating Columbus College. On the day of the 1954 *Brown* ruling, the *Enquirer* reported, "Educational leaders in the Chattahoochee Valley [anticipated] no changes" in the school system. Six months later 54 percent of Georgia voters—and 57 percent of those in Muscogee County—approved an amendment to the state constitution to close public schools rather than integrate. The General Assembly quickly enacted legislation to put the amendment into effect. However, most local middle- and upper-class whites and nearly all African Americans wanted to keep the public schools open. In 1958, as education officials across the South dragged their heels on integration and the NAACP continued its legal push to force compliance, Atlantans formed Help Our Public Education (HOPE), an apolitical organization that sought to preserve public education, even if doing so required the elimination of separate school systems for whites and blacks. On July 21, 1960, white Columbus-area homemakers—the wives of lawyers, doctors, and chamber of commerce members—formed a chapter of the group, enlisting parental, newspaper, business, and legislative support for the idea that schools should remain open. Parson Jack Johnston and others who sought to maintain white supremacy shouted their defiance and redoubled their efforts to recruit members for the White Citizens' Council, predicting that integration would lead to "atheism, communism, and mongrelization."[35]

In 1960, Governor Ernest Vandiver faced a dilemma. He had won election in 1958 in part by promising that "no, not one" Negro child would attend a white school, but in 1959, a U.S. district court had ordered Atlanta to admit black students. Rather than shut down the city's public schools, as state law required if integration were mandated, Vandiver appointed Atlanta banker John Sibley, a segregationist who nonetheless took a pragmatic view, to head a commission to study the problem. Sibley saw two choices: change state law to preserve public schools and work to keep them as segregated as possible, or reject all integration and follow the "private school plan." The Sibley Commission held hearings across the state, including one in Columbus on March 31, 1960. Local newspapers urged residents to back keeping the public schools open, while WRBL's Big Johnnie Reb editorials rejected HOPE and school integration, encouraging white parents to send their children to private schools rather than integrated public schools.[36]

Three hundred people attended the hearing, with most of the African Americans, middle- and upper-class whites, and members of the chamber of commerce who testified expressing support for continuing public education, and labor organizations, working-class whites, and members of the White Citizens' Council lining up in opposition. More African Americans appeared before the commission in Columbus than at any other hearing. Speakers included school supporters Primus King, A. J. McClung, and Albert Thompson, who declared, "I believe in integration; I think that we are all citizens; I think that the future of this country lies only in utilizing the full resources and materials of this country. It cannot be done in a segregated society." George Ford took a different tack, however, praising Spencer as one of the best high schools in the district and expressing confidence that Superintendent Shaw would hire teachers able to instruct both black and white students. When asked directly whether segregation or integration were best, Ford answered, "I think freedom of the people is best." Though 60 percent of those who testified before the commission across the state favored closing the schools, Sibley ignored the hard-line segregationists and advocated maintaining public schools, though school districts should allow students freedom of choice to preserve "the maximum segregation possible within the law." In January 1961, Vandiver pushed through a bill repealing the "private school" law. In September, nine African Americans enrolled in previously white Atlanta schools.[37]

In mid-July 1963, several dozen black Columbus teenagers staged read-ins to desegregate the Bradley Library. On the third day, police arrested a protester and a white youth who got into a scuffle. The Recorder's Court fined the African American $37.50 but acquitted the white man. The library closed a day later. On July 17, African American young people began playing baseball and football and using the playground equipment at previously all-white Weracoba/Wildwood Park, attracting a crowd of several hundred whites. After fights broke out between white and black boys the next day, police restored calm and then temporarily closed the park on July 19. Black youths also tried to enter city swimming pools; they, too, shut down, remaining closed for years. The all-white board of education formed the Special Committee on Desegregation and voted to integrate public libraries on September 1. On September 16, the day after white terrorists bombed Birmingham's Sixteenth Avenue Baptist Church, killing four young girls, the board unanimously approved a freedom-of-choice plan to desegregate the city's public schools one grade per year, starting with the twelfth grade in September 1964. Under freedom of choice, a student could choose to go to any school. When all-white school boards across the South enacted these plans, a few black students chose to go to formerly all-white schools, but virtually no white children chose to attend all-black schools.[38]

The proposed plan was too slow for the NAACP, and it filed suit in January 1964 on behalf of Jerry, Gwendolyn, and Jim Lockett, children of a Columbus woman married to a Fort Benning soldier. *Lockett v. the Board of Education of the Muscogee County School District* charged that the MCSD operated "a superior public school system for whites" and an inferior one for Negroes. The case wound its way through the courts for more than three decades, in part because of the role of district judge J. Robert Elliott, a staunch segregationist appointed to the federal bench in 1962. In 1963, Elliott declared, "The chief function and primary concern of the Board of Education is not ... social revolution," and he spent decades obstructing the NAACP's efforts to achieve meaningful desegregation. In *Lockett*, Shaw argued that the gradual approach would prevent "chaos" from erupting as schools abandoned the "long and universal custom" of segregation; in actuality, however, Shaw and the board of education were working to maintain racial and class privilege and societal control as well as to avoid legal coercion. Elliott approved the MCSD plan, the NAACP appealed, and Shaw and the board continued to negotiate with black leaders, following the same strategy that had desegregated public facilities. In September 1964, African American twelfth-grader Robert Leonard began attending Baker High School without incident. Shaw portrayed himself as "marching in the front lines of public education today," and he and the board enjoyed strong white community support during the freedom-of-choice period, with local newspapers urging citizens to obey the courts. Die-hard segregationists, however, perceived Shaw and the board as too willing to desegregate, and resentment began to grow.[39]

In 1967, a U.S. Supreme Court decision required school districts to create unitary systems that eliminated all vestiges of segregation. In response, the board desegregated all grades through freedom of choice and placed at least two minority-race teachers at each school. But freedom of choice produced little significant integration: though forty of Columbus's sixty-seven schools had both black and white students, only 12.5 percent of the district's black students attended formerly white schools and less than 1 percent of white children were enrolled in black schools. Federal court decisions in 1968 and 1969 ordered desegregation using student racial ratios and crosstown busing. To "forestall the possibility of having the federal courts take over the operation of the schools," the board announced on January 5, 1970, that effective February 1, 110 white teachers and 120 black teachers—about 17 percent of the district's total—would be transferred to create a balanced ratio of 75 percent white teachers and 25 percent African American teachers at each school.[40]

The community erupted. Opponents of the plan jammed the January board meeting, 250 white students walked out at Jordan High School, and two white parents petitioned to stop the transfers, winning a legal victory. On May 29, 1971, however, the U.S. Fifth Circuit Court ordered Muscogee County to dismantle its dual system, and the board quickly approved a pupil assignment plan that used busing to redistribute students so that each school's student body was 70 percent white and 30 percent black. The 75/25 ratio for faculty remained in place, with a directive that "the oldest teachers in point of service in each school shall be given their choice of remaining in such school or being assigned to a different school." But whites continued to take precedence: though nearly all white teachers transferred to black schools were novices, black teachers sent to white schools tended to be veterans with advanced degrees.[41]

Over Labor Day weekend, before schools opened, 350 white parents formed Citizens against Forced Busing, whose members voted to boycott the schools and burned an effigy of Shaw. Despite the opposition, 37,000 of the roughly 40,000 students expected attended on opening day, and by September 16, enrollment reached 40,471. Business and civic leaders' support prevented Columbus from suffering much of the disorder and strife that accompanied desegregation in other southern cities, although three elementary buildings were firebombed that fall. Students from two prestigious white neighborhoods were assigned to former black junior high and high schools, and the mayor, the area's congressional representative, and other white leaders sent their children to those schools rather than enrolling them in private academies. Citizens against Forced Busing remained active for the rest of the academic year, most notably with its participation in a February 28, 1972, statewide boycott to protest forced busing. In the absence of support from the leaders of Columbus's white community, the boycott produced absentee rates between 10

Dr. William H. Shaw, 1973.
Columbus Ledger-Enquirer.

and 20 percent above normal, far below the group's 60 percent goal, and it faded away.[42]

Muscogee County experienced much less white flight between 1970 and 1980 than did other Georgia districts. Enrollment boomed in the exclusive all-white Brookstone private school and in St. Anne and Pacelli, the Catholic K–12 schools, but MCSD's white enrollment declined only 4.6 percent more than the overall population decline for white school-age children. White parents kept their children in the public schools for several reasons. Whites tended to flee when African Americans constituted more than 30 percent of the population, but Columbus was only 26 percent black in 1970. In addition, MCSD was a consolidated district, meaning that no whiter suburban schools existed within the county. Further, district leaders maintained majority-white schools, especially in prestigious North Columbus. In 1972–1973, the school board allowed students in kindergarten through second grade to remain at their neighborhood schools. Twelve of the fifty elementary schools returned to black majorities, but by 1975, every Columbus high school maintained a white majority of at least 57 percent. Columbus High and Hardaway, the two north-side high schools attended by affluent whites, had white majorities of 70 percent. Many north-side elementary and junior high schools had even larger white majorities. Wealthy white parents perceived "their" schools as "protected."[43]

This "protection" came at a cost to the black community. The middle-class children whose families formed the bedrock of support for black schools were targeted for transfer to white schools, and in the words of one African American teacher, "We had a certain racial pride for excelling that we lost in integration.... The black students felt that the whites were coming and taking over their school." Perhaps most damaging to black students was the dispersal of veteran African American teachers and the consequent loss of what one educator termed their "loving, nurturing touch." White teachers lacked the experience, the training, and perhaps the desire to relate effectively to black students. One white teacher described feeling almost as if she had joined the Peace Corps, "going to a place you've never been, living with people you've never dealt with, not understanding their culture, where they were coming from." Columbus's black principals and teachers did not experience the large-scale demotions and firings that occurred elsewhere in the South, constituting about a quarter of the workforce from 1970 to 1990 and growing to a third by 1997. But regardless of how much experience they had, African American teachers in white schools were treated as if they were novices. They taught in white teachers' classrooms, had to develop new courses, were assigned to teach low-level classes, and received students known to have behavior problems. Seating in teachers' lounges and lunchrooms generally remained segregated.[44]

But integration also meant that for the first time, African American students had access to the same resources as their white counterparts. One student at Spencer High remembered a "remarkable improvement" in textbooks, supplies, lockers, and facilities. In 1973, the board proposed converting Spencer to a junior high and special education center and changing its name to Southside School, leading to protests as the black community "refused to allow them to put Spencer High School on the blacklist," as one alumnus declared. A black teacher remembered, "Everybody got up in arms. They were about to have the whole town burned down." After the two black members of the school board negotiated behind the scenes, and Thompson and other leaders made Spencer's case before the board, it voted unanimously against the change.[45]

Principals, teachers, and students, black and white, viewed the period during and after desegregation as "a lost educational time." Teachers felt that standards were lowered as "we were so intent on everybody passing so that you would not be perceived as prejudiced or discriminatory in any way." Students of both races described negative educational outcomes. Buddy Nelms, a white student at Baker High, believed that academics "suffered extremely." An African American woman who attended a predominantly white high school thought that teachers and administrators "just got us in and got us out like cattle." All schools offered exactly the same curriculum during this period as a way to prevent parents from complaining about the relative merits of different schools. But as one teacher pointed out, "If we make all the schools the same, we would tend to make all the schools move toward mediocrity."[46]

Every high school experienced significant racial conflict, most seriously at Baker, whose white students came primarily from surrounding blue-collar neighborhoods or families of enlisted personnel stationed at Fort Benning and whose black students came from nearby housing projects and working-class enclaves. Fights between individuals escalated into riots, with students wielding chains, belt buckles, combs, sticks, stones, and even trophies displayed in the entrance hall. Watching black students enter the courtyard from one direction and whites from the other reminded one white teacher of "a military maneuver": when the students met in the middle, "they'd fight, fight, fight." Hiding on the second floor, Nelms was reminded of "watching gladiators." Rioters threw large garbage cans into the crowd, injuring many students, and when an ambulance arrived to help the injured, someone cut the hoses under the hood. "The students owned the school," creating a state of near anarchy.[47]

In an attempt to counter the violence, undercover police infiltrated the high schools. By late December 1971, burly off-duty firefighters patrolled the corridors. Principals cracked down, usually by forcing African American children to adapt to the way education had "always" taken place. As a result, disproportionate numbers of black students were suspended and expelled. Such punishments had been virtually nonexistent prior to 1972 but subsequently became increasingly common, mainly among students from Carver and Spencer and often for offenses such as using profanity, possessing weapons, and engaging in violence. Though black students made up less than half the MCSD population, they received two-thirds of suspensions. African American teachers and students believed discipline was harsher for black students: "A lot of black students [were] paddled and a lot of white parents called on the telephone." According to an African American coach, many black boys who "perhaps were just being themselves in terms of their culture" found themselves "penalized because some of the white teachers felt a little threatened."[48]

Shaw retired as superintendent in 1973. His successor, Braxton Nail, relaxed the transfer criteria, and in 1975–1976, the board allowed students to remain at the schools they had attended the previous year. In addition, Columbus's African American population rose from 34 percent in 1980 to nearly 40 percent in 1990. By 1985, whites accounted for less than 50 percent of MCSD's enrollment, and that number hovered around 45 percent five years later. In the face of these leadership and demographic changes, Columbus schools quickly resegregated. By 1982, all four south-side high schools and fifteen of the nineteen south-side elementary schools had black majorities. Carver High School and eleven south-side elementary and middle schools had student bodies that were at least 80 percent black. Yet in 1990, the four north-side high schools retained white majorities, and eleven north-side elementary and middle schools had white majorities exceeding 70 percent. Many in the African American community believed that the majority-white school board had intentionally preserved white schools and allowed academic standards and financial support for black schools to decline. As of 1990, Carver's building was in disrepair, and its tenth-graders' reading and math test scores were ten points lower than the next high schools' scores and more than twenty points below the district average.[49] Dysfunctional schools, especially for poor and black students, continued to plague the city into the twenty-first century.

Columbus's African Americans recorded many civil rights gains in the quarter century after World War II. Many of these accomplishments were achieved via negotiations with the white power structure, with occasional assistance from the federal government. But the community suffered some losses as well, and the school system's descent into mediocrity foreshadowed decades of difficult times that included violent racial conflict, economic stagnation, rising crime rates, and the near death of downtown.

CHAPTER 8

From Optimism to Malaise

Economics, Politics, and Culture, 1950s–1980s

In the flush postwar years, Columbus experienced economic growth and implemented successful urban planning, using annexation and consolidation to position for the modern era. But by the 1970s, Columbus was beset by malaise. The upscale businesses that had once helped downtown thrive had relocated to suburban shopping centers, and the city's industrial economy stagnated as the country endured recession and high inflation. Racial conflict spiked, with firebombings and rioting. Crime was on the rise, including multiple horrific serial murders.

A diversion from the malaise arrived on a Friday in February 1973, when a surprise storm dumped a record fourteen inches of snow on the city, causing schools to scramble to get children home safely and leading to eighty car crashes as inexperienced drivers navigated icy roads. With police cars not equipped for snow, officers rode in heavy garbage trucks. Many children had never before seen snow, and they delighted in throwing snowballs, making snow cream, and building snowmen—and in one case, a thirteen-foot Buddha. But by Monday, the snow had turned to dirty slush, and the city was once again mired in the bleak 1970s.[1]

The joy occasioned by the end of World War II was accompanied by concerns about Columbus's economic fortunes as Benning downsized and war industries converted to domestic products. Formed in 1944, the Columbus Planning Association declared that its goal was to "enable Columbus to meet its post-war destiny." It joined with the chamber of commerce in commissioning George J. Simons's 1948 comprehensive city plan, which recommended street improvements, increased downtown parking, and slum clearance in the Bottoms and North Highlands. Annexations of county land in 1945 and 1949 made Columbus's metropolitan area the second-largest in Georgia by 1950, and more land was annexed nine years later. Electors approved bonds for construction of a city auditorium, renovation of Golden Park, enlargement of Memorial Stadium, additions to City Hospital and the jail, and other improvements to streets and lighting, sidewalks and sewers, parks and recreation. The airport became a modern facility served by Delta, Eastern, and Southern airlines. In March 1950, the Catholic Sisters of the Third Order opened Columbus's second medical center, St. Francis Hospital, which the *Columbus Ledger* praised as "the first private hospital in the state to treat men of all races and faiths." St. Francis doubled in size over the next four decades. The City Hospital underwent a major expansion in 1955–1956, changing its name to the Medical Center on January 1, 1957. Another expansion in 1965 doubled its capacity again, with further additions including a coronary care unit in 1968 and an emergency wing three years later. In 1986, after still more growth, the Medical Center became the core of the Columbus Regional Healthcare System.[2]

The Columbus Housing Authority carried out slum clearance. Dreaming "of a city that will be free of these miserable little shacks," chair Theo McGee and executive director Brown Nicholson Sr. identified seventy blocks of substandard houses and eighty blighted blocks, and E. E. Farley declared that the city's African Americans were "yearning for better living conditions." Many white citizens, however, criticized the authority as socialistic, with the Real Estate Board in particular advocating that "free enterprise" rather than government should take the lead. Undeterred, McGee countered, "I suppose if these public housing projects are called 'social housing,' we could with equal propriety describe the eliminated shacks as 'capitalistic housing.'" He observed that the Bottoms and other run-down African American areas were "as much a part of the city" as wealthier white neighborhoods. The *Ledger* backed McGee, publishing a 1953 series, "The Shame of Columbus," that stung the public conscience with descriptions of terrible living conditions. McGee also badgered the city commission to toughen building codes, an effort that bore fruit in 1955 with minimum requirements for structural soundness, lighting, heating, ventilation, and sanitation and with Columbus's first zoning ordinance the following year. The Housing Authority redeveloped the Bottoms, clearing and subdividing the land and selling it to private developers. Displaced residents were relocated to the newly constructed E. E. Farley Homes and Elizabeth F. Canty Homes. By the time McGee left the Housing Authority in 1973, it had built eleven projects. Starting in 1965, it concentrated on the needs of the elderly poor, creating "retirement villages" in South Columbus and in the old Ralston Hotel. Nevertheless, by 1980, 20 percent of Columbus residents were living below the poverty level, and the demand for low-cost housing remained unfilled, with 15 percent of city residences failing to meet the minimum standards.[3]

Postwar population growth meant that private housing remained in high demand. Developers built large apartment complexes, including the four-hundred-unit Camellia Apartments, which opened in 1949 near Fort Benning. From 1946 to 1949, the Jordan Company built not only apartments but also between five hundred and six hundred houses. At the same time, increased automobile ownership allowed Columbus residents, like people across the country, to flee congested urban areas for the suburbs. In 1954–1955, Columbus developers built thirty-one subdivisions, and by 1956, more than 90 percent of new single-family residences were located in subdivisions outside the city. Developed by Farley, Carver Heights (1950) and Willis Plaza (1954) became the first suburbs targeted at African Americans. With the 1959 completion of Oliver Dam at the old Clapp's Factory site, the Jordan Company realized a bonanza from its Green Island lakeshore property. Within two years, the company had developed the Green Island Golf Club and renovated the Big Eddy Club into an exclusive private dining facility. Columbus's first true shopping center, St. Elmo, near Wildwood Park, had opened in 1939, and the next two decades saw a proliferation of suburban shopping centers and fast-food restaurants. Cross-Country Plaza, the city's largest shopping center, opened on Macon Road in May 1956. The city's first McDonald's drive-in, which had no indoor seating, opened there in 1962 and featured plate-glass walls that allowed customers to admire the gleaming stainless steel efficiency within as the restaurant turned out hamburgers at assembly-line speed. Columbus Square, the region's first air-conditioned covered mall, opened across Macon Road in 1965, while Peachtree Mall, farther north on the four-lane Manchester Expressway, welcomed its first customers ten years later.[4]

As local wages and purchasing power increased, retail sales grew almost 300 percent between 1942 and 1948. By 1950, Columbus's retail sales made up nearly 5 percent of Georgia's total. But as was the case across the country, the growth of suburban shopping centers began to kill downtown businesses. In 1957, the commission and chamber again hired Simons, this time asking him to solve the commercial business district's

Arthur Cotton Moore's 1975 redevelopment plan for Broadway included routing the Chattahoochee into a canal with glass-topped excursion boats. Columbus State University Archives, Columbus State University, Columbus, Georgia.

problems. His report became the first in a series of proposals aimed at modernizing downtown Columbus, launching a twenty-year war on cars that included a proposal for a perimeter loop highway around downtown that would be lined with parking garages as well as a grassy pedestrian mall on Broadway that was described as "a veritable paradise where the eternal battle between man and motors would be eliminated." Studies in the 1960s and 1970s also proposed downtown open-air malls. Depending on perspective, Arthur Cotton Moore's 1975 plan was either the most visionary or the most bizarre: believing that the "the City now turns its back on" the Chattahoochee River, its greatest asset, he argued for construction not only of a pedestrian mall but also of a canal connected to the river flowing down Broadway that would enable glass-topped touring boats to shuttle shoppers to stores. The city commission's refusal to go along with any of these plans left the downtown Columbus landscape so bleak that in 1975, a city council member suggested flattening the entire city center and starting over. That idea, too, was a nonstarter.[5]

Among the businesses that left downtown during these years were Sears, Penney's, Metcalf's, Davison's, Kiralfy's, and Schwobilt, all of which moved to Columbus Square. Kirven's opened a location at the mall in 1985 but kept the downtown store for another year. When the mall store closed in 1993, the company's 117 years in business came to an end. The last large urban retail establishment to go was H. L. Green in 1994. Most notable among the few downtown construction projects during the 1960s and 1970s was a six-story tower added to the *Ledger-Enquirer* building in 1970. Many residents viewed the old business district as ugly, inconvenient, even dangerous. A similar fate befell the African American commercial center, known since the 1990s as the Liberty District, though the city hired no consultants to revive it. By 1980, crime, drugs, and prostitution dominated the area, and in the early 1990s, the Housing Authority's urban renewal project cleared houses and shops, sparing only the Liberty Theatre and a few historic churches and active businesses. In 1996, the Public Safety Building was completed at the district's northern end. The derelict theater received a $1 million federal grant in 1993 and in 1996 opened as an African American cultural arts center. In 2015, the Housing Authority began clearing Booker T. Washington Apartments to make way for a mixed-use development, Columbus Commons, but the Liberty District's heart remained a virtual moonscape, with few residents and businesses.[6]

Columbus's economy had remained fairly prosperous through the 1960s, thanks to activity at Fort Benning during the Vietnam War. By decade's end, however, in line with national trends, its industrial economy stagnated. By 1976, the unemployment rate topped 15 percent, median income was just three-quarters of the national average, and 16.4 percent of citizens lived in poverty. Textiles remained dominant, employing 45 percent of manufacturing workers. Among the lowest-paid industrial workers, millhands earned an average of just $6,500 annually. The biggest economic change had begun with W. C. Bradley's 1947 death: the family sold the Eagle & Phenix and Columbus Manufacturing to outside corporations, making them the first mills to pass from local control. Muscogee Manufacturing expanded to surround the Mott House and Carnegie Library, and George Parker Swift IV opened a carpet mill on River Road in 1950. But the Swifts followed the Bradley family's lead, selling Swift Spinning to a New York firm in 1961 and Muscogee Manufacturing to Fieldcrest in 1963. By 1974, Fieldcrest, one of the world's largest towel producers, had become the only local mill that still started with raw cotton and turned it into finished products. Fieldcrest also purchased the Eagle & Phenix in 1978. Swift focused on denim for the booming jeans market, opening a large plant and distribution center on Flat Rock Road in 1981. In just over a decade, the facility had mostly become automated, and the fifteen hundred operatives who worked there produced one hundred miles of denim each day. The Swift family gradually sold off its textile interests, ending the dynasty with the carpet mill's sale in 1998.[7]

Bibb Mill resisted the trend, expanding under existing ownership. During World War II, white employees left for better-paying jobs, creating openings for black laborers, seven hundred of whom were hired for the formerly all-white carding room. The wide looms it used during World War II produced sixty thousand sets of king and queen sheets a day, giving the mill a local monopoly on those products for several years. In the 1960s, "Rovmatic" machines in the carding room halved the workforce. At the same time, desegregation ended Bibb City's corporate welfare: after passage of the 1964 Civil Rights Act, owners filled in the swimming pool, gave Comer Auditorium to Columbus, and discontinued club activities. The next year, the Bibb sold its houses to operatives to avoid integrating the village. Bibb City continued to operate as an entity within Muscogee County, though the superintendent was no longer automatically also mayor, who was instead popularly elected.[8]

All Columbus textile mills began hiring African American operatives, but they continued to experience discriminatory treatment. A black sweeper at the Eagle & Phenix recalled that in the early 1950s, he was to be "invisible" and was not allowed in the walkway between looms if whites were standing there. According to a male Fieldcrest worker, "If you were black you had to work twice as hard as the white worker." Black women faced additional challenges. Although their wages were higher than those for domestic labor, African American females received more work than white women and were fired for "slow" work, even when they matched the pace of their white counterparts. When Fieldcrest's towel mill did away with separate water fountains and bathrooms, whites refused to use the same facilities as blacks, and even in the absence of "white" and "colored" signs, the Eagle & Phenix's bathrooms remained segregated until 1972, when two black workers began using the customarily white restroom. Fieldcrest's loom fixers intimidated African Americans who signed up for training for higher-paying jobs. Friction arose when black operatives became supervisors, with many whites quitting their jobs rather than working under African Americans. Though conditions were difficult, textile labor improved African Americans' standard of living, providing them with money to purchase homes and automobiles. Nevertheless, black millhands felt that they had to be careful about showing prosperity: a black Eagle & Phenix worker who bought a Cadillac, for example, feared that if he drove it to work, his boss would be harder on him and would look for any excuse to fire him.[9]

Conditions in the mills improved by the 1950s, but the work remained difficult and dangerous. Two sisters working at Swift got their hair caught in machinery and barely escaped injury. One woman had her shirt torn off when her sleeve caught as she reached to free tangled yarn. In the weave room, sharp-ended shuttles flew out of looms, threatening the eyes of those in the vicinity. The deafening noise damaged hearing. Brown lung remained a long-term health hazard. Under federal guidelines instituted in the late 1970s, millowners provided workers with respirators, though millhands often refused the masks. As late as 1988, some workers believed brown lung to be an allergy and themselves not susceptible to it. The Textile Workers Union of America launched another southern organizing drive, finally achieving some success in Columbus in the early 1970s. Fieldcrest employees approved unionization in June 1971, and the Eagle & Phenix organized in 1979, after its acquisition by Fieldcrest. However, union efforts at Swift Spinning failed after a bitter fight in which management played the race card: a Swift supervisor told an employee that if the union won, "the niggers will run it." In addition, the owners threatened that Swift might have to close if the company were forced to pay the union scale—$3.75 per hour. A female worker was fired after ignoring her boss's order to stop taking notes on antiunion intimidation. After the unionization vote failed, the National Labor Relations Board rejected workers' claims of unfair labor practices, finding that the woman taking notes had been insubordinate and that the "nigger" comment was protected free speech. In 1988, a vote at Swift's carpet mill failed after another divisive campaign. This time charges that the company had engaged in unfair practices resulted only in a slap on the wrist from the board, which merely required Swift to post a notice promising fair treatment. After an acrimonious 1991 Fieldcrest dispute, however, the board declared that management's unfair practices had been "numerous, pervasive and outrageous" and required the company to pay $2 million to union workers who had been denied a raise given to nonunion workers and to reinstate workers fired for union activities.[10]

Union membership improved working conditions for African Americans at Fieldcrest. For example, seniority rules meant that they could not be laid off while recently hired whites were retained. But the union was no panacea. A 1978 lawsuit charged that areas of the Fieldcrest mill remained segregated, with African American workers required to perform "menial and servile jobs" that required strenuous physical exertion or that were unpleasant. Only a small percentage had moved into higher-paying jobs. By 1990, however, unionization issues became almost moot, as global trends foreshadowed the demise of Columbus's textile mills. The number of operatives had declined by nearly 40 percent over the preceding two decades, as international competition and technology and labor costs drove mills overseas, and that trend continued into the twenty-first century.[11]

Industrial growth remained moribund through the 1970s. The only factories that moved to Columbus between 1945 and 1975 were Sunshine Biscuits in 1952 and Dolly Madison, a subsidiary of Interstate Bakeries, in 1971. Some observers blamed textile owners, who allegedly "tied up the Chamber of Commerce" to block industrial competition. A 1978 report advised that Columbus needed to abandon its "protectionist stance toward existing industries" to achieve economic growth. The city developed a significant junk food industry, with food manufacturers employing nearly 20 percent of industrial workers by 1975. The venerable Tom Huston Peanut Company employed a thousand nonunionized workers to process twenty-seven million pounds of peanuts annually by 1956. A decade later, General Mills bought the company and changed its name to Tom's Foods. Although sales grew at an average of 10 percent each year, Tom's changed hands three times over the next two decades, and by 1990 the company was in trouble. Heico Acquisitions bought Tom's in 1993 but failed to turn a profit, and in April 2005 it defaulted on Tom's $60 million debt, declaring bankruptcy. Lance bought Tom's in October 2005 for $37.9 million and merged with Snyder's of Hanover five years later. The new Snyder's-Lance retained a production facility in Columbus and kept Tom's as a brand for chips, but the famous peanuts were a thing of the past.[12]

Nehi Corporation, bottler of RC Cola, followed a similar trajectory. RC was a noted beverage innovator, marketing the first canned soda in 1954 and later the first aluminum can and pop-top. The company also introduced the sixteen-ounce bottle in 1958. In 1951, downtown Columbus candy maker Alex Mitchell persuaded a friend at Nehi to produce a sugar-free cola for Mitchell's diabetic daughter. The original saccharin-sweetened cola was bitter, but after a decade of research, RC had Diet Rite, the first diet soda, an instant sensation that catapulted

RC ahead of Coke and Pepsi for the first (and last) time. The *Los Angeles Times* declared the drink the Leading New Product of the 1960s, but the company's brief stay at the top of the soft drink world ended in 1969, when the U.S. Food and Drug Administration banned Diet Rite's sweetener, cyclamate, as a potential carcinogen. Company officials determined that Royal Crown would never again tie itself so closely to a single product, diversifying into fruit juice and home furnishings. RC moved its headquarters to Atlanta in 1975 and then to Miami in 1984, though Columbus retained RC's concentrate-manufacturing facility, which pumped millions into the local economy. Cott Beverages bought that enterprise in 2001 and established an international headquarters in Columbus. After operating at a loss from 2006 to 2008, Cott bounced back to post an $81.5 million profit in 2009, but profits steadily declined, falling below $11 million in 2014.[13]

Other longtime industries left Columbus. Lummus Cotton Gin Company had operated since 1869 and had prospered with the new synthetic fibers after World War II. Forming Lummus International Sales in 1972, the company moved half its production overseas. Its fortunes declined, and after a 1993 bankruptcy, outside investors bought it and moved it and its 250 jobs to Savannah. The Bradley Company's Iron Works began producing the Char-Broil grill in 1953, and the W. C. Bradley Company stopped storing cotton on Front Avenue in 1985, its centennial year. Though D. Abbott Turner had decreed that the company would maintain its downtown roots, he died in 1982, and in 2006 the Bradley Company moved Char-Broil manufacturing to China. No longer an industrial player in the city, it expanded into leisure and lifestyle products, and its real estate division thrived. Goldens' Foundry, which had operated on Sixth Avenue since 1890, expanded and modernized, prospering through the 1990s. But it, too, succumbed to bankruptcy in 2009. Under its fifth-generation local management, Goldens' restructured and continued to provide iron castings for transportation, construction, agriculture, and energy.[14]

As Columbus's industry declined, other local businesses thrived. J. Tom Morgan was the genius behind the "Litho-Krome Process," which applied standardized photographic masking methods to achieve brilliant four-color lithography. Hallmark began a relationship with Litho-Krome in the mid-1950s, seeking "large-volume, accurate color reproduction." Morgan printed Hallmark cards as well as items for RC Cola, Whitman's Chocolates, Crayola, and IBM, among other national companies. In the mid-1960s Litho-Krome moved across the Thirteenth Street viaduct to a one-hundred-thousand-square-foot facility that employed 150 workers. When Morgan retired in 1979, Hallmark purchased Litho-Krome. In 2003, Hallmark restructured the company and moved it into a state-of-the-art printing plant in Midland. But business declined as electronic greeting cards became increasingly popular, and Litho-Krome closed in February 2015.[15]

Sidney Simons, the Pecan King, made his first fortune with the Southland Pecan Company. In 1941, after several bad crop years, he built a refrigerated warehouse for pecan storage and started U.S. Security Warehouse, which eventually outgrew Southland Pecan. The warehouse stored peanuts for Jimmy Carter's family, frozen vegetables from McKenzie and Company in Moultrie, and food for Fort Benning. After Simons's 1968 death, his son-in-law bought additional warehouses, and on December 31, 1981, U.S. Security merged with two other companies to become New York–based Americold, the world's largest refrigerated warehouse company. Simons's most lasting local legacy, however, grew from his real estate interests. In 1952, the Harmony Club moved next to his North Columbus property. In 1988, after the completion of I-185, the Harmony Club property became the Harmony Place shopping center. IBH Properties of Atlanta first leased and then purchased the Simons tract for Simons Plaza on Airport Throughway, and the city named the access road Sidney Simons Boulevard. In 2004, the property was incorporated into a Woodruff Company redevelopment, the Landings.[16]

By the late 1940s, Roy Martin operated 140 theaters across the Southeast and had acquired large numbers of hotels, amusement parks, and business properties. After Martin died in a 1948 plane crash, his sons further expanded Martin Theatres before selling the company to Fuqua Industries in 1969. Carl Patrick, who had been associated with Martin Theatres since 1945, became president and CEO, and under his stewardship, the chain's revenues mushroomed from $300 million per year to more than $2 billion. In 1982, Patrick and his sons, Carl Jr. and Mike, bought the company, returning it to Columbus and renaming it Carmike Cinemas. Carmike then built a $6.5 million headquarters at Broadway and Thirteenth Street, and the chain grew to more than three hundred theaters in thirty-five states. By the mid-1990s, Carmike had become the second-largest theater chain in the United States.[17]

In 1953, Columbus's First National Bank, founded in 1876 and housed in the Iron Bank on Broadway, merged with the Merchants and Mechanics Bank, chartered in 1871. In 1985, the bank moved into a modern facility on Thirteenth Street, becoming the first local bank to install automated teller machines. After mergers with First National Bank of Atlanta and First Union Corporation, the bank changed its name to Wachovia, which was purchased by Wells Fargo in 2008. Columbus Bank and Trust experienced even greater success with an innovative offshoot that became a foundation of the local economy. W. C. Bradley had presided over CB&T until his death in 1947, when his son-in-law, Abbott Turner, took over. In 1957, Turner hired James W. Blanchard as president. After thirteen years at the helm, Blanchard died, and his twenty-eight-year-old son, James H. Blanchard, assumed the mantle. In 1972 the bank formed CB&T Bancshares as a holding company, and in 1989, after CB&T expanded across the Southeast, Blanchard renamed it Synovus Financial Corporation. Over the next three decades, the bank developed software to manage bank accounts, operations, and credit cards, and in 1974, CB&T became the first bank to process transactions online for BankAmericard (now Visa). CB&T developed procedures of scale, adding millions of accounts, and in 1983 incorporated its highly profitable card-processing division as a publicly held subsidiary, Total System Services, known locally as TSYS. The company thrived through the 1980s, adding millions to Columbus's economy.[18]

Although heavy industry was generally declining, Columbus landed a major manufacturer in 1980, when Pratt & Whitney jet engines, a division of high-tech conglomerate United Technologies, built a seven-hundred-thousand-square-foot robotic plant on 321 acres in North Columbus. At the time, Pratt & Whitney's engines powered three-quarters of the world's commercial airliners and almost half of U.S. military aircraft. The company reached full production in 1986, with eight hundred nonunionized employees and an annual payroll of $13 million. But profits soon plummeted as a consequence of increased competition, cuts to the U.S. defense budget, flagging air travel, airlines' excess jet inventory, and economic recession, and the city struggled to hold onto Pratt & Whitney.[19]

Another company that had an enormous impact on Columbus was the American Family Insurance Company. Charismatic founder John B. Amos, a Florida native, began selling stock in Columbus in 1955, going door-to-door and offering buyers one-hundred-share lots for $11.10 per share. By April 1956, he had raised enough capital, but the company struggled, and at one point, he had to sell his office furniture to keep go-

John Amos (*center*) and his brothers, Paul (*left*) and William, 1976.
Courtesy of Aflac.

ing. In 1958, a year after the surgeon general had declared that a causal relationship existed between smoking and lung cancer, Amos, a lifelong chain smoker, began to sell cancer insurance to business groups. In 1964, Amos renamed the company American Family Life Assurance, and by 1970, its total earnings had reached $18 million. That year, Amos visited the Osaka World's Fair and noticed that many Japanese were wearing surgical masks because they were extremely concerned about disease, and he sought to tap into that market. In 1974, American Family became the first foreign insurance company licensed to sell policies in Japan; the following year, it sold $25 million in policies there, and by the mid-1980s, the company insured 10 percent of the Japanese people. Back home, American Family was listed on the New York Stock Exchange in 1974 and in 1975 built an eighteen-story tower on Wynnton Road that became Columbus's tallest building. Within two years, the company was Georgia's highest-earning insurance business.[20]

Columbus was fascinated by Amos's wealth, perhaps because he was a maverick who did not "give a damn about the higher society in Columbus" and because he had earned rather than inherited his money. Amos eschewed exclusive Green Island in favor of a South Columbus home on the edge of an African American neighborhood. In the 1960s and 1970s, when racial tensions in the city peaked, Amos and his wife, Elena, whose father was a crusading anticommunist Cuban journalist, entertained culturally diverse guests. Amos and his company prioritized family, and he quipped, "We not only believe in nepotism. We practice it": with at least eight of his relatives serving as company officers—among them his brothers, William and Paul; Paul's son, Dan; and Elena's brother, Salvador Diaz-Verson—the company's name could have been "Amos Family Life." A pragmatic Democrat, Amos saw himself as a populist and supported George Ford, president of Columbus's chapter of the NAACP, when he ran for the state legislature. Though Ford lost, he became a member of American Family's board of directors and called Amos his "best friend in the world." In 1986, Amos shocked the members of the all-white Big Eddy Club by bringing Ford to lunch, making him the first African American to eat there. Dead silence greeted them until a member shrugged toward Amos and remarked, "Well, what do you expect? He's not from here." In 1974, Georgia governor Jimmy Carter unofficially opened his presidential bid at a racially integrated eight-hundred-guest reception held at Amos's home. Amos also contributed to Republicans, sometimes donating to candidates facing off against each other and telling them that he hoped the best man won. "They both appreciate it," he said.[21]

Amos's political connections and his fervent anticommunism brought international recognition for Columbus when the School of the Americas relocated from Panama to Fort Benning in 1984. A Cold War center for anticommunist resistance, it provided Latin American military officers with training in logistics, weapons, intelligence, and psychological operations. The school's presence and its $3.5 million budget also had economic benefits for Columbus. The Amoses formed the School of the Americas Support Group to welcome the students and their families and ease their adjustment to Columbus and later to defend the school against its critics, who linked graduates to atrocities committed in Central America.[22]

By the late 1970s, American Family faced charges that it used fear and high-pressure tactics to scare elderly consumers into buying policies. The U.S. House Committee on Aging called cancer insurance a "rip-off." American Family's stock dropped 12.5 percent, its revenues declined, and it lost a few policyholders, but it soon roared back. Bolstered by its Japanese earnings, American Family was ranked as the top U.S. insurance company in profitability and sales in both 1979 and 1980. In

1989, Amos was Georgia's highest-paid executive, and his company adopted the acronym "Aflac." A heavy smoker, Amos was diagnosed with lung cancer in 1986, and he subsequently spearheaded the creation of what became the John B. Amos Cancer Center at Columbus Medical Center, raising more than $3 million. At the time of his death on August 13, 1990, Aflac insured thirty million people in six countries; had three thousand employees, fifteen hundred of them in Columbus; and was valued at $8 billion. Amos's successor as head of the company, his nephew, Dan, worked there part-time at age fourteen and sold insurance at eighteen. After graduating from college, he directed sales in Alabama and Florida before moving into the top echelons of management in 1984. Under Dan Amos's guidance, Aflac grew to even greater heights.[23]

In 1956, the U.S. government began creating an interstate highway system. Unfortunately for Columbus, none of the new roads initially reached the city, a decision some critics attributed to the influence of textile owners who sought to keep local laborers from seeking opportunities elsewhere. Construction did begin on some local routes, including the Lindsay Creek Bypass, a four-lane corridor between Fort Benning and the airport that was completed in May 1970, and the Manchester Expressway, another four-lane route between Columbus and Ellerslie that opened in 1965 and was intended eventually to extend to Atlanta. By the mid-1960s, boosters had seized on the idea that improving transportation would ease Columbus's economic woes, and local leaders instead sought a connection to I-85 to the north. I-185 construction began in 1975 and was completed in September 1979, prompting great excitement, with Columbus celebrating "as if the city had just become part of the United States." Effused the *Columbus Ledger*, "At long last [the highway] gives us a gateway to the world." The chamber of commerce still seemed to feel a bit isolated, however, branding Columbus the Brightest Light on the Georgia Horizon. Completed in 1989, the four-lane Corridor Z connected Columbus with Brunswick to the south, providing a route banker Jim Blanchard described as critical to Southwest Georgia's economic health. In 1998, the Fall Line Freeway between Columbus and Macon opened, with additional sections extending the road to Augusta completed in late 2017.[24]

After decades of inactivity, the Chattahoochee reemerged as a transportation link. Since the 1920s, wealthy entrepreneur James W. Woodruff had advocated the construction of dams to create a nine-foot navigable channel for barge traffic, produce hydroelectric power, and control flooding. In the mid-1930s, he helped form the Chattahoochee Valley Chamber of Commerce (later the Three-Rivers Development Association). Local pressure on Congress helped to produce the Rivers and Harbors Act of 1946, which authorized the U.S. Army Corps of Engineers to construct three dams south of Columbus that the chief of the Corps predicted would "lead to a revolutionary industrialization of this section." Woodruff Dam at the confluence of the Flint and Chattahoochee Rivers was completed in 1957, with George Andrews Dam at Columbia, Georgia, and Walter F. George Dam at Eufaula, Alabama, and Fort Gaines, Georgia, beginning operations three years later. In 1959, Georgia Power opened Oliver Dam at the old Clapp's Factory site, backing water up eight and a half miles to the foot of Goat Rock Dam and generating hydropower for the region. The Georgia Ports Authority built state docks at Columbus: they opened with a "Port Festival" on September 6, 1964. With river traffic resuming, boosters saw "unlimited potential" for industry, tourism, and recreation. But as with other moments when Columbus saw itself on the brink of greatness, the anticipated "revolutionary industrialization" never materialized. The dock operation had lost $131,000 by 1972, averaging just over one barge arrival per month, and barge traffic declined further through the 1980s before dropping precipitously in the 1990s and ceasing completely in 2001.[25]

Keeping the channel navigable had required the Corps of Engineers to dredge above the dams, an environmentally questionable practice that cost millions each year. Critics placed maintaining the Chattahoochee's navigable channel among the nation's "10 most-wasteful projects." The dams exacerbated pollution, blocking the natural flow that flushed impurities. In 1964, the city began treating raw sewage in settling ponds at a new $8 million plant on the river in South Columbus, but a 1966 U.S. Department of Interior report found that the river was "grossly polluted [with] bacterial contamination." Columbus College biology professor George Stanton demanded that the city control the clear-cutting of trees on construction projects to prevent sediment from clogging the creeks that flowed into the river. He advocated the creation of buffers along creeks, the setting aside of natural areas, and the protection of the watershed. The 1972 Clean Water Act outlawed dumping raw sewage and industrial chemicals into rivers, but whenever a hard rain fell, the city's "combined overflow" sewers sent raw sewage into the Chattahoochee. As a consequence of this and other factors, Georgia missed by more than a decade the U.S. Environmental Protection Agency's 1983 deadline to make the river "fishable and swimmable."²⁶

Fort Benning remained a major pillar of the Columbus-area economy—so much so that a 1978 analysis warned that the city depended too heavily on the dual base of manufacturing and Fort Benning. Active and retired members of the military comprised 12 percent of Columbus's population from the 1950s through the 1970s. By 1976, Benning had a total annual payroll of about $300 million, an amount that more than doubled to $660 million by the mid-1980s, equivalent to thirty-five Pratt & Whitney plants.²⁷

Although President Harry S. Truman had officially desegregated the armed forces in 1948, Benning changed little over the next two decades. After black military policemen ticketed a state senator's wife for speeding, they were moved to the post's back gate. White troops lived in Baker Village, but Negroes were banned from the complex. When a mixed-race couple came to Benning in the mid-1960s, they were threatened and quickly moved off base. In the 1960s, the army finally did away with the separate white and black USOs and post exchanges and named Roscoe Chester's son, Frank, to head the base's PX. The Vietnam draft brought large numbers of black soldiers to Benning, though most were enlisted men and noncommissioned officers. Race relations at Fort Benning reflected national conflicts, with frequent brawls breaking out, especially when white officers ordered African American enlisted men to perform menial tasks. In 1969, the infantry commander created the Race Relations Coordinating Group, organizing seminars where soldiers could express concerns. Many African American soldiers objected to discrimination on the duty roster and in promotions, noting that "white NCOs always put black soldiers on the dirtiest details." Reflecting the increasing disaffection with the war, a mock trial held on May 16, 1970, attracted 500 people, including 150 troops: Benning soldiers heard testimony from audience members and ultimately found the army guilty of war crimes and genocide. Benning, like many other military bases, also had an underground newspaper that criticized the war. Begun in 1969, *RAP!* focused on the concerns of African American soldiers.²⁸

The base captured national attention during the trial of Lt. William Calley for ordering the massacre of about five hundred Vietnamese villagers at My Lai. With the national media in attendance, the courts-martial lasted four and a half months, the longest in military history. On March 31, 1971, the jury found Calley guilty of premeditated murder, sentencing him "to be confined at hard labor for the length of your natural life; to be dismissed from the service; to forfeit all pay and allowances." Across the country, the public strongly disapproved of the verdict, viewing Calley as a scapegoat. Thirty-five hundred local supporters attended the Rally for Calley, and the Fourth National Bank started a defense fund on his behalf as the marquees of local motels demanded, "Free Calley." The trial nevertheless turned many people against the war, and a poll taken two weeks after Calley's conviction revealed that for the first time, a majority of Americans opposed the conflict. Three days after Calley was placed in the Fort Benning stockade, President Richard Nixon ordered him moved to house arrest, and in November 1974, former congressman Secretary of the Army Howard "Bo" Callaway, the son of a Chattahoochee Valley textile tycoon, paroled Calley. He subsequently married a Columbus woman and worked for many years in his father-in-law's Cross Country Plaza jewelry store. After decades of silence regarding the massacre, Calley told the Columbus Kiwanis Club in 2009, "There is not a day that goes by that I do not feel remorse for what happened that day in My Lai." He continued, "I was a second lieutenant getting orders from my commander and I followed them—foolishly, I guess."[29]

During World War II and the Korean conflict, Benning soldiers and Columbus citizens slaked their thirst and found entertainment across the river in Phenix City. In 1935, Phenix City had become the Russell County seat, making it easier for local organized crime to control the city and county governments. Illegal gambling flourished, including "the bug," a numbers racket based on daily sales on the New York Stock Exchange. Slot machines were everywhere, even the post office, and clubs offered casino games and high-quality floor shows. A prostitution syndicate connected Miami, Jacksonville, Savannah, and New Orleans—as well as Phenix City, which was the source of 60 percent of the cases of sexually transmitted disease found among soldiers at Benning. The army's efforts to crack down on prostitution occasionally ensnared innocent bystanders: a young woman on her way to work at Fort Benning was waiting at a

Phenix City bus stop at 5:30 one morning when police arrested her as a prostitute and held her until an officer vouched for her.[30]

The problem was not limited to the Alabama side of the river. A 1945 grand jury found that the bug was "flourishing as never before" in Columbus and that slot machines "operated openly." In February, a sheriff's department "flying squadron" raided bars that dispensed liquor by the drink and provided "havens for 'playing the bug.'" The grand jury indicted Phenix City kingpins Hoyt Shepherd and Jimmie Matthews, whose Army Club on Broadway violated Columbus's liquor laws. The man who signed their bail bonds, Fate Leebern, was shot to death in Phenix City's Southern Manor Club the following year in the presence of Matthews, Shepherd, and his brother, Grady "Snooks" Shepherd, who admitted to having pulled the trigger but claimed to have acted in self-defense. Snooks had a very shallow knife wound on his abdomen that police described as a "pin scratch," while Leebern's penknife was folded in his pocket and showed no sign of blood. Insiders claimed that the wound was self-inflicted (or Hoyt-inflicted). The Shepherds hired every lawyer in Russell County for their defense team, and the jury acquitted Snooks after five hours of deliberation.[31]

Phenix City's organized vice trade came to a crashing halt in 1954. Albert Patterson, an attorney who had helped to defend Snooks Shepherd, fell out with the gangsters and ran for Alabama attorney general, promising to end organized crime and winning despite the mob's vote buying and ballot-box stuffing. On June 18, shortly after the election, however, Patterson was shot four times outside his Coulter Building office. He died without identifying his killer. The next day, Governor Gordon Persons ordered Gen. Walter J. "Crack" Hanna and the Alabama National Guard to work with local authorities to apprehend the assassin, but Hanna quickly learned that Phenix City "was a whole damn town of ill repute" where local law enforcement was allied with the gangsters. On July 22, in an unprecedented move, Persons placed Phenix City under martial law. Backed by guardsmen with fixed bayonets, Hanna took over the Russell County Courthouse and city hall, firing the sheriff, deputies, and police. Describing the mission as "the moral equivalent of war," Hanna sent troops to raid every vice establishment. In addition to liquor, prostitution, and gambling, they uncovered narcotics, a baby-selling operation, abortion facilities, a safe-cracking school, and a factory that produced marked cards and loaded dice. A total of 749 indictments were obtained against 152 people, all but 2 of whom were convicted. Taped telephone calls revealed that Columbus commissioner Jesse Binns was in Hoyt Shepherd's pocket, and in September a grand jury censured Binns for "hobnobbing... with a known underworld racketeer." The *Columbus Ledger*'s coverage of the mess won the paper a 1955 Pulitzer Prize for the "vigor, consistency and fearlessness of its pursuit against chronic civil cancer in Phenix City." In January 1956, the cleanup finished, *Look* magazine designated Phenix City an All-American City.[32]

Those in search of more highbrow fare could attend concerts put on by the Columbus Symphony Orchestra, which was organized in 1949 and conducted for fifteen years by Jordan High School's popular band director, Bob Barr. In 1963, the Three Arts League, with major support from the Woodruff family, renovated the Royal Theatre to serve as the Symphony's home. In the late 1970s, the Symphony became a professional orchestra. Columbus College contributed many musicians to the Symphony, including Harry Kruger, who succeeded Barr in 1965 and held the post until 1986, when George Del Gobbo took up the baton.[33]

Television came to Columbus on October 6, 1953, when WDAK-TV went on the air with NBC and ABC network programming. Five weeks later, James W. Woodruff Jr.'s CBS affiliate, WRBL-TV, began broadcasting, and in August 1962, its antenna was recognized in the *Guinness Book of World Records* as the world's tallest structure. Early Columbus TV was live and locally focused, with personalities such as weatherman Doug Wallace, *Sportsman's Lodge* host Ridley Bell, and Dick McMichael, who spent five decades as a news anchor, becoming fixtures on the Columbus airwaves. Rozell Fabiani's *At Home with Rozell* aired 8,599 shows between 1954 and 1988, offering viewers a daily mix of cooking and craft segments, music, news, conversations with guests, and other "women's programming." In addition to her role as a trailblazer for women, Fabiani opened the airwaves to minority groups at a time when they rarely appeared on screen. African American contralto Fredye Marshall frequently sang on Rozell's show, and she hosted guests from Tuskegee University in 1956. For nearly two decades, Fabiani also produced an annual "Salute to the First Americans" week, bringing a total of about 150 tribal groups to Columbus. During the Vietnam War, Fabiani sent Christmas packages overseas to the Fort Benning–based First Cavalry, including gifts for Vietnamese children. After hearing that the Vietnamese people bathed in creeks, she launched a campaign to send them Ivory Soap,

Still photograph from a Hillbilly Bread commercial that appeared on *At Home with Rozell*, early 1960s.
From the Collection of Virginia E. Causey.

whose advertising slogan highlighted the fact that the bars floated. Her efforts brought in donations of four thousand cases. On one occasion, Fabiani's craft demonstration involved putting citric acid in a fishbowl and dropping in mothballs, which moved up and down. A viewer then called in and asked, "What do I do with the dead goldfish?" Fabiani won three McCall's Gold Mike Awards, the highest honor given to women in radio and television, as well as innumerable local prizes. In 1988, when the station's new management abruptly canceled her show, Rozell stripped the solid oak cabinets from her kitchen set and took them with her.[34]

Between 1964 and 1966, Columbus sports fans headed to Golden Park to watch the New York Yankees' AA farm team play. To counteract the potential negative associations of the team's name, the owners added Confederate flags to the uniforms and over the ballpark entrance, and the team became known as the Confederate Yankees. African American players not only wore the Confederate emblem but endured harassment from white fans. Four years after the Yankees' departure, the Houston Astros' AA team arrived. Known as the Columbus Astros through 1988 and for the next two seasons as the Columbus Mudcats, the team fielded such future Major Leaguers as right-handed fireballer J. R. Richard, three-time All-Star and 1996 National League MVP Ken Caminiti, and Bruce Bochy, who went on to manage the San Francisco Giants to three World Series titles. After a decade in the Big Leagues with the Houston Astros and Baltimore Orioles and two years playing in Japan, former All-Star slugger Glenn Davis returned to Columbus, where he had played at Golden Park from 1982 to 1984, and won a seat on the city council in 2002. Between 2003 and 2008, Columbus was home to a South Atlantic League team, known for one year as the South Georgia Waves and subsequently as the Columbus Catfish.[35]

Highlighting the area's military history, the Fort Benning Infantry Museum opened in 1959 in an old wooden building. Formed in 1967, the Infantry Museum Association began raising money to find a permanent location for the exhibits tracing the role of the American infantryman since the French and Indian War. A decade later, the museum moved into the old Fort Benning Hospital. In 1962, after a two-year salvage operation in the Chattahoochee raised the hull of the Confederate ironclad *Jackson*, it was transported along with the gunboat's armor-plated fantail, propellers, and cannonballs for storage on the South Commons. The ruined *Chattahoochee* gunboat, including two Columbus Iron Works engines, was salvaged in 1964. In 1970, the Confederate Naval Museum featuring the two vessels opened to the public. The museum's facilities were less than ideal, leaving the hulls outdoors and vulnerable to the elements and to humans: the museum's director extinguished "two fires in the *Jackson* from people thumping cigarettes down in it." Financial struggles also plagued the institution.[36]

The Columbus Little Theatre had brought life to the venerable Springer Opera House in the postwar years, but by 1959, it stood vacant and decaying. In 1963, the theater was slated for demolition when young members of the city's elite formed the Springer Trustees. Clason Kyle, the great-grandson of George Parker Swift, gave more than two hundred speeches urging the opera house's preservation, and the trustees raised $100,000 to buy and begin restoring the historic building. In October 1965, the Little Theatre hosted a black-tie gala in the partially renovated theater, presenting a musical adaptation of *St. Elmo*. In September 1971, Governor Jimmy Carter designated the Springer the State Theater of Georgia, and eight years later it was named a National Historic Landmark. The Springer Theater's revitalization provided the impetus for a historic preservation movement that ultimately brought life back to Columbus's downtown.[37]

Seeking more efficient government and concerned about outmigration from the city, which reached as high as one in eight households during the 1960s, Columbus leaders began considering a county-city merger. In June 1961, the city and county commissions created the joint Citizens Committee on Consolidation. Headed by John Amos, the committee had twenty-one members chosen from among the local elite, but it included only two women and no African Americans. When the committee recommended consolidation into one government, county commissioners denounced the proposal. Area state legislators supported the plan, however, and pushed through a bill setting April 11, 1962, for a referendum. In the run-up to the vote, the chair of the county commission labeled the plan "communistic" and called consolidation a "metro-Castro government" and Amos an "immigrant" to the area. On Election Day, a slight majority in Columbus and nearly 60 percent of county voters rejected the proposal.[38]

Proponents regrouped and tried again, creating a second Consolidation Study Committee in February 1967 but once again failing to include African Americans among the powerful community leaders on the panel. In November 1968, voters in the city overwhelmingly approved a constitutional amendment creating a commission to draft a new city charter in the event of consolidation. At the same time, Republican J. R. Allen, a charismatic, young former chair of the county commission and a strong supporter of consolidation, won the mayor's office. Early in 1969, the General Assembly passed enabling legislation for an amendment creating a Muscogee County Charter Commission. It prohibited any changes to state courts, the sheriff's department, the school district, or Bibb City. The November 1968 ballot also included an annexation proposal for most of the rest of the county still outside the city limits, effective in time for inclusion in the 1970 census. Though a large majority of county residents opposed the Charter Commission and annexation, more than two-thirds of all voters approved.[39]

The Charter Commission met in May 1969 and selected Columbus College president Thomas Whitley as chair. Its members included Bill Turner, G. Gunby Jordan II, four active or retired RC executives, and other influential businessmen and lawyers but no women or black leaders. George Ford protested, and in October the city commission appointed three nonvoting "negro advisers," including Robert Wright and

Albert Thompson. The Charter Commission proposed reorganizing local government to create a council of ten nonpartisan members, six at-large and four from districts. A steering committee of African American and white leaders, the chamber of commerce, and newspapers strongly promoted the merger. City commissioners, state legislators, and all but one county commissioner also supported the idea, and on May 27, 1970, voters approved the plan by a four-to-one margin. It went into effect on January 1, 1971. Columbus–Muscogee County became Georgia's first consolidated government and the fifth in the South. Consolidation's success grew from what was described as an "accelerated spirit of progress" that began with Allen's election. The Charter Commission worked hard at transparency, and the 1969 annexation left fewer than fourteen hundred registered voters in the county, diluting the opposition. Consolidation enabled the local government to eliminate duplicated services, and by 1999, Columbus boasted a lower per-person cost of government than twenty-five other southeastern cities.[40]

Allen easily won reelection in November 1970. Though none of the newly drawn council districts had a black majority, voters elected Robert Wright and A. J. McClung to the city council, making them the body's first African American members. Inspired by Allen to run as a Republican, Wright won in the district with the largest black population and went on to serve three terms. McClung took an at-large district, and his fellow councillors unanimously chose him to serve as mayor pro-tem, a position he held for twenty-eight years. Consolidation was less effective at bringing women into the higher echelons of local government, and as of 1974 they accounted for only 17 percent of all city workers, with none of those in higher pay grades. Under pressure from the League of Women Voters and Urban League, the mayor appointed the Commission on the Status of Women. The commission found ample evidence of discrimination: male bus drivers' pay was higher than more-educated female clerk/typists; female assistants to the tax commissioners earned 40 percent less than male assistants in the Planning Office, who essentially performed the same jobs; no women held supervisory positions; only 3.3 percent of the city's workers were black women, and they were clustered in low-paid service occupations. In May 1976, the council approved an affirmative action plan, but in 1989, women still comprised only a quarter of the city workforce, and most remained concentrated in clerical and service positions. Some gains did occur, however. In 1976, Columbus College librarian Mary Jane Galer became the first local woman elected to the General Assembly since Love Tolbert in the 1930s. Two years

Dr. Robert Wright, February 4, 1977.
From the Collection of Virginia E. Causey.

J. R. Allen, September 13, 1970.
From the Allen Family Collection.

Mary Jane Galer, ca. 1981.
Columbus State University
Archives, Columbus State
University, Columbus, Georgia.

later, businesswoman Edna Kendrick became the first female to serve on the council since Anna Griffin in 1921. And in 1984, South Columbus voters made Republican Rose Strong the first African American woman to join the council.[41]

Allen continued to promote progressive city government, recruiting new industry and securing federal revenue sharing for recreation, urban development, and comprehensive planning. A devout Christian, Allen fought the presence of adult bookstores downtown yet supported the sale of mixed drinks as an economic boon. He named African Americans to city boards. He hired a black secretary as the public face of his office and promoted a black man who had formerly served as a "janitor in the basement of the court house" to deputy voter registrar. He increased the number of black police officers from four to fifty-two, so that they accounted for 17 percent of the force. Nevertheless, the police department remained plagued by scandals, including a burglary ring. To combat these problems, Allen pushed through a September 1969 departmental reorganization, improved training, added a public safety director, and instituted a civil service system. The department hired its first black policewoman in 1971.[42]

Despite these changes, systemic racism persisted. Referred to as "boy" and "nigger" by white colleagues, black officers, many of whom had served in Vietnam, drank from a hose in the basement while whites had refrigerated fountains. African American officers believed that discriminatory hiring denied them promotions (in 1970, the highest-ranking black policeman was a sergeant) and that they received disproportionate punishments for minor infractions. Excluded from the Fraternal Order of Police, black officers formed the Afro-American Policemen's League in early 1971. Led by Robert Leonard, whose nephew had desegregated Baker High School, the League met with the city council, Allen, and the police chief, but got no relief. On May 29, twenty League members called in sick to protest the firing of a black policeman. After the chief refused to meet with League representatives, black officers picketed the police station during off-duty hours. On May 30, Wright, Allen, and twenty-five black and white businessmen met with League leaders. One black officer tried to spit on Allen. When another pulled a gun and said, "I'm just back from Vietnam and I'm ready to have a shoot-out right here," he was pinned to the wall by an African American policeman who defended the mayor's record on blacks. Civic leaders asked the League for a cooling-off period, but on May 31, seven officers resumed picketing, dramatically cutting the American flag insignia from their uniform

Afro-American Policemen's League picketing the police station, May 30, 1971.
From the Collection of Judge Bobby Peters.

sleeves in front of representatives of the press. The officers explained that they were doing so carefully out of respect for the flag and the ideals of liberty and equality it represented but that they believed the police department's actions ran contrary to those principles.[43]

Allen, the police chief, and the public safety director fired the officers, on the grounds that they had desecrated the flag. The League members sued, claiming that removing the flag constituted symbolic speech protected under the First Amendment. Frank "Butch" Martin, a young white attorney who went on to become mayor of Columbus, was a member of the League's defense team. On June 19, Atlanta civil rights activist Hosea Williams led a five-hundred-person march through Columbus that culminated in a speech on the old courthouse steps during which he threatened an African American boycott of white businesses if the policemen were not rehired within forty-eight hours. On the night of June 21, police killed Willie J. Osborne, a twenty-year-old black robbery suspect, with Leonard claiming that the young man had been "shot down in cold blood, shot in the back." A few days later, the Reverend Ralph Abernathy of the Southern Christian Leadership Conference delivered a eulogy before two thousand angry mourners at the young man's funeral as his body lay in a casket draped with the Black Nationalist flag.[44]

Though Wright and McClung pleaded for order, the African American community exploded. Twenty-seven arsons over the weekend damaged white businesses. The city council granted emergency powers to Allen, who called in one hundred "riot-trained" highway patrolmen and banned sales of liquor, guns, and ammunition. At a June 21 press conference, a tearful Allen asked every citizen "to turn his attention to God" and promised to restore order. Allen, the *Ledger*, Governor Jimmy Carter, and Congressman Jack Brinkley characterized Williams as an outside agitator provoking the violence, with Brinkley referring to the activist as "the chief racist of them all." Rudy Allen and Robert Leonard chaired the Community Action Group (CAG) leading the boycott. White property owners posted guards or sat with shotguns on roofs, and the Jaycees set up an information center to dispel rumors. Nightly firebombings continued, reaching a total of eighty-one by the end of June and causing $800,000 in damage. Police and firefighters complained of sniper fire, cut hoses, and brick throwing.[45]

The violence continued to escalate. On July 24, CAG sponsored a march that drew four hundred people to the police station, where protesters staged a sit-in. After forty-five minutes of speeches, police ordered those in the crowd to disperse, and they complied. On the march back to CAG headquarters, however, a melee broke out as a hundred club-wielding officers and state troopers beat marchers, sending five to the hospital. That evening, multiple police cars and fire engines were fired on, with a policeman and two firefighters injured. At 11:00 p.m., Allen declared a state of emergency. Over the next three days, police responded to thirty-one calls reporting snipers, arson, and brick throwing. A July 26 rally that brought Abernathy back to Columbus attracted a thousand people. CAG demanded that the city hire African Americans for white-collar positions and that members of the black community receive appointments to city boards, announcing a July 31 mass march in support of those changes. Mayor Allen refused to issue a parade permit and secured an injunction, but CAG went ahead and staged the march, which drew two hundred protesters. The police arrested eighty-one marchers; they were convicted of unlawful assembly and disorderly conduct, and the U.S. Fifth Circuit Court of Appeals upheld the convictions nearly two years later. The emergency ordinance remained in effect until August 25, when the most destructive period of racial violence in Co-

Guards at Little Joe's liquor store, summer 1971.
From the Collection of Jim Cannon.

lumbus history finally came to an end. From June through September 1971, a total of 161 fires had caused more than $1 million in damage.[46]

African American leaders found themselves in the hot seat. Accused of firebombing, Rudy Allen retorted that he had not burned anything, but "if I saw somebody with a match, I wouldn't blow it out." In Allen's view, "Firebombing was symbolic of the injustices happening.... White folk don't understand anything but buildings, bodies, and budgets." Wright criticized the Fraternal Order of Police, charging that some of its actions made him "question [officers'] dedication to law and order" and blaming their "attitudes" for low morale in the department. McClung noted that the controversy revealed underlying problems, including substandard housing, unpaved streets, and inadequate street lighting in Negro neighborhoods. Wright and McClung occupied a difficult position: the white community expected them to control African Americans, but many blacks viewed them as tools of the white power structure.[47]

As with Columbus's earlier civil rights issues, resolution came through negotiation. A committee of seven white and six black civic leaders—among them Bill Turner, Nolan Murrah, Rudy Allen, George Ford, and NAACP leader Margaret Belcher—met soon after the first firebombing. Turner later said that the whites were called "nigger lovers" and the African Americans "Uncle Toms." Another member recalled, "It was a war refought, but it gradually grew into communication." At J. R. Allen's request, the federal government granted Columbus $58,000 for a police-community relations commission and agreed to review the police department. Allen and the police chief continued to refuse to rehire the seven police officers, so negotiators concentrated instead on economic issues, setting up an informal job exchange at Friendship Baptist Church. Most significantly, on September 28, 1972, Columbus's African American and white leaders established a chapter of the Urban League, which focused on practical ways to improve the black community. Under the leadership of Jessie Taylor for the next two decades, the Urban League had notable success in improving African Americans' employment opportunities, health care, education, and housing.[48]

The Afro-American Policeman's League lawsuit came before Judge Elliott. The right-wing jurist ruled the flag patch's removal was not symbolic speech, but "a calculated show of contempt for the City authority." According to Elliott, if the officers' action was protected by the First Amendment, then "punching the Police Chief in the nose" would also be symbolic speech. But he cited no case law, and in 1983, the Eleventh Circuit Court threw out his judgment and found in favor of the Policemen's League, declaring that the removal of the flag patch was constitutionally protected speech and that the officers' dismissal was "contrary to every promulgated City of Columbus rule," including the city charter, due process under the Police Hearing Board, and the police manual. When the U.S. Supreme Court refused to review the case, the officers asked to be rehired, with credit for the thirteen years they had spent fighting the case. The lawsuit dragged on, but in 1993, twenty-two years after the officers had initially filed suit, the city settled, awarding $133,000 to each policeman.[49]

On February 16, 1973, exactly one week after snow blanketed Columbus, residents woke to the shocking news that J. R. Allen had died in a plane crash the night before when ice formed on the wings of the aircraft carrying him back home from a speaking engagement in Rome, Georgia. The city mourned its young mayor, with Governor Jimmy Carter and Vice President Spiro Agnew sending condolences. As mayor pro-tem, McClung succeeded Allen, becoming the city's first African American chief executive and serving until the April 3 special election.[50]

As it did across the rest of the country, crime in Columbus spiked during the 1960s and 1970s, fueled by racial and social unrest and economic dislocation. Most distressing to local residents, three serial killers were active in the area in the late 1970s and 1980s, with other murders horrifying the community as well. On September 16, 1977, a sixty-year-old public health educator was found beaten, raped, and strangled with a nylon stocking in her Wynnton home. Over the next seven months, the Stocking Strangler raped and garroted six more older women, all of them well-to-do and all but one living in Wynnton. Area residents put bars on their windows, alarm buttons by their beds, floodlights outside, and deadbolt locks on doors. Police patrolled the neighborhood, focusing particularly on African Americans after the coroner said that pubic hair taken from the crime scenes displayed "negroid characteristics." Police took samples from black men, sparking charges of harassment.[51]

Six years later, on May 4, 1984, police matched fingerprints found at the crime scenes with those of an African American man, Carlton Gary, and charged him with three of the murders. The prosecution spent tens of thousands of dollars building its case over the next two years, but the court refused to pay Gary's Atlanta attorney, a situation his lawyer later described as a "legal lynching." On August 26, 1986, a jury that included only three African Americans found Gary guilty despite some inconsistencies in the evidence—Gary's shoe size and blood did not match what was found at the crime scenes. The next day, jurors sentenced him to death.[52]

Over the next two decades, new attorneys discovered that the prosecution had concealed significant evidence and found other evidentiary discrepancies: a cast of the killer's teeth from a wound on one of the victims did not match Gary's mouth; his semen was a different biochemical type than the murderer's; Gary's unsigned "confession" was compiled two months after his interrogation by three detectives who had neither taken notes nor used a tape recorder. The Georgia courts nevertheless refused to grant him a retrial, and he was scheduled to die on December 16, 2009. Three hours before his scheduled execution, the Georgia Supreme Court halted proceedings while it determined whether DNA testing, which had not been a possibility in the 1980s, should be conducted. Tests subsequently found that Gary's DNA was not a match for the semen found on the women whom he had been charged with raping, though it did match semen found on one of the other victims. In September 2017, thirty-one years after Gary moved to death row, a superior court judge denied him a new trial. The Georgia Supreme Court unanimously rejected his appeal, and on March 15, 2018, he was executed despite the persistent doubts about whether he had received fair treatment. As one of Gary's attorneys noted bitterly, "The crime happens, the mob gathers. Far too often, the question is, which nigger's neck are we going to put the noose around?"[53]

In the spring of 1978, while the Stocking Strangler was active, police and the *Columbus Ledger* received letters in which someone who signed himself "Forces of Evil" threatened to kill black women. After finding two African American prostitutes and a white female soldier beaten to death, police arrested William Henry Hance, a black soldier at Fort Benning. Psychologists determined that Hance was not psychotic but declared that his mental functioning was so low that he was incapable of assisting in his defense "in an appropriate, rational way." The court nevertheless allowed Hance to act as his own lead counsel, and he was convicted and sentenced to death in December 1978. After prosecutors were found to have engaged in misconduct, the Eleventh Circuit Court of Appeals reversed the death penalty and ordered a new sentencing trial. The new jury was leaning toward imposing a life sentence, but a prosecutor warned that Hance posed a danger to the community, and all of the jurors except one changed their votes to death. The holdout was the panel's only African American, and the other jurors threatened she could be charged with perjury since she had sworn that she could impose the death penalty. She finally told her fellow jurors, "You do what you have to do, but I won't vote for a death sentence." The jurors then told the judge that they had reached a unanimous decision, and Hance was executed on March 31, 1994.[54]

A decade passed before Columbus's third serial killer struck. In 1988, thirty-three-year-old Curtis Grantham, a white man known to downtown residents for his violent temper and erratic behavior, murdered at least three women, slitting the throats of two women and stabbing the third to death in front of her eighteen-month-old son. He was convicted of two of the murders in June 1990 and was spared the death penalty after providing authorities with the location where he had buried the bodies.[55]

Other notable murders that occurred in Columbus during this period included those of Ann Curry, who was eight months pregnant, and her two children, four-year-old Erika and twenty-month-old Ryan, on August 29, 1985. Michael Curry told police that he had returned home from work and found his family hacked to death with a bush ax. Suspicion soon fell on Curry, who was having an affair and wanted to leave his wife but had told a coworker that he could not afford alimony and child support. However, the district attorney felt that he did not have enough evidence to convict Curry, and he remained free until 2009, when a grand jury indicted Curry after the case was reopened. On April 27, 2011, twenty-six years after the murders, Curry was convicted of the crimes and sentenced to life in prison.[56]

In December 1989, twenty-six-year-old Kalvin Bailey walked into police headquarters and pumped four bullets into an officer's back, killing him, and then wounded another officer in a spray of gunfire. Bailey, who had been diagnosed with schizophrenia a decade earlier, explained his crime by declaring that he had "just snapped" and pled not guilty by reason of insanity. Despite this history of mental illness, the district attorney sought the death penalty against Bailey, an African American; after just an hour of deliberation, the jury found him guilty of capital murder and recommended a life sentence. Bailey's attorney believed that his client was punished unfairly because he had killed a police officer.[57]

Two additional deaths struck the Columbus school system. In July 1989, William Henry Shaw's successor as superintendent, Braxton Nail, hanged himself with a garden hose in his backyard. Nail had inherited an $890,000 deficit and a bookkeeping scandal when he took over in 1973 but within three years had righted the ship, and the district posted an $883,000 surplus. However, Nail's tenure had also been plagued by race-related issues, as the schools essentially resegregated under his watch. In addition, critics charged that the system was top-heavy with administrators and that the superintendent was aloof and hands-off, better with buildings than with people. Nail was reportedly despondent about the state of MCSD affairs.[58]

Nail's replacement, Jim Burns, also proved controversial. He upset the status quo by hiring new personnel, transferring principals, and giving longtime administrators poor performance reviews. Burns was accused of wielding his power autocratically, and the conversion of Baker High School to a middle school brought him at least one death threat. In the summer of 1992, the school board began pressing for his resignation, with one member leading an anti-Burns rally at Weracoba Park. Matters appeared headed toward a climactic confrontation at the October 19 school board meeting, with rumors swirling that the board would fire him and that Burns would raise damning allegations about board members.[59]

Just after midnight on the night of October 18–19, screams awakened Burns's neighbors. Police found the superintendent dead in a pool of blood by his open front door and a trail of blood leading upstairs to his bedroom. An intruder apparently entered the house using a key that was under the doormat, went upstairs, and stabbed Burns in the back with a six-inch hunting knife as he slept. Wounded, he shouted "Get out of here, you son of a bitch!" and chased the man downstairs before collapsing and dying. Police chief Jim Wetherington confidently predicted that police would catch the killer before the sun rose. Soon after the murder, a neighbor reported that a suspicious man in a small gray pickup was speeding the wrong way on a one-way street, and police subsequently stopped Kareem Lane, an African American high school student, driving a truck that matched that description. In the vehicle, officers found an empty knife sheath, a dark jacket, and a hood with eye holes. Officers questioned Lane for hours and then let him go, keeping the sheath as evidence. When they went to Lane's home two days later, police found that his clothes and the truck's interior had been cleaned. In addition, officers had allowed thirty-one people to pass through the crime scene on the morning of October 19, leaving fingerprints and otherwise contaminating evidence. Coroner Don Kilgore called the investigation "messed up" but also raised the absurd possibility that Burns had fastened a knife to the wall and backed into it to garner public sympathy. Police considered a variety of other suspects in Burns's murder, including his wife, but made no arrests.[60]

In 2008, a cold-case investigator sent the knife for DNA testing, and in November 2009, police obtained a warrant for Lane's DNA. In April 2010, police announced that the DNA matched, and Lane was arrested on May 3. At Lane's September 2012 trial, prosecutors offered no motive for the murder, and an expert testified that there was in fact no DNA match—while Lane could have been the source, so could thousands of other people. After three days of deliberation, the jury deadlocked, and the judge declared a mistrial. At an August 2014 retrial, Lane was acquitted. The case remains unsolved but is officially closed.[61]

Despite the tribulations of the 1970s and 1980s, Columbus's citizens began to look at their city with new eyes and to find value in what they saw. The Springer Theatre's renovation proved that people recognized Columbus's rich architectural heritage and supported saving city landmarks. That seed blossomed into a full-fledged renaissance in downtown Columbus in the 1990s.

CHAPTER 9

Renaissance

Columbus since the 1990s

Columbus's revitalization beginning in the 1990s was based on adaptive reuse of downtown's historic structures, a cultural renaissance centered on Columbus College and arts organizations, growth in technology and white-collar industries, and a renewed focus on the Chattahoochee. Visionary civic, political, and philanthropic leaders laid the foundation for cultural growth, economic prosperity, and increased tourism. Though serious problems remained with education, crime, race relations, and poverty, the city's future was brighter than any time since the end of World War II.

After the historic City Market's demolition in the 1920s, other landmarks fell to the wrecking ball. "Progress" swept aside Augusta Howard's Sherwood Hall; the Martin J. Crawford, Eli S. Shorter, and John Winter mansions downtown; Raphael Moses's Esquiline in South Columbus; William H. Young's Beallwood; and the Gothic Redd Mansion, James C. Cook's Belmont, and L. H. Chappell's Glen Lora in Rose Hill. In 1972 the Government Center tower replaced the graceful 1896 courthouse. As similar "urban renewal" projects swept across the nation, historic preservation efforts grew, with the local movement spurred by the raising of the Confederate gunboats and the saving of the Springer Theatre in the early 1960s. As in the City Market fight, the elite were at the forefront. In January 1966, the Columbus Junior League donated $5,000 to have a renowned architectural historian survey historic buildings: the study identified 364 significant structures that provided the blueprint for preservation. In June of that year, Janice Biggers and Sarah Turner Butler, daughter of D. Abbott Turner, led seventy people in forming the

Historic Columbus Foundation (HCF), which was modeled on the Historic Savannah Foundation. The HCF restored five downtown houses and established a fund to buy threatened structures for resale to owners willing to renovate.[1]

In October 1966, the National Historic Preservation Act established the National Register of Historic Places, with listing on the register qualifying a property for grants, loans, and tax incentives. In 1969, HCF listed a deteriorating twenty-six-block downtown historic district with two hundred antebellum and Victorian houses. HCF had a strong ally in the Columbus Housing Authority, which pumped millions into an urban renewal project between Fourth and Ninth Streets, the river, and what is now Veterans Parkway. The authority landscaped streets, put benches and gaslights at the Confederate monument on Broadway, and built nine pocket parks. It authorized federal rehabilitation loans totaling about $3 million by 1978, stabilizing houses to be sold to private owners and consequently attracting more homeowners to the district. Among the threatened houses that the HCF moved from elsewhere in the city into the historic district were the Goetchius House, which became a restaurant; the John Pemberton House; Pemberton's country house; E. E. Farley's house; David Rothschild's house, which became a bed and breakfast; and three houses originally in High Uptown that were relocated to Front Avenue. These relocations invoked the specter of the moveable houses that Basil Hall had noted on these same streets in 1828.[2]

To commemorate the nation's two-hundredth birthday, HCF teamed with a local Bicentennial Committee to create the Promenade, a three-block outdoor history museum on a once-neglected stretch of riverbank. The Housing Authority built a plaza and donated a Victorian cottage that the Junior League renovated. The Coastal Plains Regional Commission granted funds to build a 430-seat amphitheater and Founders' Park, and D. Abbott Turner donated a Liberty Bell replica. The city, HCF, and civic groups paid for gazebos, a fountain, a formal garden, and exhibits along the Promenade and in the restored cottage. Biggers saw the Promenade as "the beginning of turning [the city's] face toward the river instead of putting tin warehouse sheds" along it. In the summer of 1977, HCF and the U.S. Department of the Interior sponsored a Historic American Engineering Record team that documented the riverfront mills, providing the basis for the designation of the Iron Works, Eagle & Phenix, Muscogee Mills, City Mills, and Bibb Mill as the Historic Riverfront Industrial District National Landmark.[3]

Historic preservation spurred downtown economic development. Local leaders had long discussed the possibility of constructing a convention center, but the city council abandoned those plans in the early 1970s when costs soared. The 1975 closing of the Ralston Hotel, which offered the city's only large meeting space, made the need more urgent. Businesswoman Edna Kendrick chaired a 1975 committee that recommended the city renovate the vacant Iron Works. The council agreed to buy the antebellum industrial complex for $400,000, giving rise to the city's first major preservation project. Architects kept as much of the buildings' historical character as possible, saving massive exposed timbers and iron beams, brick walls and vintage machinery. When the Iron Works Convention and Trade Center opened September 15, 1979, twenty thousand people crowded inside, marveling at its metamorphosis from gritty industrial facility to modern meeting space. The $8 million cost was about a third less than a new facility of the same size. Three years later, a Hilton Hotel opened across the street, adapting the historic structure of the antebellum Empire Mills to serve as the lobby, bar, and restaurant.[4]

Adaptive reuse of historic buildings spread into the downtown business district under the leadership of developer Harry Kamensky. Inspired by Denver's redevelopment of a block of historic buildings, Kamensky formed Rankin Square Properties, selling forty shares at $5,000 each in 1976. Kamensky planned to renovate the block bounded by Broadway, First Avenue, Tenth Street, and Eleventh Streets, including the 1880 Rankin Hotel and the white Iron Bank. Promotional materials declared the project "one of the largest non-governmental attempts in the country to revitalize Main Street." He acquired "porno shops, peep shows, pool halls, and beer joints"; removed modern facades to reveal elegant nineteenth-century brickwork; took down overhead neon signs; and turned the properties into upscale retail establishments, restaurants, and offices. In 1977, Rankin Square was added to the National Register of Historic Places, and by the following summer, property taxes on the block had nearly tripled and sales tax receipts were five times greater than in 1976. But by 1979, Kamensky had trouble raising money, a problem he blamed on anti-Semitism: "Anytime you have a country club that refuses membership to Jews and blacks, then you have a bias that extends to the point you must have a closed society." Though Kamensky did not achieve all he wanted for Rankin Square, it became the first step on the long path to bringing new life downtown.[5]

City leaders continued to work to attract dollars and people downtown. In June 1983, a group led by Bill Turner, Jim Blanchard, and architect Rozier Dedwylder formed Uptown Columbus, a nonprofit that focused on the economic revitalization of the central business district and along the riverfront. It bought distressed properties and resold them at low interest. The Seaboard Freight office and the Southern Plow building on Front Avenue were renovated in the mid-1980s, with the latter, renamed One Arsenal Place, becoming home to the chamber of commerce. Merchants Square in the 900 block of Front and Broadway adapted the Loeb warehouses for commercial space. The W. C. Bradley Company cemented its downtown commitment by renovating its warehouses along Front Avenue to serve as the corporate headquarters. The Iron Bank was remodeled for office space, while the Hardaway Company adapted the antebellum Webster Building. Carmike completed a modern black-glass corporate headquarters on Thirteenth Street in 1983. The following year, when Norfolk Southern Railway threatened to demolish the Sixth Avenue passenger depot, which had opened in 1901 but been defunct since 1971, HCF launched a Save Our Station crusade, raising $50,000 to buy the building. In 1987, TSYS agreed to renovate the depot into its headquarters, and in 1999 the chamber of commerce moved into the building. By 1990, downtown had two million square feet of office space housing twelve thousand workers. Among the first restaurants were Chris Losonsky's Tavern on the Square on Eleventh Street; Jim Morpeth and Scott Ressmeyer's Country's Barbecue, in a renovated bus station; and Buddy Nelms's the Loft, a Broadway restaurant with a music venue on the second floor.[6]

The boom had a homogenizing effect. Upper Broadway had been home to bars, adult theaters, and pornographic bookstores, which were prohibited from operating within six hundred feet of churches, teen centers, and playgrounds. Though the area was peaceful—as one reporter observed, "the gays don't bother the patrons at the porno parlor, and the people after lurid magazines leave the transvestites alone"—it was a "doomed habitat," as revitalization plans included sweeping clean the 1300 block. Uptown's enthusiasm also did not extend to the historic black business district at Sixth Avenue and Eighth Street. The William H. Spencer Memorial Restoration Society raised funds to save the 1912 Spencer House on Fourth Avenue. African American preservationists advocated saving the Ma Rainey House, the homes of educator Dr.

Manley Taylor and real estate agent E. E. Farley, and the First African Baptist, Friendship Baptist, and St. James African Methodist Episcopal Churches. As had historically held true for the black community, those efforts would depend mostly on self-help.⁷

The visionary leadership of the *Columbus Ledger-Enquirer*'s editors added structure and support to the city's renaissance. The country's first public journalism project, Columbus Beyond 2000: Agenda for Progress, sought input from a wide spectrum of residents. Executive editor Tom Kunkel invited local leaders to a symposium on the city's future that led to hundreds of interviews with black and white political, religious, and cultural leaders. A team of reporters began preparing a special section analyzing the city's problems and prospects. When Kunkel resigned before the project's completion, his successor, former managing editor Jack Swift, expanded the effort, and after more than a year of research, the special section was published on May 29–June 5, 1988. It reported that Columbus remained socially, racially, and economically divided. Slogans such as We're Talkin' Proud! devised by the chamber of commerce rang hollow to low-wage workers and the unemployed, while African Americans felt that they lacked equal rights and opportunities. The newspaper recommended diversifying Columbus's economy, improving roads, offering day care for working mothers, building a new civic center and public library, including minorities in city life, supporting the arts, and protecting the environment. Despite extensive publicity, the report evoked little community response. Swift refused to let the project fade, however, and in 1990 he initiated a task force, United Beyond 2000, that sponsored town meetings and interracial barbecues that in some cases brought black and white leaders together in a social setting for the first time. The task force encouraged citizens to direct their city's future, the focus of later public journalism. Many locals believed that the effort eschewed journalism's traditional objectivity, and a summer 1990 Knight-Ridder survey of the overworked newspaper staff elicited harsh condemnations of Swift. In November, he committed suicide.⁸

The newspaper then dropped the project, leading to questions about why the *Ledger-Enquirer* had failed to finish what it started. Despite the controversy, veteran newsman Billy Winn said that Beyond 2000 had a positive effect, leading progressive leaders to unite behind attorney Frank "Butch" Martin's 1990 campaign for mayor. Martin won the election on a Beyond 2000 platform that advocated economic, social, and racial progress and took aim at "cynicism and inertia." Two years into his term, he persuaded voters to pass a one-cent sales tax that dramatically changed Columbus, raising $65 million to replace the city's outdated sewer system, which was polluting the Chattahoochee; $26 million for a civic center on the South Commons; $15 million for a public safety building; and $35 million for parks and sidewalks.[9]

On March 30, 1990, the Georgia Environmental Protection Division had given Columbus five years to comply with the Federal Clean Water Act by replacing the antiquated sewer system, which poured raw sewage into the Chattahoochee after heavy rains. Water Works president Billy Turner suggested placing a large collection pipe on the riverbank with an asphalt maintenance road atop it. The city added lighting, benches, and drinking fountains, turning a sewer spill into an attraction, the Columbus RiverWalk. The first fifteen miles of the trail opened in 1993, drawing thousands to the Chattahoochee to run, bike, walk, and fish. By 2019, the RiverWalk stretched twenty-two miles from Oliver Dam to Fort Benning. The project inspired Columbus to take a fresh look at the Chattahoochee, and Martin believed that it convinced residents that their city could accomplish great things: "Instead of people looking down at the dirt on their shoes, [the RiverWalk] caused them to look up, where they saw something that was a symbol of civic pride." Also during the 1990s, the city and Water Works developed Oxbow Meadows on sixteen hundred acres along the river in South Columbus, with a science and ecology education center and an eighteen-hole golf course. The Bradley Company donated land for the exclusive River Club just below the Fourteenth Street dam and renovated the Eagle & Phenix mill into luxury condominiums and apartments. The city and United Cities Gas cleaned up the historic gasworks site by the Dillingham Bridge and it became part of Woodruff Park, high on the bank overlooking the RiverWalk. For their part, the chamber of commerce and Uptown focused on developing the urban riverfront.[10]

In 1994, American Rivers identified the Chattahoochee as one of the country's most threatened rivers. The U.S. Environmental Protection Agency found the river south of Atlanta to be "one of the nation's five worst" for dangerous pollutants. The city also found itself embroiled in the decades-long Apalachicola-Chattahoochee-Flint water wars, as the states of Georgia, Alabama, and Florida fought over the river system's water. In 1990, Alabama had filed suit to stop the U.S. Army Corps of Engineers from building reservoirs for Atlanta, arguing that the state

The Columbus RiverWalk opened in 1992. Columbus State University Archives, Columbus State University, Columbus, Georgia.

needed river flow for nuclear power plants. Florida joined in the suit to ensure freshwater to flush oyster beds in Apalachicola Bay. Columbus, which sought to protect the flow needed for its hydropower and drinking water, aligned with downriver interests against Atlanta. Years of negotiation and litigation produced no conclusion, and in 2014, the U.S. Supreme Court appointed a special master to mediate the dispute. After collecting testimony at a monthlong fall 2016 trial, the special master ruled in February 2017 that Georgia should have no cap on the water it draws from the Chattahoochee. Florida protested to the Supreme Court, but the Trump administration sided with Georgia in August 2017. The Supreme Court deferred a final ruling the following June, finding merit in Florida's claim of harm from upstream water consumption. A narrow Court majority ordered the special master to reconsider the evidence that Florida would benefit if Atlanta capped its water usage.[11]

Despite its many benefits, the creation of the RiverWalk did not entirely solve the problem of sewage being released into the Chattahoochee after heavy rains. The Columbus Water Works received its first National Pollutant Discharge Elimination System permit required by the EPA to operate a combined sewer system in 1992, and over the next twenty-five years, the Georgia Environmental Protection Division attempted to impose upgrades on Columbus's sewer system. The Water Works successfully rebuffed the state's efforts to require more stringent limits for fecal coliform bacteria in its discharges into the river. When the Water Works sought renewal of its permit in September 2017, the Georgia Environmental Protection Division again requested that the Water Works accept limits on effluents comparable to every other municipality on the Chattahoochee. The Water Works refused, arguing that its testing showed Columbus was compliant with acceptable average ranges for fecal coliform bacteria counts. However, testing by the Chattahoochee Riverkeeper showed that bacteria levels in the river after thunderstorms far exceeded the EPD's safe limit. Despite the Water Works' objections, in August 2018, the Environmental Protection Division issued a draft permit requiring more stringent limits on bacteria and more extensive monitoring of the river after heavy rain. Environmental regulators required that the Water Works post signs warning of health risks at downtown Columbus's dozen sewer outfalls emptying into the Chattahoochee and inform the public of sewage discharge events using "websites, newspaper, radio or TV announcements."[12] In late 2018, negotiations were ongoing between the EPD and the Water Works.

Mayor Martin was also responsible for bringing Olympic softball to Columbus in 1996, when the sport made its debut in the Games. The city beat out Augusta and DeKalb County by offering a "financial/cash incentive" of $2.75 million. Columbus, Phenix City, Fort Benning, and Columbus College collaborated to host the event, attracting millions of dollars in private donations to assist with what ultimately totaled $50.25 million in capital improvements, including the softball complex, with its $2 million stadium; the new civic center; the South RiverWalk; and renovations to Memorial Stadium and Golden Park. Fort Benning and Columbus College provided food, housing, security, medical care, and transportation for the eight teams. Carmen Cavezza, a former commanding general at Fort Benning, served as executive director of Columbus '96, heading a committee of more than one hundred local leaders. The ten-day Olympic competition opened on July 21, with sold-out crowds watching the U.S. team's 10–0 victory over Puerto Rico and subsequent contests. In the wake of the July 27 Olympic Park bombing in Atlanta, officials declared that the Games would continue with security tightened, as local leaders pointed out that the two hundred athletes and officials in the Olympic Village at Fort Benning were "with the guys with the M-16's on the roofs." The mostly American crowd thrilled to the U.S. gold medal victory over China, and Columbus received high marks for its "splendidly run" competition.[13]

The Olympics brought short- as well as long-term benefits to Columbus, with Martin enthusing, "The publicity we received from having the Olympics here...is probably the most important thing to happen in the history of Columbus." The Olympics generated $12.6 million in revenue as tourism spiked during and immediately after the Games. For the year as a whole, tourism brought $316.9 million to Columbus, up 15.7 percent from 1995—a greater increase than Atlanta experienced. The number of visitors grew 19.2 percent between 1995 and 1996, reaching almost a million. Three new hotels opened or were renovated during the Olympic year, with a fourth opening in 1997. Though the number of visitors declined to 828,000 in 1998, sports tourism boomed, as the city's Sports Council recruited tournaments for the softball complex and other recreation facilities. Athletic events' economic impact peaked at more than $20 million in 2008 before dropping to around $17 million in 2016, with nearly a third of that generated by the South Commons softball complex.[14]

The 1996 Columbus Challenge, a public-private campaign that raised more than $100 million for the arts, built on the optimism engendered by the Olympic success. A 1994 Uptown Master Plan had proposed the idea of a performing arts center, and leaders focused on bringing the idea to fruition with the understanding that it would have to be funded by a combination of public and private contributions and could not sit empty between shows. Adding to the momentum was the slated demolition of the Three Arts Theatre, which was home to the Columbus Symphony and the Miss Georgia Pageant, and Columbus College's desire for a new performing arts center. The school's president, Frank Brown, initially resisted a downtown site, but relocating the institution's arts programs downtown would enable music students to use the performing arts center during the day. Columbus's powerful state legislators, led by Tom Buck and Calvin Smyre, convinced Governor Zell Miller to make a $24 million appropriation in 1994. In November 1995, Bill Turner assembled the directors of the Columbus Symphony, the Springer Theatre, the Liberty Theatre, the Columbus Museum, the Historic Columbus Foundation, the Civil War Naval Museum, and the nascent Space Science Center at Columbus College and told them that the Bradley-Turner Foundation would put up a $20 million challenge grant for the new arts center and the participating cultural institutions. The money was donated within three months, and the foundation raised its goal, ultimately putting up $35 million. Members of the public donated $29 million, the state kicked in $24 million,

Bill Turner, 1995. From the W. C. Bradley Company.

and the city donated land and a parking deck, bringing the total to $101 million. The RiverCenter opened on May 5, 2012, with a performance by soprano Jessye Norman, who praised the hall.[15]

Opening in June 1996, the Coca-Cola Space Science Center was a part of the city's riverfront development initiative and was funded by the Columbus Challenge as well as by a grant from the soft drink giant. A replica of the Challenger space shuttle allows schoolchildren and other visitors to fly simulated moon missions, while the Omnisphere Theatre hosts solar system programs and night sky representations. The center also boasts an observatory and telescope, which it opens to the public at no charge about forty nights each year. Between 2012 and 2016, 1.73 million people viewed the cosmos via the observatory's website, while thirty-seven thousand people visited in person in 2016 alone. The center has also enabled students and professors to collaborate on research.[16]

The Columbus Challenge aided a $12 million renovation of the Springer Opera House in 1998–1999. The project maintained historic authenticity while installing state-of-the-art theatrical lighting, equipment, and spaces. The building's old hotel was made into offices and apartments for visiting artists. Director Paul Pierce credited the Challenge and CSU's RiverPark campus with enlivening downtown, as "the presence of that many students on our streets, in our stores, cafes and things has really brought the level of energy up downtown." A 2014 Springer renovation added a new children's theater, the Dorothy W. McClure Springer Theater Academy Education Center. As the project came to a close, Pierce touted the arts' $52 million annual economic impact in Columbus and highlighted the city's robust "theater district," which featured the Springer, three stages at the RiverCenter, and Columbus State's theater program. Despite help from the Columbus Challenge, however, the Liberty struggled to attract visitors. By 2015, the old black business district had few residents and fewer businesses, and many Columbus citizens thought the area was dangerous.[17]

By 1992, the concrete foundations under the Confederate Naval Museum's salvaged *Chattahoochee* and *Jackson* were sinking, and the ship remnants were falling apart. Wealthy donors as well as the Columbus Challenge came to the rescue, funding a new facility on the South Commons, overlooking the Chattahoochee. Renamed the National Civil War Naval Museum at Port Columbus, it opened in a new forty-thousand-square-foot building in March 2001, becoming the nation's only museum focused exclusively on Civil War navies. In addition to the *Chattahoochee* and *Jackson*, exhibits illustrate Civil War naval exploits and lives of common sailors. But the September 11 terrorist attacks caused Americans to curtail travel, and the 2008 recession worsened the museum's budget problems, with the number of visitors never topping more than about half of the expected fifty thousand to seventy-five thousand each year. In 2011, the city significantly cut its support, forcing reductions in staff and programming. Isolated as anticipated development never came to the South Commons, the museum lost support from some people who were angered at the decision to drop "Confederate" from the name; at the same time, it failed to attract interest from African Americans, who wanted nothing to do with the Confederate relics. The staff works to present more diverse perspectives, but just twenty thousand people visited in 2016.[18]

By the 1990s, Fort Benning's Infantry Museum had outgrown the post's old hospital building, but the institution was not included in the Columbus Challenge. The National Infantry Association launched a fund-raising drive in 1998, initially seeking $35 million but later raising its sights after Bill Turner urged the association to create a first-class institution. The association bought ninety acres across from Oxbow Meadows, and donations flooded in, including $5 million each from Congress and the Georgia legislature; millions from corporations, including Aflac, AT&T, and Samsung; and millions more from foundations, with the Bradley-Turner Foundation the largest private donor. With a final price tag of $91 million, the National Infantry Museum and Soldier Center opened on June 19, 2009, with a keynote address delivered by former secretary of state Colin Powell, who had been stationed at Fort Benning early in his career. The 190,000-square-foot facility showcases thousands of donated artifacts and averaged 300,000 visitors per year over its first seven years, making it Columbus's most popular attraction.[19]

The 1950 Bradley Library had also become outdated and overcrowded, but voters rejected a $700,000 bond issue for a new library in 1995. Turner lent his support two years later, leading the school board to endorse the idea as long as it required no new school taxes. In 1999, supporters considered the closed Columbus Square Mall site on Macon Road. Since the 1970s, the thoroughfare had delineated the predominantly African American lower-income neighborhoods in South Columbus from the wealthier and whiter northern enclaves. A public library on this "Macon-Dixon Line" might act as a community bridge. At around the same time, community activists near Weracoba Park defeated a proposal to turn Thirteenth Street into a six-lane thoroughfare that would have divided midtown neighborhoods. In 2001, the Historic Columbus Foundation created six midtown historic districts. These projects bonded community activists and led to the MidTown Project, which sought to sustain and enhance neighborhoods bordering Macon Road. The library location fit that vision perfectly.[20]

In November 1999, voters barely approved a one-cent special purpose local option sales tax that would generate $50.4 million for the library, but the plan continued to generate controversy. Many in North Columbus considered the Macon Road location unsafe. In addition, many of those who had voted in favor of the tax expected that the new library complex would include substantial green space, but the plan proposed only twenty acres of park and added government, commercial, and residential development. The condominiums were soon dropped from the proposal, leaving more open land, but then the Library Board provoked public ire by commissioning a $250,000 abstract sculpture for the entrance. In the wake of the Water Works' installation of a $239,000 seventeen-foot rock sculpture popularly known as "Viagra Falls" in front of the RiverCenter, members of the public felt that officials were out of touch with public sentiment, a perception enhanced by one library board member's statement that "if it's not controversial, then we will have failed miserably." After weeks of dispute, the Library Board withdrew the commission, though it still had to pay $35,000 to the sculptor.[21]

The new library opened on January 3, 2005, with three thousand people in attendance. Land near the library went to the school board, which four years later built an elegant administration building derided by critics as the Taj Mahal. The school district gave the city six acres for a natatorium, a citizens' service center, and a parking garage. Most of the remaining acreage was to become a park, resolving a decadelong fight over green space around the library. In 2005, MidTown commissioned a twenty-five-year master plan for six square miles from I-185 to Tenth Avenue along the Macon/Wynnton Road corridor. A 2015 Knight Foundation grant provided $200,000 for the development of walkable and bikeable corridors between midtown and Uptown. In 2016, the Mid-Town and Uptown organizations partnered with the Community Foundation to use Columbus Challenge funds to create "civic commons" where diverse citizens could mingle.[22]

Columbus College grew along with the city and helped in creating a vibrant middle class. The school offered a solid education for both African Americans and whites whose jobs, family, or economic limitations meant that they could not leave the city to pursue higher education. Graduates populated middle- and high-level management in local government and industry. Ray Lakes, the first African American to occupy a high-level administrative position at the college, called the institution the "great equalizer of Columbus," moving the city from dependence on low-wage jobs and Fort Benning to an "automated/knowledge-based economy." In October 1990, Columbus College teamed with TSYS and Columbus Tech to train computer programmers, graduating its first students with degrees in applied computer science in 1993. By that time, TSYS had become the world's largest credit card processor, and its leaders wanted to ensure that they had enough qualified programmers. After considering the possibility of moving the company elsewhere, they settled on the strategy of collaborating with Columbus College to develop an accelerated program that awarded students a data-processing certificate after just six to eight months of intensive coursework, a pace "unheard of in higher education." Students could finance their education with a state-backed loan repayable by working four years in a Georgia computer-related job. By 2008, the program had graduated about one thousand programmers, 99 percent of them hired by TSYS, which not only remained in Columbus but expanded and became a leading employer. In 2003, the college named its computer science department after the company, and the mutually beneficial relationship thrived, with TSYS donating $5 million to the College of Business in 2015 to establish the TSYS Cybersecurity Center for Financial Services.[23]

Columbus College's enrollment declined during the 1970s and 1980s, requiring cuts in programs, faculty, and staff. By 1986, it faced $800,000 in budget cuts, and campus morale plummeted. In January 1988, Frank Brown, formerly the school's vice president for finance, took over as president and began to revitalize the school. Columbus College opened its first student housing, transitioning away from an exclusively commuter school, and used repurposed bricks from the Shannon Hosiery Mill to construct the Thomas Y. Whitley clock tower, which became the institution's symbol. The college solidified its connection to the community with new outreach programs, including the Columbus Regional Mathematics Collaborative (1989), the Center for Excellence in Science and Education (1993), Oxbow Meadows Environmental Learning Center (1995), and the Coca-Cola Space Science Center (1996). Enrollment rose in the early 1990s, and the college evolved into a regional institution.[24]

On June 12, 1996, the board of regents granted the institution university status and renamed it Columbus State University. In 2001, the school launched a capital campaign to raise $67 million to enhance learning and service, teacher preparation, arts and culture, and technology and commerce. When the campaign closed in October 2005, CSU had raised more than $100 million, enabling enhancements to the RiverCenter's Schwob School of Music and the relocation of the fine and performing arts programs to the downtown RiverPark campus. The university transformed the Rankin Hotel into the Rankin Arts Center, with housing for 350 students on the top floors and administrative offices below. In 2007, an empty Pillowtex mill was converted into the Corn Center for Visual Arts and the Riverside Theater Complex, with studios, exhibition space, and a theater. In the same year, the Yancey Center at One Arsenal Place opened, housing the art, theater, communications, and history and geography departments. On the main campus, the capital campaign produced the Davidson Student Center, the Schuster Student Success Center, the Lumpkin athletic arena, and the Cunningham Center for leadership development. The capital campaign also permitted the school to purchase the Spencer House in Oxford, England, to use as a residential facility for study abroad, making CSU one of only a handful of American universities with a residence at the world's oldest English-speaking university—"pretty doggone high cotton," as President Brown noted.[25]

In January 2017, CSU's College of Education and Health Professions moved into the renovated 1930 *Ledger-Enquirer* building, meaning that about a third of the university's more than eight thousand students were taking classes downtown. By 2015, the RiverPark campus had an economic impact on Uptown that topped $21 million a year as faculty, staff, and students sought housing, dining, shopping, and entertainment. Overall, the university contributed $263.5 million to the local economy. That year, CSU launched the First Choice Campaign, another capital effort aimed at generating $105 million to "cement CSU's status as a favored destination for top students and faculty." It included funds for the RiverPark campus, scholarships and student support, new professors, an addition to the main campus Center for Commerce and Technology, and athletics. Within three years, the campaign had reached its goal.[26]

Columbus State had evolved into a diverse institution with a broad liberal arts and professional curriculum, offering forty-six undergraduate degree programs as well as master's, educational specialist, and doctoral degrees. In the 2017–2018 academic year, ethnic minorities accounted for almost half of the student body and nearly 30 percent of faculty, while women comprised 45 percent of the faculty and six of the school's nineteen administrators. By 2015, the school had granted around 60 percent of local residents' college degrees. Brown stressed the importance of CSU's relationship to local business and philanthropic leaders, noting that especially on the downtown campus, the college's growth came from "Columbus dollars": "The state does not have a single penny invested in the housing downtown and very little money invested in the buildings downtown."[27]

In 1992 Columbus voters for the first time elected the members of the board of education. Many observers saw the change as a step forward, and it indeed increased diversity, as three white men, two white women, two black men, and two black women won seats. However, turf battles became increasingly frequent. In May 1991, the local NAACP had revived the *Lockett* desegregation suit, charging the appointed board with preserving white-majority schools by ignoring the racial ratios that had been mandated in 1971. Following a June 1993 vote along racial lines, the board sought to have the suit dismissed. In May 1997, the Eleventh Circuit Court granted the Muscogee County School District (MCSD) unitary status, indicating that it had removed all vestiges of intentional segregation. The NAACP chose not to appeal, instead asking the board to work toward desegregation, increase the number of African American teachers and administrators, and raise minority achievement.[28]

In the early 1990s, MCSD established elementary and secondary magnet schools as one way to promote desegregation. Though some gains occurred, the magnet schools did not prove to be a panacea. Despite $8 million in upgrades, Carver High School, the science, technology, and engineering magnet, remained nearly 95 percent African American. At Downtown Elementary School, which opened in 1995 to serve inner-city African American students, the principal developed a magnet program by surveying predominantly white downtown workers whose children were a target population, and the number of white students who "volunteered" to attend determined the number of black children admitted. Columbus High School started a "school within a school" liberal arts magnet in 1991 and became a total magnet school a decade later, choosing students through competitive testing and interviews. Black enrollment declined from 37 percent in 1999 to less than 25 percent in 2016, evoking charges that it was a private school for elites. By 2018, magnet schools in traditionally white neighborhoods were fairly diverse, but with the exception of Hannan Elementary, all magnets in African American neighborhoods had student populations more than 85 percent black.[29]

Students in most Columbus public schools performed below the state average on standardized tests. In 2015, only one middle and two elementary schools had a majority of students pass the tests. The two high schools that recorded pass rates above the state average were the district's whitest and wealthiest. All but two failing elementary and middle schools were Title I schools that served the poorest students. Increasing poverty among school-age children complicated efforts to improve their education. By 2016, 71 percent of MCSD students lived in poverty, an increase of 10 percent in five years. Thirty-seven of the district's fifty-three schools were Title I, receiving almost $10 million in federal allocations to equalize educational quality between haves and have-nots.[30]

In 2016, 92 percent of Columbus's school-age children attended public educational institutions, indicating support from even well-off families. For more prosperous students in north-side schools and in exclusive schools such as the Britt David Elementary Computer Magnet Academy and Columbus High, the future looked bright. Those schools attracted the ablest teachers, the highest-achieving students, and the most parental support. Hired in 2013, superintendent David Lewis tackled the north-south split and the "insidious impediment" of poverty, proposing graduation coaches, a program to encourage dropouts to return to school, and an "early warning system" to track at-risk students. He divided the district into three decentralized supervisory zones to erase the Macon-Dixon Line. With local property taxes frozen since 1982 and state budget reductions after the 2008 recession, Lewis cut more than 10 percent in plant services, transportation, nutrition, and central administration, realizing $1 million in savings for the district by 2015 and raising graduation rates at every high school so that the MSCD exceeded the state average. In 2015, 54 percent of voters approved another special purpose local option tax for capital projects, among them rebuilding Spencer High School. Nevertheless, stark inequities persisted between schools in North and South Columbus, but many residents, including the chamber of commerce president, recognized that "education is the only way" to improve the quality of life for students living in poverty.[31]

In 2016, about 20 percent of Columbus residents—and more than 30 percent of the city's children—lived in poverty. Per capita income was close to the national average, but median household income was $40,388, below both the state and national averages. Between 2008 and 2013, the number of local households with incomes greater than $150,000 increased by 23.2 percent, while the percentage of families earning less than $50,000 changed little. Recognizing that such high poverty rates and persistent inequities would prevent Columbus from thriving, public, private, and nonprofit leaders launched the Regional Prosperity Initiative (subsequently renamed Columbus 2025) to improve the area's quality of life. The program's strategies included a "cradle-to-career" alignment of education, training, business, and social services; expanding prekindergarten programs, career and apprenticeship opportunities; mentoring for at-risk students; and adult education. In addition, a dynamic marketing campaign aimed to attract talented workers, new firms, and investment.[32]

Other efforts sought to combat the problem of homelessness. In 1987, a coalition of individuals and service providers formed the Metropolitan Columbus Task Force for the Homeless, which incorporated as a nonprofit in 1990. Six years later, the Housing Authority asked the task force to administer an Emergency Shelter Grant Program with a full-time office and staff to assist the estimated eighteen hundred people living on the streets or in temporary shelters. The program was renamed the Homeless Resource Network in 2004 and offered mail service, storage, help in obtaining identification, and transportation as well as temporary grants that would enable people to pay rent or utilities and thus avoid becoming homeless. Columbus joined seventy-one other U.S. cities in the Zero: 2016 (now Built for Zero) campaign to end veteran and chronic homelessness. The goal was to get the most at-risk individuals off the street by providing first housing and then health and social services. A $1.4 million grant from the U.S. Department of Housing and Urban Development increased the number of beds in Columbus's temporary shelters, but homelessness persisted. In December 2016, the Homeless Resource Network served about 450 individuals living in shelters or on the street; thirteen months later, 201 individuals were in shelters, while another 78 were unsheltered.[33]

As of 2016, one in four of Columbus's children and one in five of the city's adults faced chronic hunger. Feeding the Valley, one of Georgia's seven regional food banks, focused on providing food to soup kitchens, food pantries, senior and youth centers, churches, and other nonprofits, serving more than 260 partner agencies. Its Mobile Pantry program delivered boxes to rural families in need, while its kitchen prepared about one hundred hot meals each day for seniors through Meals on Wheels. In addition, donations from grassroots food drives and grocery stores enabled Feed the Valley to distribute seven million pounds of food annually to forty thousand people—nearly 10 percent of the population in its coverage area. Feeding the Valley opened a new distribution center in North Columbus in 2017, predicting that in five years, it would provide ten million pounds of food to fifty-five thousand people.[34]

Around 1988, Columbus began to have issues with organized gangs. The first gang-related death occurred in April 1990 during a Friday night shootout in the Baker High School parking lot. Three days after the killing, the police department created a special gang task force, but it had little initial success. In 1991 and 1992, shootings occurred at the Columbus Square Mall and at several middle and high schools. Police expanded the task force, and over a nine-day span in October 1993, officers arrested seventeen gang members on more than fifty charges, including armed robbery, auto theft, burglary, kidnapping, and rape. Gang membership peaked at an estimated thirty-five hundred in 1997, before the Gang Resistance Education and Training program in schools and

MCSD's zero-tolerance policy reduced gang activity by one-third the following year. Nevertheless, gangs have remained a major factor in Columbus crime.[35]

Overall crime rates declined significantly between the early 1990s and 2015, but the number of violent and property crimes remained higher than state and national levels. Police acknowledged a direct correlation between crime and poverty, as most perpetrators came from low-income neighborhoods with few economic opportunities, family instability, and blighted property. Moreover, the public did not perceive the city's crime situation as improving, with more than one-third of respondents to Regional Prosperity Initiative surveys rating their personal and property safety "below average" or "very poor." This discrepancy may have resulted from some isolated but sensational acts of violence. In July 1996, for example, a nineteen-year-old randomly shot passersby at Thirtieth Avenue and Radcliff Street, killing three and critically wounding four. After a February 2005 dispute with his wife, Clarence Moore grabbed a hunting knife and killed his two sons before slitting his own throat. On March 4, 2008, angered at his girlfriend's infidelity, Eddie Harrington drove their three-year-old son and twenty-three-month-old twin girls to a wooded area in Midland, shot each in the head and then shot himself. A week later, a retired teacher walked into Doctors Hospital and gunned down two hospital workers and a bystander, apparently seeking to avenge his mother's 2004 death at the facility. And on January 4, 2016, three young men bludgeoned to death a Upatoi woman and her two grandchildren before stealing a car, clothes, and jewelry.[36]

The perpetrators of all of these crimes were African American, and Muscogee County's black residents were responsible for a disproportionate share of offenses, including the majority of violent crimes in black neighborhoods. Columbus experienced an all-time high of thirty-five murders in 2017, with thirty-two of the victims African Americans and twenty-three of them in their teens or twenties. But the true cause of these high rates was not race but poverty: African Americans were far more likely than whites to live in conditions incubating crime. In 2016, 25 percent of the city's black residents lived in poverty, more than three times the 8 percent rate for whites. African Americans were twice as likely to be unemployed as whites and were more likely to attend the lowest-performing schools, to drop out, and to live in the most blighted areas. Further, African Americans' long history of mistrust of law enforcement was reinforced when a white Muscogee deputy sheriff killed an unarmed black man during a traffic stop on December 10, 2003. Ken-

A march protesting the shooting of Kenneth Walker, January 15, 2005.
The Militant/Bill Arth.

neth Walker, a thirty-nine-year-old Blue Cross/Blue Shield employee with no police record, was shot after the black SUV in which he was a passenger was mistaken for one belonging to a drug dealer. On February 19, 2004, the deputy was fired for refusing to cooperate with investigators. Walker's wife, Cheryl, filed a $100 million civil suit in U.S. District Court against the sheriff's office, the sheriff, and the deputy, but the court granted the sheriff immunity. In November 2004, a special prosecutor allowed the deputy to give unsworn testimony to a grand jury. Though he initially had said he fired intentionally, the deputy cried, apologized, and told the grand jury he tripped and shot accidentally. The grand jury declined to indict him, fanning popular outrage over the killing.[37]

On the first anniversary of Walker's shooting, his family filed another $100 million civil suit in Muscogee Superior Court against the county, the sheriff, and the deputy. On January 11, 2005, 150 white people demonstrated on behalf of the deputy on the Government Center steps. That turnout was dwarfed by the eight thousand people who attended a Martin Luther King Jr. Day rally honoring Walker at which the Reverend Jesse Jackson, Southern Christian Leadership Conference founder Joseph Lowery, and television judge Greg Mathis called for justice. But the deputy was never charged. Mayor Jim Wetherington worked with former mayor Frank Martin and wealthy donors to settle with Cheryl Walker for $280,000 in 2008, and the Columbus Council approved $200,000 to be placed in trust for the Walkers' daughter. Both the sheriff and the district attorney had won reelection in 2004, eleven months after Walker's death, but both were defeated four years later. Despite the calls for change in the Columbus police department's relationship with members of the African American community, the percentages of African American and female police officers changed little in the decade after Kenneth Walker's death, and many black residents continue to believe that officers have treated them unfairly. Numerous entities—the local government, churches, corporations, and civic groups—have worked to improve race relations, and the city's black population has continued to grow, reaching 45.5 percent in 2010. By 2016, Columbus ranked ninth among U.S. cities for African American households making $100,000 or more. Yet the racial divide persists. Only in 2000 were the first African American members admitted to the Columbus Country Club. A decade and a half later, people of different races work together and have equal access to public accommodations, but neighborhoods, churches, private social clubs, and schools largely remain segregated.[38]

African Americans and women have continued to make gains in officeholding. African American Calvin Smyre has represented Columbus in the Georgia General Assembly since 1975, while Ed Harbison and Carolyn Hughley have served there since 1993. Voters chose the first black county marshal in 1988. In 2018, the ten members of the Columbus Council included four women—two of them African American and one Hispanic—and two black men. The first female mayor won election in 2010 and reelection four years later. Voters chose Columbus's first female sheriff in 2016. In 1988, the council had established the Mayor's Commission on Women and Minorities in response to complaints of racial and gender disparities in hiring, treatment, and promotion. The number of women and minorities in city government has slowly increased, and as of 2015 women accounted for 36 percent of government workers and held one-third of upper management and professional positions. Minorities held 43 percent of city jobs but nearly two-thirds occupied lower-level clerical or service positions. The city's 2015 affirmative action report acknowledged that women and minorities were underrepresented as administrators, technicians, and professionals.[39]

From the 1950s through the mid-1980s, Columbus's economy stagnated, with only six new local businesses opening. As the national economy expanded in the 1990s, the city attracted nineteen new businesses, capital investments exceeding $500,000, and seven thousand jobs, but the economy sagged again after the turn of the millennium. The city's growth lagged behind that of Georgia as a whole: between 1970 and 2013, Georgia's population increased by 117 percent, but Columbus grew by only 24 percent. Troop levels at Fort Benning fluctuated wildly from year to year. In 2005, the Base Realignment and Closure Commission consolidated the Armor School at Fort Knox with Fort Benning's Infantry School to create the new Maneuver Center for Excellence. Columbus leaders expected this reorganization to create a "seismic shift," with an influx of thirty-five thousand soldiers, dependents, and civilian workers by 2011. As the country headed into recession in 2008, city leaders believed that these new residents would insulate Columbus from some of the effects of the weakening economy, and voters approved a one-cent sales tax to put one hundred more police officers on the streets and fund transportation improvements. Such projections proved overly optimistic: although the $3.5 billion that the army spent on the move benefited the local economy, Benning's population grew by only eighty-six hundred between 2008 and 2012, the city's unemployment rate hovered around 10 percent through 2009 and 2010, and its March 2016 unemployment rate of 6.8 percent remained the highest in the state. To make matters worse, in 2016, the army announced a force reduction at Fort Benning, which was expected to lead to the loss of hundreds of local jobs, depress the housing market, and hurt restaurants and retailers. Unemployment had dropped to 4.8 percent by March 2018, still the highest among Georgia's major cities.[40]

Columbus's once-dominant textile industry had faded into history by the early 2000s. The Bibb was the first major mill to close. After declining from a peak of five thousand operatives during World War II to about eighteen hundred in the early 1970s, the Bibb announced layoffs of between three hundred and four hundred workers in 1997 and filed for bankruptcy. In March 1998, the mill shut down, throwing its remaining 250 millhands out of work. The closure left Bibb City with no income, and in December 2000, the town's council dissolved its ninety-one-year-old charter and became part of Columbus. Shortly after midnight on October 20, 2008, a fire swept through the empty mill, destroying the 750,000-square-foot structure and leaving only the facade, its clock stopped forever. In 1997, Fieldcrest sold the former Muscogee Mills and the Eagle & Phenix to Pillowtex for $700 million, but within five years, Pillowtex had shut down the last of the river mills. In December 2003 the W. C. Bradley Company repurchased the Eagle & Phenix and in 2005 announced plans to turn Mill No. 3 into luxury condominiums. It also renovated Mill No. 2 into apartments. Upriver at the North Highlands dam, the former Columbus Manufacturing, too, became loft apartments. Swift Mills, at one time the second-largest producer of denim in the United States, furloughed its thirteen hundred workers in the late 1990s as a consequence of the depressed market and Mexican competition. In 2006, Swift shut down its Sixth Avenue spinning mill and moved operations to the Flat Rock Road plant, but that facility soon closed as well. A developer bought the Sixth Avenue mill in 2007, intending to renovate it into loft apartments and commercial and office space, but on November 5, 2011, a fire destroyed more than half the mill. In 2016, after the developer had renovated the surviving structures, technology firm Delta Data moved from North Columbus into the first floor, lured by "the resurgence and vibrance of downtown."[41]

In April 1996, as TSYS was considering leaving Columbus, the city agreed to give the company fifty riverside acres that included the Muscogee Mill complex, antebellum Mott House, and 1907 Carnegie Library, all of which were part of the Historic Riverfront Industrial District National Landmark. If the construction went forward, the National Trust threatened to remove the district's designation. After lengthy negotiations, the Historic Columbus Foundation, Georgia Historic Preservation Division, and local Board of Historic Architectural Review agreed to Muscogee Mills' demolition if TSYS would preserve the Mott House and the Carnegie Library facade. Though preservationists bemoaned the loss of the mill, the new downtown campus was expected to pump $3.7 billion into city coffers over five years and anchor downtown's rebirth. In 2013, TSYS began a major renovation of the Mott House, Columbus's last antebellum riverfront mansion, but on September 7, 2014, an early morning fire gutted the building. TSYS demolished the remainder in 2015 and the following year created a memorial on the site featuring a re-created facade and historical panels.[42]

TSYS grew robustly through the early 2000s. After spending five years and more than $100 million developing a state-of-the-art processing platform, the company signed a deal for AT&T's Universal Card in 1990, adding thirty-five million accounts and more than $300 million in annual income. TSYS added Bank of America and Sears by 1996, more than doubling its business again. By the mid-1990s, it had become a bulwark of the local economy. It built a 110,000-square-foot processing facility to accommodate its thousands of local workers. On December 31, 2007, TSYS and its parent company, Synovus, parted ways, leaving TSYS free to use its stock and dividends for acquisitions. Despite periodic setbacks and layoffs, especially during the 2008 global recession, the firm did business in more than eighty countries and handled seven hundred million accounts by 2015, when it ranked as the top third-party card processor in the United States, Canada, and China and second in Europe. Its 47.8 percent total shareholder return made it the ninth-best stock in the S&P 500. TSYS employed about 10,500 people worldwide, 4,800 of them in Columbus, where it was the largest private local employer. It has been rated among the best companies to work for in America as well as among the world's most ethical companies.[43]

Synovus fared less well after the split. Though it was highly profitable through the 1990s and in 1998 was named *Fortune*'s best U.S. company to work for, Synovus nearly collapsed in the 2008 global financial crisis. Its market value dropped by more than one-third, it posted twelve consecutive quarterly losses, its stock plummeted from nearly $100 per share in 2007 to less than $2 in 2011, and it laid off 850 employees and closed thirty-nine bank branches. The company borrowed almost $1 billion from the federal Troubled Asset Relief Program to stay afloat. The crisis stemmed from a questionable $220 million insider loan that CEO Jim Blanchard had offered in 2000 to the head of the Sea Island Company, a family friend, as part of a plan to renovate the Sea Island resort into a five-star destination. When the 2007 housing slump hit, the resort scheme crumbled under the mountain of debt. Synovus shareholders filed suit in July 2009, charging Blanchard, who had retired as CEO in 2005 but remained a board member, and other executives with gross mismanagement. According to the suit, company officials had issued "materially false and misleading statements" about the Sea Island deal to artificially inflate stock prices. Blanchard retired from the board in April 2012, ending his forty-two-year relationship with the bank, and just under two years later, Synovus settled with its shareholders for $11.8 million, with the board agreeing to adopt policies to prevent "excessive risk."[44]

Kessel Stelling came to Synovus as president and COO in February 2010, took over as CEO in May, and led the company to sound financial footing. Synovus returned to profitability in the fourth quarter of 2011, and its stock slowly climbed out of the cellar. After paying off its federal loan in 2013, Synovus became Georgia's second-largest bank in terms of deposits, posting a $215.8 million profit in 2015. The company employed about one thousand people in the Columbus area and had $29 billion in assets spread throughout the Southeast. In 2017, it announced that Columbus Bank and Trust, a local institution since 1930, would change its name to Synovus.⁴⁵

By far Columbus's most successful company in the 1990s and early 2000s, Aflac became an international powerhouse. In 2016, it not only ranked as the top U.S. individual voluntary insurance provider but also insured 25 percent of Japanese households. Between 1984 and 2004, the value of Aflac stock increased by an astounding seventy-eight times, with shareholders enjoying 20 percent annual gains and dividends increasing every year. After Dan Amos took the helm in 1991, revenue grew from $2.7 billion to more than $20 billion in 2015. The company's North Columbus campus added two thousand jobs in 2005 and a 165,000-square-foot technology facility in April 2009. Its 3,670 local jobs made it Columbus's second-largest private employer, and it had another 4,500 employees spread around the world. The 2008 financial crisis had little effect on Aflac's trajectory, with sales increasing annually from 2008 to 2013. The stock outperformed the S&P 500 by 12 percent in 2008. Japan, the source of 74 percent of the company's revenue, proved a drag on Aflac's profitability during this period, however. The yen declined 30 percent against the dollar from 2012 to 2015, and Japan's recession caused profits to decline by 6 percent between 2014 and 2015 despite a 10 percent jump in medical and cancer insurance sales. Amos mitigated the damage by diversifying Aflac's products and expanding its U.S. market so that accident, critical illness, life, hospital, short-term disability, dental, and vision insurance accounted for 75 percent of its sales. Much of this growth was spurred by an enormously successful advertising campaign that began in 2000 and featured the company mascot, the Duck, quacking "Aflac!" By 2016, Aflac's brand recognition had soared to 94 percent, making it among the world's best-known enterprises.⁴⁶

Fortune has regularly named Aflac as one of the world's most admired companies, as one of the best companies to work for, and as one of the most ethical companies. *Black Enterprise* has also consistently given Aflac high marks for diversity, reflecting Amos's view that surrounding himself with people from a variety of backgrounds "is a living, breathing philosophy that also makes good business sense." In 2016, Aflac's U.S. workforce was composed of roughly equal numbers of white women, women of color, and men. Forty-three percent of employees were minorities. Among the company's leaders, 28 percent were female and 22 percent were nonwhite.⁴⁷

Manufacturing still played a significant role in Columbus's economy. More than 7 percent of local workers—nearly eleven thousand people—held industrial jobs in 2014. Pratt & Whitney was Columbus's largest industrial employer in 2016, with a thousand skilled workers in its Engine Repair Center. After the plant hit full production in the late 1980s, its parent company in Connecticut, United Technologies Corporation, lost 76 percent in profits as global recession and conflict reduced air travel, leading the company to announce impending job cuts and plant closures. On April 14, 1993, after meeting with A. J. McClung, the president of the Columbus Chamber of Commerce, and Georgia's lieutenant governor, company officials declared that the Columbus plant would stay open. The facility's nonunion workforce, which received lower wages and reduced benefits than were offered elsewhere, and its modern technology also helped the plant weather the 2008–2012 global recession. In 2009, Pratt & Whitney partnered with Columbus Tech to train gas turbine engine certified manufacturing specialists. Major upgrades to the plant in 2013 and 2016 allowed heavy maintenance, refurbishment, repair, and testing of Pratt & Whitney's new fuel-efficient geared turbofan engine. In February 2017, the company announced that its Columbus operations would undergo a $386 million expansion that would add five hundred jobs and a twenty-thousand-square-foot facility to manufacture turbine disks and jet engine compressors.[48]

In the early 2000s, Hostess Brands, the parent company of Dolly Madison Bakery, whose Victory Drive facility had enticed passersby with its aromas since 1971, filed two bankruptcies, amassed a huge debt, and lost market share. On November 14, 2012, embroiled in a bitter dispute with its bakers' union, Hostess abruptly closed 565 distribution centers and 33 snack-food factories, including the one in Columbus. The company reorganized and in April 2013 reopened the plant, hiring about two hundred workers to make Twinkies and Ding Dongs. Forty more joined in 2016, with employment projected eventually to rise to about three hundred. Snack food giant Snyder's-Lance completed a $10.5 million expansion in 2010 but announced six years later that it would stop shelling peanuts in Columbus. In 2018 Campbell Soup acquired Snyder's-Lance for $6.1 billion, combining it with Pepperidge Farms to create Campbell Snacks.[49]

Columbus's economy received a shot in the arm from the arrival of additional industries in the early 2000s. In 2000, Kodak opened a 276,000-square-foot facility that made high-tech digital plates to print books, magazines, boxes, and bumper stickers. It added a third production line in 2009 and expanded again in 2015. In 2010, Fortune 500 company Nash-Finch/MDV spent $25 million on a four-hundred-thousand-square-foot building that would distribute food to military commissaries and post exchanges. NCR Technologies (formerly National Cash Register) moved its headquarters to Georgia in 2009 and invested $27 million in a high-tech Columbus facility at which five hundred employees built ATMs. In 2012, the plant expanded to make self-service point-of-sale machines for hotels and restaurants. But a 2018 consolidation resulted in the closing of all of NCR's Columbus plants and the loss of more than one thousand jobs.[50]

By 1996, Carmike Cinemas had become the largest U.S. theater chain, with three hundred theaters in thirty-five states. Faced with cutthroat competition and few hit films, however, Carmike filed for bankruptcy in 2000. The company struggled after emerging from bankruptcy in 2002, recording a $127 million loss in 2007. After its stock fell below three dollars a share, the board of directors fired longtime CEO Michael Patrick and hired David Passman. The company expanded over the next five years, acquiring additional theater chains, posting healthy profits, and raising the stock's value to thirty-four dollars per share by 2016, when the Carmike board approved a $1.1 billion buyout offer from Chinese-owned AMC Entertainment Holdings. AMC decided to retain the Carmike brand but close the company headquarters at First Avenue and Thirteenth Street, bringing to an end the firm's century-long history in Columbus.[51]

By 1995, only eighteen of the sixty-three storefronts at the Columbus Square Mall were occupied, and that number fell even further over the next few years. With plaster flaking and ceilings leaking, the mall closed its doors in March 2001. Peachtree Mall and Main Street Village opened in North Columbus in 1985, while Columbus Park Crossing, farther north off Veterans Parkway, opened in 2002. Expansions north to the county line created suburban sprawl and its accompanying traffic, safety, and pollution issues. Retail in those areas hurt Peachtree Mall, which was named one of Georgia's ten worst malls in 2014 and which struggled to hold onto high-end stores, particularly in the wake of two 2016 shootings. Conversely, Uptown experienced a renaissance, bolstered by a $14 million Broadway streetscape renovation. By 2015, the area boasted forty-four retail stores and twenty-nine restaurants, although rent increases forced out longtime lower-end stores such as the Movin' Man. Seeking retail rents lower than those in North Columbus, some businesses moved downtown.[52]

Fort Benning retained its status as Columbus's major economic engine. In 2014, more than 45,500 soldiers and civilians worked at what had become the third-largest U.S. base in terms of troop strength. It annually poured $5 billion into the local economy. Including dependents and retired service members, more than one hundred thousand local residents had ties to Benning. After the military decreed that all jobs were open to women, the first females seeking positions as Army Rangers trained at Fort Benning in the summer of 2015, with two successfully completing the rigorous program. In late 2015, however, the army announced that to comply with the Budget Control Act of 2011, it was cutting more than thirty-four hundred positions in Benning's Third Brigade, removing twenty-four hundred soldiers by the end of fiscal year 2017 and leading to the elimination of another thousand local jobs. These reductions were partially offset when eight hundred members of the new Security Force Assistance Brigade arrived at Benning in late 2017. The brigade's senior NCOs and officers were tasked with advising and assisting foreign security forces.[53]

The School of the Americas (SOA), brought to Fort Benning by John and Elena Amos, trained more than sixty-four thousand soldiers "to promote military professionalism, foster cooperation among the multinational military forces in Latin America, and expand Latin American armed forces' knowledge of United States customs and traditions." But SOA graduates were also responsible for such atrocities as the assassination of Archbishop Oscar Romero and the rapes and murders of four American nuns in 1980 in El Salvador as well as for torture and executions in Chile, Colombia, and Argentina. In 1990, Maryknoll priest Roy Bourgeois, who knew two of the nuns, formed the School of the Americas Watch, whose prayer vigils at Benning's gates drew thousands of participants, most of them Catholic students from northern universities. In 1995, when thirteen protesters trespassed on base property, J. Robert Elliott sentenced them to serve between three and six months in prison, galvanizing the movement. It gained further momentum the following year, when the public learned that SOA training manuals provided instruction on methods of torture, and subsequent protests attracted as many as twenty thousand participants. Despite local support for the SOA and resentment of these "outside agitators," their presence constituted an economic boon, with local motels and restaurants courting protesters "like any other convention group." The army closed the SOA in 2000 and replaced it with the Western Institute for Security Cooperation, which offered essentially the same curriculum and instructors and continued to face charges that it was exporting "death squads." Starting in 2016, SOA Watch scaled down the Columbus event and shifted its focus to immigration, urging supporters to join a Convergence at the Border to decry "criminalization of migrants, asylum seekers, refugees and people of color."[54]

In the early 2000s, new restaurants, stores, and lofts crept northward from Tenth Street, mainly along Broadway but also expanding on cross streets toward Front and First Avenues. By 2015 developers' attention spread to blighted and underutilized areas. In March 2016 the city council approved the creation of tax allocation districts (TADs), allowing public funds to attract private development. After the project's completion, increases in property taxes would repay the public investment. As CSU's College of Education building opened, the Uptown business district TAD promoted development in the 1200 block of Broadway. Investors renovated the four-story Raymond Rowe Furniture building to house a mix of retail shops, restaurants, offices, and apartments. At the other end of the block, a technology company moved from a North Columbus office park into the old Holiday House furniture store, which the Bradley Company refurbished. Other new tenants included a hotel, liquor store, confectionary, fitness center, athletic store, and craft beer bar.[55]

A second TAD ran along the Chattahoochee between TSYS and Bibb City, a neighborhood filled with public housing and dilapidated mill cottages. A February 2016 task force produced a master plan for City Village, an ambitious decade-plus redevelopment that called for public housing to be relocated to a new mixed-income neighborhood farther north. The plan included renovation and new construction of river-view mixed-income homes as well as commercial development and pedestrian and bike paths that would connect to the RiverWalk. Historic Columbus partnered in a project aimed to redevelop the derelict City Mills and in March 2018 announced plans to attract a brewery, restaurant, bike shop, and exercise studio to the historic building.[56]

The third TAD encompassed the Liberty District and South Commons in accordance with a 2003 master plan. In 2012–2013, the city spent $37 million to install storm sewers and a streetscape on Sixth Avenue, but a Housing Authority proposal to erect one hundred mixed-income apartments near the Liberty Theatre hit a roadblock. Some stakeholders, including Lizzie Lunsford's granddaughter, objected that the master plan had called for mixed commercial, civic, entertainment, and residential development rather than the high-density housing contained in the proposal. City officials warned that if this proposal were rejected, future residential development would be unlikely and "the Liberty District will sit dormant for at least a decade." The neighborhood's historic churches, funeral homes, and Masonic lodges were alive and well, but the district's core remained gutted buildings and vacant lots. In 2017, the city designated $3.4 million to add sidewalks and bike lanes to Martin Luther King Jr. Boulevard east of the Liberty District, enhancing a planned Martin Luther King Jr. Outdoor Learning Trail to highlight local African American history. Soon thereafter, the Alpha Kappa Alpha sorority purchased 1.78 acres near the Liberty Theatre to build an event center.[57]

In 2016, the Housing Authority demolished Booker T. Washington Apartments, replacing them with Columbus Commons, a 106-unit mixed-income complex that opened in November 2017. The land fronting Victory Drive was reserved for commercial development, while directly across the road, the South Commons received fresh scrutiny. The last of Columbus's historic commons was home to Golden Park, Memorial Stadium, the Civic Center, the Ice Rink, and Olympic softball fields, but by 2016, Golden Park could no longer keep a professional baseball team, and the city wanted to sell the stadium. However, in 1910, the General Assembly had restricted the South Commons to recreational use. A citizens group, Friends of the South Commons, organized to develop a comprehensive plan for the Commons and repurpose the historic ballpark. A major step forward occurred in 2018, when the state docks returned to the city with a plan for the chemical tanks overlooking the RiverWalk to be removed.[58]

The fourth TAD covered Benning Technology Park in South Columbus, a $72 million defense contractor hub that could employ more than one thousand people. Traditionally working class and majority African American, South Columbus had long been the city's stepchild and was moribund by the 1980s. After retiring from the U.S. Army in 1968, Lonnie Jackson settled in South Columbus and began working to improve the area. In 1983, he started Combined Communities of Southeast Columbus, which fought illiteracy by offering free tutoring. By the time of Jackson's death in 2006, the program had served more than twenty thousand people. Jackson also led voter registration drives and cleanup campaigns, and his efforts earned him recognition from President Bill Clinton in 1992. In 2009–2010, the Housing Authority demolished Baker Village and built 296 mixed-income units at Arbor Pointe. Three private apartment complexes replaced nearby trailer parks, while five new motels opened their doors, four along Victory Drive and one at the National Infantry Museum. A twenty-four-hour Super Walmart opened on Victory Drive in June 2016, bringing two hundred new jobs. Despite such promising economic growth, crime and poverty persist, and the area remains isolated and bisected by six-lane Victory Drive.[59]

On March 21, 2012, hundreds of people thronged the Chattahoochee's banks to watch dynamite blow apart the Eagle & Phenix dam. A year later, a similar crowd witnessed the City Mills dam's demolition. For the first time since 1828, the river flowed freely through downtown Columbus, creating the longest urban whitewater course in the United States. In 1998, John Turner, Bill Turner's son and a Bradley Company executive, had started a crusade to return the river to a natural state. Boosters had for years been searching for a unique tourist attraction, and in 1994, a consultant had proposed a virtual reality ride down simulated rapids. Turner thought the real thing would be better. Historic Columbus backed the project but wanted to preserve the powerhouses and wings of the historic dams. The Chattahoochee River Restoration Project used enhanced technology to explore the riverbed and create a challenging yet safe 2.5-mile whitewater course. Despite the daunting $23 million price tag, a Columbus State University study suggested that the benefits would be worth it: seven hundred new jobs, nearly two hundred thousand annual visitors, $300,000 annually in new revenue from hotel/motel taxes, and $1.7 million in sales taxes—a total impact of $42 million. An added benefit was environmental. With whitewater restored, endangered shoal lilies and shoal bass would reappear. Construction of the course began in August 2011. The Fourteenth Street bridge, closed to cars since the opening of the Thirteenth Street bridge in 2000, was renovated as a pedestrian walkway. Turner stood on it in March 2013 as he announced that the whitewater course would open on Memorial Day weekend. That summer, sixteen thousand visitors rode the rapids, a number that had topped one hundred thousand by the end of 2016.[60]

Columbus finally had embraced the river that birthed it. The whitewater park attracted locals and tourists downtown. In 2015, nearly two million visitors spent $340 million in the area, contributing to forty-five hundred jobs. After CSU moved downtown, the green space above the RiverWalk became Woodruff Park, popular for festivals, bike and road

Whitewater rafting on the Chattahoochee, 2012.
Photograph by Tim Chitwood.

races, and other gatherings. The country's only zip line across state lines opened over the river in 2014, and two years later, fifteen thousand adventure seekers experienced the one-hundred-foot, forty-mile-per-hour ride from Georgia to Alabama. Property values along the Chattahoochee were expected to increase up to 60 percent after completion of the whitewater course. In March 2017, the W. C. Bradley Company announced plans for the Rapids at Riverfront Place, a $52 million residential and retail development between the Thirteenth Street and Fourteenth Street bridges. The river had come full circle, once again powering Columbus.[61]

No longer was Columbus the Electric City or the Lowell of the South, but on the free-flowing Chattahoochee, it was still Georgia's West Coast. The city's nineteenth-century red clay brick buildings hummed with commerce day and night. Thousands of rafters shot its whitewater rapids each year. The blues floated from Uptown clubs and festivals. With the rebirth of the Chattahoochee and the city's downtown, the Brightest Light on the Georgia Horizon had perhaps finally come close to achieving the long-cherished dreams of its boosters.

NOTES

Abbreviations

AR	*Annual Reports of the Officers of the City of Columbus, Georgia,* Hargrett Library, University of Georgia
Baldwin Papers	George Johnson Baldwin Papers, Collection 850, Southern Historical Collection, Wilson Library, University of North Carolina
Causey Collection	Virginia Causey Collection, MC 121, Columbus State University Archives
CE	*Columbus Enquirer*
CE-S	*Columbus Enquirer-Sun*
CL	*Columbus Ledger*
CL-E	*Columbus Ledger-Enquirer*
CS	*Columbus Sun*
CSUA	Columbus State University Archives
CSU Collection	Columbus State University Collection, Columbus State University Archives
CT	*Columbus Times* [antebellum]
GDAH	Georgia Department of Archives and History
GHQ	*Georgia Historical Quarterly*
GOHC	General Oral History Collection, MC 303, Columbus State University Archives
GT	*Georgia Trend*
HAER Collection	Historic American Engineering Record Collection, MC 14, Columbus State University Archives
HLUGA	Hargrett Library, University of Georgia
Lupold Collection	John S. Lupold Collection, MC 197, Columbus State University Archives
MARBL	Manuscript, Archives, and Rare Book Library, Emory University
NYT	*New York Times*
RC	*Report of the Committee of the Senate upon the Relations between Capital and Labor* (Washington, D.C.: U.S. Government Printing Office, 1885), vol. 4
Saber	*The Saber* [Columbus State University student newspaper], Columbus State University Archives

SHC   Southern Historical Collection, Wilson Library, University of
                North Carolina
Smith Collection   A. C. Smith Collection, MC 34, Columbus State University
                Archives

Chapter 1. "Stepping to the Music of Jingling Dimes"

1. Cyprian Willcox Diary, Oct. 27, 31, Nov. 9, 1844, Mar. 3, July 4, 21, 1845, Coulter Historical Manuscripts, pt. I, MS 2018, box 9, folder 14, HLUGA.

2. "An Act to Dispose of and Distribute Lands," "An Act to Lay Out a Trading Town," Founding of Columbus folder, Vertical File, CSUA; John S. Lupold, *Columbus, Georgia, 1828–1978* (Columbus: Columbus Sesquicentennial, 1978), 3; John H. Martin, *Columbus, Geo., from Its Selection as a "Trading Town" in 1827, to Its Partial Destruction in Wilson's Raid, in 1865* (Columbus: Gilbert, 1874), 1:5.

3. Edward Lloyd Thomas, "Notes Taken on the Survey of the Reservation of the Cowetah Falls," Edward Lloyd Thomas Papers, MSS 479, folder 4, MARBL; William W. Winn, *Line of Splendor: The Life and Times of St. Luke United Methodist Church, Columbus, Georgia, 1828–2008* (Columbus: St. Luke, 2010), 25; Lynn Willoughby, *Flowing through Time: A History of the Lower Chattahoochee River* (Tuscaloosa: University of Alabama Press, 1999), 36–37, 44; Etta Blanchard Worsley, *Columbus on the Chattahoochee* (Columbus: Columbus Office Supply, 1951), 41–45; Nancy Telfair, *A History of Columbus, Georgia, 1828–1928* (Columbus: Historical Publishing, 1929), 29; Aidel Sherwood, *Gazetteer of the State of Georgia* (Philadelphia: Martin and Boden, 1829), 97.

4. Sherwood, *Gazetteer*, 98; Martin, *Columbus, Geo.*, 1:6, 8, 10; "Thick Forest Marked Site of Columbus," *CLE*, May 28, 1961; *CE*, May 29, 1828; "First Issue of Enquirer Published in Cabin Amid Broadway Oak Grove," *CE*, May 29, 1958.

5. Martin, *Columbus, Geo.*, 1:9, 12, 14; Minutes of the Commissioners, Feb. 6, Mar. 24, 1828, Microfilm, drawer 37, box 21, GDAH; Basil Hall, *Travels in North America in the Years 1827 and 1828* (Edinburgh: Cadell, 1829), 3:83; John Bethune, "Statement of the Sale of Lots at Columbus," July 12, 1828, I. A. Few, Elias Beall, Edwin de Graffenreid, Philip H. Alston, and James Hallam, "To His Excellency John Forsyth," Oct. 31, 1828, both in file II, box 39, Muscogee County—Commissioners folder, GDAH; *CE*, July 21, 1828; Winn, *Line of Splendor*, 28.

6. Martin, *Columbus, Geo.*, 1:17; I. A. Few, Elias Beall, Edwin de Graffenreid, Philip H. Alston, and James Hallam, "To His Excellency John Forsyth," Oct. 31, 1828, file II, box 39, Muscogee County—Commissioners folder, GDAH.

7. Sherwood, *Gazetteer*, 97; Martin, *Columbus, Geo.*, 1:18; "James Stuart, 1830," in *The Rambler in Georgia*, ed. Mills Lane (Savannah: Beehive, 1973), 91; Winn, *Line of Splendor*, 30, 35, 39; Worsley, *Columbus on the Chattahoochee*, 145–146, 149–151; "Young Men's Catholic Union," *CE-S*, July 8, 1880; "Trinity Episcopal Church," *CE-S*, Aug. 2, 1891.

8. Martin, *Columbus, Geo.*, 1:13, 20; *CE*, Jan. 14, May 19, 26, 1832; Sol Smith, *Theatrical Management in the West and South for Thirty Years* (New York: Blom, 1968), 78; Helen B. Keller, "History of the Theatre in Columbus, Georgia from 1828 to 1865" (master's thesis, University of Georgia, 1957), 38; Joseph Jefferson, The *Autobiography of Joseph Jefferson* (New York: Century, 1889), 86.

9. Smith, *Theatrical Management*, 79–80.

10. Lupold, *Columbus, Georgia*, 9; Martin, *Columbus, Geo.*, 1:49, 77, 95; Elizabeth Carrow Woolfolk, *Pioneers, Patriots, and Planters: First Settlers in Virginia, Kentucky,*

North Carolina, South Carolina, Tennessee and Georgia (Houston: Wynnton, 2004), 479.

11. John E. Lamar, "Reminiscences of Columbus," *CE-S*, Sept. 27, 1891; "C. D. Arfwedson, 1833," "Tyrone Power, 1834," both in Lane, *Rambler in Georgia*, 105-106, 114-115.

12. Virginia Causey, "The Milton-Camp Murder: Honor and Violence in Old Columbus," *Muscogiana* 25, no. 2 (2014): 1-6; Bertram Wyatt-Brown, *Honor and Violence in the Old South* (New York: Oxford University Press, 1986), 26-31, 149; Martin, *Columbus, Geo.*, 1:32; Woolfolk, *Pioneers, Patriots, and Planters*, 316-320; *CE-S*, Sept. 3, 1887; *Augusta Chronicle*, Jan. 28, 1832; *CE*, Jan. 28, 1832.

13. *CE*, July 6, 20, Oct. 12, 1833; Martin, *Columbus, Geo.*, 1:48; Wyatt-Brown, *Honor and Violence*, 30, 152.

14. Martin, *Columbus, Geo.*, 1:49; *CE*, Aug. 17, Sept. 28, Oct. 5, 12, 1833; Ridgeway Boyd Murphree, "Rebel Sovereigns: The Civil War Leadership of Governors John Milton of Florida and Joseph E. Brown of Georgia, 1861-1865" (PhD diss., Florida State University, 2006), 7-9.

15. John T. Ellisor, The *Second Creek War: Interethnic Conflict and Collusion on a Collapsing Frontier* (Lincoln: University of Nebraska Press, 2010), 18, 43, 47-49, 63-104; William W. Winn, *Triumph of the Eccunna Nuxulgee: Land Speculators, George M. Troup, State Rights, and the Removal of the Creek Indians from Georgia and Alabama, 1825-1838* (Macon: Mercer University Press, 2015), 311-355; Telfair, *History of Columbus, Georgia*, 45-46; *CE*, June 23, 1832.

16. *CE*, Jan. 10, May 1, 1835; Winn, *Triumph of the Eccunna Nuxulgee*, 388-412; Ellisor, *Second Creek War*, 145.

17. Ellisor, *Second Creek War*, 186-193, 199-202, 302; *CE*, May 13, 1836; Martin, *Columbus, Geo.*, 1:58-59, 62-68; A. O. Blackmar, "The Unwritten History of Columbus," Nov. 7, 1920, Thomas J. Peddy Collection, MC 36, Miscellaneous, box 1, Blackmar Columns folder, CSUA; John Fontaine to William Schley, May 19, 1836, file II, box 36, Muscogee County—Indians folder, GDAH; John H. Howard to William Schley, May 20, 1836, file II, box 68, John H. Howard folder, GDAH.

18. Ellisor, *Second Creek War*, 240-307; Martin, *Columbus, Geo.*, 1:68-74; *CE*, Dec. 1, 1836; *Columbus Herald*, Nov. 29, 1836.

19. Lamar, "Reminiscences," Oct. 11, 1891; Raphael J. Moses, "Autobiography of Raphael J. Moses," 1892, 48, Smith Collection; Winn, *Triumph of the Eccunna Nuxulgee*, 468-473; Lupold, *Columbus, Georgia*, 11, 27.

20. W. C. Bard to Ruth Blair, Sept. 8, 1939, file II, box 78, Mirabeau B. Lamar folder, GDAH; Martin, *Columbus, Geo.*, 1:149-150; *CE*, Sept. 18, 1849.

21. Ellisor, *Second Creek War*, 418-419; Martin, *Columbus, Geo.*, 1:76-77, 80-82; Banks Family Papers, MS 1571, box 1, folders 6-27, HLUGA.

22. "Arfwedson," 102; Hall, *Travels*, 69-70; Henry deLeon Southerland Jr. and Jerry Elijah Brown, *The Federal Road through Georgia, the Creek Nation, and Alabama, 1806-1836* (Tuscaloosa: University of Alabama Press, 1989), 62.

23. John S. Lupold and Thomas L. French, *Bridging Deep South Rivers: The Life and Legend of Horace King* (Athens: University of Georgia Press, 2004), 45-70, 63-68, 86-87; Martin, *Columbus, Geo.*, 1:32, 43, 46, 84-85, 88, 104, 117-118, 154; *CE*, Dec. 27, 1834, Mar. 17, 1841.

24. Willoughby, *Flowing through Time*, 70-72; Lupold, *Columbus, Georgia*, 16-18; *CE*, Dec. 27, 1834.

25. John S. Lupold, J. B. Karfunkle, and Barbara Kimmelman, "Water Power Development at the Falls of the Chattahoochee," 1977, HAER Collection, box 1, folder 14; Barbara Kimmelman, John S. Lupold, and J. B. Karfunkle, "The City Mills," 1977, HAER Collection, box 1, folder 7; *CE*, May 18, 1833, June 5, 1849; Martin, *Columbus, Geo.*, 1:92.

26. Martin, *Columbus, Geo.*, 1:19, 89, 110; Winn, *Triumph of the Eccunna Nuxulgee*, 322–325; Lynn Willoughby, *Fair to Middlin': The Antebellum Cotton Trade of the Apalachicola/Chattahoochee River Valley* (Tuscaloosa: University of Alabama Press, 1993), 74–75.

27. Willoughby, *Fair to Middlin'*, 58, 72, 74–75, 84; *CE*, Mar. 10, Aug. 18, 1841, Jan. 26, 1842; Hines Holt to Farish Carter, Mar. 28, 1841, Farish Carter Papers, Collection 2230, subser. 1.2, folder 20, SHC; Seaborn Jones to William Schley, June 7, 1837, file II, box 74, Seaborn Jones folder, GDAH; *CT*, July 15, 22, 1841; Robert B. Murdock to "Aunt and Girls," June 16, 1841, Murdock and Wright Family Papers, Collection 532, ser. 1, folder 5, SHC.

28. Martin, *Columbus, Geo.*, 1:119; *CE*, Oct. 13, 1841, May 24, 1843; Lupold, Karfunkle, and Kimmelman, "Water Power Development," 4; John S. Lupold, "Some Preliminary Observations on the Textile and Waterpowered Industries of Antebellum Columbus, Georgia," n.d., 8–11, Lupold Collection, ser. 6, box 4, folder 1.

29. *CT*, Dec. 25, 1844, May 14, 1845; Martin, *Columbus, Geo.*, 1:138, 147, 158; Lupold, Karfunkle, and Kimmelman, "Water Power Development," 4; Lupold, "Preliminary Observations," 9–15; Deeds from Josephus Echols to John H. Howard, Apr. 30, 1845, John H. Howard to Farish Carter and John B. Baird, Apr. 21, 1845, Carter Papers, subser. 2.1.5, folder 94, Jan.–Apr. 1845; Deed from John H. Howard to William L. Jeter, May 13, 1845, Carter Papers, subser. 2.1.5, folder 97, Jan.–Mar. 1847.

30. John R. DeTreville, "The Little New South: Origins of Industry in Georgia's Fall-Line Cities, 1840–1865" (PhD diss., University of North Carolina, 1985), 110, 113–114; Lupold, Karfunkle, and Kimmelman, "Water Power Development," 5–6; Jesse Williams, "The Rock Island Paper Mill," *Muscogiana* 21, no. 2 (2010): 35–39.

31. DeTreville, "Little New South," 116, 154–155; *CE*, Jan. 23, 1850; Barbara Kimmelman, John S. Lupold, and J. B. Karfunkle, "The Columbus Iron Works," 1977, 3, HAER Collection, box 1, folder 8; Moses, "Autobiography," 48.

32. *CE*, Oct. 19, 1841; Faye Lind Jensen, "Power and Progress in the Urban South: Columbus, Georgia, 1850–1885" (PhD diss., Emory University, 1991), 21, 57; Willoughby, *Flowing through Time*, 77.

33. "William H. Young," in *Biographical Souvenir of the States of Georgia and Florida: Biographical Sketches of the Representative Public and Many Early Settled Families in These States* (Chicago: Battey, 1889), 817–818; Jensen, "Power," 35; "William H. Young," in *Men of Mark of Georgia*, ed. William J. Northen (Atlanta: Caldwell, 1911): 3:53–54; John S. Lupold, *Heritage Park: A Celebration of the Industrial Heritage of Columbus, Georgia* (Columbus: Historic Columbus Foundation, 1999), 31–32.

34. DeTreville, "Little New South," 143–144; John B. Baird to Farish Carter, June 1, 1851, Carter Papers, subser. 1.3, folder 43; Martin, *Columbus, Geo.*, 2:59, 75; *CE*, Nov. 30, Dec. 7, 1852; Frederick Law Olmsted, *A Journey in the Seaboard Slave States, with Remarks on Their Economy* (New York: Dix and Edwards, 1856), 548.

35. DeTreville, "Little New South," 145–146, 149, 152, 155–156; Martin, *Columbus, Geo.*, 2:75; John Banks, *A Short Biographical Sketch of the Undersigned by Himself* (photocopy), Family of C. Dexter Jordan, Sr. Collection, MC 64, box 1, folder 4, CSUA; *CE*, Apr. 10, 1860; William H. Young, testimony, in *RC*, 510–511.

36. Jensen, "Power," 19–20, 35; DeTreville, "Little New South," 147–148; *CT*, Feb. 18, 1846, Apr. 6, 1861; *Augusta Chronicle*, July 21, 1854; Martin, *Columbus, Geo.*, 2:76, 82; David Dodd, "Randolph Lawler Mott, 1799–1881: Columbus Businessman, Civic Leader, Unionist," *Muscogiana* 8, no. 3–4 (1997): 57–58.

37. Bunyan Hadley Andrew, "Georgia's Chattahoochee Riverbank: A Recapitulatory Note," *GHQ* 4, no. 1 (1964): 74–77; *Howard v. Ingersoll*, 54 U.S. 13 (1851).

38. *CT*, Nov. 4, 1846; *CE*, May 14, Dec. 10, 1845, Dec. 9, 16, 1851, Jan. 6, 1852, Apr. 5, 1853; Willoughby, *Fair to Middlin'*, 122–129; Martin, *Columbus, Geo.*, 2:27, 36, 65–66; Jensen, "Power," 11, 39–40.

39. *CE*, May 24, 1853; Willoughby, *Fair to Middlin'*, 127–129; Martin, *Columbus, Geo.*, 2:66, 81–82, 102, 118; Paris Tillinghast to Samuel Tillinghast, Nov. 20, 1853, Tillinghast Family Papers, Collection 01297, box 4, Rubenstein Rare Book and Manuscript Library, Duke University.

40. *A River Runs through It: A 100-Year History of the Columbus Water Works* (Columbus: Water Works, 2002), 7–9, 15; Martin, *Columbus, Geo.*, 1:125–126, 147, 162, 2:75, 113; "Vivid History of Columbus Fire Dept., Now 100 Years Old, Given by Pearce," *CL-E*, Aug. 22, 1937.

41. Martin, *Columbus, Geo.*, 2: 63–65, 119; *River Runs through It*, 8; *CT*, Nov. 8, 1852; "Charles Lyell, 1845–46," in Lane, *Rambler in Georgia*, 207.

42. Martin, *Columbus, Geo.*, 2:57; *CL*, Oct. 10, 1939; Jensen, "Power," 38.

43. Victoria MacDonald Huntzinger, "Birth of Southern Public Education: Columbus, Georgia, 1864–1904" (EdD diss., Harvard University, 1992), 23–25; Lupold, *Columbus, Georgia*, 16; John Johnson, School Report to Governor for 1859, file II, box 36, Muscogee County—Schools folder, GDAH; "George Lewis, 1844," in Lane, *Rambler in Georgia*, 188.

44. Liza Benham, "Slaves Basis of Local Cotton Wealth," *CL-E*, June 7, 1982; V. J. Jones testimony, in *RC*, 626–627; Willcox diary, Jan. 1, 13, July 4, 1845.

45. *CE*, Jan. 1, 1850, Jan. 14, 1851; Keller, "History," 39–44, 118, 99–105, 139; Mary Levin Koch, "Entertaining the Public: Music and Drama in Antebellum Georgia," *GHQ* 68, no. 45 (1984): 25–33; *CT*, Dec. 12, 1859, Sept. 31, 1860; *CS*, Oct. 3, 13, 23, 1860.

46. Willcox diary, Oct. 31, 1844; Martin, *Columbus, Geo.*, 2:67, 72, 76, 82, 89, 90, 105, 121, 1:134, 136–137; "James Silk Buckingham, 1839," in Lane, *Rambler in Georgia*, 162; Laurence Eugene O'Keeffe diary, May 9, 1853, O'Keeffe Diary and Letters Collection, MC 218, CSUA; *CE*, Jan. 11, 1843.

47. DeTreville, "Little New South," 279–280; Anthony Gene Carey, *Sold Down the River: Slavery in the Lower Chattahoochee Valley of Alabama and Georgia* (Tuscaloosa: University of Alabama Press, 2011), 100–106, 131, 138; O'Keeffe diary, n.d., 1853; *CE*, Sept. 20, 1859.

48. Carey, *Sold Down the River*, 63, 142; Carrie Davis and W. B. Allen, in "Born in Slavery: Slave Narratives from the Federal Writers' Project, 1936–1938," Library of Congress, http://memory.loc.gov/ammem/snhtml/mesnbibnarrindex.html; "James Silk Buckingham," 162–163.

49. Stephen Barber, "Blacks and Whites Together: The Experience of Some Baptist Churches in Muscogee County, Georgia, 1825–1872," *Muscogiana* 11, nos. 1–2 (2000): 4–6, 11; Carey, *Sold Down the River*, 143–168; Martin, *Columbus, Geo.*, 2:105, 151; Winn, *Line of Splendor*, 1101–107.

50. Deirdre O'Connell, *The Ballad of Blind Tom* (New York: Overlook Duckworth, 2009); "Tom the Blind Musician," *CE*, Oct. 8, 1857; "Blind Tom," *CE*, Oct. 14, 1862.

51. O'Connell, *Ballad of Blind Tom*; "Blind Tom's Story Told," *CE*, June 17, 1908; Mike Haskey, "Walk of Fame Unveiled at Liberty Theatre Sunday," *CL-E*, Nov. 9, 2008.

52. Carey, *Sold Down the River*, 54–57; *CE*, Feb. 28, 1860; Callie McGinnis, "Hatcher & McGehee Negro Book," *Muscogiana* 4, nos. 1–2 (1993): 8–16, nos. 3–4 (1993): 59–63.

53. Tom Henderson Wells, *The Slave Ship Wanderer* (Athens: University of Georgia Press, 1967), 45, 58; *Ninth Census of the United States: Population Schedule, 1870*, Muscogee County, Georgia, City of Columbus, dwelling 19, family 23, Randolph Mott household.

54. Anthony Gene Carey, *Parties, Slavery, and the Union in Antebellum Georgia* (Athens: University of Georgia Press, 2012), 190; Henry L. Benning to Howell Cobb, July 1, 1849, in *The Correspondence of Robert Toombs, Alexander H. Stephens, and Howell Cobb*, ed. Ulrich B. Phillips (Washington, D.C.: American Historical Association, 1913), 171; James C. Cobb, "The Making of a Secessionist: Henry L. Benning and the Coming of the Civil War," *GHQ* 40, no. 4 (1976): 313–323; "Speech of Hon. M. J. Crawford, of Georgia, on the Election of Speaker " Dec. 15, 1859, Open Library, https://openlibrary.org/books/OL13512032M/Speech_of_Hon._M._J._Crawford_of_Georgia_on_the_election_of_speaker; *CS*, Nov. 4, Dec. 17, 1860; Banks, *Biographical Sketch*, 21.

55. Martin, *Columbus, Geo.*, 2:119–120, 127–128; *CT*, Dec. 20, 21, 1860; *CE*, Jan. 8, 1861; "Henry L. Benning's Secessionist Speech, November 19," in *Secession Debated: Georgia's Showdown in 1860*, ed. William W. Freehling and Craig M. Simpson (New York: Oxford University Press, 1992), 117–120.

56. Martin, *Columbus, Geo.*, 2:119, 128; Eliza Frances Andrews, *The War-Time Journal of a Georgia Girl, 1864–1865* (New York: Appleton, 1908), 309; *CE*, Jan. 20, 1861; Banks, *Biographical Sketch*, 21–22; "William H. Young," 3:57; *CE*, quoted in the *Macon Weekly Telegraph*, Jan. 31, 1861.

57. R. T. Simmons to Jefferson Davis, Sept. 25, 1861, in The *Papers of Jefferson Davis*, ed. Lynda Lasswell Crist and Mary Seaton Dix (Baton Rouge: Louisiana State University Press, 1992), 7:349; L. P. Graf and R. W. Haskins, eds., "Letters of a Georgia Unionist: John G. Winter and Secession," *GHQ* 45, no. 4 (1961): 391; *CS*, Apr. 16, 1861.

58. Carey, *Sold Down the River*, 194.

Chapter 2. The "Last Battle" and "Black Reconstruction"

1. Chappell to wife, Dec. 12, 1860, Lamar-Chappell Collection, CSUA.

2. John S. Lupold, "Muscogee County in 1860," Lupold Collection, ser. 6, box 1, folder 69; David Williams, *Rich Man's War: Class, Caste, and Confederate Defeat in the Lower Chattahoochee Valley* (Athens: University of Georgia Press, 1998), 66–67, appendixes; Diffee William Standard, *Columbus, Georgia, in the Confederacy: The Social and Industrial Life of the Chattahoochee River Port* (New York: William-Frederick, 1954), 33, 36–44; *CS*, July 31, 1862; Stewart C. Edwards, "'To Do the Manufacturing for the South: Private Industry in Confederate Columbus,'" *GHQ* 85, no. 4 (2001): 544–550; *CE*, Nov. 4, Sept. 26, 1862; Barbara Kimmelman, John S. Lupold, and J. B. Karfunkle, "The Columbus Iron Works," 1977, 4–6, HAER Collection, box 1, folder 8.

3. John S. Lupold, Barbara Kimmelman, and J. B. Karfunkle, "The Eagle and Phenix Mills," 1977, 5, HAER Collection, box 1, folder 10; Edwards, 539–542, 552; Standard, *Columbus, Georgia, in the Confederacy*, 33–34, 37; *Atlanta Intelligencer*, Nov. 30, 1862; *CE*, June 14, 1863; John H. Martin, *Columbus, Geo., from Its Selection as a "Trad-*

ing Town" in 1827, to Its Partial Destruction in Wilson's Raid, in 1865 (Columbus: Gilbert, 1874), 2:144, 168; *CT*, Jan. 21, 1864; A. S. Matheson testimony, in *RC*, 537.

4. Standard, *Columbus, Georgia, in the Confederacy*, 22–23; *CS*, Feb. 21, May 26, 27, 1861, Feb. 24, 1862; Albert Moses Luria, War Journal of Albert Moses Luria [typescript], Collection 438-Z, SHC; Raphael J. Moses, "Autobiography of Raphael J. Moses," 1892, 49, Smith Collection; "Columbus, Georgia," *Encyclopedia of Southern Jewish Communities*, Goldring/Woldenberg Institute of Southern Jewish Life, http://www.isjl.org/georgia-columbus-encyclopedia.html; John S. Lupold, "Like an Extended Family: Israelites in Early Columbus," ser. 7, box 1, folder 15, Lupold Collection.

5. *CE*, July 29, Aug. 6, 1864; Williams, *Rich Man's War*, 74, 77.

6. *CE*, June 10, 18, 1861, Mar. 4, Nov. 21, 1862; Standard, *Columbus, Georgia, in the Confederacy*, 43, 25; *CS*, Apr. 9, Dec. 13, 1863; Williams, *Rich Man's War*, 138; L. P. Graf and R. W. Haskins, "Letters of a Georgia Unionist: John G. Winter and the Restoration of the Union," *GHQ* 46, no. 1 (1962): 49–51; John S. Lupold, *Columbus, Georgia, 1828–1978* (Columbus: Columbus Sesquicentennial, 1978), 30; Faye Lind Jensen, "Power and Progress in the Urban South: Columbus, Georgia, 1850–1885" (PhD diss., Emory University, 1991), 105.

7. *CE*, Aug. 1, 1861, July 27, 30, 1862; Standard, *Columbus, Georgia, in the Confederacy*, 25, 66n18; *CS*, June 5, 1861, June 5, 1862; Lupold, *Columbus, Georgia*, 30.

8. Thomas Conn Bryan, *Confederate Georgia* (Athens: University of Georgia Press, 1953), 57, 60–61; Williams, *Rich Man's War*, 83; *CE*, Apr. 17, 1864; Lizzie to Samuel Spencer, September 1, 1862, Samuel Spencer Papers, box 1, folder 5, SHC; *CS*, Apr. 4, 1864; Lizzie DeVotie to brother, Feb, 20, 1861, James H. DeVotie Papers, box 1, Columbus, Georgia, Correspondence: 1860–1863 folder, Rubenstein Rare Book and Manuscript Library, Duke University; Laura Beecher Comer diary, Dec. 19, 1862, Collection 169, ser. 1, vols. 1–3, SHC.

9. Williams, *Rich Man's War*, 108, 75; Martin, *Columbus, Geo.*, 2:168; Etta Blanchard Worsley, *Columbus on the Chattahoochee* (Columbus: Columbus Office Supply, 1951), 291; Standard, *Columbus, Georgia, in the Confederacy*, 51; Tillman and Norman Ledgers, Collection 2901, Aug. 26, 1860, SHC.

10. Robert Toombs to George Hill et al., June 11, 1862, in *The Correspondence of Robert Toombs, Alexander H. Stephens, and Howell Cobb*, ed. Ulrich B. Phillips (Washington, D.C.: American Historical Association, 1913), 2:595; *CE*, Sept. 16, 1862; Teresa Crisp Williams and David Williams, "'The Women Rising': Cotton, Class, and Confederate Georgia's Rioting Women," *GHQ* 86, no. 1 (2002): 59–60; H. E. Faber to George Parker Swift, Jan. 18, 1865, Louis Hamburger Papers, Rubenstein Rare Book and Manuscript Library, Duke University; G. Gunby Jordan to Theodore Price, Nov. 9, 1912, G. Gunby Jordan Collection, MC 12, box 1, folder 3, CSUA; *Georgia*, vol. 23, pp. 125, 1, R. G. Dun and Co. Collection, Harvard Business School, in John S. Lupold and Thomas L. French, *Bridging Deep South Rivers: The Life and Legend of Horace King* (Athens: University of Georgia Press), 299n3; *Mustian v. Mott*, Benning-Jones Collection, MC 6, box 4, folder 19, CSUA; Oscar S. Straus, *Under Four Administrations: From Cleveland to Taft* (Boston: Houghton Mifflin, 1922), 16; Bryan, *Confederate Georgia*, 52–53; *CS*, Sept. 24, 1863.

11. *CE*, Nov. 10, Apr. 3, 1863; *CS*, Oct. 13, Apr. 8, 14, 1863; Louise Calhoun Barfield, *History of Harris County, Georgia, 1827–1961* (Roswell, Ga.: Wolfe, 1978), 758; Williams and Williams, "Women Rising," 71.

12. *CE*, Oct. 9, 14, 1863, Sept. 5, 6, June 29, 1864; *CS*, Oct. 13, July 11, 1863, Sept. 6,

1864; Nancy to Thomas Mann, Jan. 2, 1864, Nancy O. and Thomas A. Mann Family Civil War Papers, Manuscripts, MF 153, GDAH; Williams, *Rich Man's War*, 134; *CT*, Feb. 11, 1864; Moses, "Autobiography," 50–51.

13. Moses, "Autobiography," 64; Worsley, *Columbus on the Chattahoochee*, 278–279; Martin, *Columbus, Geo.*, 2:154; Frank Rowsey, "From the Seminole Wars to the Battle of Atlanta," *Inn Dixie*, December 1939, 15, file II, box 11, John Banks folder, GDAH; Homer Blackmon to John Banks, Aug. 21, 1864, Banks Family Papers, MS 1571, box 2, folder 5, HLUGA; *Atlanta Constitution*, Sept. 24, 1970.

14. Williams, *Rich Man's War*, 71; *CS*, Dec. 14, 1862, Apr. 9, 1864; Standard, *Columbus, Georgia, in the Confederacy*, 55; *CT*, Sept. 3, 1862; *CE*, June 22, 23, 1864.

15. *CE*, Sept. 14, 15, 1864, Apr. 9, 1862; B. W. Clark to Joseph E. Brown, Jan. 30, 1864, Governor's Correspondence, DOC 289, C 115261, GDAH; S. E. L. H. Bomar to Daughter, July 14, 1864, Bomar Family Collection, MS 86, MARBL; Martin, *Columbus, Geo.*, 2:176; Mary Gladdy, in "Born in Slavery: Slave Narratives from the Federal Writers' Project, 1936–1938," Library of Congress, http://memory.loc.gov/ammem/snhtml/mesnbibnarrindex.html.

16. James Pickett Jones, *Yankee Blitzkrieg: Wilson's Raid through Alabama and Georgia* (Lexington: University Press of Kentucky, 2000); Standard, *Columbus, Georgia, in the Confederacy*, 59–61; Charles A. Misulia, *Columbus, Georgia, 1865: The Last True Battle of the Civil War* (Tuscaloosa: University of Alabama Press, 2010), 44–65; *CS*, Apr. 12, 1865; Charles F. Hinrichs, "Diary of Charles F. Hinrichs, Captain, 10th Missouri Cavalry, U.S.A., July 1863 to May 1865," 36, Western Historical Manuscript Collection, University of Missouri; *The War of the Rebellion: A Compilation of the Official Records of the Union and Confederate Armies* (Washington, D.C.: U.S. Government Printing Office, 1897), ser. 1, vol. 49, pt. 2, 1193; Williams, *Rich Man's War*, 175; *CT*, Feb. 15, 1865; Charles Todd Quintard, *Doctor Quintard: Chaplain C.S.A. and Second Bishop of Tennessee, Being His Story of the War (1861–1865)*, ed. Arthur Howard Noll (Sewanee: University Press of Sewanee, Tennessee, 1905), 137–138; Josiah Conzett, *My Civil War: Before, during and After, 1861–1865*, http://conzett.org/civilidx.htm; *CE*, June 27, 1865.

17. Kate Cumming, *A Journal of Hospital Life in the Confederate Army of Tennessee* (Louisville, Ky.: Morton, 1864), 175; Jones, *Yankee Blitzkrieg*, 138, 140; T. L. Ingram letter, Mar. 14, 1932, file II, box 70, Porter Ingram folder, GDAH; Mary B. Browne Slade, "John Rhodes Browne," Rhodes Browne Collection, MC 3, CSUA; "Report of the 1st Brigade, Brig. General Edward F. Winslow of the 4th Division, Maj. Gen Emory Upton, Wilson's Cavalry," *War of the Rebellion*, ser. 1, vol. 49, pt. 1, 391–392; Misulia, *Columbus, Georgia, 1865*, 119–170; Theodore F. Allen to James H. Wilson, Jan. 17, 1908, Papers of James Harrison Wilson, box 1, Theodore Allen folder, Library of Congress; Nancy Telfair, *A History of Columbus, Georgia, 1828–1928* (Columbus: Historical Publishing, 1929), 137; James Harrison Wilson, *Under the Old Flag* (New York: Appleton, 1912), 2:267.

18. Wilson, *Under the Old Flag*, 2:266–267; Standard, *Columbus, Georgia, in the Confederacy*, 61; Jones, *Yankee Blitzkrieg*, 141; "1st Brigade"; Misulia, *Columbus, Georgia, 1865*, 171–203; Slade, "John Rhodes Browne"; Wilson, *Under the Old Flag*, 2:268.

19. Hinrichs, "Diary," Apr. 17, 1865; Conzett, *My Civil War*, 80; Standard, *Columbus, Georgia, in the Confederacy*, 61; Rhodus Walton and W. B. Allen, in "Born in Slavery"; Charles B. Mitchell, "Field Notes on the Selma Campaign," in *Sketches of War History, 1861–1865, Papers Prepared for the Commandery of the State of Ohio, Military*

Order of the Loyal Legion of the United States, 1903–1908, vol. 6, ed. Theodore F. Allen (Cincinnati: Clarke, 1908), 192.

20. *A History of the Origin of Memorial Day as Adopted by the Ladies' Memorial Association of Columbus, Georgia* (Columbus: Gilbert, 1898), 6, CSUA; Jones, *Yankee Blitzkrieg*, 57; Lucy Banks, "A Letter from Columbus Shortly after the 'Last Battle,'" ed. Mike Bunn, *Muscogiana* 22, no. 1 (2011): 2–3; James William Howard diary, 46, Howard-Odum-Lifrage Collection, SMC 6, CSUA; Cumming, *Journal of Hospital Life*, 175; Wilson, *Under the Old Flag*, 2:267; A. O. Blackmar Sr., list of destroyed property, *CE*, Apr. 17, 1908.

21. *War of the Rebellion*, ser. 1, vol. 49, pt. 1, 486, 301; Misulia, *Columbus, Georgia, 1865*, 217–221; Hinrichs, "Diary," 37; Virginia Ridenhour interview, Jan. 11, 14, 20, Feb. 10, 1976, GOHC; Quintard, *Doctor Quintard*, 139.

22. Rowsey, "From the Seminole Wars"; Comer diary, Apr. 30, 1865, Dec. 25, 1866; Moses, "Autobiography," 49; *War of the Rebellion*, ser. 1, vol. 49, pt. 1, 486, 301; George Brooks, in "Born in Slavery."

23. Virginia Causey, "The Battle of Columbus and Historical Memory," *Muscogiana*, 19, no. 1 (2008): 18–28; Charles Jewett Swift, *The Last Battle of the Civil War* (Columbus: Gilbert, 1915), 21, CSUA; "By-Laws and Minutes of the Historical Society of Columbus, 1915, and Chronology of Events Pertaining to the Erection of a Monument to the Battle of Columbus," Smith Collection; Charles J. Swift to James H. Wilson, Jan. 11, 17, 23, 31, Feb. 6, 1908, James H. Wilson to Charles J. Swift, Jan. 13, 20, 27, 1908, Wilson Papers, box 24, Charles J. Swift folder.

24. "Columbus: Was It the Last Battle of the Civil War?," Appendix, Report of the Research Staff, National Park Service, Arno B. Cammerer to Bryant Castellow, both in Smith Collection, box 39, folder 12.

25. Telfair, *History of Columbus, Georgia*, 150–156; Worsley, *Columbus on the Chattahoochee*, 302.

26. *CS*, Sept. 14, Nov. 1, Dec. 9, 30, 1865, Apr. 1, 1866.

27. George Wagner diary, 1868, George Wagner Papers, MS 895, box 3, folders 23, 24, HLUGA; *CS*, Nov. 18, 1865; *CE*, Oct. 20, 1865, Apr. 12, 1866; Raphael Moses to Iverson D. Graves, Feb. 13, 1867, Graves Family Papers, MS 327, box 1, folder 6, MARBL.

28. Lupold and French, *Bridging Deep South Rivers*, 197; Dave Gillarm, "Prince Hall Masons," YouTube, May 6, 2012, http://www.youtube.com/watch?v=0mCuwiHsrNo; *CE*, Jan. 31, 1866; St. James AME Church, http://www.waymarking.com/waymarks/WM4NPF; Barber, "Blacks and Whites Together," 13; John S. Lupold, "Black Retailers and Tradesmen," Lupold Collection, ser. 6, box 1, folder 17.

29. Victoria MacDonald Huntzinger, "Birth of Southern Public Education: Columbus, Georgia, 1864–1904" (EdD diss., Harvard University, 1992), 4, 40–56, 63, 119–144; Alan Conway, *The Reconstruction of Georgia* (Minneapolis: University of Minnesota Press, 1966), 88–91; *CS*, Mar. 31, 1867, Sept. 11, 1865, May 21, 1866.

30. *Reports of the Superintendent, of the Public Schools of Columbus, Georgia for Years 1868 to 1874, Inclusive*, HLUGA; *CE*, Aug. 15, 1873.

31. *CE*, Oct. 12, Nov. 16, 17, Dec. 20, 1865, Feb. 13, 15, 21, 22, 1866; Robert M. Howard, *Reminiscences* (Columbus: Gilbert, 1912), 31–32.

32. Olive Hall Shadgett, *The Republican Party in Georgia: From Reconstruction through 1900* (Athens: University of Georgia Press, 1964), 30, 37; Edmund L. Drago, *Black Politicians and Reconstruction in Georgia: A Splendid Failure* (Athens: University of Georgia Press, 1992), appendixes A, B.

33. Telfair, *History of Columbus, Georgia*, 178; Huntzinger, "Birth of Southern Public Education," 149; Conway, *Reconstruction of Georgia*, 148–150; *CS*, Mar. 24, 1868; Elizabeth Otto Daniell, "The Ashburn Murder Case in Georgia Reconstruction, 1868," *GHQ* 65, no. 4 (1975): 299.

34. *Atlanta Intelligencer*, Mar. 14, 1868; *CS*, Mar. 14, 18, 21, 23, 24, 28, 29, Apr. 1, Nov. 27, 1868; David Rose, *The Big Eddy Club: The Stocking Stranglings and Southern Justice* (New York: New Press, 2007), 67; Martin, *Columbus, Geo.*, 2:93.

35. Daniell, "Ashburn Murder Case," 300–301; *CS*, Apr. 1, 1868; Kenneth H. Thomas, "The Ashburn Case—A New Look," paper presented at the Georgia Association of Historians annual meeting, 2000, Lupold Collection, ser. 6, box 1, folder 4.

36. *CE*, July 1–26, 1868; *Radical Rule: Military Outrage in Georgia* (Louisville, Ky.: Morton, 1868); John B. Gordon testimony, in *Report of the Joint Select Committee Appointed to Inquire into the Condition of Affairs in the Late Insurrectionary States* (Washington, D.C.: U.S. Government Printing Office, 1872), 6:317; Moses, "Autobiography," 80–81; *Report of Maj. Gen. Meade's Military Operation and Administration of Civil Affairs in the Third Military District and Department of the South* (Atlanta: Assistant Adjutant General's Office, Department of the South, 1868), 54.

37. Elizabeth Studley Nathans, *Losing the Peace: Georgia Republicans and Reconstruction, 1865–1871* (Baton Rouge: Louisiana State University Press, 1968), 100; *Radical Rule*, 42–49; Conway, *Reconstruction of Georgia*, 174–175; Lee W. Formwalt, "The Camilla Massacre of 1868: Radical Violence as Political Propaganda," *GHQ* 71, no. 3 (1987): 399–426.

38. *CE*, Nov. 1, 4, 1868, Dec. 13, 1870, Nov. 19, 1872, Jan. 7, 1875; Conway, *Reconstruction of Georgia*, 177; Lambert Spencer to Samuel Spencer, Apr. 4, 1869, Samuel Spencer Papers, box 2, folder 20.

39. *CS*, Apr. 1, 1868; C. Mildred Thompson, *Reconstruction in Georgia: Economic, Social, Political, 1865–1872* (Gloucester, Mass.: Smith, 1964), 385, 391; Telfair, *History of Columbus, Georgia*, 156–157; *Radical Rule*, 143, 111; Stirling Price Gilbert, *A Georgia Lawyer: His Observations and Public Service* (Athens: University of Georgia Press, 1946), 4.

40. *Committee Appointed to Inquire into the ... Late Insurrectionary States*, 6:425, 431–434; 452–453; Rose, *Big Eddy Club*, 67, 70; *CS*, Nov. 27, 1867.

41. *CE*, June 2, 5, 6, Apr. 26, 1865.

42. John S. Lupold, "The Industrial Reconstruction of Columbus, Georgia, 1865–1881," paper presented at the Georgia Historical Society annual meeting, October 1975, Lupold Collection, ser. 6, box 2, folder 5; Howard diary, 52; J. Rhodes Browne, "Oath of Allegiance," Rhodes Browne Collection, box 1, folder 2, CSUA; Lupold, Kimmelman, and Karfunkle, "The Eagle and Phenix Mills," 6; *CE*, Apr. 5, 1867; J. B. Karfunkle, Barbara Kimmelman, and John S. Lupold, "Muscogee Manufacturing," Aug. 1977, HAER Collection, box 1, folder 13; Louis Hamburger to Toodie, Sept. 14, 1867, Hamburger Papers.

43. Faye Lind Jensen, "'Let Us Not Be So Far Behind: Columbus, Georgia, and the Struggle of a New South Town,'" in *Making a New South: Race, Leadership, and Community Perspectives on the History of the South*, ed. Paul A. Cimbala and Barton C. Shaw (Gainesville: University Press of Florida, 2007), 39, 42; Lupold, "Industrial Reconstruction"; *CE-S*, Oct. 12, 1878, Nov. 6, 1877, Nov. 24, 1880, Nov. 23, 1890; Jensen, "Power," 187; "Columbus," *Encyclopedia of Southern Jewish Communities*; Louise DuBose interview, Sept. 1975, GOHC; Robert W. Williams testimony, in *RC*, 615, 619.

44. Jensen, "Let Us Not Be," 32, 35-39; Lupold, "Industrial Reconstruction"; John S. Lupold, "Columbus in 1886," Lupold Collection, ser. 6, box 1, folder 60; Karfunkle, Kimmelman, and Lupold, "Muscogee Manufacturing," 4; William H. Young testimony, in *RC*, 511.

45. Lupold, "Industrial Reconstruction"; *CE-S*, Mar. 19, 1876; Lupold, *Columbus, Georgia*, 55; Clason Kyle, "Young, Swift Were Textile Pioneers," *CL-E*, May 7, 1978; *CL-E*, May 16, 1937; Ben House, "Scenes Tell City's Story," *CL-E*, Sept. 7, 1958; Young testimony, 517, 523; John S. Lupold, J. B. Karfunkle, and Barbara Kimmelman, "Water Power Development at the Falls of the Chattahoochee," 1977, 7, HAER Collection, box 1, folder 14; John S. Lupold, *Heritage Park: A Celebration of the Industrial Heritage of Columbus, Georgia* (Columbus: Historic Columbus Foundation, 1999), 32, 35; John R. DeTreville, "Little New South: Origins of Industry in Georgia's Fall-Line Cities, 1840–1865" (PhD diss., University of North Carolina, 1985), 331–333.

Chapter 3. "Plethoric, Laborious, Well-Fed, Jolly, and Complacent"

1. J. E. Land, ed., *Columbus: Her Trade, Commerce, and Industries, 1892–93* (Columbus: Land Publishing, 1892), 15, 21, 24.

2. *CE*, Sept. 18, 1873, June 27, July 4, 7, 1874.

3. William H. Young testimony, in *RC*, 510–511; *Annual Report to the Stockholders of the Eagle and Phenix Manufacturing Company*, 1888, HLUGA; J. Rhodes Browne testimony, in *RC*, 525; J. A. Walker, *The Industries of Georgia, Her Advantages as a Business Centre, Manufacturing Locality, and Healthful Habitation* (Columbus: Gilbert, 1887), 41; "A History of Innovation," W. C. Bradley Company, https://wcbradley.com/index.php?/about/history.

4. John S. Lupold, *Heritage Park: A Celebration of the Industrial Heritage of Columbus, Georgia* (Columbus: Historic Columbus Foundation, 1999), 50–52; Eugene Granberry testimony, in *RC*, 498; John S. Lupold, "Like an Extended Family: Israelites in Early Columbus," 10, Lupold Collection, ser. 7, box 1, folder 15; Barbara Kimmelman, John S. Lupold, and J. B. Karfunkle, "The Columbus Iron Works," 1977, 11–14, HAER Collection, box 1, folder 8; H. S. Reynolds to George Baldwin, Apr. 10, 1902, Baldwin Papers, box 19, folder 851.

5. *CE*, Oct. 8, 1865, July 7, 1869, Mar. 19, 1872; John S. Lupold and Thomas L. French, *Bridging Deep South Rivers: The Life and Legend of Horace King* (Athens: University of Georgia Press, 2004), 202; Lupold, *Heritage Park*, 42–46; "City Mills," *CL*, Feb. 22, 1934; Thomas J. Chappell diary, Mar. 12, 1872, Loretto Chappell Collection, MC 29, box 5, folder 13, CSUA; Lambert Spencer to Samuel Spencer, Mar. 12, 1872, Samuel Spencer Papers, Collection 3477, box 3, folder 51, SHC.

6. Faye Lind Jensen, "Power and Progress in the Urban South: Columbus, Georgia, 1850–1885" (PhD diss., Emory University, 1991), 180–183; *CE*, Aug. 18, 1868; Etta Blanchard Worsley, *Columbus on the Chattahoochee* (Columbus: Columbus Office Supply, 1951), 384–385; "Georgia Midland & Gulf Railroad," Georgia's Railroad History and Heritage, http://railga.com/gmidgulf.html.

7. John S. Lupold, *Columbus, Georgia, 1828–1978* (Columbus: Columbus Sesquicentennial, 1978), 58–62; Faye Lind Jensen, "'Let Us Not Be So Far Behind: Columbus, Georgia, and the Struggle of a New South Town,'" in *Making a New South: Race, Leadership, and Community Perspectives on the History of the South*, ed. Paul A. Cimbala and Barton C. Shaw (Gainesville: University Press of Florida, 2007), 37–38; Lynn Wil-

loughby, *Flowing through Time: A History of the Lower Chattahoochee River* (Tuscaloosa: University of Alabama Press, 1999), 132–148; *CE-S*, Sept. 12, 1897, Feb. 6, Dec. 18, 1900, Apr. 16, 1901; D. Abbott Turner interview, 1976, GOHC.

8. Land, *Columbus*, 39, 74; Worsley, "William Clark Bradley," in *Columbus on the Chattahoochee*, appendix; Tom Sellers, "Dixie Is No Longer 'Land Of Cotton,'" *CL-E*, May 28, 1961; John S. Lupold, "An Historical Synopsis of the W. C. Bradley Co., 1885–1983," 1983, Lupold Collection, ser. 6, box 1, folder 21; Willoughby, *Flowing through Time*, 104.

9. Worsley, "James Philips Kyle," in *Columbus on the Chattahoochee*, appendix; Land, *Columbus*, 33–34, 85, 91; Nancy Telfair, "Henry Clifford Smith" and "Joseph Albert Kirven," in *A History of Columbus, Georgia, 1828–1928* (Columbus: Historical Publishing, 1929), appendix; *CE-S*, Mar. 2, 1890, Sept. 10, 1886; Mrs. W. M. Fambrough, "Progressive Spirit of Founders of Businesses in Columbus Has Built the City into Trading Center," *CE*, Mar. 24, 1950.

10. Lupold, "Like an Extended Family," 9–10; Oscar S. Straus, *Under Four Administrations: From Cleveland to Taft* (Boston: Houghton Mifflin, 1922), 21; *CE*, Dec. 2, 1865; *CE-S*, Dec. 9, 14, 1878; "The Jewish Fair," *CE-S*, Dec. 9, 1886; "A Brilliant Beginning," *CE-S*, Dec. 15, 1886; Raphael J. Moses, "Autobiography of Raphael J. Moses," 1892, Smith Collection; Stephen J. Whitfield, "Jewish Fates, Altered States," in *Jewish Roots in Southern Soil: A New History*, ed. Marcie Ferris and Mark I. Greenberg (Waltham, Mass.: Brandeis University Press, 2006), 314; Howard N. Rabinowitz, *Race, Ethnicity, and Urbanization: Selected Essays* (Columbia: University of Missouri Press, 1994), 266.

11. David Gerson interview, New South Miscellany, box 1, folder 9, MARBL; Land, *Columbus*, 75–135; Lynn Willoughby, *Judge Aaron Cohn: Memoirs of a First Generation American* (n.p.: BookSurge, 2008), 15–16; Margaret Byrne interview, Feb. 19, 26, 1975, GOHC.

12. "Columbus, Georgia," *Encyclopedia of Southern Jewish Communities*, Goldring/Woldenberg Institute of Southern Jewish Life, http://www.isjl.org/georgia-columbus-encyclopedia.html; "Notice of Dissolution," *CE-S*, Feb. 2, 1889; "Moses Simons Passes Away," *CE-S*, Feb. 22, 1907.

13. "Company History—Spanning Three Centuries," David Rothschild Company, http://www.davidrothschildco.com/history_%20of_%20david_%20rothschild_%20co.htm; J. B. Karfunkle, "Sol Loeb Warehouse," 1977, HAER Collection, box 2, folder 5; Sol Loeb Scrapbook, CSUA; Stuart Rockoff, "The Jews of Columbus, Part II," *Jewish Georgian* 24, no. 3 (2012): 29; Willoughby, *Judge Aaron Cohn*, 10–30.

14. Craig Lloyd, "The Origins and Development of the Black Middle Class in Columbus, Georgia," Lift Every Voice Collection, MC 205, ser. 2, box 1, folder 13, CSUA; John Hill testimony, in *RC*, 593, 595; Alfred H. Hendricks testimony, in *RC*, 631; Lupold and French, *Bridging Deep South Rivers*, 197; Billy Winn, "The City's Oldest Black Business," *CL-E*, Mar. 14, 1995; Judith Grant-Shabazz and Margaret Dawson, *Black Pioneers in the Historical Development of Columbus, Georgia* (Columbus: Columbus Consolidated Government, 1990); "Clippings from Papers Edited by Colored Men," *American Missionary* 43, no. 3 (1889): 70, http://www.gutenberg.org/files/16103/16103-h/16103-h.htm; John S. Lupold, "Black Businessmen and Professionals, 1900," Lupold Collection, ser. 6, box 1, folder 17; *CE-S*, Jan. 16, 1886; Roger Harris, "Some Childhood Memories of Miss Loretto Chappell," *Muscogiana* 1, no. 3 (1990): 141.

15. Land, *Columbus*, 53, 142–43; *CE*, May 7, 1873; "Vivid History of Columbus Fire

Dept., Now 100 Years Old, Given by Pearce," *CL-E*, Aug. 22, 1937; Kenneth H. Thomas, *Columbus, Georgia in Vintage Postcards* (Charleston, S.C.: Arcadia, 2001), 31, 59; *CE-S*, Jan. 5, 1879, Oct. 8, 1901; J. Ralston Cargill, "Register of Reasons for a Modern Hotel in Columbus, Georgia," [1914], Baldwin Papers, box 24, folder 1049; Paul Timm, "Ralston Hotel to Close to Transients Sept. 6," *CL*, Aug. 5, 1974; Theo Jackson McGee, *A Pleasant Journey* (Columbus: n.p., 1975), 106.

16. Land, *Columbus*, 35; *CE*, Dec. 27, 29, 1874, June 15, 22, 1875; *CE-S*, Oct. 16, 1896; Telfair, *History of Columbus, Georgia*, 203–204; *AR*, 1878, 1892, 1898, 1910, 1915.

17. "Officer Harvey Dead, Stokes Wounded," *CE-S*, May 21, 1920; "Clues Chased Down but Double Murderer Remains a Fugitive," *CE-S*, May 25, 1920; "Will Maddox Dies in Okla. Reports State," *CE-S*, Sept. 8, 1920; *AR*, 1878, 1892, 1898, 1910, 1915.

18. *CE-S*, Apr. 21, 23, May 8, 1878, Jan. 20, 1880, July 6, 1889; Ken Elkins, "Courageous Editor Gives Life in Line of Duty," *CL-E*, May 7, 1878; John F. Flournoy, D. P. Dozier, Cliff B. Farnie, Wm. A. Little, and T. E. Blanchard to Gunby Jordan, July 6, 10, 1889, Hoke Smith to Gunby Jordan, July 11, 1889, all in G. Gunby Jordan Collection, MC 12, box 1, folder 1, CSUA.

19. "A Terrible Tragedy," *CE-S*, Nov. 12, 1890; "The Crime Is Murder," *CE-S*, Nov. 13, 1890; "The Court of Inquiry," *CE-S*, Dec. 3, 1890; "The Third Day's Trial," *CE-S*, Dec. 4, 1890; "Judge Fort's Decision," *CE-S*, Dec. 20, 1890.

20. "The Trial Commenced," *CE-S*, Nov. 10, 1891; "The Trial Moves On," *CE-S*, Nov. 12, 1891; "The Evidence All In," *CE-S*, Nov. 15, 1891; "They Are Not Guilty," *CE-S*, Nov. 20, 1891.

21. Sheldon Hackney, *Populism to Progressivism in Alabama* (Princeton: Princeton University Press, 1969), 138; *New Charter of the City of Columbus, Ga.*, 1891, HLUGA; *AR*, 1895; *CE-S*, Oct. 13, 1887, Aug. 17, Nov. 25, 30, Dec. 5, 1897; "Purity of the Ballot," *CE-S*, Aug. 19, 1898; "The Colored Politicians," *CE-S*, Nov. 19, 1897; "Today's Election," *CE-S*, May 18, 1898; "Local Laconics," *CE-S*, Nov. 17, 1898; John S. Lupold, untitled manuscript on progressive reform in Columbus, n.d., Lupold Collection, ser. 6, box 1, folder 75; Robert M. Howard, *Reminiscences* (Columbus: Gilbert, 1912), 68; A. O. Blackmar Sr., Scrapbook, Katherine Mahan Collection, MC 165, CSUA.

22. "Columbus Fire Department," *CL-E*, Aug. 22, 1937; W. C. Woodall, "Big Sweep: Fifth Ave.'s 2nd Fire," *CL*, n.d. (clipping), W. C. Woodall, "Volunteer Firemen," *CL*, Apr. 6, 1964 (clipping), both in W. C. Woodall Collection, MC 33, box 5, CSUA; Fred H. Schomburg Sr., *Memories of Fred H. Schomburg, Sr., 1881–1972*, 3, CSUA; *AR*, 1892, 1898, 1912; *CE-S*, May 4, 1898, July 31, 1906; Thomas, *Columbus, Georgia*, 50.

23. *CE-S*, Dec. 11, 1900, May 11, 1901, June 1, 1902, Apr. 6, 1904, May 10, 1895; Susan Schley Gristina and Philip Schley interview, Mar. 28, 2012, GOHC; William Winn, "The Medical Center, 1836–1991: An Institutional History of Public Service, Education, and Leadership in Medicine" [unpublished manuscript], 13, 28–40, Causey Collection; "Mud, Water Long Aroused Ire Here," *CL*, n.d. (clipping), Chappell Collection, box 2, folder 25; *AR*, 1895, 1898.

24. D. Abbott Turner interview, 1976, Loretto Chappell interview, Feb. 1975, both in GOHC; *CE-S*, Apr. 12, 1900, May 19, 1901.

25. *CE-S*, Oct. 8, 1901, Aug. 9, 1903, July 19, 1910, Nov. 24, 1912; Thomas, *Columbus, Georgia*, 20, 21; *AR*, 1910.

26. *CE-S*, Aug. 14, Oct. 7, 1900, Aug. 24, 1901, Apr. 7, 1903, May 8, 1904.

27. Robert P. Clapp to Stone and Webster, May 15, 1901, Baldwin Papers, box 19, folder 819; J. B. Karfunkle, Barbara Kimmelman, and John S. Lupold, "The Power Station of the Columbus Railroad Company at the City Mills Dam," 1977, 1–2, 26–31,

HAER Collection, box 1, folder 14; Schomburg, *Memories*, 9–10; W. C. Woodall, "A Trip 'Around the Belt,'" *CL*, Sept. 12, 1966; W. C. Woodall, "Street Cars Played Great Role in Life of City in Old Days," *CL*, Feb. 22, 1934.

28. "Consolidation Is Effected," *CE-S*, Nov. 23, 1894; H. S. Reynolds to George Baldwin, Jan. 2, 1902, Baldwin Papers, box 19, folder 841; "An Ordinance," [May 1901], Baldwin Papers, box 19, folder 819; L. F. Garrard to George Baldwin, Mar. 31, 1905, Baldwin Papers, box 22, folder 953; DuBose interview.

29. John S. Lupold and Richard Coss, "Nomination of St. Elmo/Weracoba for National Register of Historic Places," 15–17, Lupold Collection, ser. 8, box 1, folder 1; Land, *Columbus*, 57, 59; *CE-S*, Mar. 30, 1890, Aug. 25, 1897; W. C. Woodall, "When Lakebottom Was a Lake," *CL*, July 13, 1970; Karfunkle, Kimmelman, and Lupold, "Power Station," 27; Mary Hannah Flournoy interview, GOHC.

30. "Annexation Will Soon Be an Accomplished Fact," *CE-S*, July 4, 1909; *AR*, 1915; Land, *Columbus*, 128; Joyce Bassett, "Rose Hill: Columbus's First Suburb," July 23, 1979, Lupold Collection, ser. 6, box 3, folder 89; Sara Crawford, ed., *Gunby Jordan Remembers: A History of the Jordan Company, 1904–1986* (Columbus: Columbus Productions, 1986), 4, 9–13.

31. Callie B. McGinnis, "The First Decade of Telephone Service in Columbus, Georgia: Subscribers from 1880–1890," *Muscogiana* 22, no. 1 (2011): 9–25; Worsley, *Columbus on the Chattahoochee*, 375; *CE-S*, Apr. 22, 1880.

32. *CE-S*, Mar. 27, 1881; Land, *Columbus*, 88; Martin, *Columbus, Geo.*, 2:57; Worsley, *Columbus on the Chattahoochee*, 335, appendix A, 393–395; *CE*, Dec. 7, 1865; *AR*, 1898; "Report on the Gas Light Co. of Columbus," n.d., Baldwin Papers, box 19, folder 842; H. S. Reynolds to George Baldwin, Sept. 20, 1901, Baldwin Papers, box 19, folder 831; Barbara Kimmelman, John S. Lupold, and J. B. Karfunkle, "The City Mills," 13–15, 1977, HAER Collection, box 1, folder 7; "Hydroelectric Power Development at North Highlands," 2–8, HAER Collection, box 1, folder 15; "Water Power Development at the Falls of the Chattahoochee," 1977, 11, 16, HAER Collection, box 1, folder 14; "Columbus Manufacturing Company," 1977, 2–3, HAER Collection, box 1, folder 9; Karfunkle, Kimmelman and Lupold, "Power Station," 5, 11.

33. "George Johnson Baldwin, Columbus Companies Series, 1901–1914," Baldwin Papers, box 1, folder 1A; George Baldwin to Joseph F. Gray, Nov. 16, 1903, Baldwin Papers, box 23, folder 1040; George Baldwin to J. F. Hanson, Dec. 27, 1899, Baldwin Papers, box 2, folder 75; J. F. Hanson to George Baldwin, July 25, 1901, Baldwin Papers, box 3, folder 115; "Memorandum of Water Powers in the Chattahoochee River between Columbus and West Point, Ga., Taken from Bulletin 3A of Georgia Geological Survey," June 13, 1901, Baldwin Papers, box 19, folder 823; George Baldwin to Stone and Webster, June 14, 1902, box 19, folder 858, Baldwin Papers; "Development of East Highlands Reads Like a Fairy Story Book," *CE-S*, May 16, 1914; Lupold, Karfunkle, and Kimmelman, "Water Power Development," 12–13.

34. H. S. Reynolds to George Baldwin, Jan. 2, 1902, Baldwin Papers, box 19, folder 841; H. S. Reynolds to George Baldwin, Jan. 6, 1905, John F. Flournoy to George Baldwin, Jan. 11, 1905, both in Baldwin Papers, box 21, folder 945; J. F. Hanson to George Baldwin, Jan. 2, 1903, George Baldwin to Stone and Webster, Jan. 7, 1903, both in Baldwin Papers, box 20, folder 878; J. F. Hanson to George Baldwin, Dec. 4, 1903, Baldwin Papers, box 21, folder 916; George Baldwin to Stone and Webster, Mar. 3, 1904, Baldwin Papers, box 21, folder 925; George Baldwin to J. F. Hanson, Feb. 26, 1903, Baldwin Papers, box 20, folder 886; George Baldwin to L. H. Chappell, Nov. 3, 1903, Baldwin Papers, box 21, folder 915; "Falling Waters Reveal Damage," *CE-S*, Jan. 4,

1902; "Record Shows That January Was an Eventful Month Here," *CE-S*, Feb. 2, 1902; *CE-S*, Feb. 28, 1902; "Mills Will Start Up about Apr. 15," *CE-S*, Mar. 27, 1902; "Water Power," 13–14.

35. Stone and Webster to George Baldwin, Feb. 10, 1904, Baldwin Papers, box 21, folder 922; Stone and Webster to George Baldwin, Dec. 14, 1904, Gunby Jordan, Minutes of the Riparian Rights Committee, Dec. 13, 1904, both in Baldwin Papers, box 21, folder 942; "Columbus Power Consolidation," Mar. 2, 1903, Baldwin Papers, box 20, folder 887; Lupold, Karfunkle, and Kimmelman, "Water Power Development," 14–16; *CL*, Dec. 6, 1905.

36. "Citizens' Ticket," [Nov. 12, 1906], Baldwin Papers, box 22, folder 1000; George Baldwin to Stone and Webster, Mar. 19, 1909, Baldwin Papers, box 23, folder 1018; Stone and Webster to John S. Bleecker, Sept. 9, 1909, Baldwin Papers, box 23, folder 1029; "Chattahoochee Power Company," Nov. 3, 1909, Baldwin Papers, box 23, folder 1030; "Tentative Agreement between B. H. Hardaway and John S. Bleecker," Feb. 6, 1910, "Memorandum of Agreement," Feb. 14, 1910, both in Baldwin Papers, box 23, folder 1036; "Chattahooche Waters Christen Goat Rock," *CE-S*, Dec. 20, 1912; "Columbus to Have New Light and Power Plant," *CL*, Oct. 6, 1909; Lupold, Karfunkle, and Kimmelman, "Water Power Development," 16–24; Board of Trade, *Columbus, Georgia: The Place with the Power and the Push*, [1913], HLUGA; *CE*, Aug. 5, 1934.

37. "Mud, Water Long Aroused Ire Here," *CL*, n.d. (clipping), Chappell Collection, box 2, folder 25; B. M. Hall, *Report on Water Supply of Columbus, Georgia* (Columbus: Stewart, 1894), file II, box 59, GDAH.

38. H. S. Reynolds to George Baldwin, Baldwin to Reynolds, Nov. 3, 1902, Baldwin Papers, box 20, folder 872; George Baldwin to T. E. Golden, Jan. 10, 1903, Baldwin Papers, box 20, folder 878; "Mud, Water Long Aroused Ire Here," *CL*, n.d. (clipping), Chappell Collection, box 2, folder 25; *A River Runs through It: A 100-Year History of the Columbus Water Works* (Columbus: Water Works, 2002), 10–17; "Overwhelming Victory for Waterworks Bonds," *CE-S*, Oct. 19, 1913.

39. Michael F. Harkins, "Camp Conrad," Lupold Collection, ser. 6, box 1, folder 28; Worsley, *Columbus on the Chattahoochee*, 388–389; *CE-S*, Dec. 8, 1898; Telfair, *History of Columbus, Georgia*, 223.

40. Worsley, *Columbus on the Chattahoochee*, 409–414; Telfair, *History of Columbus, Georgia*, 268–278; Loretto Chappell interview; Winn, "Medical Center," 40.

41. Peggy A. Stepflug and Richard Hyatt, *Home of the Infantry: The History of Fort Benning* (Macon: Mercer University Press, 2007), 1–40; "Columbus Gets Big Army Camp," *CE-S*, Aug. 18, 1918; Louise DuBose, "Women in Columbus," 1975, Louise Jones DuBose Collection, MC 2, box 1, folder 1, CSUA.

42. Stepflug and Hyatt, *Home of the Infantry*; Elizabeth Carrow Woolfolk, *Pioneers, Patriots, and Planters: First Settlers in Virginia, Kentucky, North Carolina, South Carolina, Tennessee and Georgia* (Houston: Wynnton, 2004), 355; "The Boundaries of Fort Benning Are Designated by Colonel Eames," *CE-S*, Nov. 14, 1918; Sharyn Kane and Richard Keeton, *Fort Benning: The Land and the People* (Fort Benning: U.S. Army Infantry Center, 1994), 167–170.

43. A. Elizabeth Taylor, "The Origin and Development of the Convict Lease System in Georgia," *GHQ* 26, no. 2 (1942): 113, 117–118, 120, 127; Douglas A. Blackmon, *Slavery by Another Name: The Re-Enslavement of Black Americans from the Civil War to World War II* (New York: Doubleday, 2008), 53, 108; *CE-S*, Sept. 16, 1881; Matthew J. Mancini, *One Dies, Get Another: Convict Leasing in the American South, 1866–1928* (Columbia: University of South Carolina Press, 1996), 59–60, 78; "Joint Investigation

of the Convict Lease System," SR 37 (microfilm), 1908, Legislature—Commissions and Committees—Reports and Investigations, 1866-1968, 1:4-9, GDAH; *CL*, Oct. 31, 1897; *Twentieth Annual Report of the Commissioner of Labor: Convict Labor* (Washington, D.C.: U.S. Government Printing Office, 1906), 208, 354-355.

44. *Marion County Patriot*, May 21, 1886; "Penitentiary Investigation," *CE-S*, Sept. 9, 1887; "The Convict Investigation," *CE-S*, Sept. 22, 1887; Gunby Jordan to W. C. Woodall, Feb. 24, 1928, G. Gunby Jordan Collection, box 1, folder 4; Bruce Hall, "Plans for Road Work in Georgia," *Good Roads* 13, no. 3 (1917): 31-32.

45. E. P. Holmes testimony, in *RC*, 607-610; Thomas Jefferson Bates testimony, in *RC*, 491-493; Frederick Barret Gordon, "Industrial Progress and Possibilities of the Negro," Mar. 5, 1907, 15-17, HLUGA.

46. Eugene Granberry testimony, in *RC*, 494; W. H. Hinde testimony, in *RC*, 533; William H. Young testimony, in *RC*, 522; G. Gunby Jordan, speeches to the Georgia Industrial Association, May 30, 1901, June 16, 1911, both in G. Gunby Jordan Collection, box 1, folder 6; Jensen, "Let Us Not Be," 41-42.

47. John S. Lupold, "The Growth and Influence of the Eagle and Phenix Manufacturing Company, a Pioneer Large-Scale New South Textile Mill, 1865-1914," paper presented at the Citadel Conference on the New South, 1979, 7-9, Lupold Collection, ser. 7, box 1, folder 1; "The Weavers Strike," *CE-S*, Mar. 29, 1896; "The Eagle and Phenix Strike," *CE-S*, Mar. 31, 1896; "In Receivers' Hands," *CE-S*, June 14, 1896, "Purchased by Bondholders," *CE-S*, June 8, 1898; John S. Lupold, Barbara Kimmelman, and J. B. Karfunkle, "The Eagle and Phenix Mills," 1977, 5, HAER Collection, box 1, folder 10.

48. "A New 20,000 Spindle Mill!" *CE-S*, Mar. 11, 1900; Barbara Kimmelman, John S. Lupold, and J. B. Karfunkle, "The Columbus Plant of the Bibb Manufacturing Company," 1977, HAER Collection, box 1, folder 4; John S. Lupold, "Bibb City Historic District," National Register of Historic Places, Lupold Collection, ser. 6, box 1, folder 12; Lupold, "Growth and Influence of the Eagle and Phenix," 10.

49. *Constitution and By-Laws of Weavers Union No. 1111*, Apr. 18, 1896, HLUGA; "Winn and Greene Are Appointed," *CE-S*, Feb. 18, 1899; "Georgia Labor in Annual Convention," *CE-S*, Apr. 18, 1901; Frank Joseph Byrne, "The Columbus Strikes of 1918-1921: Textile Unionism and Violence in Post-World War I Georgia," (master's thesis, University of Georgia, 1994), 34-35, 30; *Preamble, Constitution, and Rules of Order of the Central Federation of Labor*, 1902, HLUGA; "Bibb City Club Formaly Opened," *CL*, Mar. 29, 1908; Board of Trade, *Columbus, Georgia*.

50. John F. Flournoy to George Baldwin, June 28, 1901, Stone & Webster to George Baldwin, July 30, 1901, Rollin Jefferson to H. S. Reynolds, Aug. 2, 1901, Baldwin Papers, box 19, folder 824; H. S. Reynolds to George Baldwin, July 8, 1903, Baldwin Papers, box 20, folder 907; "Street Railway Employees Are Out on a Strike," *CE-S*; July 31, 1901, "Supper to the Street Car Men," *CE-S*, Jan. 11, 1903, May 2, 1900.

51. Byrne, "Columbus Strikes," 14, 21, 27; Lupold, "Bibb City"; Lupold, untitled manuscript on progressive reform.

52. Byrne, "Columbus Strikes," 36-45; Lupold, untitled manuscript on progressive reform; "400 Employees Quit When Eagle & Phenix Mill Posts Notice Banning Union Help," *CE-S*, Apr. 2, 1918; "City and Suburbs Put under Martial Law by Gov. Dorsey," *CE-S*, Aug. 15, 1918.

53. Byrne, "Columbus Strikes," 45-46; Lupold, untitled manuscript on progressive reform; "Injunction Obtained by Swift Spinning Mill against Thomas and Others," *CE-S*, Aug. 16, 1918; "To the Law-Abiding Citizens of Columbus, Georgia," *CE-S*,

Aug. 18, 1918; "Strikers Return to Work This Morning in All Textile Mills," *CE-S*, Aug. 21, 1918; Frederick B. Gordon, "Mill Workers and the War," Nov. 15, 1918, HLUGA.

54. Lupold, untitled manuscript on progressive reform; Byrne, "Columbus Strikes," 50–53; *CL*, Feb. 2, 1919; "Big Nationwide Textile Strike Effective Today," *CE-S*, Feb. 3, 1919; "Textile Mills Close as Operatives Quit after 8 Hours Work," *CE-S*, Feb. 4, 1919.

55. Byrne, "Columbus Strikes," 54–60, 77, 81–82; "Strikers Will Picket Plants That Refused Eight Hour Work Day," *CE-S*, Feb. 5, 1919, "Labor Organizer Charged with Inciting to Riot," *CE-S*, Feb. 22, 1919; "Twenty-Seventh Passes into History," *CE-S*, Mar. 26, 1919; "Textile Strike Is Voted Off; Is Effective Mon. A.M.," *CE-S*, Apr. 4 1919; Teresa Griffin to Murray, Feb. 9, 1919, Lewis Neale Whittle Papers, Collection 777, SHC.

56. James Walker to Samuel Gompers, June 8, 1919, C. F. McLaughlin to Hugh M. Dorsey, May 30, 1919, "Resolution Adopted Unanimously by the Convention of the American Federation of Labor, Atlantic City, N.J." (photocopies), all in Lupold Collection, ser. 6, box 4, folder 20; "Seven Are Shot in Labor Riot Here," *CE-S*, May 22, 1919; "Carr and Clark Are Acquitted of Murder by Jury," *CE-S*, July 26, 1919; "Over 200 Workers Joined Strikers Is Claim," *CE-S*, Apr. 1, 1921; Byrne, "Columbus Strikes," 62, 83–84; *CL*, Mar. 30, 1921.

Chapter 4. Lynching, Industrial Education, Babe Ruth, and Christian Communism

1. Liz Barton to Nora Johnson, Oct. 2, 1977, Margaret S. Sullivan Papers, MC 298, ser. 1, box 2, folder 2, CSUA; Margaret Byrne interview, GOHC; "A Mad Mule on Broad Street Today," *CL*, Jan. 15, 1908.

2. "Emancipation Proclamation," *CE-S*, Jan. 2, 1898; C. H. Johnson, testimony, in *RC*, 637.

3. "Will Demand Separation," *CE-S*, May 16, 1900; "Lincoln Park Root of Evil," *CE-S*, May 23, 1900; "Things of Interest Before the Council," *CE-S*, June 7, 1900; "Car Ordinance Was Violated," *CE-S*, Aug. 23, 1900; John F. Flournoy to George Baldwin, Oct. 25, 1901, George Baldwin to F. E. Reidhead, July 11, 1905, both in Baldwin Papers, box 19, folder 834.

4. Richard Wright, *Black Boy* (1945; New York: Harper, 2007), 172; "SWIFT JUSTICE!" "Slaton's Crime," "Yesterday's Tragedy," both in *CE-S*, June 2, 1896; Billy Winn, "Racial Violence in the Chattahoochee Valley," presentation at the Columbus Public Library, May 3, 2007, Causey Collection.

5. "Retribution Came Quickly," *CE-S*, June 10, 1900; Winn, "Racial Violence"; William W. Winn, "Lynching on Wynn's Hill," *Southern Exposure* 14, no. 3–4 (1987): 17–24.

6. Winn, "Lynching on Wynn's Hill"; "It's Murder Says Coroner," *CE-S*, July 2, 1912; "Taken from Courthouse by a Mob and Lynched," *CE-S*, Aug. 14, 1912.

7. Winn, "Lynching on Wynn's Hill"; "Solemn Protest Is Made against Mob Violence," *CE-S*, Aug. 21, 1912; "Three Men Are Indicted," *CE-S*, Aug. 31, 1912; "Grand Jury Finds Bill against Land," *CE-S*, Sept. 6, 1912; "Lands and Lynn in Jail," *CE-S*, Nov. 24, 1912; Nathan Straus to Lucian Lamar Knight, Dec. 2, 1914, file II, box 148, Straus folder, GDAH; Phoebe Farris, ed., *Women Artists of Color: A Bio-Critical Sourcebook to 20th Century Artists in the Americas* (Westport, Conn.: Greenwood, 1999), 360–365.

8. *AR*, 1910; Victoria MacDonald Huntzinger, "Birth of Southern Public Education: Columbus, Georgia, 1864–1904" (EdD diss., Harvard University, 1992), 155–157; Eugene Granberry testimony, in *RC*, 502–503; George Dews testimony, in *RC*, 601–604; Katherine Hines Mahan and William Clyde Woodall, *A History of Public Schools in*

Columbus, Muscogee County, Georgia (Columbus: Muscogee County Board of Education, 1977), 92, 157, 233.

9. Huntzinger, "Birth of Southern Public Education," 164–175; Mahan and Woodall, *History of Public Schools*, 163–165.

10. Huntzinger, "Birth of Southern Public Education," 176–213; *Thirty-Fifth Annual Report of the Public Schools of Columbus, Georgia*, 1902, 28–29, Columbus Public School Report Collection, box 6, CSUA.

11. Huntzinger, "Birth of Southern Public Education," 185–195; "The Free Kindergarten Inaugurated," *CE-S*, Apr. 7, 1895; "Kindergarten Established for Children of the Operatives of the Eagle & Phenix Mills," *CE-S*, Nov. 15, 1903; F. B. Gordon, "President Mill, Columbus, Ga.: Answers 'The Last Stronghold of Infant Mill Slavery,'" *Social Service* 4, no. 5 (1902): 148–149; Carleton Gibson to George Foster Peabody, Aug. 29, 1901, George Foster Peabody Papers, box 73, YMCA Columbus, Georgia folder, Library of Congress; G. Gunby Jordan, Speech to the Georgia Industrial Association annual meeting at Warm Springs, May 30, 1901, G. Gunby Jordan Collection, MC 12, box 1, folder 6, CSUA.

12. "Educating Southern Factory Children; Mrs. Leonora Beck Ellis' Description of Columbus's Primary Industrial School," *CE-S*, Apr. 26, 1903; Huntzinger, "Birth of Southern Public Education," 196–203; Carleton Gibson to George Foster Peabody, May 9, 1904, George Foster Peabody Papers, box 73, YMCA, Columbus, Georgia folder.

13. "McIlhenny Name of New School on N. Highlands," *CE-S*, Apr. 28, 1915; Huntzinger, "Birth of Southern Public Education," 196–203; Roland B. Daniel, "Industrial Education in Columbus," *Journal of Proceedings and Addresses of the Twenty-Fourth Annual Meeting of the Southern Educational Association* (Nashville: Southern Educational Association, 1913), 192.

14. Carleton Gibson, The *Secondary Industrial School of Columbus, Georgia*, Jan. 1909, 45–47, HLUGA; "School Board Decides to Build $50,000 Secondary Industrial School on Rose Hill," *CE-S*, Jan. 10, 1906; George Baldwin to F. E. Reidhead, Feb. 9, 1907, Baldwin Papers, box 23, folder 1004; Mabel Longshore Bryan, "History of the Jordan Vocational High School" (master's thesis, University of Georgia, 1943), 6–7; Lauren Yarnell Bradshaw, "Practical Paternalism: G. Gunby Jordan's Quest for a Vocational School System in Columbus, Georgia" (PhD diss., Georgia State University, 2016).

15. Bryan, "History," 7–14; Gibson, *Secondary Industrial School*, 48; "First Graduating Exercises There," *CE-S*, July 26, 1908; "Name of Industrial Changed to Jordan Vocational High at Cornerstone Exercises," *CE-S*, Mar. 13, 1937.

16. Huntzinger, "Birth of Southern Public Education," 203–212; Carleton Gibson, "The Negro Schools of Columbus, Georgia," *Southern Workman* 39, no. 11 (1910): 596–598; Daniel, "Industrial Education in Columbus," 190; Frederick Barret Gordon, "Industrial Progress and Possibilities of the Negro," Mar. 5, 1907, 15–17, HLUGA.

17. Mahan and Woodall, *History of Public Schools*, 226–228, 230, 234–237; Huntzinger, "Birth of Southern Public Education," 212–213.

18. W. C. Woodall, "Woodall Says Enquirer City's Oldest Business Institution," *CE*, May 26, 1948; "Opening of the New Library Yesterday," *CE-S*, Oct. 16, 1907; "Children Flock to the New Library," *CE-S*, Oct. 19, 1907; *AR*, 1915; Loretto Chappell interview, Feb. 1975, GOHC.

19. *CE*, Feb. 10, 21, 23, May 17, 1871; Helen B. Keller, "History of the Theatre in Columbus, Georgia from 1828 to 1865" (master's thesis, University of Georgia, 1957), 51–55; *CL*, Jan. 19, 1902; Clason Kyle, *In Order of Appearance: Chronicling Thirty-*

Five Years on America's Most Celebrated Stage (Columbus: Communicorp, 2006), 42–44, 136, 140, 149, 281, 311; "Entertainments in Columbus," Robert Harold Brisendine Papers, box 3, folder 32, MARBL; Theatrical handbills, Smith Collection, box 8, Springer Opera House Handbills (1909–1914) folder; Board of Trade, *Columbus, Georgia*, [1913], HLUGA; John S. Lupold, *Columbus, Georgia, 1828–1978* (Columbus: Columbus Sesquicentennial, 1978), 116; "The 'Bonita' Opens Nov. 1," *CE-S*, Oct. 2, 1910; Etta Blanchard Worsley, "Roy Elmo Martin, Sr.," in *Columbus on the Chattahoochee* (Columbus: Columbus Office Supply, 1951), appendix.

20. Ads for Buffalo Bill Wild West Show, *CE-S*, Oct. 6, 1895; "Programme of the Chattahoochee Valley Exposition," *CE-S*, Sept. 28, 1888; "Colored People's Day," *CE-S*, Nov. 27, 1888; "Columbus and the Exposition," *CE-S*, Nov. 9, 1890; "The Biggest Day Yet over 12,000 Visitors to Exposition Park," *CE-S*, Nov. 1, 1892; "Big Opening of Chattahoochee Valley Fair Held with Many Exhibits—Is Largely Attended," *CE-S*, Oct. 23, 1917; Fred H. Schomburg Sr., *Memories of Fred H. Schomburg, Sr., 1881–1972*, 1, 6, CSUA.

21. Worsley, *Columbus on the Chattahoochee*, 355–359; "The Rink at Villa Reich," *CE-S*, Jan. 22, 1902; Samuel Spencer to Louisa Benning, Dec. 3, 1870, Samuel Spencer Papers, Collection 3477, box 3, folder 34, SHC.

22. George Foster Peabody to J. A. Kirven, Sept. 20, 1901, George Foster Peabody to L. H. Chappell, Feb. 7, 1907, J. E. Moorland to George Foster Peabody, Oct. 9, 1906, A. T. Maycock to George Foster Peabody, June 29, 1908, all in Peabody Papers, box 73, YMCA Columbus, Georgia folder; "Y.M.C.A. Organized," *CE-S*, Apr. 25, 1901; "To Organize a Colored Y.M.C.A.," *CE-S*, Apr. 28, 1901; "Opening of the Y.M.C.A. Today," *CE-S*, Dec. 2, 1903; "Booker T. Washington Speaks," *CE-S*, Oct. 9, 1907.

23. *CE*, Aug. 8, 1867, Oct. 26, 1870; "The Pennant Ours," *CE-S*, July 14, 1888; "The Southern League," *CE-S*, Sept. 4, 1897; "Jim Fox as Manager of Columbus Ball Team," *CE-S*, Nov. 21, 1908; "Outlook for Sally League Dark This Year," *CE-S*, Feb. 24, 1918; Lupold, *Columbus, Georgia*, 117.

24. *CE-S*, Feb. 23, 1912; "Columbus Is Glad to Be Spring Training Camp for Pittsburgh National League Baseball Squad," *CE-S*, Mar. 11, 1917; "Braves' Boss in Columbus; Likes Grounds," *CE-S*, Feb. 18, 1919; "Braves Hold First Spring Practice Wednesday," *CE-S*, Mar. 4, 1920; "Yankee–Rochester Game Arrangements Complete; Rotarians to Dine Ruth," *CE-S*, Mar. 9, 1924; "Yanks Downed by Rochester," *CE-S*, Apr. 3, 1924.

25. "'Foxes' Chosen as Name for Columbus Team," *CE-S*, Apr. 18, 1926; "South Commons Selected as Site for Ball Park," *CE-S*, Apr. 11, 1926; "Theodore E. Golden Dies at Home Here After Long Illness," *CE-S*, Oct. 9, 1937; "Negro Teams Play at Golden Park," *CE-S*, Apr. 24, 1929; "Pinch Hittin'," *CE-S*, May 19, 1932; "Columbus Only Pennant-Winner in Cardinal System," *CE-S*, Oct. 7, 1936; John S. Lupold, *Heritage Park: A Celebration of the Industrial Heritage of Columbus, Georgia* (Columbus: Historic Columbus Foundation, 1999), 52.

26. "Columbus Has Opportunity to Secure Big Game," *CE-S*, Sept. 7, 1916; "Athletic Stadium to Honor Memory World War Heroes," *CE-S*, Mar. 24, 1923; Lupold, *Columbus, Georgia*, 117; Tuskegee-Morehouse, http://www.tuskegee-morehouse.com/.

27. Mahan and Woodall, *History of Public Schools*, 225; "The Baseball Team," *CE-S*, Mar. 26, 1899; "Saturday's Football Game," *CE-S*, Nov. 1, 1900; "Girl Athletes of the High School Organize," *CE-S*, Oct. 24, 1909; "Sheridan Elected to Police Board," *CE-S*, July 7, 1921; "Smith Again Named Mayor of Columbus," *CE-S*, Jan. 4, 1933;

Edwina Wood, Department of Recreation, Reports for July 1924, Feb., Mar. 1925, Smith Collection, box 6, 1917–1926 City Miscellaneous folder.

28. John S. Lupold, "Bibb City Historic District," National Register of Historic Places, Lupold Collection, ser. 6, box 1, folder 12; "Movement to Buy North Highlands Park Given a Strong Endorsement," *CE-S*, May 29, 1908; "Mother and Child Dead under Debris of North Highlands Pavilion," *CE-S*, Apr. 25, 1908.

29. "Trains Will Be Held," *CE-S*, July 25, 1896; "Money Cannot Overcome Racial Characteristics," *CE-S*, Apr. 3, 1908.

30. W. C. Woodall, "When Lakebottom Was a Lake," July 13, 1970, *CL*; "No Necessity to Go Off," *CE-S*, July 6, 1890; "Thousands Went out to Wildwood," *CE-S*, Apr. 1, 1902; "Picnic Day Was Enjoyed," *CE-S*, May 8, 1910; "Labor Day Program for Wildwood Park," *CE-S*, Sept. 4, 1908; "Public May Lose Wildwood Park," *CE-S*, Sept. 1, 1920; "Wildwood Offer Submitted to City," *CE-S*, Feb. 17, 1922.

31. "Down the Chattahoochee," *CE-S*, Mar. 18, 1894; "Social News," *CE-S*, Jan. 6, 1921; "Massachusetts Man Writes of Hospitality and Cordiality of Columbus and Her People," *CE-S*, Apr. 17, 1921; Louise DuBose interview, Sept. 1975, GOHC; David Rose, *The Big Eddy Club: The Stocking Stranglings and Southern Justice* (New York: New Press, 2007), 2.

32. "The Country Club of Columbus Is Organized," *CE-S*, June 8, 1909; "Dynamite and Golf Balls Explode at the Country Club," *CE-S*, July 19, 1919; "Standard Club Asks for Charter," *CE-S*, Dec. 7, 1907; "Application for Charter," *CE-S*, Oct. 8, 1909; *Constitution and Rules, Muscogee Club, Columbus, Georgia*, 1900, HLUGA; Lynn Willoughby, *Judge Aaron Cohn: Memoirs of a First Generation American* (n.p.: BookSurge, 2008), 36, 48; "Columbus, Georgia," *Encyclopedia of Southern Jewish Communities*, Goldring/Woldenberg Institute of Southern Jewish Life, http://www.isjl.org/georgia-columbus-encyclopedia.html.

33. "Many Secret Orders in Columbus, and the Fraternal Spirit Is Strong," *CE-S*, Nov. 15, 1903; "Handsome Temple, Erected by Masons, Is One of the Finest Buildings in the City," *CE-S*, Nov. 15, 1903; "The Eagle & Phenix Club, for Cotton Mill Operatives," *CE-S*, Nov. 15, 1903; "Colored Masons Here," *CE-S*, June 25, 1896; "Colored Odd Fellows," *CE-S*, Feb. 18, 1899; "Colored K.P.'s to Celebrate Today," *CE-S*, Mar. 28, 1909; "Int. Ben. Society Having a Fine Annual Session," *CE-S*, Aug. 29, 1919; Daniel Levine, "A Single Standard of Civilization: Black Private Social Welfare Institutions in the South, 1880s–1920s," *GHQ* 81, no. 1 (1997): 53, 55, 61–63; *International Order of Twelve: Constitution, By-Laws and Rules of Order* (Columbus: Gilbert, n.d.), CSUA; Robert W. Williams testimony, in *RC*, 615.

34. "The King's Daughters," *CE-S*, July 30, 1887; Mrs. J. S. Gordy, "Century Club Card Party Lovely," *CE-S*, June 8, 1919; "City Federation Formed Yesterday," *CE-S*, May 21, 1912; "Negro Committee Thanks Donors," *CE-S*, July 22, 1923; *CE-S*, Mar. 15, 1916; "Free Clinic for Children Opens Today," *CE-S*, June 4, 1917; "City Federation Endorses Dental Clinic and Pure Milk Movement," *CE-S*, Feb. 20, 1919; "Club Women to Ask City Council for Health Dept.," *CE-S*, June 1, 1918; "Federation Co-Operates in Crusade," *CE-S*, Nov. 27, 1917; Levine, "Single Standard of Civilization," 64.

35. James A. Dombrowski, The *Early Days of Christian Socialism in America* (New York: Octagon, 1977), 14–22, 132–170; Josiah Strong, *The New Era; or, The Coming Kingdom* (New York: Baker and Taylor, 1898), 345; "Muscogee Now Has a Colony," *CE-S*, Nov. 24, 1896; "Much Interest in Commonwealth," *CE-S*, Dec. 31, 1898; John O. Fish, "The Christian Commonwealth: A Georgia Experiment," *GHQ* 57, no. 2 (1973):

213–220; Paul D. Bolster, "Christian Socialism Comes to Georgia: The Christian Commonwealth Colony," *Georgia Review* 26, no. 1 (1972): 61–70.

36. Fish, "Christian Commonwealth," 220–223; "The Colony Is Now in Court," *CE-S*, May 18, 1899; "No Receiver for Colony," *CE-S*, June 8, 1899; "Receiver's Sale," *CE-S*, Nov. 7, 1900; "Enterprises at the Commonwealth," *CE-S*, Oct. 13, 1903.

37. Barbara Welter, "The Cult of True Womanhood: 1820–1860," *American Quarterly* 18, No. 2 (1966): 152–173; A. Elizabeth Taylor, "The Origin of the Woman Suffrage Movement in Georgia," *GHQ* 28, no. 2 (1944): 64–78; "Address of Miriam Howard DuBose," *Woman's Tribune*, Feb. 19, 1894, Women's Suffrage, Ga., Collection, GDAH; "What One Woman Thinks," [1895] (clipping), National American Woman Suffrage Association Papers, Reel 62, Library of Congress; Susan B. Anthony diary, Feb. 3, 4, 1895, Susan B. Anthony Papers, Reel 3, Library of Congress.

38. Anthony diary, Feb. 6, 7, 8, 1895; "Mrs. McLendon to Mr. Callaway," *Macon Telegraph*, July 10, 1916; Taylor, "Origin," 79.

39. *State of Georgia v. Augusta Howard*, Nov. 1920, Richard Howard, application for pardon, Application for Executive Clemency, Dec. 2, 1921, Governor, Convict and Fugitive Records—Applications for Clemency, GDAH; "Love for Magnolias May Cost Willie Lee his Life," *CE-S*, May 21, 1920; "Miss Howard's Case Be Called in Superior Court Today," *CE-S*, Aug. 5, 1920; "Miss Howard's Trial Set for August 5th," *CL*, July 18, 1920.

40. *Georgia v. Howard*, Howard application for pardon, Application for Executive Clemency; "Miss Howard Makes Statement to Jury," *CE-S*, Nov. 25, 1920; "Convicted on Charge of Unlawful Shooting," *CE-S*, Nov. 27, 1920; "Prison Board Urges Pardon," *CL*, Nov. 30, 1921; "Mrs. Napier Gets Pardon for Woman of Columbus," *Macon Telegraph*, Dec. 13, 1921; Chris Hart e-mail, July 1, 2015, Causey Collection.

41. "Franchise League Formed," *CL*, Nov. 26, 1913; Gunby Jordan, "Cheerful Results of the Agitation," Frank J. Dudley, "Not Governed by Dictates of Bossism," both in *CL*, June 28, 1914; A. Elizabeth Taylor, "Revival and Development of the Woman Suffrage Movement in Georgia," *GHQ* 42, no. 4 (1958): 353; Anna Caroline Benning to Louisa Benning, Dec. 15, 18, 1872, Samuel Spencer Papers, box 4, folder 57, SHC.

42. Eugene Anderson, *Unchaining the Demons of the Lower World or A Petition of Ninety-Nine Per Cent. against Suffrage*, Georgia Association Opposed to Woman Suffrage, Rare Pamphlets Collection, GDAH; "She Belongs to Columbus," *CE-S*, Nov. 3, 1896; "Women's Party Demonstrations," *CE-S*, Aug. 17, 1918; "Equal Suffrage," *CL*, Aug. 29, 1915.

43. "That Suffrage Amendment," *CL*, July 15, 1919; "Muscogee Women Are Active for Woman Suffrage," *CL*, Dec. 19, 1920; "Snakes in Ireland," *CE-S*, Aug. 29, 1920; "Women Register to Vote for First Time in County," *CE-S*, Jan. 18, 1921; A. Elizabeth Taylor, "The Last Phase of the Woman Suffrage Movement in Georgia," *GHQ* 43, no. 1 (1959): 16–17, 23.

Chapter 5. The Klan and Coca-Cola

1. "Modern Things for Modern Women," *CE-S*, July 1, 1920; Bruce Bliven, "Away Down South: Casual Notes of a Traveler in the Land of the New Frontier," *New Republic*, Oct. 1927, 296.

2. "The Sentiment for Commission Government Almost Unanimous," *CL*, June 6, 1913; "Commission Government Charter Is Defeated," *CL*, Dec. 11, 1913; "New City Charter Gets Overwhelming Approval by People," *CL*, Sept. 28, 1921; Democratic City

Government Committee, "To Each and Every Voter," "Why the Commission-Manager Bill?," both in Smith Collection, box 1, 1920 State Election folder.

3. "Primary Victors among Columbus Leading Citizens," *CE-S*, Nov. 27, 1921; "Clements Slain; Huling and Son Are Held," *CE-S*, Sept. 10, 1922; "County Board Contests Lost by Incumbents," *CE*, Sept. 13, 1934; Katherine McDuffie, "Mrs. Tolbert Receives Golden Rule Foundation Scroll Honoring Her as American Mother of '54," *CL*, May 7, 1954.

4. "H. Gordon Hinkle, City Manager, Is Victim of Attack," *CE-S*, Apr. 22, 1922; Gregory C. Lisby and William F. Mugleston, *Someone Had to Be Hated: Julian LaRose Harris—A Biography* (Durham: Carolina Academic, 2002), 103–142; "Non Silba Sed Anthar," Smith Collection, box 9, folder 3.

5. Lisby and Mugleston, *Someone Had to Be Hated*; "Lives of Dimon and Hinkle Threatened," *CE-S*, Apr. 23, 1922; "Front of Mayor's Home Shattered by Bomb in Attempt to Assassinate Him," *CE-S*, May 21, 1922; "Threatening Letter to Mayor," *CE-S*, May 23, 1922; "City Manager Hinkle Leaves Dissatisfied," *CE-S*, May 27, 1922; "Police Chief Moore Discharged," *CE-S*, Dec. 24, 1922; "Bomb Plot Bared; Grand Jury to Act," *CE-S*, Dec. 28, 1922; "Columbus Klan Disbanded by Kleagle," *CE-S*, Jan. 12, 1923; "Enquirer-Sun Awarded Pulitzer Medal," *CE-S*, May 4, 1926.

6. "City Budget Is Approved," *CL*, Apr. 7, 1922; "Community Leaders Hear Final Report on City Planning," *CE-S*, Jan. 14, 1926; "Airplane Field Sign for Columbus Urged," *CE-S*, Jan. 14, 1926; "Plane Service Is Inaugurated," *CE-S*, June 25, 1929.

7. "Paving All Main Highways in Muscogee County," *Industrial Index* 22, no. 46 (Apr. 18, 1928): 18; "Harllee Branch, in the Atlanta Journal, Says Columbus, Rich in All Resources, Is Moving Unitedly on to City of 75,000," *CE-S*, Mar. 2, 1925; "New Names Urged for 120 Streets," *CE-S*, July 6, 1927; "Army Truck Caves in Flooring 14th Street Structure," *CE-S*, Aug. 2, 1923; "Viaduct Contract Support Is Asked," *CE-S*, Aug. 2, 1923; "Hundreds See the Unveiling," *CL*, July 27, 1922.

8. "Much Construction Here Is Shown by Big Issue of Industrial Index," *CE-S*, Mar. 20, 1924; Jordan Company ad, *CL*, Sept. 9, 1929; Sara Crawford, ed., *Gunby Jordan Remembers: A History of the Jordan Company, 1904–1986* (Columbus: Columbus Productions, 1986), 17–18.

9. Lynn Willoughby, *Flowing through Time: A History of the Lower Chattahoochee River* (Tuscaloosa: University of Alabama Press, 1999), 148, 168; "Columbus Inland Port When President Signs Rivers-Harbors Bill," *CE-S*, Mar. 3, 1925; "The Waterways Conference in Atlanta," *CE-S*, Nov. 28, 1929; "Chattahoochee Valley and Gulf Association Formed," *CL*, Aug. 15, 1928.

10. Willoughby, *Flowing through Time*, 165; "Chattahoochee Roars to Record Stage as Thousands Flee from Their Homes," *CE-S*, Mar. 17, 1929; "City Gas Supply Fails Saturday," *CE-S*, Mar. 17, 1929; "Fight against Flood to Maintain Electric Service Is Described," *CE-S*, Mar. 20, 1929.

11. Rothschild Furniture ad, *CE-S*, Oct. 10, 1920; "Textile Manufacturing Chief Industry of Columbus," *CE-S*, July 5, 1921; W. C. Bradley Company ads, *CE-S*, Oct. 8, 1920, Apr. 6, 1925; "W. C. Bradley Buys Iron Works Stock," *CE-S*, Sept. 27, 1925; Chamber of Commerce, *Columbus, Georgia, the Electric City* (Columbus: Columbus Office Supply, [1925]), Smith Collection, box 37, folder 9; "The Lummus Cotton Gin Co., Pioneer in its Line in the South," *CL*, Nov. 6, 1910.

12. Virginia Causey, Jean Simons Hyman, and Sydney Simons, "Sidney Simons: The Man behind the Boulevard," *Muscogiana* 26, no. 2 (2015): 1–16; Etta Blanchard Worsley, "Tom Huston Peanut Company," in *Columbus on the Chattahoochee* (Colum-

bus: Columbus Office Supply, 1951); "Tom Huston—Fact or Fancy," typescript, n.d., Tom Huston Collection, MC 37, box 2, folder 19, CSUA; Linda O. McMurry, *George Washington Carver: Scientist and Symbol* (Oxford: Oxford University Press, 1981), 220–225.

13. "Tom Huston—Fact or Fancy"; "Huston Builds Freezing Plant," *CE*, May 23, 1930.

14. George Baldwin to F. E. Reidhead, Mar. 12, 1907, F. E. Reidhead to George Baldwin, Mar. 15, 1907, both in Baldwin Papers, box 23, folder 1006.

15. Mark Pendergrast, *For God, Country, and Coca-Cola*, 2nd ed. (New York: Basic Books, 2000), 17–33; Pemberton and Carter ad, *CE*, Mar. 2, 1860; "Capt. Pemberton's Cavalry," *CE*, Aug. 14, 1864; Pemberton resignation, "Georgia, Civil War, Confederate Soldiers Compiled," Microfilm Reel M266, National Archives and Records Administration; Tillman and Norman Ledgers, vols. 1–2, 1859–1868, SHC.

16. "The Eagle Drug and Chemical House," *CE*, Dec. 8, 1865; "Dissolution," *CE*, Feb. 11, 1870; E. D. Murphy, "Coca-Cola's Ghost," 1997, Lupold Collection, ser. 6, box 3, folder 65; Pendergrast, *For God, Country, and Coca-Cola*, 14–16.

17. Murphy, "Coca-Cola's Ghost"; Pendergrast, *For God, Country, and Coca-Cola*, 7, 19–43, 88–89, 473n22; "Pemberton's Coca Wine," *Southern World*, May 1, 1885; "Of Coca-Cola," *CE-S*, Feb. 28, 1902.

18. Pendergrast, *For God, Country, and Coca-Cola*, 130–142; "Robert W. Woodruff," Lupold Collection, ser. 6, box 4, folder 32; William B. Turner, *The Learning of Love: A Journey toward Servant Leadership* (Macon: Smith and Helwys, 2000), 14; Tim Chitwood, "Columbus Helped Make Coke's Success 'The Real Thing,'" *CL-E*, Mar. 27, 2011; Susan Wiggins interview, Aug. 2, 2002, D. Abbott Turner interview, 1976, Loretto Chappell interview, Feb. 1975, all in GOHC.

19. Glenn Vaughn, "The Fizz and Fizzle of Royal Crown: Georgia's Other Cola," *GT*, Oct. 1995, 28; Bill Winn, "R.C. Cola Gets Start in Basement," *CL-E*, May 7, 1978; "Thousands View New Electric Sign," *CE-S*, Dec. 25, 1913; Pendergrast, *For God, Country, and Coca-Cola*, 142.

20. "Hatcher Offer Was Declined," *CL*, Aug. 14, 1914; Vaughn, "Fizz and Fizzle"; Bill Winn, "R.C. Cola Gets Start in Basement," *CL-E*, May 7, 1978.

21. Sharyn Kane and Richard Keeton, *Fort Benning: The Land and the People* (Fort Benning: U.S. Army Infantry Center, 1994), 173; Billy Winn, "African American Soldiers at Fort Benning," Causey Collection; Papers of the NAACP, pt. 9, ser. A, ed. John H. Bracey Jr. and August Meier, http://cisupa.proquest.com/ksc_assets/catalog/1536_PapersNAACPPart9SerA.pdf, xix, 9.

22. "Twenty-Fourth Wins from the Grey Sox," *CE*, Aug. 13, 1922; "Twenty Fourth Will Give Two Programs," *CE*, Feb. 19, 1926; Ellis B. Kohs newsletters, Dec. 12, 20, 1943, Ellis B. Kohs Papers, MSS 877, box 1, folder 3, MARBL.

23. Peggy A. Stepflug and Richard Hyatt, *Home of the Infantry: The History of Fort Benning* (Macon: Mercer University Press, 2007), 56–57, 65–87, 72, 134; Worsley, *Columbus on the Chattahoochee*, 433–435; Jean Edward Smith, *Eisenhower in War and Peace* (New York: Random House, 2012), 74–76; H. Paul Jeffers and Alan Axelrod, *Marshall: Lessons in Leadership* (New York: Macmillan, 2010), 65–70.

24. *Annual Report of the Columbus Public Schools for 1920–1921, 1924–1925*, HLUGA; *CL*, Sept. 14, 1924; "Five Offers for New School Site," *CE*, Aug. 20, 1924; "City Commission Votes to Buy Wildwood Site," *CE*, Oct. 7, 1924; "Wildwood School Site Wins," *CE*, Dec. 14, 1924; Paul B. Austin interview, Jan. 3, 1976, GOHC.

25. Becky Matthews, "The Development of Secondary Education for Black Stu-

dents in Columbus, Georgia, 1920–1932," 1990, Lupold Collection, ser. 6, box 2, folder 7; Genie King interview, Jan. 15, 22, 1975, GOHC; Roscoe Chester, "Low School: End of the Line for Blacks," *CL-E Chattahoochee Magazine*, Oct. 17, 1976, 9; John Henrik Clarke, "A Search for Identity," National Black United Front, http://www.nbufront .org/MastersMuseums/JHClarke/ArticlesEssays/SearchForIdentity.html; "Negro Baptists Here Plan High School," *CE-S*, Aug. 20, 1922; "Bond Issues Win by Big Margin," *CE-S*, May 19, 1929.

26. Matthews, "Secondary Education for Black Students"; Clarke, "Search for Identity"; Roscoe Chester, "Spencer Near Golden Anniversary," *CE*, Apr. 23, 1977; Liza Benham, "Freedmen's Bureau Lifesaver for Blacks," *CL*, June 10, 1982.

27. John S. Lupold, "Black Businessmen, 1921," Lupold Collection, ser. 6, box 1, folder 18; "Columbus, Georgia: The City Beautiful," Souvenir Program for the Georgia State Medical Association, May 14–17, 1928, Alfonso Biggs Collection, MC 154, box 1, folder 1, CSUA; William Winn, "The Medical Center, 1836–1991: An Institutional History of Public Service, Education, and Leadership in Medicine" [unpublished manuscript], 42, Causey Collection; Richard Hyatt, "From Two Worlds to One," *CL-E*, May 3, 2007; Billy Winn, "Brewer's Life, Death Helped Shape Our History," *CL-E*, Apr. 24, 1988.

28. John S. Lupold, "Historical Background: Site of New Columbus Police Station," Lupold Collection, ser. 6, box 2, folder 60; *Lift Every Voice: Columbus Georgia's African American Heritage* (Columbus: Pope Johnson Video, 2003); Judith Grant-Shabazz and Margaret Dawson, *Black Pioneers in the Historical Development of Columbus, Georgia* (Columbus: Columbus Consolidated Government, 1990).

29. Grant-Shabazz and Dawson, *Black Pioneers*; "Columbus, Georgia: The City Beautiful"; "Colored Population Prosperous, Valued, and Contented, in Columbus," *CE-S Columbus Centennial Edition* (Columbus: Ledger and Enquirer-Sun, 1928); Primus King interview, July 16, 1979, GOHC; John Henrik Clarke, "A Great and Mighty Walk," Hunter College Department of Africana, http://www.hunter.cuny.edu/afprl /clarke/a-great-and-mighty-walk.

30. Jason L. Ellerbee, "African American Theatres in Georgia: Preserving an Entertainment Legacy" (master's thesis, University of Georgia, 2004), 65–66; *Lift Every Voice*; "A Rebirth for the Liberty Theatre," Lupold Collection, ser. 6, box 3, folder 10; Buzzy Jackson, *A Bad Woman Feeling Good: Blues and the Women Who Sing Them* (New York: Norton, 2005), 21–22.

31. Jackson, *Bad Woman Feeling Good*, 12–23; Sandra R. Lieb, *Mother of the Blues: A Study of Ma Rainey* (Amherst: University of Massachusetts Press, 1983), 1–17; Karl Gert zur Heide, "Ma Rainey—Part 6," *Doctor Jazz Magazine*, June 2011, 12–14.

32. Jackson, *Bad Woman Feeling Good*; Daphne Duval Harrison, *Black Pearls: Blues Queens of the 1920s* (New Brunswick, N.J.: Rutgers University Press, 1988), 13; Angela Y. Davis, *Blues Legacies and Black Feminism: Gertrude "Ma" Rainey, Bessie Smith, and Billie Holiday* (New York: Pantheon, 1998), 39–41.

33. Harrison, *Black Pearls*, 11, 35; Lieb, *Mother of the Blues*, 22–23; Steve Goodson, "Gertrude 'Ma' Rainey: 'Hear Me Talkin' to You,'" in *Georgia Women*, ed. Ann Short Chirhart and Kathleen Ann Clark (Athens: University of Georgia Press, 2014), 2:154; Sterling A. Brown, *Southern Road* (New York: Harcourt, Brace, 1932), 62–63.

34. Davis, *Blues Legacies and Black Feminism*, 8–24, 138; Lieb, *Mother of the Blues*, 2, 45–48.

35. "Liberty Theatre Cultural Center, Inc.," Columbus Jazz Society, http://www

.columbusjazzsociety.com/liberty.htm; Shaila Dewan, "After Years of Neglect, Rebirth for a Blues Singer's House," *NYT*, Mar. 28, 2008; Dusty Nix, "Rainey House Saved—At Last," *CL-E*, Feb. 19, 2004; Brad Barnes, "Ma Rainey House Opens as Blues Museum," *CL-E*, Sept. 6, 2006.

36. Bill Winn, "Du Bois Helped Shape the American Mind," *CL-E*, Mar. 27, 1988; Charles T. Butler, "Alma Thomas (1891–1978)," *New Georgia Encyclopedia*, https://www.georgiaencyclopedia.org/articles/arts-culture/alma-thomas-1891-1978; Stephen Townsend, "The Cantey Family: What Became of Them?" *Muscogiana* 24, no. 2 (2013): 16–22.

37. Tim Chitwood, "The Prison," *CL-E*, Dec. 23, 2007; Brad Barnes, "Behind the Bars," *CL-E*, Dec. 23, 2007; Clason Kyle, "Fate Unsure, Stockade 'Way Down,'" *CL-E*, Apr. 23, 1978; Columbus Stockade Nomination Form, Georgia Heritage Trust, 1973, Lupold Collection, ser. 6, box 1, folder 73.

38. Ed Kahn, *Complete Recordings: Darby & Tarlton*, liner notes (Hambergen, Germany: Bear Family Records, 1995), 6–11, 16; Jake Fussell e-mail, Apr. 16, 2015, Ricky Whitley e-mail, May 23, 2015, both in Causey Collection; Graham Wickham, *Darby and Tarlton* (Denver: Blue Yodeler, 1966), 6–13; George Mitchell, "Tarlton Is Still Singing His Blues," *CL-E*, June 23, 1968.

39. Kahn, *Complete Recordings*, 11, 45–46; "'Today's Program," *CE*, Dec. 11, 1928; "'Blues' Composer Dead at Age 78," *CL*, Aug. 20, 1974; Wickham, *Darby and Tarlton*, 12–15; Richard Hyatt, "Please Don't Forget the Columbus Stockade Blues," *CL-E*, Sept. 25, 1994; Tim Chitwood, "Remembering a Forgotten Legend," *CL-E*, May 24, 1998; "Guitarists Featured by Symphony," *CL*, June 24, 1963; Ann Cohen, "Jimmie Tarlton: Steel Guitar Rag," *Testament Record Catalog* (Los Angeles: Testament Records, 1969).

40. Richard Hyatt, "Tarlton's Grave Does Have a Marker," *CL-E*, Sept. 30, 1999; Kaffie Sledge, "Ailing Singer Quits 'Stockade,'" *CL*, Sept. 13, 1978; "'Stockade Blues' Composer Dies; to Be Buried Saturday," *CL*, Nov. 30, 1979.

41. "WRBL—The City's First Radio Station," typescript, n.d., Joseph A. Gamble file, GOHC; "Three Arts League Announces Program for Artists Series," *CE*, Oct. 14, 1928; Worsley, *Columbus on the Chattahoochee*, 460–61.

42. "Columbus Centennial Program Will Be Featured by Mammoth Military Demonstration, Colossal Pageants, and an Impressive Street Parade," *CL* and *CE-S* Centennial Edition, Apr. 21, 1928; Nancy Telfair, *History of Columbus, Georgia, 1828–1928* (Columbus: Historical Publishing, 1929), 312–326; "Kirven's Centennial Display Attracts Thousands to Store," "Twenty-Five Thousand at Opening Events of Columbus Centennial Celebration," "Pageant at Stadium Proves to Be Spectacular Event," all in *CE-S*, Apr. 26, 1928; "Program, Columbus Centennial, 1828–1928," Smith Collection, box 39, folder 13.

43. Telfair, *History of Columbus, Georgia*, 326–336; "Tribute Paid South's Heroes," *CE-S*, Apr. 27, 1928; "Centennial Ends as Thousands Witness Spectacular Parade and Coronation," *CE-S*, Apr. 28, 1928.

44. "Our New City Market," *CE*, Nov. 10, 1867; "Ordinance to Abolish Present Board City Hospital Heads Is Read," *CE-S*, May 6, 1920; "Mayor Couch Signs Market Ordinance; Structure Stays," *CE-S*, Dec. 19, 1920; Robert McKnight interview, Feb. 1982, GOHC; "Fight to Save Market House," *CL*, Nov. 3, 1920.

45. "Opening of City Market Great Occasion; Hundreds Take Part in the Attending Festivities," *CE*, Apr. 24, 1921; "Tearing Away Part of the City Market," *CE*, July 7, 1923; "Effort to Halt Removal Fails," *CE*, July 2, 1924.

Chapter 6. Columbus in the 1930s and 1940s

1. John S. Lupold, untitled manuscript on progressive reform in Columbus, n.d., Lupold Collection, ser. 6, box 1, folder 75.

2. Marshall Morton, "Morton Reviews Success of City Manager Government," *CL-E*, Jan. 6, 1952; *CE*, July 26, Dec. 28, 1932; "Head of City Schools Appeals to Tax Payers," *CE*, May 15, 1934; "The Negroes Celebrate," *CE*, May 21, 1933; "Miss Fornie Holmes Retires from Duty with Public Schools," *CE*, Sept. 12, 1934; "Georgia Bi-Centennial Pageant, 1733–1933 Program," May 19, 1933, Smith Collection, box 6, Miscellaneous folder; Katherine Hines Mahan and William Clyde Woodall, *A History of Public Schools* (Columbus: Board of Education, 1977), 252, 255, 259, 264; B. B. Littlejohn interview, Dec. 12, 1975, GOHC; Iola Florence interview, May 19, 1997, Causey Collection, Muscogee County School District Desegregation ser., folder 6.

3. *Columbus News*, Mar. 23, 1932; "Needy Receive Help of Board," *CE*, Nov. 10, 1929; "Welfare Work Grows Harder," *CE*, Jan. 15, 1930; "Public Works or Dole?," *CE*, Sept. 3, 1933; "Relief Rolls Be Curtailed," *CE*, Oct. 6, 1935; Beatrice Kerr, "Welfare Head Says Families Live on Less Than 10 Cents Per Day in Some Cases Here," *CE*, May 23, 1936; "City May Aid Welfare Work," *CL*, Apr. 13, 1922; "Ask Increased Aid of County Commissioners," *CL*, May 17, 1922; "City of Columbus, 1933 Expenditures for Charity and Miscellaneous," Smith Collection, box 6, 1934, City Miscellaneous folder.

4. "Negro Soup Kitchen Serves Hungry Here," *CE*, Feb. 4, 1930; "County Would Receive Large Welfare Fund," *CE*, May 6, 1937; "Relief Bureau to Quit Here," *CE*, July 15, 1938; Mary Elizabeth Langdon interview, Feb. 22, 1975, GOHC.

5. "Slum Clearance Work Recommended to City," *CE*, Mar. 29, 1938; "Columbus Slum Clearance Locations Announced," *CE*, Feb. 18, 1939; "Housing Units to Open Today," *CE*, Jan. 31, 1941; "Georgia's Modern Apartment Complexes," National Register of Historic Places Nomination, Georgia DNR, http://georgiashpo.org/register/research.

6. "New Federal Building to Provide Work," *CE*, Apr. 20, 1932; "Projects for FERA Approved," *CE*, May 20, 1934; "New Site and Plant for Industrial High Urged at Exercises," *CE*, July 12, 1935; "Columbus Citizens Approve Bonds for Great Program of Improvement," *CE*, Sept. 15, 1938; Marshall Morton, "A Brief History of Federal Relief in Columbus, Georgia, 1933–1937," Smith Collection, box 29, folder 5.

7. "Camp Inspection Reports," 23, Records of the Civilian Conservation Corps, www.magsgen.com/images/RG35_CCC_Camp_Inspection_File_List.pdf; Michael S. Holmes, "The New Deal and Georgia's Black Youth," *Journal of Southern History* 38, no. 3 (1972): 443–460; "Training Class Is Open for Negroes," *CE*, Sept. 20, 1936; "NYA Projects Show Results," *CE*, Oct. 8, 1936.

8. Michael S. Holmes, "The Blue Eagle as 'Jim Crow Bird': The NRA and Georgia's Black Workers," *Journal of Negro History* 57, no. 4 (1972): 276–280; Arthur F. Raper, *Preface to Peasantry: A Tale of Two Black Belt Counties* (Chapel Hill: University of North Carolina Press, 1936), 237.

9. Harry Harden interview, Feb. 17, 1988, Mill Workers Oral History Collection, MC 109, CSUA; "Textile Mills Aided by NRA," *CE*, June 27, 1934; John A. Salmond, *The General Textile Strike of 1934: From Maine to Alabama* (Columbia: University of Missouri Press, 2002), 28–30; "A Committee" to Franklin D. Roosevelt, Lupold Collection, ser. 6, box 1, folder 80; John S. Lupold, "Bibb City Historic District," National Register of Historic Places, Lupold Collection, ser. 6, box 1, folder 12; Mae Phillips to National Labor Relations Board, Oct. 29, 1934, Lupold Collection, ser. 6, box 3, folder 8.

10. Barbara Kimmelman, John S. Lupold, and J. B. Karfunkle, "The Columbus Plant of the Bibb Manufacturing Company," 1977, 13–16, HAER Collection, box 1, folder 4; Carolyn Smith, "Minnie Clyde Balkcom and the Bibb City Experience, 1936–1998," *Muscogiana* 12, no. 2 (2001): 1–5; Jesse McKinney, *Memoirs of a Mill Town* (Columbus: Brentwood Academic, 1998), 6–52; Brooks Griffin and Plez Johnson interview, June 28, 1977, William B. Turner interview, July 11, 2002, D. Abbott Turner interview, 1976, Loretto Chappell interview, Feb. 1975, Susan Wiggins interview, Aug. 2, 2002, all in GOHC; Lupold, "Bibb City."

11. Salmond, *General Textile Strike of 1934*, 31, 40; Janet Irons, *Testing the New Deal: The General Textile Strike of 1934 in the American South* (Urbana: University of Illinois Press, 2000), 115–116; Russell Pryor, "The Uprising in Columbus: Race and Class in the 1934 General Textile Strike," *Muscogiana*, 20, no. 1 (2009): 8, 11–13; "Fourteen Are Arrested as Settlement Move Is Made in Strike," *CE*, June 23, 1934; "Workers Hold Mass Meeting," *CE*, June 26, 1934; "Employes of Local Mill Suspend Work," *CE*, July 18, 1934; "Alabama Mill Strike Begins," *CE*, July 17, 1934; "Workers Take Strike Action," *CL*, May 29, 1934.

12. "Strike Sympathizer Fatally Shot," *CE*, Aug. 11, 1934; "Textile Union Leaders Order General Strike," *CE*, May 31, 1934; "Impressive Labor Day Program to Be Given at Exposition Grounds," *CE*, Sept. 2, 1934; "Funeral Held for Gun Victim Here Sunday," *CL*, Aug. 13, 1934; Irons, *Testing the New Deal*, 116–119.

13. "Doors Closed at Bibb Mill by Officials," *CE*, Sept. 5, 1934; "Talmadge Appeals for Labor's Vote," *CE*, Aug. 18, 1934; "Talmadge Wins by Wide Margin," *CE*, Sept. 13, 1934; "Guardsmen Arrive in Bibb City," *CE*, Sept. 17, 1934; "Two Placed under Arrest as Guardsmen Start Drive against Forming of Crowds," *CE*, Sept. 19, 1934; Pryor, "Uprising in Columbus," 13, 17–19; Dora Watson interview, Feb. 4, 1988, Eulis Pippin interview, Feb. 16, 1988, both in Mill Workers Oral History Collection; Lloyd Davis interview, July 1986, Janet Irons Collection, SMC 17, CSUA; John Earl Allen, "The Governor and the Strike: Eugene Talmadge and the General Textile Strike, 1934" (master's thesis, Georgia State University, 1977).

14. "Quick Termination of Textile Walkout Bright Prospect Friday Night," *CE*, Sept. 22, 1934; "Textile Mills Ready to Open in This City," *CE*, Sept. 24, 1934; "More Textile Workers Get Jobs Tuesday," *CE*, Sept. 26, 1934; Pryor, "Uprising in Columbus," 18–19; Luther Morris interview, Mar. 10, 1988, Mill Workers Oral History Collection.

15. "Textile Mills Will Increase Wages of Workers Effective in Week Beginning December 7," *CE*, Nov. 24, 1936; Roger Biles, *The South and the New Deal* (Lexington: University Press of Kentucky, 2015), 62.

16. Irons, *Testing the New Deal*, 5, 161, 175; "Textile Union Groups Have Active Council," *CE*, Apr. 15, 1936; "Meritas Mills Close Temporarily," *CE*, Sept. 12, 1935; "Mill Sale Deeds Filed for Record," *CE*, Nov. 13, 1937; Davis interview; Griffin and Johnson interview.

17. "Mill to Hold Election Here," *CE*, Jan. 20, 1938; "Wilbur Holds Mill 'Unfair,'" *CE*, Aug. 28, 1938; "Mill Workers Cast Ballots against TWOC," *CE*, Apr. 15, 1939.

18. "WRBL—The City's First Radio Station," typescript, n.d., Joseph A. Gamble file, GOHC; "Daily Radio Programs," *CE*, Oct. 13, 1945; "Withering Heights," *CE*, Oct. 13, 1945; "Three Arts League to Bring to Columbus Renowned Artists," *CE*, Oct. 27, 1935; "Three Arts League and Its President," *CE*, Feb. 6, 1940; "3 Arts Moves to Jordan High," *CE*, Mar. 30, 1943; Joseph Gamble interview, Oct. 1981, GOHC.

19. Margaret Mitchell to Nelson Shipp, July 11, 20, 1938, Margaret Mitchell Collection, MSS 265, box 1, folders 75, 76, MARBL; "Charter Granted to Museum Group,"

CE, Oct. 29, 1941; "Edward S. Shorter Is One of Six Georgia Artists Selected to Show Their Paintings at World's Fair," *CE*, Jan. 26, 1939; "Gifts Are Made to Establish Museum of Art," *CE*, Nov. 2, 1941; William W. Winn, *Building on a Legacy: The Columbus Museum* (Columbus: Columbus Museum, 1996), 14–17; Edward Shorter interview, Mar. 1976, GOHC.

20. "Publisher's Announcement," *CE*, May 27, 1930; "Georgia-Alabama Marathon Dance," *CE*, June 26, 1932; "It's Here—Now—The Colored Marathon Dance," *CE*, Sept. 3, 1932; "Police Close Dance Here," *CE*, Aug. 14, 1932; "The Municipal Golf Course," *CE*, Oct. 11, 1930; "Coach Austin Takes New Job," *CE*, May 19, 1941; "Million Residents and Soldiers Enjoyed Columbus Recreational Facilities during the Last Year," *CE*, Feb. 4, 1945; *Columbus News-Record*, Feb. 5, 1935; Langdon interview; Paul B. Austin interview, Jan. 3, 1976, GOHC.

21. Tom Stempel, *Screenwriter: The Life and Times of Nunnally Johnson* (San Diego: Barnes, 1980), 17–24; Craig Lloyd, "Nunnally Johnson in Columbus," *Muscogiana* 9 nos. 1–2 (1988): 29–32, 35; Pete Martin, *Hollywood without Makeup* (New York: Lippincott, 1948), 62, 68, 72–73.

22. "Nunnally Johnson," *Life*, Sept. 18, 1944, 85, 87; Pete Martin, *Hollywood without Makeup*, 56–59, 63–64, 82–83; *Nunnally Johnson's 'Riverside' Stories and Other Selected Works*, ed. Thornton F. Jordan (Columbus: Historic Columbus Foundation, 1997), introduction.

23. Virginia Spencer Carr, introduction to *Collected Stories of Carson McCullers* (Boston: Houghton Mifflin, 1987), viii; Virginia Spencer Carr, *The Lonely Hunter: A Biography of Carson McCullers* (Garden City, N.Y.: Doubleday, 1975), 20–31, 82–83, 97–98, 131, 139; "Story of Life on Army Post Appears," *CE*, Oct. 7, 1940; Virginia Doss, "McCullers' New Novel," *CE*, Aug. 15, 1943; Carlos Dews, "Carson McCullers: 'The Brutal Humiliation of Human Dignity' in the South," in *Georgia Women*, ed. Ann Short Chirhart and Kathleen Ann Clark (Athens: University of Georgia Press, 2014), 2:291–292.

24. Dews, "Carson McCullers," 294–296; Carson McCullers, "The Member of the Wedding," in *Collected Stories of Carson McCullers*, ed. Virginia Spencer Car (Boston: Houghton Mifflin, 1987), 302; McCullers, *The Heart Is a Lonely Hunter* (Boston: Houghton Mifflin, 1940), 4.

25. McCullers, *The Heart Is a Lonely Hunter*, 51; *CE*, "Miss Augusta Howard," June 13, 1934; Lamar Smith to Thomas Hardwick, Sept. 28, 1921, Governor, Convict and Fugitive Records—Applications for Clemency, GDAH; McCullers, "The Ballad of the Sad Café," in *Collected Stories of Carson McCullers*, 252; Jacqueline R. Pierce, "The Virgin Ogre: Subverted Southern Belles in O'Connor and McCullers," paper presented at the Midwest Modern Language Association Convention, Chicago, Nov. 8, 1997.

26. Dews, "Carson McCullers," 284–286, 288, 291; Carr, *Lonely Hunter*, 100, 136–37; Sarah Schulman, "White Writer," The *New Yorker*, Oct. 21, 2016; Latimer Watson, "Carson McCullers Gets Guggenheim Fellowship," *CE*, Apr. 6, 1942.

27. Carr, *Lonely Hunter*, 38–40, 57.

28. Ibid., 21; Richard Wright, "Inner Landscape," *New Republic*, Aug. 1940, 195.

29. Carson McCullers to editor, *CL-E*, Feb. 26, 1948; Carson McCullers to Director of the Library, Aug. 21, 1958, Carson McCullers Collection, 1924–1976, box 24, folder 2, Ransom Humanities Research Center, University of Texas.

30. "Columbus Nearing Legal Sale of Liquor as City Approves Measure Fixing License Fees," *CE*, Mar. 29, 1938; Dr. W. F. Gann to editor, Nov. 23, 1925, Smith Collection, box 18, folder 33.

31. Peggy A. Stepflug and Richard Hyatt, *Home of the Infantry: The History of Fort Benning* (Macon: Mercer University Press, 2007), 92, 128, 161–162, 163; John B. McDermott, "General Patton Has Interesting Career in Army," *CE*, Nov. 13, 1940; Sara Spano, *I Could've Written "Gone with the Wind" but Cousin Margaret Beat Me to It: Sara Spano's Most Popular Newspaper Columns* (Ann Arbor, Mich.: McNaughton and Gunn, 1990), 81; "Clason Kyle," in *Columbus and the Home Front: Memories of Columbus, Georgia, during World War II* (Columbus: Shaw Young Historians, 2007), 34; Jesse Helms, "Mrs. Tibbets Is Proud of Noted Fighter," *CE*, Aug. 8, 1945.

32. "Thousands of Colored Troops Processed Here," *Benning Bayonet*, Nov. 12, 1942; "555th Parachute Infantry Battalion: The 'Triple Nickels,'" U.S. Army Center of Military History, http://history.army.mil/news/2014/140200a_tripleNickel.html.

33. Mary Penick Motley, *The Invisible Soldier: The Experience of the Black Soldier, World War II* (Detroit: Wayne State University Press, 1987), 39, 100, 103; "Dead Soldier Is Identified," *CE*, Apr. 8, 1941; Alexa Mills, "A Lynching Kept out of Sight," *Washington Post*, Sept. 2, 2016; A. Philip Randolph, interview by Norman Thomas, in *Work and Struggle: Voices from U.S. Labor Radicalism*, ed. Paul le Blanc (London: Routledge, 2011), 222.

34. "Colored YMCA Dedication Set Today," *CE*, July 27, 1941; E. E. Farley to editor, *CE*, Oct. 10, 1943; "Walter T. Lunsford, Sr.," in *Columbus and the Home Front*, 40; Lillian "Bunky" Clark interview, Jan. 26, 2007, GOHC.

35. "Walter T. Lunsford, Sr.," 40–41.

36. "Talmadge Will Sign Measure for Fast Time," *CE*, Mar. 21, 1941; "Hands of Clock Should Be Turned Forward," *CE*, Aug. 9, 1941.

37. "Benning Road Opening Ready for Saturday," *CE*, Aug. 11, 1943; "County Commissioners Name Marker for Vets," *CE*, Aug. 16, 1945; Frances Rothwell, "Full Air Service Opens in Columbus Tuesday," *CE*, July 30, 1944; "City Bus Line Transfer Recalls 56-Year History," *CL*, July 27, 1943.

38. "Solons Will Inspect Fort Benning Today," *CE*, Aug. 14, 1940; "Building Activity in Columbus," *CE*, Oct. 3, 1941; "Summerfield Again," *CE*, Oct. 12, 1940; "Housing Men Urging Speedy Authorization of Home Construction," *CE*, Nov. 21, 1944; Sara Crawford, ed., *Gunby Jordan Remembers: A History of the Jordan Company, 1904–1986* (Columbus: Columbus Productions, 1986), 27; "Laurette Rosenstrauch," in *Columbus and the Home Front*, 59; "Eleanor White," in *Columbus and the Home Front*, 72–73; Janet Fitzgerald, "Surviving Hard Times in Boogerville: Erin R. M. Bagley and Her Family through Depression and War, 1930–1950," 1998, Lupold Collection, ser. 6, box 1, folder 20.

39. Mahan and Woodall, *History of Public Schools*, 277–280, 308; "Overcrowding in City Schools Is Considered," *CE*, Dec. 10, 1940; "Dr. E. M. Boyce to Go to Navy," *CE*, May 17, 1944.

40. Alfred A. Crowell, "Acute Labor Shortage Strikes War Work Here," *CE*, Feb. 17, 1943; "Georgia Dollars in War Textiles," *CE*, Nov. 21, 1943; "Golden's Wins 'M' Production Award," *CE*, Mar. 30, 1943; Griffin and Johnson interview; Curtis Parker interview, Jan. 30, 1975, GOHC.

41. "Sugar Stocks of Coca-Cola Are Sufficient," *CE*, Jan. 22, 1942; "25 Years of Progress: The Story of the Tom Huston Peanut Company," Tom Huston Collection, MC 37, box 2, folder 24, CSUA; Mark Pendergrast, *For God, Country, and Coca-Cola*, 2nd ed. (New York: Basic Books, 2000), 184–186; "John R. Kinnett, Jr.," in *Columbus and the Home Front*, 31; "Earnings of Nehi Show Sharp Drop during Past Year," *CE*,

Feb. 12, 1945; Glenn Vaughn, "The Fizz and Fizzle of Royal Crown: Georgia's Other Cola," *GT*, Oct. 1995, 28.

42. "Eddie Lindsey," in *Columbus and the Home Front*, 36; "Janet L. Cohn," in *Columbus and the Home Front*, 14–15; "Louise Griner," in *Columbus and the Home Front*, 16–17; "Rebecca Hardaway King," in *Columbus and the Home Front*, 27; John Daniel Fourham interview, Mar. 18, 2011, GOHC; William W. Winn, *Line of Splendor: The Life and Times of St. Luke United Methodist Church, Columbus, Georgia, 1828–2008* (Columbus: St. Luke, 2010), 336.

43. Stepflug and Hyatt, *Home of the Infantry*, 388–391; Etta Blanchard Worsley, *Columbus on the Chattahoochee* (Columbus: Columbus Office Supply, 1951), 484–485; "Local Red Cross Completes Quota before Schedule," *CE*, Oct. 14, 1944; "Registration for Blood Bank Will Start Wednesday," *CE*, Jan. 9, 1945; Clark interview; "Swift-Kyle House—Statement of Significance," n.d., Quillian-Ansley-Gates Collection, MC 180, ser. 5, box 3, folder 81, CSUA.

44. "Fifty Held Here as Officers Wage Anti-Vice Drive," *CE*, Feb. 14, 1940; "Hygiene Group Urges Clean-Up," *CE*, Feb. 14, 1940; "Dr. Aufranc Asks Cities and Fort Benning to Help Control Vice in this Area," *CE*, Apr. 15, 1942; "Army, Russell to Make War on Diseases," *CE*, Mar. 5, 1943; "Palmer Calls for Control of Vice Here," *CE*, May 5, 1942; "Phenix City Vice Fight," *CE*, Sept. 25, 1942.

45. "Drive against Dives Planned," *CE*, Dec. 1, 1942; "Negroes Ask VD Authority," *CE*, Apr. 7, 1943; "Venereal War to Be Pushed," *CE*, Aug. 19, 1944; "Case of 'Bathing Suiters,' Set Aside by Local Judge " *CE*, Sept. 23, 1944; "Negroes Sentenced for Not Taking Venereal Treatment," *CE*, June 14, 1945.

46. George Johnston, "Operation Dixie: Union Organizing for the CIO in the American South in 1946," George Johnston–*Operation Dixie* Collection, MC 272, box 1, folder 7, CSUA.

47. Ibid.; *The Trumpet*, Aug. 16, 1947, Smith Collection, box 25, folder 21; Calvin Kytle and James A. Mackay, *Who Runs Georgia?* (Athens: University of Georgia Press, 1998), 283.

48. Kimmelman, Lupold, and Karfunkle, "Bibb Manufacturing," 14–15; McKinney, *Memoirs of a Mill Town*, 12; John Wells interview, Nov. 5, 1996, Bibb City Historical Collection, MC 166, box 1, folder 17, CSUA; Jesse Williams e-mail, Nov. 6, 2015, Causey Collection; Johnston, "Operation Dixie."

49. Johnston, "Operation Dixie."

50. Ibid.

Chapter 7. Violence, Direct Action, Negotiation

1. Billy Winn, "Brewer's Life, Death Helped Shape Our History," *CL-E*, Apr. 24, 1988; Primus King interview, July 16, 1979, GOHC; "Steady Stream of Voters Moving on Polling Places," *CL*, July 4, 1944; "Negro Voting Right Upheld by U.S. Court," *CL*, Mar. 7, 1946; "Highest Court Affirms Negro Right to Vote," *CL*, Apr. 1, 1946.

2. Theo Jackson McGee, *A Pleasant Journey* (Columbus: n.p., 1975), 76–77; Eugene Talmadge speech, July 13, 1946, WSB Radio Collection, Special Collections and Archives, Georgia State University; Calvin Kytle and James A. Mackay, *Who Runs Georgia?* (Athens: University of Georgia Press, 1998), 251; Stephen G. N. Tuck, *Beyond Atlanta: The Struggle for Racial Equality in Georgia, 1940–1980* (Athens: University of Georgia Press, 2001), 78–79.

3. *We Charge Genocide: The Historic Petition to the United Nations for Relief from a Crime of the United States Government against the Negro People* (New York: Civil

Rights Congress, 1951), 19, Civil Rights Movement Veterans, www.crmvet.org/info/genocide2_intro.pdf; "Blast Aimed at Police Sets Off Near Riot," *CE*, May 1, 1951; "2 Police Officers Targets in 2nd Grenade-Throwing," *CE*, May 21, 1951; "2 Negroes Freed in Bus Incident," *CE*, May 31, 1951; "4 GIs Convicted of Bombing Police of Georgia Town," *Indianapolis Recorder*, Aug. 25, 1951, http://indiamond6.ulib.iupui.edu/cdm/ref/collection/IRecorder/id/8640.

4. Lieutenant Charles Stevens interview, Apr. 20, 2007, Albert Thompson interview, July 21, 2002, both in GOHC.

5. John S. Lupold, "Black Businessmen and Professionals, 1940," Lupold Collection, ser. 6, box 1, folder 17; John S. Lupold, "Historical Background: Site of New Columbus Police Station," Lupold Collection, ser. 6, box 2, folder 60; S. A. Roddenbery, *I Swear by Apollo: A Black Surgeon in the Deep South* (Hamilton, Ga.: Gandy, 1994); Billy Winn, "Brewer's Life, Death Helped Shape Our History," *CL-E*, Apr. 24, 1988; Juanita Louise Jones Crittenden, "A History of Public Library Service to Negroes in Columbus, Georgia, 1831–1959," (master's thesis, Atlanta University, 1960), 37–41; Marvin Wall, "City to Add Negro Police," *CL*, Aug. 14, 1951; "Safety Board Suspends Three Negro Policemen," *CL*, May 15, 1958.

6. Billy Winn, "Brewer's Life, Death Helped Shape Our History," *CL-E*, Apr. 24, 1988; Billy Winn, "Brewer Was on Collision Course with 1950s," *CL-E*, May 1, 1988; "NAACP Files 2nd Plea to Integrate Schools," *CL-E*, Oct. 13, 1955; "The Citizens' Council," [ca. 1956], Right-Wing Ephemera Collection, MC 2790, box 1, folder 12, HLUGA; Mrs. C. A. Scott, "Park Request Denied Effort to Encourage Integration," *CL*, Aug. 18, 1954.

7. "Physician Slain in Flowers' Store," *CL*, Feb. 19, 1956; "Flowers Is Charged in Brewer Murder," *CL*, Feb. 20, 1956; U.S. Justice Department, Civil Rights Division, "Notice to Close File," https://www.justice.gov/crt/case-document/file/950081/download; "Flowers Shot 1 Year After Brewer Death," *CL*, Feb. 11, 1957; Winn, "Collision Course"; Billy Winn, "'Shots in Rapid Succession' Death to Brewer " *CL-E*, May 8, 1988; Rudolph Allen Sr. interview, Dec. 2, 2015, GOHC; "Negro Leader Slain in Georgia Dispute," *NYT*, Feb. 19, 1956; "Freed in Negro Death: White Georgia Store Owner's Indictment Refused by Jury," *NYT*, Mar. 1, 1956; W. Montague Cobb, "Thomas Hency Brewer, Sr., MD, 1894–1956," *Journal of the National Medical Association*, May 1956, 191–193, http://www.ncbi.nlm.nih.gov/pmc/articles/PMC2641107/pdf/jnma00721-0042.pdf; Tuck, *Beyond Atlanta*, 44; Herschel Cribb, "Jury Acquits Policeman of Charge of Beating Negro Prisoner to Death," *CE*, Apr. 24, 1958.

8. Sonam Vashi, "Clarence Pickett," Georgia Civil Rights Cold Cases Project at Emory University, https://coldcases.emory.edu/baby-they-done-killed-me-the-troubled-life-and-brutal-death-of-clarence-pickett/.

9. "Bombing of Negro Residences, January 10, 1958," "Bombing of Negro Residence, July 2, 1958," Internet Archive, https://ia802702.us.archive.org/23/items/foia_Bombings-Attempted_Bombings—Chicago-3/Bombings-Attempted_Bombings—Chicago-3_text.pdf; Ben Walburn, "Fourth Avenue Blast Investigated by Police," *CE*, Jan. 10, 1958; "Dynamite Blast Rips Home Here; Sleeping Occupants Escape Harm," *CE*, July 2, 1958; Stan Zuckerman, "King Says Ruling Seed of Violence," *CE*, July 2, 1958.

10. Liza Benham, "King Led Challenge of White-Only Voting," *CL-E*, June 13, 1982; Thomas C. Humphries, "Civil Rights in Columbus: Refuge or Refuse?," CSU Collection, Record Group III, ser. B, box 2.

11. McGee, *Pleasant Journey*, 89–90, 93; Lynn Willoughby, *Judge Aaron Cohn:*

Memoirs of a First Generation American (n.p.: BookSurge, 2008), 45, 138, 154–55; Rayna Goodman interview, Apr. 12, 2014, Shalom Y'all Collection, MC 357, box 1, CSUA.

12. Jessica Stephens, "The Standoff: First Presbyterian Church of Columbus, Georgia, Robert McNeill, and Racial Equality" (master's thesis, Auburn University, 2011); Minutes of Session, Mar. 24, 1958, First Presbyterian Church Records, MC 171, ser. 1, box 3, Minutes, 1958, folder, CSUA; Robert B. McNeill, "Georgia Minister Offers a Solution for the South," *Look*, May 28, 1957, 55–58; Robert B. McNeill, *God Wills Us Free: The Ordeal of a Southern Minister* (New York: Hill and Wang, 1965), 122, 124–129.

13. McNeill, *God Wills Us Free*, 132, 145–155, 159; Stephens, "Standoff," 65–69; Minutes of Session, Mar. 24, 1958, Porter G. Pease to Frank C. King, Mar. 25, 1958, both in First Presbyterian Church Records, MC 171, ser. 1, box 3, Minutes, 1958, folder, CSUA.

14. McNeill, *God Wills Us Free*, 148–155; Ralph Emerson McGill Papers, MSS 252, box 98, Clippings, folder 3, and box 102, Sound Recordings, Audiocassette 11.1, MARBL.

15. McNeill, *God Wills Us Free*, 2, 6, 161–164; Stephens, "Standoff," 78–79; Steve Lesher, "M'Neill Says Segregation Un-Christian, Un-Democratic," *CL*, June 8, 1959; "'Mr. McNeill's 'Crime,'" *NYT*, June 9, 1959; "Fired Minister Leaves Hospital," *Marietta Journal*, July 7, 1959; "Cleric Gets New Post," *NYT*, Aug., 9, 1959.

16. "Church Men Try to Keep Rev. McNeill," *Marietta Journal*, June 9, 1959; Steve Lesher, "M'Neill Says Segregation Un-Christian, Un-Democratic," *CL*, June 8, 1959; Stephens, "Standoff," 79.

17. McNeill, *God Wills Us Free*, 116, 166–174, 177; Michael B. Friedland, *Lift Up Your Voice Like a Trumpet: White Clergy and the Civil Rights and Antiwar Movements, 1954–1973* (Chapel Hill: University of North Carolina Press, 1998), 35.

18. "Soldier Fined in Dispute on City Bus," *CE*, Dec. 24, 1956; "Negro Charged for Not Sitting in Rear of Bus," *CE*, May 29, 1957; "Commission Removes Airport Race Barriers," *CE*, July 5, 1961; "'Riders' Pass through City without Incident," *CE*, June 2, 1961; Allen interview; Lillian "Bunky" Clark interview, Jan. 26, 2007, GOHC; "Negroes Seek Desegregation of City Buses," *CL*, June 20, 1961; Delane Chappell, "A. J. McClung, Statesman," *Columbus and the Valley*, Feb.–Mar. 1977, 33; Alva James-Johnson, "Sunday Interview: Bunky McClung Clark," *CL-E*, Nov. 15, 2015.

19. Allen interview; Clark interview; "Delegation Appears before Commission," *CE*, July 18, 1961; Bill Levy, "Six Arrested in Attempt to Integrate City Buses," *CE*, July 18, 1961; "Eight Negroes Arrested in City Bus Incidents," *CL-E*, Aug. 4, 1961; Alva James-Johnson, "Sunday Interview: Bunky McClung Clark," *CL-E*, Nov. 15, 2015; John Sheftall, "Truth, Beauty, and the Preservation of Spirit," presentation for the Historic Columbus Foundation, Apr. 14, 2016.

20. Gerald Kent interview, Shalom Y'all Collection, box 1; "Lunch Counter Racial Bars Lifted at 7 Stores in City," *CE*, Jan. 24, 1962.

21. "Lunch Counter Integration Set at Several Stores Here," *CE*, Dec. 12, 1961; "Columbus Restaurants Integrate Peacefully," *CE*, July 10, 1964; Delane Chappell, "A. J. McClung, Statesman," *Columbus and the Valley*, Feb.–Mar. 1977, 33; Allen interview.

22. Ann Johnston, "NAACP Youth Group Hits Local Theatres," *Columbus News*, June 29, 1963; Quarterly Report, Georgia Council on Human Relations, June–July–Aug. 1964, Frances Freeborn Pauley Papers, MSS 659, box 10, folder 3, MARBL; Con-

stance Johnson, "City Names 25 to Biracial Unit," *CL*, Sept. 4, 1963; "County Okays Creation of Biracial Committee," *CL*, Sept. 3, 1963; Tuck, *Beyond Atlanta*, 143–145.

23. *Columbus News*, May 2, 1964; Richard Hyatt, "Let George Do It," *CL-E Chattahoochee Magazine*, Feb. 11, 1979, 10–13; "Albert Thompson: A Role Model for Youth," *Columbus Times*, Aug. 1981, Columbus Biography—Thompson, Albert folder, Chappell/Bradley Library Vertical Files, CSUA; "What! Demonstrations in Columbus?," *Columbus News*, June 29, 1963, Isaac W. Humphye, "Have Columbus Ministers Chickened Out?," *Columbus News*, June 29, 1963, both in A. J. McClung Papers, MC 200, ser. 2, box 1, Columbus Times folder, CSUA; "McClung Selected for Safety Board," *Columbus News*, Jan. 7, 1967, McClung Papers, ser. 2, box 1, Newspaper Clipping folder.

24. William W. Winn, *Building on a Legacy: The Columbus Museum* (Columbus: Columbus Museum, 1996), 19; *One System . . . First Annual Report of the Muscogee County School District, Columbus Georgia, January 2, 1950–June 30, 1950* (Columbus: Columbus Office Supply, 1950), Columbus Public Library Genealogy Room; *Eightieth Annual Report of the Public Schools, Columbus, Ga., for the Year Ending August 1, 1947*, Muscogee County Board of Education Minutes, Feb. 10, 1947, 2281, Feb. 12, 1951, 334, May 14, 1951, 441, Feb. 9, 1953, 737, all in Muscogee County School District Archives; "William Henry Shaw Chosen School Head," *CE*, July 3, 1945; "Vote Favors Merger of Schools," *CE*, May 5, 1949; "One School System," *CL*, Feb. 2, 1920; "Negroes Pay 5 Per Cent of Taxes, Get Quarter of School Funds—Board," *CL*, Mar. 11, 1952; William Henry Shaw interview, Jan. 18, 1978, GOHC; Katherine Hines Mahan and William Clyde Woodall, *A History of Public Schools in Columbus, Muscogee County, Georgia* (Columbus: Muscogee County Board of Education, 1977), 288–296.

25. Virginia Johnson Storey, "The History of the Development of Public Libraries in Columbus, Georgia," 1979, 14, Columbus Public Library Genealogy Room; Muscogee County Board of Education Minutes, Mar. 8, 1948, 2472–73, Muscogee County School District Archives; "City to Obtain Bradley Estate," *CL-E*, Aug. 31, 1947; William Rowe, "$350,000 Library Ready; Dedication Rites Tuesday," *CL-E*, Oct. 29, 1950; "Story of Newly Built W. C. Bradley Memorial Library," *Industrial Index*, Dec. 27, 1950.

26. Edward Shorter interview, Mar. 1976, GOHC; Winn, *Building on a Legacy*, 19–23, 44–45, 53; "Only Eight Years Old: Columbus Museum Is Fast-Growing, Precocious Infant," *CL-E*, May 28, 1961; Joseph B. Mahan, *Columbus: Georgia's Fall Line Trading Town* (Northridge, Calif.: Windsor, 1986), 125–126; John S. Lupold, *Columbus, Georgia, 1828–1978* (Columbus: Columbus Sesquicentennial, 1978), 114.

27. "College Hinges on Bonds Vote," *CL*, May 15, 1958; McGee, *Pleasant Journey*, 96; Craig Lloyd, "Origins and Development of Columbus College," *Proceedings and Papers of the Georgia Association of Historians* 6 (1985): 24–31; Mahan, *Columbus*, 125–126, 170; Shaw interview; Reagan L. Grimsley, *Enriching Lives: A Pictorial History of Columbus State University* (Virginia Beach, Va.: Donning, 2008), 12–20.

28. Lloyd, "Origins and Development," 24–31; Shaw interview; Grimsley, *Enriching Lives*, 21–53; "Columbus College Changing to Four Year Institution," *CE*, Apr. 13, 1965; *Plants Grow Well in Columbus Georgia Soil!* (Columbus: Chamber of Commerce, 1967), HLUGA.

29. Thomas Whitley interview, Dec. 6, 1982, GOHC; Grimsley, *Enriching Lives*, 44–48; Lloyd, "Origins and Development," 30–31; "First Negro Attends CC," *Saber*, Sept. 30, 1963; "Saber Interviews First Negro Student," *Saber*, Nov. 12, 1964; Perry S. Jones, "Issues Involving the Racial Integration of Columbus College during the Period 1963–1970," CSU Collection, Record Group III, ser. B, box 3.

30. Ray Lakes interview, Dec. 18, 2007, GOHC; Grimsley, *Enriching Lives*, 46–48;

"Rebel Mascot Question Heads List of 69's Top News Events," *Saber*, Jan. 16, 1970; "CC President Removes CC Rebel Mascot," *Saber*, Mar. 13, 1970; "'Cougar' Selected as CC's Mascot," *Saber*, May 6, 1970; Whitley interview; James H. Chappel interview, Feb. 28, 2007, CSU Collection, Record Group IV, ser. B, box 1.

31. Whitley interview; Lakes interview; John S. Lupold e-mail, Dec. 3, 2015, Causey Collection; Jones, "Issues Involving the Racial Integration"; Howard Beeth interview, Nov. 1990, CSU Collection, Record Group IV, ser. B, box 3; "Black Students Speak Out," *Saber*, Oct. 22, 1970; "Black Student Union Holds Annual Black Culture Day," *Saber*, June 1, 1971; "Blacks Claim Racial Discrimination," *Saber*, May 24, 1974; Andrea Hurley, "The Integration of Columbus College from a Female Perspective," CSU Collection, Record Group III, ser. B, box 2.

32. "Viet Nam Student Movement Receives Support of College," *Saber*, Jan. 25, 1966; "Moratorium Debate Ends in Victory for Negative Views," *Saber*, Dec. 4, 1969; Lakes interview.

33. Shirley Hok, "Columbus College, 1958–1994: Women Student Enrollments and Societal Change," CSU Collection, Record Group III, ser. B, box 2; "Blacks Claim Racial Discrimination," *Saber*, Nov. 25, 1974; Vicky Jackson, "Child Care Center," *Saber*, Nov. 25, 1974; Ferinez Phelps, "Committee on the Status of Women," Nov. 28, 1973, Bob and Mary Jane Galer Collection, MC 105, box 1, Committee on the Status of Women folder, CSUA.

34. "Streakers, Streakers," *Saber*, Mar. 8, 1974; "Columbus Nudity Laws Questioned," *Saber*, Sept. 27, 1974; Grimsley, *Enriching Lives*, 49–52; Craig Lloyd e-mail, Dec. 11, 2015, Causey Collection.

35. "$4 1/4 Million School Bond Issue Passed," *CE*, June 21, 1950; *Public Schools of Muscogee County, Georgia: A Survey Report* (Nashville: Peabody College, 1957), 287, CSUA; Mahan and Woodall, *History of Public Schools*, 285–296; "State Organization Report," June 25, 1959, Pauley Papers, box 7, folder 1; Minutes, HOPE Executive Committee, Nov. 11, 1960, and "HOPE News," Aug. 1, 1960, both in Pauley Papers, box 7, folder 4; "The Citizens' Council," Right-Wing Ephemera Collection, box 1, folder 12, HLUGA.

36. Jeff Roche, *Restructured Resistance: The Sibley Commission and the Politics of Desegregation in Georgia* (Athens: University of Georgia Press, 1998), 70–95; "Schools Hearing Highly Important," *CL*, Mar. 28, 1960; "Big Johnnie Reb" Radio Editorials, [1960], Audiocassette 11.3, McGill Papers, box 102, Sound Recordings.

37. Roche, *Restructured Resistance*, 153–155, 162–170; Sibley Commission, "Meeting of the General Assembly Committee on Schools, Columbus Sub-Committee," Columbus, Ga., Mar. 31, 1960, Vertical File "Desegregation, 1960 Sibley Committee Hearings," CSUA; Remer Tyson, "Hearings over on School Issue," *CL*, Apr. 1, 1960; "Divided Sibley Group Urges Georgia to Abandon 'No Budge' School Policy," *Marietta Journal*, Apr. 28, 1960.

38. Jim Lowrey, "Negro Fined in 'Scuffle' at Library," *CL*, July 17, 1963; "Fight Breaks Out at Weracoba Park," *CL*, July 18, 1963; Constance Johnson and Gordon Cooksey, "100 Whites Await Negroes at Park," *CL*, July 19, 1963; Constance Johnson, "Board Approves Gradual Mixing," *CL*, Sept. 17, 1963; Virginia E. Causey, "The Long and Winding Road: School Desegregation in Columbus, Georgia, 1963–1997," *GHQ* 85, no. 3 (2001): 398–434.

39. *Jerry L. Lockett et al. v. Board of Education of Muscogee County School District*, Civil Action 991, Middle District of Georgia, Columbus Division, Apr. 1, 1964, 31; Causey, "Long and Winding Road," 400–404.

40. Causey, "Long and Winding Road," 405–406.
41. Ibid., 406–408; Pat Smith, "Muscogee Ordered to Integrate Fully," *CE*, May 29, 1971.
42. Causey, "Long and Winding Road," 409–412.
43. Ibid., 412–414; *Jerry L. Lockett et al. v. Board of Education*, "Individual School Reports," 1971–1980.
44. Causey, "Long and Winding Road," 414–417.
45. Ibid., 417–418.
46. Ibid., 418–421.
47. Ibid., 421–423.
48. Ibid., 424–426.
49. Ibid., 428–429; *Norm-Referenced Achievement Test Data*, 1990, Muscogee County School District Archives.

Chapter 8. From Optimism to Malaise

1. Alfred Sawyer, "Snowfall Paralyzes Columbus; State of Emergency Declared," *CL*, Feb. 9, 1973; Howell Meddars, "Humorous Events Found in City-Crippling Storm," *CL*, Feb. 11, 1973.
2. W. C. Tucker, "Top o' the Morn," *CE*, Mar. 23, 1944; "City Seen as Second Biggest in State," *CL*, Mar. 13, 1950; Charles Ewing, "St. Francis Dedicated to Mankind's Service," *CL*, Mar. 13, 1950; "60 Years of Caring at St. Francis Hospital, 1950–2010," *Spirit of St. Francis* 8, no. 1 (2010): 2–6, Causey Collection; William W. Winn, "The Medical Center, 1836–1991: An Institutional History of Public Service, Education, and Leadership in Medicine" [unpublished manuscript], 56–71, Causey Collection.
3. Richard Beckman, "City's Newest Ordinance Is Designed to Promote Better Health, Safety," *CE*, June 25, 1957; "City OKs 'Bottoms' Redevelopment Plan," *CE*, June 25, 1957; Carlton M. Johnson, "The Shame of Columbus," *CL*, Aug. 24, 25, 26, 27, 28, 1953; "Georgia's Modern Apartment Complexes," National Register of Historic Places Nomination, Georgia DNR, http://georgiashpo.org/register/research; Margaret Laney Whitehead and Barbara Bogart, *City of Progress: A History of Columbus, Georgia* (Columbus: Columbus Office Supply, 1978), 290–300; Planning Division, *Human Services Facilities* (Columbus: Community Development, 1979), 2, 28, 33, HLUGA.
4. "E. E. Farley Wins Award as Negro Man of the Year," *CE*, Jan. 26, 1953; "2,000 Visit Plaza Opening for 11 Stores," *CL*, Mar. 10, 1956; "Hamburger Chain Will Build Macon Road Unit," *CL*, June 11, 1962; "Georgia's Modern Apartment Complexes"; Sara Crawford, ed., *Gunby Jordan Remembers: A History of the Jordan Company, 1904–1986* (Columbus: Columbus Productions, 1986), 36; "Six New Subdivisions Started This Year," *CL-E*, Sept. 11, 1955; Whitehead and Bogart, *City of Progress*, 304–305.
5. Mrs. W. M. Fambrough, "The Enquirer, Which Chronicled Establishment of Columbus, Still Recording City's Progress," *CE*, March 25, 1950; Kenneth T. Jackson, *Crabgrass Frontier: The Suburbanization of the United States* (Oxford: Oxford University Press, 1987), 231–271; "Parking Problem Becomes More Serious as Fewer and Fewer Ride City Buses," *CL*, Nov. 20, 1953; Steve Lesher, "Simons' Plan for City Is Bold and Far-Reaching," *CL*, Nov. 12, 1957; Constance Johnson, "New Face for Columbus?," *CL*, July 7, 1961; Arthur Cotton Moore, "Policy Recommendations for the Advancement of the [Columbus] Area," 1–9, Quillian-Ansley-Gates Collection, MC 180, ser. 5, box 1, folder 8, CSUA; Otis White, "Urban Revival: The Building That Changed Columbus," *GT*, July 2011, 49.

6. "Moved to the Suburbs," *CL-E Chattahoochee Magazine*, Oct. 23, 1980; Constance Johnston, "Ledger-Enquirer Building Planned," *CL-E*, May 24, 1970; Richard Hyatt, "Development Project Covers 60-Block Area," *CL-E*, Mar. 1, 1989; Alva James-Johnson, "BTW Residents Express Mixed Emotions as They Leave Complex," *CL-E*, Feb. 7, 2015; Bill Montgomery, "Downtown Wilts as Centers Flower," *Atlanta Journal*, Nov. 14, 1973; Liza Benham, "Fourth Avenue Divided 2 Columbus Downtowns," Chappell/Bradley Library Vertical Files, Downtown Columbus 1980s folder, CSUA; "Liberty Theatre Cultural Center, Inc.," Columbus Jazz Society, http://www.columbusjazzsociety.com/liberty.htm.

7. *Economy and Population, Columbus, Georgia* (Columbus: Chamber of Commerce, 1978), CSUA; *Profile: Columbus* (Columbus: League of Women Voters, 1976), CSUA; John S. Lupold, "Industrial Archaeology of Columbus, Georgia," ser. 6, box 2, folder 74, Lupold Collection; "Swift Textiles, Inc.," [mid-1990s], Delane D. Chappell Collection, MC 252, box 4, folder 35, CSUA; Joseph B. Mahan, *Columbus: Georgia's Fall Line Trading Town* (Northridge, Calif.: Windsor, 1986), 208–209, 213.

8. John S. Lupold, "Bibb City Historic District," National Register of Historic Places, Lupold Collection, ser. 6, box 1, folder 12; Brooks Griffin and Plez Johnson interview, June 28, 1977, GOHC; Timothy Minchin, *Hiring the Black Worker: The Racial Integration of the Southern Textile Industry, 1960–1980* (Chapel Hill: University of North Carolina Press, 1999), 26.

9. Minchin, *Hiring the Black Worker*, 13–14, 33, 101–105, 124, 166–192.

10. Dan East interview, Dec. 3, 1996, Mrs. Elner Greene interview, Nov. 15, 1996, both in GOHC; Celia Bailey interview, Feb. 18, 1988, James Shavers interview, Feb, 16, 1988, both in Mill Workers Oral History Collection; Minchin, *Hiring the Black Worker*, 245–247, 256–257; "Fieldcrest Employees Go Union," *CL*, June 18, 1971; "Mills Defeat Textile Union," *CL*, Nov. 18, 1988; *Swift Textiles, Inc. and Textile Workers Union of America, AFL-CIO*, Oct. 11, 1974, 36, 38–39, National Labor Relations Board, http://apps.nlrb.gov/link/document.aspx/09031d45800aa0e1; *Columbus Mills, Inc. and Amalgamated Clothing and Textile Workers Union*, May 31, 1991, 223–237, National Labor Relations Board, http://apps.nlrb.gov/link/document.aspx/09031d45800bd0ed; "N.L.R.B. Orders Stiff Penalties for Fieldcrest in Workers' Case," *NYT*, Sept. 6, 1995.

11. Minchin, *Hiring the Black Worker*, 245–300.

12. Ben Walburn and Paul Miles, "Mills Fear New Local Industry," *CL*, June 12, 1962; *Tom Huston Company Annual Report*, 1965, Tom Huston Collection, MC 37, box 2, folder 30, CSUA; Scott Shepherd, "Southern Snack Firm Has New English Parent," *Baton Rouge Advocate*, Aug. 7, 1983; "Lance Buys Tom's Assets," *Food Management* 40, no. 13 (2005): 49; "Snyder's of Hanover, Lance Set to Merge to Create $1 Billion Snack Food Firm," *Food Trade News*, http://best-met.com/news/snyders-of-hanover-lance-set-to-merge-to-create-1-billion-snack-food-firm/.

13. Glenn Vaughn, "The Fizz and Fizzle of Royal Crown: Georgia's Other Cola," *GT*, June 1995, 28, and "Royal Crown Fights Back with Old Weapon: A New Product," *GT*, July 1995, 25; "Royal Crown Company, Inc., History," Funding Universe, http://www.fundinguniverse.com/company-histories/royal-crown-company-inc-history/; Bill Winn, "R.C. Cola Gets Start in Basement," *CL-E*, May 7, 1978; "New Cyclamate-Free Drinks Being Prepared by Bottlers," *CE*, Oct. 21, 1969; "Cott Income Statement—Annual," AmigoBulls, http://amigobulls.com/stocks/COT/income-statement/annual.

14. Whitehead and Bogart, *City of Progress*, 274, 627, 641–642; Loyall Solomon,

"World's Largest Cotton Gin Manufacturer Moving to Savannah," *Savannah Morning News*, Jan. 15, 1998; Barbara Kimmelman, John S. Lupold, and J. B. Karfunkle, "The Columbus Iron Works," 1977, 18–19, HAER Collection, box 1, folder 8; Susan Wiggins interview, Aug. 2, 2002, GOHC; "A History of Innovation," W. C. Bradley Company, https://wcbradley.com/index.php/about/history; Chuck Williams, "Hometown Product Loyalty Tested," *CL-E*, Nov. 28, 2004; Larry Gierer, "Goldens' Foundry and Machine Company Files for Chapter 11," *CL-E*, Oct. 3, 2009.

15. J. Tom Morgan Jr., *Kiss Impressions: My Love Affair with Lithography* (Rochester, N.Y.: Rochester Institute of Technology, 1983); Whitehead and Bogart, *City of Progress*, 638–639; Tony Adams, "Hallmark Closing Litho-Krome Plant in Columbus, 50 Jobs Lost," *CL-E*, Feb. 17, 2015.

16. Virginia Causey, Jean Simons Hyman, and Sydney Simons, "Sidney Simons: The Man behind the Boulevard," *Muscogiana* 26, no. 2 (2015): 1–16; Sydney Simons e-mails, Feb. 16, Mar. 2, 2015, Causey Collection.

17. Etta Blanchard Worsley, "Roy Elmo Martin, Sr.," in *Columbus on the Chattahoochee* (Columbus: Columbus Office Supply, 1951), appendix; "Martin Theatres Sets Expansion," *Marietta Journal*, Jan. 11, 1970; "Fuqua to Sell Theater Unit," *NYT*, Feb. 26, 1982; "Carmike to Add Theaters," *NYT*, Sept. 14, 1995.

18. "M&M, First National to Unite at Close of Business Saturday," *CL*, Oct. 23, 1953; "Wachovia and First Union Set to Merge," *CL-E*, Aug. 4, 2001; "Wells Fargo to Buy Wachovia in $15.1 Billion Deal," *NYT*, Oct. 3, 2008; Sara Crawford and Janis Eberhardt, *A Trust to Keep: The One Hundred Year History of Columbus Bank and Trust Company* (Columbus: CB&T, 1988), 75–113; *Looking Back, Moving Forward* (Columbus: Total System Services, 2013), http://tsys.com/Assets/TSYS/downloads/br_tsys-history-30th-anniversary-book.pdf; Chuck Williams, "Sunday Interview with Jimmy Blanchard," *CL-E*, May 9, 2015.

19. Kathy Kamienski, "Jet Firm Picks Columbus," *CL*, Nov. 6, 1980; "Automation Produces Product of High Quality in Less Time," *CL*, Apr. 22, 1984.

20. Allen R. Myerson, "John Amos: A Tough Act to Follow," *GT*, Oct. 1985, 70–75; Seymour Shubin, *The Man from Enterprise: The Story of John B. Amos, Founder of Aflac* (Macon: Mercer University Press, 1998); David Everett, "The Life and Times of John B. Amos," *CL-E Chattahoochee Magazine*, Feb. 13, 1977; "'Family Life' Is Now Listed on Exchange," *CL*, June 14, 1974; Jack Swift, "Business Booms," *CL*, Apr. 7, 1975; "American Family Tops," *CL*, Aug. 31, 1977.

21. Emma Edmonds, "What Makes John Amos Worth $769,279 a Year?," *Atlanta Constitution*, Apr. 28, 1978; Everett, "Life and Times"; Shubin, *Man from Enterprise*; Myerson, "John Amos"; Constance Johnson, "AFC Is 1 of Top Political Contributors," *CL*, July 9, 1979.

22. Shubin, *Man from Enterprise*; Lesley Gill, *The School of the Americas: Military Training and Political Violence in the Americas* (Durham: Duke University Press, 2004), 25–28.

23. Christopher Bonner, "Cancer Insurance Should Be Banned," *CL-E*, Dec. 31, 1978; Nita Birmingham, "AmFam Corp. Retains Forbes No. 1 Ranking," *CL-E*, Oct. 28, 1980; "Amos Ranks as Highest-Paid," *CL-E*, May 16, 1989; Bill Winn, "AFLAC Founder Amos Dies," *CL-E*, Aug. 14, 1990; "A Turnaround for American Family," *BusinessWeek*, Sept. 17, 1984; Shubin, *Man from Enterprise*.

24. Constance Johnson, "Area's Link to Nation Opens," *CL*, Sept. 17, 1979; "Unlocking Georgia's Best-Kept Secret," *CL*, Sept. 18, 1979; "Corridor Z Called Bargain for Money," *CL*, June 7, 1983; "Fall Line Freeway," Aug. 2017, Georgia Department

of Transportation, http://www.dot.ga.gov/InvestSmart/documents/GRIP/Facts/FallLineFreewayFactSheet.pdf.

25. Lynn Willoughby, *Flowing through Time: A History of the Lower Chattahoochee River* (Tuscaloosa: University of Alabama Press, 1999), 168–174; "Pick Says City's Future Hinges on River Project," *CL*, Oct. 5, 1951; "'Mr. Jim' to Throw Switch at Woodruff Dam Friday," *CL-E*, Mar. 17, 1957; Bill Plot, "Unlimited Potential Seen," *CL-E*, Sept. 6, 1964; Jim Houston, "Ports Group Is Confident Despite Losses," *CL-E*, Dec. 1, 1972; Robert E. Van Geuns, "The Development of Barge Traffic on Georgia's Inland Waterways, 1958–1968, and Some Development Potentials," 1970, Georgia Institute of Technology, https://smartech.gatech.edu/bitstream/handle/1853/50537/e-400-500_328115.pdf.

26. Charles Seabrook, "Barging into Controversy," *Atlanta Journal-Constitution*, Sept. 11, 2000; Willoughby, *Flowing through Time*, 176–181; Otis White, "Stanton Leads Fight for Ecology," *Saber*, Oct. 9, 1972; Lisa Battle, "River Is Vulnerable," *CL-E*, Sept. 6, 1964; *A River Runs through It: A 100-Year History of the Columbus Water Works* (Columbus: Water Works, 2002), 25–41.

27. Peggy A. Stepflug and Richard Hyatt, *Home of the Infantry: The History of Fort Benning* (Macon: Mercer University Press, 2007), 173–174, 189; *Economy and Population*, 3, 54, 59, 146; Glenn Vaughn, "Columbus, Fort Benning Ties Unique," *CL*, Mar. 23, 1986.

28. Lonnie Jackson interview, July 16, 2002, GOHC; C. V. Glines, "Black vs. White: Confrontation in the Ranks Is Calling for Improved Human Relations—or Else," *Armed Forces Management*, June 1970, 24; David Zeiger, *Sir, No Sir* [documentary], "Resistance Chronology," http://displacedfilms.com/sir-no-sir-archive/timeline/chronology_riots.html; Robert Sharlet, "Searching for Jeff," http://jeffsharletandvietnamgi.blogspot.com/2014/12/last-days-of-vietnam.html.

29. Michael R. Belknap, *The Vietnam War on Trial: The My Lai Massacre and the Court-Martial of Lieutenant Calley* (Lawrence: University Press of Kansas, 2013); Doug Linder, "The My Lai Courts-Martial, 1970," University of Missouri-Kansas City, 1999, http://law2.umkc.edu/faculty/projects/ftrials/mylai/mylai.htm; Tom Dunkin and Bob Payne, "Lt. Calley Gets Life," *CL*, Mar. 31, 1971; "Crowd Laments Guilty Verdict," *CL*, Mar. 31, 1971; Don Eddins, "Calley Fund Drive Gains Speed as Support Continues to Pour In," *CL*, Apr. 1, 1971; James T. Wooten, "Officials at Fort Benning Silent on New Calley Move by Nixon," *NYT*, Apr. 4, 1971; R. W. Apple Jr., "Parole of Calley Granted by Army Effective Nov. 19," *NYT*, Nov. 9, 1974; Dick McMichael, "Calley Apologizes for My Lai Massacre," *CL-E*, Aug. 21, 2009.

30. Edwin Strickland and Gene Wortsman, *Phenix City: The Wickedest City in America* (Birmingham: Vulcan, 1955), 24, 33–34; "Army, Russell to Make War on Diseases," *CE*, Mar. 5, 1943; "Gertrude and Jack Hewitt," in *Columbus and the Home Front: Memories of Columbus, Georgia, during World War II* (Columbus: Shaw Young Historians, 2007), 21.

31. "Flying Squadron Visits Bars, Clubs as 3 Are Arrested," *CE*, Feb. 1, 1945, "G. N. Shepherd Held in Fatal Shooting at Southern Manor," *CE*, Sept. 17, 1947; "Russell Jurors Free Shepherd in Murder Case," *CE*, Apr. 4, 1947.

32. Strickland and Wortsman, *Phenix City*, 10–22, 188–273; "Persons Puts Phenix City, County under Martial Law," *CL*, July 22, 1954; "Muscogee Jury's Report Absolves Sheriff Howard but Censures Binns," *CL*, Sept. 23, 1954; John Goheen, "Phenix Raised," *National Guard Magazine*, Aug. 2004; "Sketches of the Pulitzer Prize Winners in Journalism, Letters and Music for 1955," *NYT*, May 3, 1955.

33. Mahan, *Columbus*, 128, 130; "Three Arts Theatre Dedicated in Columbus," *CL*, Nov. 1, 1964; "Harry Kruger," *Atlanta Journal-Constitution*, Oct. 10, 2009.

34. "WDAK-TV to Begin Video Operation after Official Ceremonies Tomorrow," *CL*, Oct. 5, 1953; "WRBL-TV Starts Telecast Today on VHF Channel 4," *CL*, Nov. 15, 1953; "Specialized Structures: Tallest," *Guinness Book of World Records*, 1963, http://frankosport.com/tower/index.html; Rozell Fabiani and Doug Wallace interview, July 20, 25, 1989, GOHC; Richard Hyatt, "Local TV Pioneer, Mr. 'Sportsman' Ridley Bell Dies," *CL-E*, Jan. 23, 1989; Chuck Williams, "Sunday Interview with Dick McMichael," *CL-E*, July 5, 2014.

35. Eric Pastore and Wendy Pastore, "History of Golden Park," DigitalBallParks, http://digitalballparks.com/SALLY/Golden1.html; J. Gordon Hylton, "Was There Really a Professional Baseball Team Called the Confederate Yankees?," Marquette University Law School Faculty Blog, http://law.marquette.edu/facultyblog/2011/07/11/was-there-really-a-professional-baseball-team-called-the-confederate-yankees/.

36. Mahan, *Columbus*, 130–133; "Confederate Museum Is Now Open," *CL*, Aug. 1, 1962; "Museum Charter Granted," *CL*, June 29, 1967.

37. Clason Kyle, "Old South Revisited at Restored Springer," *Marietta Journal*, May 15, 1968; Clason Kyle interview, July 8, 2008, GOHC; John S. Lupold, "Historic Columbus Foundation," 2007, Lupold Collection, ser. 6, box, 2, folder 63; *Historic Preservation in Columbus, Georgia* (Columbus: Columbus Area Bicentennial Committee, 1976), 12, CSUA; "Springer Named Georgia State Theater," *CL*, Sept. 7, 1971.

38. *Economy and Population*, 110; Danny Lawrence Dupree, "Columbus, Muscogee County, Georgia Consolidation: A Case Study" (master's thesis, Auburn University, 1974); Office of the Mayor, "Summary of Consolidation, Columbus/Muscogee County Governments, Columbus, Georgia," [ca. 1972], Lupold Collection, ser. 6, box 3, folder 73; "The Saga of Annexation," *CL-E*, June 22, 1969; Constance Johnson, "Merge Plan Is Rejected by Voters," *CL*, Apr. 12, 1962.

39. Dupree, "Columbus, Muscogee County"; Gordon Cooksey, "Allen Is Elected Mayor," *CE*, Nov. 6, 1968; "Arguments for and against Annexation," *CL-E*, June 22, 1969.

40. Dupree, "Columbus, Muscogee County"; Charles Morrow Rector, "City Government," *Columbus–Muscogee County Public Record*, file II, box 36, Muscogee County—Columbus folder, GDAH; Bob Fort, "Merger Voted In," *CE*, May 28, 1970; James V. Burgess, "Consolidation in Georgia—Columbus and Muscogee County Merge Governments January 1," *Nation's Cities*, Dec. 1970, 21; Bob Hydrick, "J. R. Allen and Consolidation: His Vision Still Leads Us," *Columbus and the Valley*, Jul.–Aug. 1999, 2.

41. Constance Johnson, "Allen, Councilmen Take Oath; McClung Named Mayor Pro-Tem," *CL*, Nov. 23, 1970; "Edna Kendrick Scores 2–1 over Jones," *CL*, Nov. 8, 1978; Angela Coleman, "Affirmative Action Becoming Reality Here," *CL-E*, June 28, 1989; Ken Edelstein, "Strong's Loss Now Her Gain," *CL-E*, Dec. 26, 1988; Mayor's Commission on the Status of Women, "Preliminary Report: Employment Status of Female Personnel of the Consolidated Government of Columbus, Georgia," June 20, 1975, Bob and Mary Jane Galer Collection, MC 105, box 1, Commission on Status of Women folder, CSUA.

42. "City Hires Four Negro Policemen," *CL*, June 15, 1961; Margaret Shannon, "God and the Millionaire," *Atlanta Journal-Constitution Magazine*, Sept. 12, 1971; Rector, "City Government"; "Police Woman Hired," *Columbus Times*, June 25–26–27, 1971.

43. *Leonard v. City of Columbus*, U.S. Court of Appeals, Eleventh Circuit, 705 F.2d 1299, 1983, CaseText, https://casetext.com/case/leonard-v-city-of-columbus-3; Shannon, "God and the Millionaire"; "Why AAPL Filed Suit," *Columbus Times*, June 25–26–27, 1971.

44. *Leonard v. City of Columbus*, 1983; "Black Police League Files Suit Here," *CL*, June 19, 1971; Tom Dunkin and Don Eddins, "Williams Leads March, Lists Demands," *CL*, June 20, 1971.

45. Constance Johnson, "Mayor Asks Law, Order of Citizens," *CL*, June 21, 2016; "Black Areas Hit Hardest," *CL*, June 21, 1971; "Fire Bomb Total at 81," *CL*, June 30, 1971; Richard Diamond, "Racism Killed Osborne Abernathy Declares," *Columbus Times*, June 29, 1971; "'CAG' Calls for Massive Boycott," *Columbus Times*, June 29, 1971; Jack Brinkley interview, June 21, 1971, WSB video clip, http://dlg.galileo.usg.edu/crdl/id:ugabma_wsbn_58178.

46. *Community Action Group v. City of Columbus*, Mar. 9, 1973, Justia.com, http://law.justia.com/cases/federal/appellate-courts/F2/473/966/225729/; Constance Johnson, "Convictions in '71 Violence Upheld," *CL*, Feb. 7, 1973; Richard Diamond, "Abernathy Speaks to Hundreds," *Columbus Times*, July 28, 1971; "Diamond Attacked Brutally," *Columbus Times*, July 27, 1971; "Troopers Scatter Blacks at Georgia Demonstration," *NYT*, July 25, 1971; "Columbus, Ga., Mayor Asks People to Keep Off Streets," *NYT*, July 25, 1971.

47. "Bob Wright Takes Issue with FOP," *CL*, June 25, 1971; Rudolph Allen Sr. interview, Dec. 2, 1975, GOHC; Charles Wheeler and Harmon Perry, "Oreos Aren't Cookies in Columbus," *Atlanta Journal-Constitution*, June 27, 1971.

48. Shannon, "God and the Millionaire"; "Columbus, Ga., Gets Funds for Police-Community Ties," *NYT*, July 28, 1971; Thomas C. Humphries, "Civil Rights in Columbus: Refuge or Refuse?," Kevin Heath, "National Urban League of Columbus GA, 1971–1990," both in CSU Collection, Record Group III, ser. B, box 2.

49. *Leonard v. City of Columbus*, 551 F.2d 974, Court of Appeals, Fifth Circuit, May 9, 1977, OpenJurist, http://openjurist.org/551/f2d/974/leonard-v-city-of-columbus; *Leonard v. City of Columbus*, 1983; "Court Sides with Fired Black Policemen," *CE*, July 3, 1984; Constance Johnson, "Fired Officers Want Jobs Back," *CL-E*, July 4, 1984; David Rose, *The Big Eddy Club: The Stocking Stranglings and Southern Justice* (New York: New Press, 2007), 43.

50. Kathy Aure, "Mayor Allen, 3 More Die in Plane Crash," *CE*, Feb. 16, 1973; A. J. McClung, "Prologue," A. J. McClung Papers, MC 200, ser. 4, box 2, Biographical Information folder, CSUA.

51. Richard Hyatt, "The Stranglings: Looking Back after 7 Years," *CL-E*, May 13, 1984; Rose, *Big Eddy Club*; David Rose, "Terminate with Extreme Prejudice," *Observer*, June 13, 2004, http://www.guardian.co.uk/theobserver/2004/jun/13/features.magazine17.

52. Phil Gast, "Grand Jury Indicts Suspect in 3 'Stocking Stranglings,'" *CE*, May 5, 1984; Jim Lynn and Clint Williams, "No One Was Surprised by Jury's Guilty Verdict," *CL*, Aug. 27, 1986; Rose, *Big Eddy Club*; David Rose, "Terminate with Extreme Prejudice," *Observer*, June 13, 2004, http://www.guardian.co.uk/theobserver/2004/jun/13/features.magazine17.

53. Richard Hyatt, "Jury Sentences Gary to Death," *CE*, Aug. 28, 1986; Rose, *Big Eddy Club*; David Rose, "Terminate with Extreme Prejudice," *Observer*, June 13, 2004, http://www.guardian.co.uk/theobserver/2004/jun/13/features.magazine17; Tim Chitwood, Chuck Williams, and Alan Riquelmy, "Gary Execution Stopped by Geor-

gia Supreme Court," *CL-E*, Dec. 16, 2009; Tim Chitwood, "40 Years after Ritual Serial Killings, 'Stocking Strangler' Carlton Gary's Appeals Are Running Out," *CL-E*, Sept. 18, 2017; "Georgia Supreme Court Rejects 'Stocking Strangler' Carlton Gary's Appeal," *CL-E*, Dec. 1, 2017; "'Stocking Strangler' Silent during Execution," *CL-E*, Mar. 17, 2018.

54. "Hance Given Death Penalty," *CL*, Dec. 17, 1978; Phil Gast, "Hance Re-Trial Begins," *CE*, May 7, 1984; Bob Herbert, "In America; Mr. Hance's 'Perfect Punishment,'" *NYT*, Mar. 27, 1994.

55. Kimball Perry, "Plea Deal Was Necessary, DA Says," *CL*, June 5, 1990; Cathy Fussell e-mail, Mar. 5, 2016, Tim Chitwood interview, Mar. 5, 2016, both in Causey Collection.

56. Tim Chitwood and Ben Wright, "Police Say Bush Ax Used to Kill Mother, Children," *CL*, Aug. 30, 1985; Tim Chitwood, "Michael Curry Found Guilty of Murder," *CL-E*, Apr. 27, 2011.

57. Kimball Perry, "Bailey Goes on Trial for His Life," *CL-E*, June 17, 1991; "Bailey Escapes the Chair for Murder," *CL-E*, June 28, 1991.

58. "Dr. Nail Dies of Hanging," *CL-E*, July 13, 1989; Richard Hyatt, "Nail Very Private Despite Public Position," *CL-E*, July 13, 1989.

59. Richard Hyatt, "Superintendent Burns' Stay Rocky from the Start," *CL-E*, Oct. 19, 1997; Tim Chitwood, "The Burns Murder Case: What We Know and Unanswered Questions," *CL-E*, Sept. 27, 2014.

60. Richard Hyatt, "Murder Scene Was Circus Atmosphere Morning after Killing," *CL-E*, Oct. 19, 1997; Tim Chitwood, "The Burns Murder Case: What We Know and Unanswered Questions," *CL-E*, Sept. 27, 2014.

61. Tim Chitwood, "Trial Date Set for Kareem Lane, Charged in Then-Superintendent Jim Burns' 1992 Homicide," *CL-E*, Apr. 30, 2012; Jim Mustian, "Mistrial Declared in Kareem Lane Murder Trial after 10–2 Deadlock," *CL-E*, Sept. 19, 2012; Chuck Williams, "Kareem Lane Found Not Guilty in Jim Burns' Murder Case," *CL-E*, Sept. 6, 2014.

Chapter 9. Renaissance

1. John S. Lupold, "Historic Preservation in Columbus," Quillian-Ansley-Gates Collection, MC 180, ser. 5, box 2, folder 45, CSUA; John S. Lupold, "Historic Columbus Foundation," 2007, Lupold Collection, ser. 6, box 2, folder 62; Ed Neal interview, Dec. 6, 2006, GOHC.

2. Lupold, "Historic Preservation in Columbus"; Lupold, "Historic Columbus Foundation"; Brown Nicholson Jr. interview, Mar. 21, 2007, GOHC; Clason Kyle, "City's Houses Have Often Played Musical Chairs," *CL-E*, Apr. 30, 1978; "Road Houses," *CL-E*, Mar. 20, 1998.

3. Lupold, "Historic Preservation," "Historic Columbus Foundation"; *Historic Preservation in Columbus, Georgia* (Columbus: Columbus Area Bicentennial Committee, 1976), 12, CSUA; Janice Biggers interview, July 12, 2002, GOHC.

4. Constance Johnson, "Citizens Stars of Trade Center Opening," *CL-E*, Sept. 16, 1979; Nan Snow, "Columbus," *American Preservationist* 4, no. 1 (1981): 44–56; *Historic Preservation in Columbus, Georgia*; Lupold, "Historic Preservation in Columbus."

5. Timothy Martin, "Rankin Square Leads Revitalization of Downtown Area," *CL-E*, Sept. 9, 1979; Constance Johnson, "Harry Kamensky Faces Tomorrow with a Dream," *CL-E Chattahoochee Magazine*, May 29, 1977; "Rankin Square, Columbus, Georgia: Description and History," Quillian-Ansley-Gates Collection, ser. 5, box 3,

folder 72; Constance Johnson, "Rankin Square's Benefits Cited," *CL*, Aug. 24, 1978; Nolan Walters, "Rankin Square's Kamensky Faces 'Who Am I' Problem," *CE*, Jan. 30, 1979.

6. "Uptown Columbus Master Plan and Tourism Strategy," Oct. 26, 1994, CSUA; Alice Robertson, "Uptown Columbus Renaissance," *Columbus and the Valley*, Holiday 1998, 24–33; "Uptown Columbus, Inc.," [2004?], Frank Brown Papers, MC 283, box 24, folder 6, CSUA; Constance Johnson, "Council OKs Plan to Save Union Station," *CE*, May 9, 1984; Rozier Dedwylder, "Uptown's Strong Gains Benefitting the Whole City," *CL-E*, Feb. 17, 1985; Chuck Williams, "In 20 Years, Buddy Nelms Grows the Loft into Multidimensional Business," *CL-E*, June 2, 2012.

7. Liza Benham, "Save Black Downtown, Spencer Society Urges," *CL-E*, Chappell/Bradley Library Vertical Files, Downtown Cols 1980's folder, CSUA; Priscilla Black Duncan, "'Uptown' Slates Clean Sweep on Broadway," *CL*, Feb. 2, 1987.

8. Don H. Corrigan, *The Public Journalism Movement in America: Evangelists in the Newsroom* (Westport, Conn.: Praeger, 1999), 49–50, 99–106; Billy Winn, "Public Journalism—An Early Attempt," *Nieman Reports* 47, no 4 (1993), https://www.questia.com/article/1G1-15003492/public-journalism-an-early-attempt; Billy Winn, "The Future Is Bright—If We Plan for It," *CL-E*, May 29, 1988; Liza Benham and Ken Edelstein, "Many People Say City Leaves Them Out," *CL-E*, June 2, 1988; "L-E Editor Swift Is Found Dead at Home," *CL-E*, Nov. 16, 1990.

9. Winn, "Public Journalism"; Chuck Williams, "Former Columbus Mayor Frank Martin Dies at 73," *CL-E*, Aug. 12, 2012; Otis White, "Urban Revival: The Building That Changed Columbus," *GT*, July 2011, 46–53.

10. Mike Gaymon, *A View from the Backhoe* (n.p.: CreateSpace, 2015), 59–61; Delane Chappell, "The Columbus Riverfront: A Place to Be Proud Of," *Columbus and the Valley*, Spring 1994, 42–53; Chuck Williams, "Sunday Interview with Billy Turner," *CL-E*, Sept. 12, 2015.

11. Ken Edelstein, "Chattahoochee Put on Endangered Waterways List," *CL-E*, Apr. 20, 1994; Anne Roberts, "A River Runs through It: An Update on the Tri-State Water Wars," Southern Legislative Conference, Dec. 2015, http://knowledgecenter.csg.org/kc/content/river-runs-through-it-update-tri-state-water-wars; Greg Blustein, "Georgia Scores," *Atlanta Journal-Constitution*, Feb. 14, 2017; Kathryn Warihay and William Droze, "Southern Water Wars Teed Up for Ruling," *Environmental Law and Policy Monitor*, August 28, 2017, http://www.environmentallawandpolicy.com/2017/08/southern-water-wars-teed-ruling/; Stuart Leavenworth, "Supreme Court Gives Florida Another Chance in Water War against Georgia," *CL-E*, June 27, 2018.

12. Georgia EPD Gets Columbus Permit Right Again," *Chattahoochee Riverkeeper Riverchat*, Summer 2018, http://old.chattahoochee.org/wp-content/uploads/2018/08/CRK_SUMMER_NEWSLETTER_2018_WEB_READY.pdf; Jeffrey Larson to Steve Davis, Sept. 21, 2017, NDPES Draft Permit, Sept. 21, 2017, John Peebles to Hwan Cho, Sept. 29, 2017, Georgia Environmental Protection Division, National Pollutant Discharge Elimination System permit for the Columbus Water Works, August 16, 2018, all in Causey Collection.

13. "Columbus, Georgia Named to Host Women's Softball for Centennial Games," Aug. 6, 1993, Olympics '96 Columbus Softball Collection, MC 93, box 12, folder 2, CSUA; Ken Edelstein and Timothy Rogers, "Columbus an Olympic City," *CL-E*, Aug. 7, 1993; Molly Blue, "USA! USA!" *CL-E*, July 31, 1996; Patsy J. Thomas, "'The Games Will Go On,'" *CL-E*, July 28, 1996.

14. Timothy Rogers, "Calculating Olympic Profits," *CL-E*, Aug. 9, 1996; Tony Adams, "Columbus Area Attractions Look to Draw More Visitors," *CL-E*, May 13, 2000; Eric S. Bruner, "Tourism Now Big Business in Columbus," *CL-E*, Aug. 5, 1997; Columbus Sports Council, "South Commons Softball Complex," "Top Venues," 2016, both in Causey Collection.

15. Otis White, "Urban Revival: The Building That Changed Columbus," *GT*, July 2011, 46–53; "Uptown Columbus Master Plan"; Frank Brown interview, Mar. 23, 2012, GOHC; Brad Barnes, "Leap of Faith," *CL-E*, Apr. 21, 2002; Timothy Rogers, "Space Science Center Opens," *CL-E*, June 13, 1996; Sandra Okamoto, "Norman Christens Theatre," *CL-E*, May 5, 2002.

16. Richard Hyatt, "Center Promises Fantastic Voyages," *CL-E*, Apr. 26, 1996; "Coca-Cola Space Science Center: Description and Fact Sheet," [2016], Causey Collection.

17. Chuck Williams, "Sunday Interview with Paul Pierce," *CL-E*, May 25, 2014; Ellen Lampert-Gréaux, "Polishing a Georgia Peach: The Springer Opera House," EntertainmentDesignMag.com, Sept. 1, 2000, http://livedesignonline.com/mag/polishing-georgia-peach-springer-opera-house-0.

18. Tim Chitwood, "Dream Comes True," *CL-E*, Mar. 10, 2001; Tim Chitwood, "Civil War Naval Museum Sails into Uncharted Waters," *CL-E*, Dec. 26, 2011; Holly Beasley Wait e-mail, Aug. 17, 2016, Causey Collection.

19. Chuck Williams, "Sunday Interview with Ben Williams," *CL-E*, Feb. 21, 2016; Mick Walsh, "Congress Approves $5 Million toward Construction," *CL-E*, Sept. 28, 2006; Alan Riquelmy, "House OKs $5 Million for Museum," *CL-E*, Mar. 21, 2007.

20. "The Next Chapter: Your Guide to the Columbus Public Library," *CL-E*, Jan. 4, 2005; Alva James-Johnson, "Sunday Interview with Anne King," *CL-E*, Nov. 8, 2015; Virginia Peebles interview, Feb. 25, 2011, GOHC.

21. *Columbus Consolidated Government Fiscal Year 2010 Capital Improvement Program Budget*, https://www.columbusga.gov/finance/Financial_Planning/FY10_BB_CIP.pdf; "GA Library Faces Firestorm over 'Pile of Junk' Sculpture," *Library Journal*, Aug. 1, 2005, http://lj.libraryjournal.com/2005/08/ljarchives/ga-library-faces-firestorm-over-pile-of-junk-sculpture.

22. Mark Rice, "Book Opens on New Era," *CL-E*, Jan. 4, 2005; Tim Chitwood and Sara Pauff, "City, School Leaders Resolve Library Land Disputes," *CL-E*, Jan. 20, 2010; Tunnell-Spangler-Walsh, *A Master Plan for MidTown Columbus* (Columbus: MidTown Project), Sept. 30, 2005, http://www.midtowncolumbusga.org/wp-content/uploads/2012/08/Master-Plan-for-MidTown-Columbus-2005.pdf; *At a Crossroads: MidTown, Inc. 2005–2015* (Columbus: MidTown, 2015), http://www.midtowncolumbusga.org/wp-content/uploads/2012/08/Final-Report-for-MidTown-Inc-At-a-Crossroads-2-17-2016.pdf.

23. Ray Lakes interview, Dec. 18, 2007, GOHC; Billy Winn, "The Future Is Bright—If We Plan for It," *CL-E*, May 29, 1988; "State Honors TSYS and CSU for Joint Computer Training," *CL-E*, Nov. 18, 1997; Reagan L. Grimsley, *Enriching Lives: A Pictorial History of Columbus State University* (Virginia Beach, Va.: Donning, 2008), 85–87; "TSYS Gives $5 Million to Columbus State University," July 13, 2015, Columbus State University, https://news.columbusstate.edu/tsys-gives-5-million-to-columbus-state-university/.

24. Grimsley, *Enriching Lives*, 62–68, 80–82; Mary Jo Whitley interview, Mar. 1, 2008, CSU Collection, Record Group IV, ser. B; Brown interview.

25. Grimsley, *Enriching Lives*, 96–104; "Capital Campaign Raises More Than

$100 Million," Oct. 31, 2005, Columbus State University, https://news.columbusstate.edu/capital-campaign-raises-more-than-100-million/; Chuck Williams, "Sunday Interview with Frank Brown," *CL-E*, May 2, 2015.

26. Tony Adams, "Columbus State University Plans 'Transformational' Expansion on Ledger-Enquirer Property," *CL-E*, Jan. 10, 2015; Sasaki Associates, *Columbus State University Master Plan*, July 2012, Causey Collection; "CSU's Economic Impact at RiverPark," *Columbus State Magazine* 23, no. 2 (2016): 19; "The First Choice Campaign," Columbus State University, https://firstchoicecampaign.columbusstate.edu/.

27. *Columbus State University Master Plan*; CSU Facts & Figures 2017–2018 Academic Year, https://ir.columbusstate.edu/reports/facts17/facts17-18.php; Chuck Williams, "Sunday Interview with Frank Brown," *CL-E*, May 2, 2015.

28. Liza Benham, "Elected School Board Will Be More Diverse," *CL-E*, Nov. 24, 1993; Jim Houston and Richard Hyatt, "School System Wins Case," *CL-E*, May 7, 1997; Virginia E. Causey, "The Long and Winding Road: School Desegregation in Columbus, Georgia, 1963–1997," *GHQ* 85, no. 3 (2001): 429–431.

29. Causey, "Long and Winding Road," 431–434; Virginia Causey, "Mostly Separate and Still Not Equal," *CL-E*, July 7, 2002; "Elementary Schools in Muscogee County," https://www.schooldigger.com/go/GA/district/03870/search.aspx?level=1; Governor's Office of Student Achievement, "K–12 Public Schools Report Card, Muscogee County," https://gaawards.gosa.ga.gov/analytics/saw.dll?dashboard.

30. Mark Rice, "Majority of Elementary Schools Fall below State Average," *CL-E*, Nov. 19, 2015; Mark Rice, "Three-Fourths of County Middle Schools below State Test Average," *CL-E*, Nov. 20, 2015; Mark Rice, "Most County High Schools below State Average," *CL-E*, Nov. 21, 2015; Alva James-Johnson and Mark Rice, "The Changing Face of Title I," *CL-E*, Dec. 13, 2015.

31. *Regional Prosperity Initiative, Phase 1*, Chamber of Commerce, http://regionalprosperityinitiative.org/project-details/; Dimon Kendrick-Holmes, "Interview with Superintendent David Lewis," *CL-E*, Jan. 17, 2015; Mark Rice, "Analysis: Lewis Saves MCSD $1M, after Adding Three Region Chiefs to Central Office," *CL-E*, Nov. 7, 2015; Mark Rice, "Every Columbus Public High School Improves Graduation Rate," *CL-E*, Nov. 9, 2015; Mark Rice, "SPLOST Passes with More Than 54 Percent after Early Votes Counted," *CL-E*, Mar. 17, 2015.

32. *Columbus, Georgia Community Profile* (Miami: Knight Foundation, [2000]), CSUA; Alva James-Johnson, "Poverty Rates a Challenge throughout the Region," *CL-E*, Dec. 5, 2015; Alva James-Johnson, "Leaders Unveil 5-Step Plan to Curb Poverty, Grow Economy," *CL-E*, Jan. 28, 2017; *Regional Prosperity Initiative, Phase 1*.

33. Metropolitan Task for Force for the Homeless, "Continuum of Care," 1995, 2000, 2010, Causey Collection; Alva James-Johnson, "$1.4 Million Awarded to Agencies for Homeless Housing Programs," *CL-E*, Jan. 6, 2017; "United Way Conducts Annual Survey," Jan. 25, 2018, https://unitedwayofthecv.org/wp-content/uploads/2018/01/PRESS-RELEASE-PIT-Count-2018.pdf.

34. Tony Adams, "New Feeding the Valley Center Nears Opening," *CL-E*, Dec. 9, 2016; Feeding the Valley, http://www.feedingthevalley.org/about-us/family-distribution/.

35. Ben Wright, "Task Force to Target City Gangs," *CL-E*, Apr. 19, 1990; Ed Hall, "Gang-Related Conflicts Reported Near Schools," *CL-E*, May 2, 1991; Demetrius Patterson, "17 Bound Over after Alleged Gang Shootout," *CL-E*, Sept. 9, 1991; Amy Wofford, "Columbus Police Say There Are 15 Gangs," *CL-E*, Nov. 10, 1997; Amy Wofford, "Program Helps Reduce Area Gang Activity," *CL-E*, Apr. 20, 1998.

36. *Regional Prosperity Initiative, Phase 1*; Mike Owen, "Columbus Crime Rate," *CL-E*, Jan. 30, 2017; Tim Chitwood, "Columbus Has More Property Crime Than Comparable Cities," *CL-E*, Mar. 9, 2016; Tim Chitwood, "A Family's Anguish," *CL-E*, Mar. 23, 2009; Tim Chitwood, "Court Hearing: Victims of Triple Homicide Suffered Extreme Trauma to the Head, Stab Wounds," *CL-E*, Jan. 15, 2016; Harold Goodridge, "Shooting Spree Leaves Three Dead, Four Critical," *CL-E*, July 1, 1996; Melanie Bennett, "Man Kills Two Sons," *CL-E*, Feb. 24. 2005; Harry Franklin, "Missing Children Found Dead," *CL-E*, Mar. 20, 2008; Tim Chitwood, Larry Gierer, and Sara Pauff, "Deadly Grudge," *CL-E*, Mar. 28, 2008.

37. Alva James-Johnson, "Chattahoochee Valley Struggles with Black-on-Black Crime," *CL-E*, Feb. 8, 2014; Tim Chitwood, "Many 2017 Murder Cases," *CL-E*, Dec. 30, 2017; Tim Chitwood, "Tragedy of Errors: Two Critical Mistakes Led to Kenny Walker's Shooting in 2003," "The Kenneth Walker Shooting: How It Happened," both in *CL-E*, Dec. 7, 2013.

38. Chuck Williams, "Walker Shooting 10 Years Later: Former Mayor Was Driving Force behind Settlement," *CL-E*, Dec. 8, 2013; Alva James-Johnson, "Columbus Ranks in Top 10 in U.S. for Black Households Making $100,000 or More," *CL-E*, Apr. 30, 2016; Ben Wright, "Hundreds Question Police Encounters at Forum on Race Relations and Policing," *CL-E*, July 22, 2016; Bill Arth, "Columbus, Georgia: 8,000 March against Police Brutality, Racism," *The Militant* 69, no. 4 (2005), http://www.themilitant.com/2005/6904/690401.html; Police Demographic Information 2000, 2005, 2010, Columbus Consolidated Government, Human Resources; Maggie Potapchuk and Carolyne Abdullah, *Columbus, Georgia*, MP Associates, http://www.mpassociates.us/uploads/3/7/1/0/37103967/mftreport52005.pdf.

39. Tim Chitwood, "Controversial Former Muscogee County Marshal Dies," *CL-E*, Oct. 27, 2016; Tim Chitwood, "Tomlinson Won Over More Black Voters in Runoff," *CL-E*, Dec. 2, 2010; Tim Chitwood, "Donna Tompkins Defeats John Darr," *CL-E*, Dec. 7, 2016; "Columbus Council," Columbus Consolidated Government, http://www.columbusga.org/council/council.htm; "Affirmative Action Annual Report, Fiscal Year 2015," Columbus Consolidated Government, http://www.columbusga.org/HR/pdfs/AAAReport_FY15.pdf.

40. Georgia Department of Community Affairs, "Business Retention and Expansion Process Summary Report for Muscogee County, Georgia," May 2001, Business and Industry: Chamber of Commerce Vertical File, CSUA; Randy Southerland, "Columbus: Seismic Shift," *GT*, June 2008, http://www.georgiatrend.com/June-2008/Columbus-Seismic-Shift/; Ben Young, "Columbus: Success Brings Success," *GT*, June 2010, http://www.georgiatrend.com/June-2010/Columbus-Success-Brings-Success/; Tony Adams, "Metro Area Jobless Rate Drops to 4.9%," *CL-E*, Mar. 25, 2016; Tony Adams, "Painful Prediction," *CL-E*, Jan. 31, 2016; "Columbus Area Unemployment Rate," Apr. 26, 2018, Georgia Department of Labor, https://dol.georgia.gov/sites/dol.georgia.gov/files/related_files/document/lf_columbus.pdf.

41. Jan Wesner Childs, "Bell Tolls for Bibb," *CL-E*, Mar. 13, 1995; Eric S. Bruner, "Bibb Co. Mill to Shut Down on March 20," *CL-E*, Mar. 7, 1998; Eric S. Bruner, "Pillowtex Buys Fieldcrest Cannon," *CL-E*, Sept. 12, 1997; Jeanine Prezioso, "Bibb City Merger Begins," *CL-E*, Dec. 9, 2000; Lily Gordon and Chuck Williams, "Devastated: Fire Claims 750,000 Square-Foot Bibb Mill," *CL-E*, Oct. 31, 2008; Tony Adams, "The Last of the River Mills in Columbus," *CL-E*, June 23, 2002; Tony Adams, "Eagle Takes Flight," *CL-E*, Jan. 22, 2007; Tony Adams, "Swift Denim Plans Furloughs in '99," *CL-E*, Dec. 18, 1998; Tony Adams, "Swift Mill Slated for $50M Face Lift," *CL-E*, May 22,

2010; Tony Adams, "Delta Data Moving from Brookstone Centre to Downtown Swift Mill," *CL-E*, February 29, 2016.

42. Eileen Zaffiro, "Fate of Historic Buildings Uncertain," *CL-E*, Apr. 13, 1996; Eileen Zaffiro, "TSYS Breaks Ground Today," *CL-E*, Sept. 10, 1977; Chuck Williams, "History in Ruins: Riverfront Mott House a Total Loss in Sunday Fire," *CL-E*, Sept. 7, 2014; Peebles interview.

43. *Looking Back. Moving Forward* (Columbus: Total System Services, 2013), http://tsys.com/Assets/TSYS/downloads/br_tsys-history-30th-anniversary-book.pdf; "History of TSYS," *CL-E*, Oct. 26, 2007; Tony Adams, "Going Their Separate Ways," *CL-E*, Oct. 29, 2007; Tony Adams "TSYS Reports $364M Profit for 2015," *CL-E*, Jan. 27, 2016; Tony Adams, "Aflac and TSYS among 'World's Most Ethical' Companies," *CL-E*, Mar. 14, 2017; Laurie Pasiuk, *Vault Guide to the Top Business Services Employers* (New York: Vault, 2006), 110.

44. Gordon Jackson, "Synovus Loans to Sea Island Co. Blamed for Bank's Woes," *Florida Times-Union*, July 15, 2009; Peter Waldman, "How Sea Island Became a Paradise Lost," *Bloomberg Businessweek*, Dec. 30, 2009, http://www.bloomberg.com/news/articles/2009-12-30/how-sea-island-became-a-paradise-lost; Tony Adams, "Synovus to Settle Shareholder Lawsuit," *CL-E*, Jan. 15, 2013.

45. Phil W. Hudson, "A Sit-Down with the CEO of the 2nd Largest Bank Based in Georgia," *Atlanta Business Chronicle*, Oct. 2, 2015; Tony Adams, "It's Over: Synovus Repays $968 Million Owed to Federal Troubled Asset Relief Program," *CL-E*, July 26, 2013; Chuck Williams, "CB&T to Change Its Name in 2018," *CL-E*, Mar. 23, 2017.

46. "Aflac (AFL): A Dividend Aristocrat Trading for Less Than 10x Earnings," Simply Safe Dividends, Dec. 29, 2015, http://www.simplysafedividends.com/aflac-afl-a-dividend-aristocrat-trading-for-less-than-10x-earnings/; Tony Adams, "Aflac Reports $730 Million Profit in Quarter, $2.5 Billion for 2015," *CL-E*, Feb. 1, 2016; Abby Brach, "Amos Credits Success to Duck," *CL-E*, July 7, 2000; K. K. Snyder, "A Household Name: Dan Amos," *GT*, Sept. 2015, http://www.georgiatrend.com/September-2015/30-Years-Of-Influence/.

47. "Aflac Is Among Fortune's 'World's Most Admired Companies' for 15th Year," *CL-E*, Feb. 22, 2016; Mike Owen, "Aflac Garners Major Awards for Workplace, Workforce," *CL-E*, Dec. 23, 2016; Chuck Williams, "Aflac CEO Dan Amos on Diversity: 'I Already Know How a 60-Year-Old White Guy Thinks,'" *CL-E*, Sept. 21, 2016; Tony Adams, "Aflac and TSYS among 'World's Most Ethical' Companies," *CL-E*, Mar. 14, 2017.

48. Jim Poole, "P&W Plant to Stay Open," *CL-E*, Apr. 15, 1993; Tony Adams, "Pratt & Whitney to Add 500 Jobs with $386M Expansion," *CL-E*, Feb. 15, 2017; Kirk Johnson, "By Pratt & Whitney's Math, Connecticut Costs Too Much," *NYT*, Apr. 23, 1993; Association for Career and Technical Education, "Taking Business to School," https://www.acteonline.org/taking-business-to-school-case-study-pratt-whitney/; "Pratt & Whitney Opens New F100 Engine Overhaul Facility in Columbus, Ga.," Dec. 12, 2013, Pratt & Whitney, http://www.pw.utc.com/Press/Story/20131212-0830/2013/All%20Categories#sthash.yfq0SepD.dpuf; "Pratt and Whitney Plans $65 Million Upgrade at Columbus, Georgia Plant," June 30, 2016, Area Development, http://www.areadevelopment.com/newsItems/6-30-2016/pratt—whitney-engine-center-columbus-georgia.shtml.

49. Tony Adams, "Sour Ending for Hostess," *CL-E*, Nov. 16, 2012; Tony Adams, "New Hostess Owner Set to Resume Snack Cake Production at Dolly Madison Plant in Columbus," *CL-E*, June 12, 2013; Tony Adams, "Hostess Brands to Hire More than

40 at Snack Cake Bakery on Victory Drive," *CL-E*, May 6, 2016; "Snyder's-Lance's Decision to Discontinue Peanut Shelling Forces Impending Layoffs," Sept. 14, 2015, WRBL, http://wrbl.com/2015/09/14/snyders-lances-decision-to-discontinue-peanut-shelling-forces-impending-layoffs/; Katherine Peralta, "Campbell Soup Completes Multibillion-Dollar Purchase," *Charlotte Observer*, Mar. 26, 2018.

50. Ben Wright, "Kodak Unveils $28 Million Expansion at Columbus Plant," *CL-E*, Aug. 8, 2015; Tony Adams, "NCR Closing Its Columbus Plants," *CL-E*, Apr. 23, 2018; "Nash Finch Company Announces Acquisition Distribution Center," Dec. 17, 2009, BusinessWire, http://www.businesswire.com/news/home/20091217005200/en/Nash-Finch-Company-Announces-Acquisition-Distribution-Center; Sara Belsole, "Second NCR Facility Brings 300 Jobs to Columbus," Mar. 28, 2012, WLTZ, http://www.wltz.com/story/17276676/second-ncr-facility-brings-300-jobs-to-columbus; Ben Young, "Columbus: Success Brings Success," *GT*, June 2010, http://www.georgiatrend.com/June-2010/Columbus-Success-Brings-Success/.

51. Tony Adams, "Carmike Board Removes CEO Michael Patrick," *CL-E*, Jan. 21, 2009; Tony Adams, "AMC Plans to Keep Carmike Brand, Not Headquarters," *CL-E*, Mar. 5, 2016; Tony Adams, "Lights, Camera, Sold! Carmike Shareholders Approve Buyout by AMC," *CL-E*, Nov. 15, 2016; "Judge Approves Chapter 11 Plan for Carmike Cinemas," *NYT*, Jan. 4, 2002.

52. Tony Adams, "Columbus Square Mall Closes Its Doors," *CL-E*, Mar. 1, 2001; Tony Adams, "Columbus Park Crossing Only Tip of What's to Come," *CL-E*, Aug. 18, 2003; Tony Adams, "Movin' On," *CL-E*, Oct. 23, 2004; Adam Carlson, "Peachtree Makes List of Georgia's Worst Malls," *CL-E*, July 11, 2014, Larry Gierer, "Anthony Meredith Shot at Peachtree Mall while Easter Shopping," *CL-E*, Mar. 27, 2016; "Uptown Vibrancy Report," *Columbus State Magazine*, 23, no. 2 (2016): 20.

53. *Regional Prosperity Initiative, Phase 1*; "Fort Benning Army Base, Georgia," Military Standard, http://www.themilitarystandard.com/army_base/ga/fort_benning.php; Chuck Williams, "Women Starting Ranger School over Earning Respect," *CL-E*, June 1, 2015; Chuck Williams, "First Two Female Rangers Showing 'Quiet Professionalism,'" *CL-E*, Oct. 15, 2015; Gary Sheftick, "New Academy Will Train Security Force Assistance Brigades," U.S. Army, https://www.army.mil/article/182572/new_academy_will_train_security_force_assistance_brigades.

54. Richard Grimmett and Mark P. Sullivan, "United States Army School of the Americas: Background and Congressional Concerns," Congressional Research Service, http://fas.org/irp/crs/soa.htm; "Most Notorious SOA Graduates," "Update from the Convergence at the Border," both in SOA Watch, http://www.soaw.org/; Leslie Gill, *The School of the Americas: Military Training and Political Violence in the Americas* (Durham: Duke University Press, 2004), 199–221; Ben Wright, "SOA Watch to Hold One-Day Protest outside Fort Benning," *CL-E*, Oct. 11, 2016.

55. Mike Owen, "How Do TADs Help Develop Blighted Areas?," *CL-E*, Mar. 11, 2016; "Columbus Council Approves All Three TADs," *CL-E*, Mar. 16, 2016; Chuck Williams, "The 1200 Block," *CL-E*, Jan. 17, 2016; Chuck Williams, "1200 Block a Prime Piece of Real Estate for Small Investors," *CL-E*, Jan. 18, 2016.

56. Mike Owen, "$60 Million Transformation," *CL-E*, Feb. 14, 2016; Chuck Williams, "Vacant Riverfront Mill May Get New Life as Downtown Brewery," *CL-E*, Mar. 22, 2018.

57. Mike Owen, "Sixth Avenue Flood Abatement Project Turns Final Corner," *CL-E*, May 13, 2013; Alva James-Johnson, "Plans to Improve MLK Boulevard Move Forward to Preserve Legacy," *CL-E*, Jan. 16, 2017; JRA Architects and KPS Group,

"Master Plan for the Liberty District," Columbus Consolidated Government, http://www.columbusga.org/pdfs/Liberty%20District%20Master%20Plan%20(clean%20copy).pdf.

58. Mike Owen, "Demolition Begins at Booker T. Washington Apartments," *CL-E*, June 8, 2015; Chuck Williams, "The Play That May Have Saved Golden Park," *CL-E*, Mar. 29, 2016; Alva James-Johnson, "Plans to Remove Eyesore from Columbus Riverfront," *CL-E*, Mar. 25, 2018; "Columbus, City of, Title to Commons," *Acts and Resolutions of the General Assembly of the State of Georgia* (Atlanta: Byrd, 1910), 482.

59. Mike Owen, "How Do TADs Help Develop Blighted Areas?," *CL-E*, Mar. 11, 2016; "Arbor Pointe Kicks Off New Phase of Mixed-Income Housing Complex," *CL-E*, Jan. 27, 2012; Ben Wright, "Clinton to Honor Local Man," *CL-E*, Apr. 13, 1992; John F. Greenman, "Major Economic Progress You Just Might Not Have Noticed," *CL-E*, Aug. 6, 2016; Tony Adams, "Wal-Mart Supercenter on Victory Drive Opens," *CL-E*, June 14, 2016; Urvaksh Karkaria, "New Fort Benning Biz Park to Be Defense Hub," *Atlanta Business Chronicle*, July 26, 2010, http://www.bizjournals.com/atlanta/stories/2010/07/26/story1.html; Lonnie Jackson interview, July 16, 2002, GOHC; "South Columbus Hero: Mr. Lonnie Jackson," *Columbus Times*, Black History ser., 1990, 10–11; University of Georgia Environment and Design Summer Studio, "Revitalizing Columbus South," 2003, http://aqg.uga.edu/documents/columbus_south_report_final.pdf; "Newton D. Baker Village Revitalization Project," Columbus Housing Authority, http://www.columbushousing.org/page.asp?urh=NewDevelopmentsViewer&id=5.

60. Tim Chitwood and Tiffany Stevens, "City Mills Dam Blast Bigger Than Eagle & Phenix," *CL-E*, Mar. 11, 2013; Ed Hall, "Forum Seeks the 'IT,' to Draw Tourists " *CL-E*, Mar. 31, 1994; Chuck Williams, "Sunday Interview with Mat Swift," *CL-E*, July 28, 2014; Chuck Williams, "Chattahoochee River Whitewater," *CL-E*, Mar. 7, 2013; Chuck Williams, "Sunday Interview with Richard Bishop," *CL-E*, Aug. 16, 2016; Chuck Williams, "Whitewater Express, Uptown Whitewater Approach 100,000-Rafter Mark," *CL-E*, Aug. 16, 2016; Mike Owen, "14th Street Bridge Opening Delayed until October," *CL-E*, Aug. 23, 2013; Tim Chitwood, "$23 Million Chattahoochee River Whitewater Project's Ready to Launch," *CL-E*, Apr. 26, 2010; Tim Chitwood, "Stick Around to See the Shoal Lilies Resurrect," *CL-E*, Apr. 13, 2016; Tim Chitwood, "Crews Install First Steel Piece of 'Wave-Shaper' for New Whitewater Rapid," *CL-E*, Nov. 8, 2012; Tony Adams, "$24.4 Million Chattahoochee River Restoration Project a Blend of Public, Private Funding," *CL-E*, Apr. 6, 2013; Karen Rosen, "Columbus Roaring Ahead," *GT*, June 2014, http://www.georgiatrend.com/June-2014/Columbus-Roaring-Ahead/; Sam A. Williams, *The CEO as Urban Statesman: Harnessing the Power of CEOs to Make Cities Thrive* (Macon: Mercer University Press, 2014), 99–132; "Uptown Columbus Master Plan"; K. K. Snyder, "Columbus: Seeing the Big Picture," *GT*, June 2016, http://www.georgiatrend.com/June-2016/Columbus-Seeing-the-Big-Picture-Prosperity-revitalization-and-the-military/.

61. Tony Adams, "Columbus Tourism Heating Up," *CL-E*, Mar. 18, 2016; Stephanie Pedersen, "Zip Line Named Blue Heron Adventure to Open Saturday," *CL-E*, Sept. 12, 2014; Michael J. Daniels and Frank R. Lazzarra, "Chattahoochee River Restoration Columbus, Georgia and Phenix City, Alabama: Market and Economic Impact Analysis," *CL-E*, June 3, 2005, http://docplayer.net/7438385-Chattahoochee-river-restoration-columbus-georgia-and-phenix-city-alabama-market-and-economic-impact-analysis.html (copy in Causey Collection).

SELECTED BIBLIOGRAPHY

Primary Sources

"Bombing of Negro Residences, January 10, 1958, Columbus, Georgia," and "Bombing of Negro Residence, July 2, 1958, Columbus, Georgia." FBI Reports, Internet Archive, https://ia802702.us.archive.org/23/items/foia_Bombings-Attempted_Bombings—Chicago-3/Bombings-Attempted_Bombings—Chicago-3_text.pdf.

"Born in Slavery: Slave Narratives from the Federal Writers' Project, 1936–1938." Library of Congress, http://memory.loc.gov/ammem/snhtml/mesnbibnarrindex.html.

Daniel, Roland B. "Industrial Education in Columbus." *Journal of Proceedings and Addresses of the Twenty-Fourth Annual Meeting of the Southern Educational Association*. Nashville: Southern Educational Association, 1913.

Gibson, Carleton. "The Negro Schools of Columbus, Georgia." *Southern Workman* 39, no. 11 (1910): 596–598.

Hall, Basil. *Travels in North America in the Years 1827 and 1828*. Vol. 3. Edinburgh: Cadell, 1829.

"Henry L. Benning's Secessionist Speech, November 19." In *Secession Debated: Georgia's Showdown in 1860*, ed. William W. Freehling and Craig M. Simpson, 117–120. New York: Oxford University Press, 1992.

Howard, Robert M. *Reminiscences*. Columbus: Gilbert, 1912.

Johnson, Nunnally. *The Letters of Nunnally Johnson*. Ed. Dorris Johnson and Ellen Leventhal. New York: Knopf, 1981.

Land, J. E., ed. *Columbus: Her Trade, Commerce, and Industries, 1892–93*. Columbus: Land, 1892.

Lane, Mills, ed. *The Rambler in Georgia*. Savannah: Beehive, 1973.

Martin, John H. *Columbus, Geo., from Its Selection as a "Trading Town" in 1827, to Its Partial Destruction in Wilson's Raid, in 1865*. Columbus: Gilbert, 1874.

Minutes of the Columbus Council and Ordinances of the Mayor and Council of the City of Columbus, Clerk of Council, Columbus Consolidated Government.

"Papers of the NAACP, Part 9, Discrimination in the U.S. Armed Forces, 1918–1955." Series A. Ed. John H. Bracey Jr. and August Meier. http://cisupa.proquest.com/ksc_assets/catalog/1536_PapersNAACPPart9SerA.pdf.

Radical Rule: Military Outrage in Georgia. Louisville, Ky.: Morton, 1868.

Report of the Committee of the Senate upon the Relations between Capital and Labor. Vol. 4. Washington, D.C.: U.S. Government Printing Office, 1885.

Turner, William B. *The Learning of Love: A Journey toward Servant Leadership.* Macon, Ga.: Smith and Helwys, 2000.

The War of the Rebellion: A Compilation of the Official Records of the Union and Confederate Armies. Washington, D.C.: U.S. Government Printing Office, 1897.

Wilson, James Harrison. *Under the Old Flag.* Vol. 2. New York: Appleton, 1912.

Secondary Sources

Belknap, Michal R. *The Vietnam War on Trial: The My Lai Massacre and the Court-Martial of Lieutenant Calley.* Lawrence: University Press of Kansas, 2013.

Bradshaw, Lauren Yarnell. "Practical Paternalism: G. Gunby Jordan's Quest for a Vocational School System in Columbus, Georgia." Ph.D. diss., Georgia State University, 2016.

Bryan, Mabel Longshore. "A History of the Jordan Vocational High School, Columbus, Georgia." Master's thesis, University of Georgia, 1943.

Byrne, Frank Joseph. "The Columbus Strikes of 1918-1921: Textile Unionism and Violence in Post-World War I Georgia." Master's thesis, University of Georgia, 1994.

Carey, Anthony Gene. *Sold Down the River: Slavery in the Lower Chattahoochee Valley of Alabama and Georgia.* Tuscaloosa: University of Alabama Press, 2011.

Carr, Virginia Spencer. *The Lonely Hunter: A Biography of Carson McCullers.* Garden City, N.Y.: Doubleday, 1975.

Causey, Virginia E. "The Long and Winding Road: School Desegregation in Columbus, Georgia, 1963-1997." *Georgia Historical Quarterly* 85, no. 3 (2001): 398-434.

Cobb, James C. "The Making of a Secessionist: Henry L. Benning and the Coming of the Civil War." *Georgia Historical Quarterly* 40, no. 4 (1976): 313-323.

Daniell, Elizabeth Otto. "The Ashburn Murder Case in Georgia Reconstruction, 1868." *Georgia Historical Quarterly* 65, no. 4 (1975): 296-312.

Dews, Carlos. "Carson McCullers: 'The Brutal Humiliation of Human Dignity' in the South." In *Georgia Women: Their Lives and Times*, ed. Ann Short Chirhart and Kathleen Ann Clark, 2:281-298. Athens: University of Georgia Press, 2014.

Dupree, Danny Lawrence. "Columbus, Muscogee County, Georgia Consolidation: A Case Study." Master's thesis, Auburn University, 1974.

Edwards, Stewart C. "'To Do the Manufacturing for the South': Private Industry in Confederate Columbus." *Georgia Historical Quarterly* 85, no. 4 (2001): 538-554.

Ellisor, John T. *The Second Creek War: Interethnic Conflict and Collusion on a Collapsing Frontier.* Lincoln: University of Nebraska Press, 2010.

"Encyclopedia of Jewish Communities—Columbus, Georgia." Goldring/Woldenberg Institute of Southern Jewish Life, http://www.isjl.org/georgia-columbus-encyclopedia.html.

Fish, John O. "The Christian Commonwealth: A Georgia Experiment, 1896-1900." *Georgia Historical Quarterly* 57, no. 2 (1973): 213-226.

Gill, Lesley. *The School of the Americas: Military Training and Political Violence in the Americas.* Durham: Duke University Press, 2004.

Goodson, Steve. "Gertrude 'Ma' Rainey." In *Georgia Women: Their Lives and Times*, ed. Ann Short Chirhart and Kathleen Ann Clark, 2:148-165. Athens: University of Georgia, 2014.

Graf, LeRoy P., and Ralph W. Haskins, eds. "The Letters of a Georgia Unionist: John G. Winter and Secession." *Georgia Historical Quarterly* 45, no. 4 (1961): 385-402.

———. "The Letters of a Georgia Unionist: John G. Winter and the Restoration of the Union." *Georgia Historical Quarterly* 46, no. 1 (1962): 44-58.

Grimsley, Reagan L. *Enriching Lives: A Pictorial History of Columbus State University.* Virginia Beach, Va.: Donning, 2008.

Huntzinger, Victoria MacDonald. "The Birth of Southern Public Education: Columbus, Georgia, 1864–1904." EdD diss., Harvard University, 1992.

Jensen, Faye Lind. "Power and Progress in the Urban South: Columbus, Georgia, 1850–1885." PhD diss., Emory University, 1991.

Jones, James Pickett. *Yankee Blitzkrieg: Wilson's Raid through Alabama and Georgia.* Lexington: University Press of Kentucky, 2000.

Keller, Helen B. "The History of the Theatre in Columbus, Georgia from 1828 to 1865." Master's thesis, University of Georgia, 1957.

Kyle, Clason. *In Order of Appearance: Chronicling Thirty-Five Years on America's Most Celebrated Stage.* Columbus: Communicorp, 2006.

Lift Every Voice: Columbus Georgia's African American Heritage. Columbus: Pope Johnson Video Productions, 2003.

Lisby, Gregory C., and William F. Mugleston. *Someone Had to Be Hated: Julian LaRose Harris—A Biography.* Durham: Carolina Academic, 2002.

Lloyd, Craig. "Nunnally Johnson in Columbus." *Muscogiana* 9, nos. 1–2 (1988): 29–36.

———. "The Origins and Development of Columbus College." *Proceedings and Papers of the Georgia Association of Historians* 6 (1985): 24–31.

Lupold, John S. *Columbus, Georgia, 1828–1978.* Columbus: Columbus Sesquicentennial, 1978.

———. *Heritage Park: A Celebration of the Industrial Heritage of Columbus, Georgia.* Columbus, Ga.: Historic Columbus Foundation, 1999.

Lupold, John S., and Thomas L. French, Jr. *Bridging Deep South Rivers: The Life and Legend of Horace King.* Athens: University of Georgia Press, 2004.

Misulia, Charles A. *Columbus, Georgia, 1865: The Last True Battle of the Civil War.* Tuscaloosa: University of Alabama Press, 2010.

O'Connell, Deirdre. *The Ballad of Blind Tom.* New York: Overlook Duckworth, 2009.

Pendergrast, Mark. *For God, Country, and Coca-Cola.* 2nd ed. New York: Basic Books, 2000.

A River Runs through It: A 100-Year History of the Columbus Water Works. Columbus: Water Works, 2002.

Rose, David. *The Big Eddy Club: The Stocking Stranglings and Southern Justice.* New York: New Press, 2007.

Salmond, John A. *The General Textile Strike of 1934: From Maine to Alabama.* Columbia: University of Missouri Press, 2002.

Shubin, Seymour. *The Man from Enterprise: The Story of John B. Amos, Founder of AFLAC.* Macon: Mercer University Press, 1998.

Standard, Diffee William. *Columbus, Georgia, in the Confederacy: The Social and Industrial Life of the Chattahoochee River Port.* New York: William-Frederick, 1954.

Stelpflug, Peggy A., and Richard Hyatt. *Home of the Infantry: The History of Fort Benning.* Macon, Ga.: Mercer University Press, 2007.

Stephens, Jessica. "The Standoff: First Presbyterian Church of Columbus, Georgia, Robert McNeill, and Racial Equality." Master's thesis, Auburn University, 2011.

Strickland, Edwin, and Gene Wortsman, *Phenix City: The Wickedest City in America.* Birmingham: Vulcan, 1955.

Taylor, A. Elizabeth. "The Origin of the Woman Suffrage Movement in Georgia." *Georgia Historical Quarterly* 28, no. 2 (1944): 63–79.

Telfair, Nancy. *A History of Columbus, Georgia, 1828–1928*. Columbus: Historical Publishing, 1929.

Vaughn, Glenn. "The Fizz and Fizzle of Royal Crown: Georgia's Other Cola." *Georgia Trend* 10, no. 10 (1995): 28.

Whitehead, Margaret Laney, and Barbara Bogart. *City of Progress: A History of Columbus, Georgia*. Columbus: Office Supply, 1978.

Williams, David. *Rich Man's War: Class, Caste, and Confederate Defeat in the Lower Chattahoochee Valley*. Athens: University of Georgia Press, 1998.

Williams, Sam A. *The CEO as Urban Statesman: Harnessing the Power of CEOs to Make Cities Thrive*. Macon: Mercer University Press, 2014.

Willoughby, Lynn. *Flowing through Time: A History of the Lower Chattahoochee River*. Tuscaloosa: University of Alabama Press, 1999.

Winn, William W. *Line of Splendor: The Life and Times of St. Luke United Methodist Church, Columbus, Georgia, 1828–2008*. Columbus: St. Luke Methodist Church, 2010.

———. "Lynching on Wynn's Hill." *Southern Exposure* 14, nos. 3–4 (1987): 17–24.

———. *Triumph of the Eccunna Nuxulgee: Land Speculators, George M. Troup, State Rights, and the Removal of the Creek Indians from Georgia and Alabama, 1825–1838*. Macon: Mercer University Press, 2015.

Worsley, Etta Blanchard. *Columbus on the Chattahoochee*. Columbus: Office Supply, 1951.

INDEX

Allen, J. R., 223, 224, 225–228, 230
Allen, Rudy, 182–185, 228, 229
Alston, Philip H., 6
Amos, Dan, 215, 259
Amos, John, 212–215, 223, 262
Ashburn, George W., 52–54, 55–56
Austin, Paul B. ("Pops"), 131, 154

Baldwin, George J., 78–81, 87–88, 96, 102, 126
Banking, 18–19, 21, 23, 57, 61, 66, 211–212, 258–259; Bank of Columbus, 18, 23, 31, 61 (*see also* Jones, Seaborn; Young, William H.); Bank of St. Marys, 23 (*see also* Winter, John); Columbus Bank & Trust (originally the Eagle & Phenix Savings Bank, then Columbus Savings Bank, merged with Third National Bank), 61, 86, 211, 259 (*see also* Blanchard, James H.; Jordan, G. Gunby; Young, William H.); First National Bank (merged with Merchants and Mechanics Bank, then with Wachovia Bank, then with Wells Fargo Bank), 61, 211 (*see also* Browne, J. Rhodes); Fourth National Bank (merged with Trust Company Bank, then SunTrust Bank), 61, 218; Insurance Bank, 19, 27; Laborers' Savings and Loan, 66; Merchant and Mechanics Bank, 61, 211; Synovus, 212, 258–259 (*see also* Blanchard, James H.)
Banks, John, 17, 183; the Cedars, 16, 183; Civil War, 32, 41–42, 46; slave owner, 16, 31, 47; Howard Factory, 22; Wynnton Academy, 26
Bates, Asa, 9, 12, 85
Beall, Elias, 6
Benning, Anna Caroline, 82, 118
Benning, Henry L., 31, 32, 37, 48, 82, 123
Betjeman, John A., 82

Biggers, Janice, 235, 236
Blanchard, James H., 212, 215, 238, 258
Boogerville, 145, 158, 164
Booth, John Wilkes, 26–27
Bottoms, the, 95, 133, 174, 203
Bradley, W. C., 2, 57, 90, 116, 165, 187, 206; anti-union, 88, 89, 93, 148; Bibb Mill, 78, 88; Coca-Cola, 128; Columbus Bank & Trust, 61, 212; Columbus Iron Works, 125; Eagle & Phenix Mill, 88, 89, 93, 148, 149; Merchants & Planters Line (steamboats), 63; philanthropy, 2, 63, 128, 149; W. C. Bradley Company, 63, 125
Bradley-Turner Foundation, 2, 128, 243, 246; Columbus Challenge, 243–245, 247. *See also* Bradley, W. C.; Coca-Cola; Turner, D. Abbott
Brewer, Thomas H.: civil rights activism, 132, 133, 172–173, 175; death, 175, 177, 178, 180
Brown, Frank, 243, 248, 249
Browne, J. Rhodes, 45, 57, 61
Browne, Rhodes, 65, 71, 75, 78, 110
Butler, Sarah Turner, 235

Calhoun, Alfred R., 60–61
Calley, William, 217–218
Camp, Joseph, 11–12
Camp, Leon, 74–75
Camp Conrad, 81–82
Carr, Paddy, 13, 14, 15
Chappell, Absalom H., 34
Chappell, L. H., 79, 80, 116, 123, 131, 235; Camp Conrad, 81–82; "City Beautiful," 74; modernized fire and police departments, 72; municipal water system, 81; paved streets, 73–74; white primary, 71
Chappell, Loretto, 74, 104, 141

Chattahoochee (Civil War gunboat), 45, 222, 235, 245. *See also* Civil War; Industry/manufacturing
Chattahoochee River, 60, 110, 148, 205, 235; Apalachicola-Chattahoochee-Flint water wars, 240–241; boundary with Alabama, 23; Civil War, 43, 45; fall line, 1, 6; floods, 16–17, 21–22, 74, 78, 124, 216; lynching, 97, 173; pollution, 25, 60, 81, 216–217, 240, 241; riverboats and river trade, 7, 17–18, 21, 24, 28, 61, 62–63, 85, 94, 111, 215–216; Riverwalk, 240; salvage of Civil War vessels, 222; tax allocation district, 263; water supply, 80–81, 241–242; whitewater course, 265–266
—bridges: Civil War, 43, 45, 47; crime, 68; destroyed by flooding, 16–17, 74; lower bridge (Dillingham Street), 16–17, 18, 25, 27, 54, 74, 94, 124, 240; slave market, 30; upper bridge (Thirteenth/Fourteenth Street) 17, 43, 74, 123, 124, 265, 266. *See also* King, Horace
—dams and hydropower, 124, 215; City Mills, 18, 77, 265; Eagle & Phenix dam, 58, 240, 265; Goat Rock dam, 80; John H. Howard's dam, 19–20, 22, 23; Oliver dam, 18, 204; North Highlands dam, 77–79, 257; Woodruff dam, 216
Chattahoochee Valley Exposition/Fair, 69, 105
Chester, Frank, 217
Chester, Roscoe, 131, 132
Christian Commonwealth, 113–114
Churches, 83, 94, 98, 112, 156, 185, 238, 255; antilynching, 97; antiunion, 169; antiwoman suffrage, 118; attitudes toward slavery, 28–29; Christian Commonwealth, 114; Civil War hospitals in, 39; Confederate Memorial Day, 141; First African Baptist, 49, 66, 239; First Baptist, 8, 29, 37, 133; First Presbyterian, 8, 179–182; Friendship Baptist, 133, 136, 230, 239; Great Depression charity, 145; Hamp Stevens Methodist, 149; Holy Family Catholic (originally Church of St. Philip and St. James), 9; Independent Baptist Tabernacle, 169, 173 (*see also* Johnston, Evall G.); opposition to blues music, 137 (*see also* Rainey, Gertrude); in original town plan, 6; St. Christopher Episcopal, 133; St. James African Methodist Episcopal, 49, 133, 239; St. Luke Methodist, 8, 29, 167, 179; support for African American education, 26, 49–50; Trinity Episcopal, 9, 43, 104, 112 (*see also* de Graffenreid, Edwin L.); World War II, 162
City Market, 71, 117, 142–143, 235. *See also* Historic preservation
Civil War, 1, 3, 15, 25, 64, 141; Battle of Columbus, 34, 42–48, 56; "Blind Tom" Wiggins's fund-raising for Confederacy, 30; class conflict, 32, 40–41, 56; Committee of Public Safety, 37, 39; food shortages, 34, 37, 38, 46; destruction of property / looting, 45–46; emancipation of slaves, 42, 45–46, 47; historical memory, 37, 46, 48; industry, 35–36, 42; loss of younger generation, 41–42; opposition to war / divisions among population, 32, 33, 37–38, 40–41 (*see also* Winter, John); politics, 40–41; slave labor, 42, 43; speculation/profiteering, 35, 38–40; support for Confederacy, 32–33, 35, 36–37; women's bread riot, 40; women's contributions, 33, 37–40
Clarke, John Henrik, 131, 132, 134
Clarke, Joseph, 133, 134
Coca-Cola, 2, 56, 126, 127–128, 129, 166, 210, 244. *See also* Bradley, W. C.
Coca-Cola Space Science Center, 243, 244, 248
Cohn, Aaron, 66, 179
Cohn, Sam, 66
Columbus, founding of, 6–9
Columbus Beyond 2000, 239–240
Columbus Centennial (1928), 140–141
Columbus Challenge (1996), 243–245, 247
Columbus College / State University, 172, 216, 235; Confederate mascot, 189, 190–191; desegregation, 190–192; effect on local economy, 247–248; establishment of, 189; feminist movement, 192–193; granted university status, 248; growth since 1990s, 247–250; participation in Columbus Symphony, 220; revitalization of downtown, 243, 248–249; role in 1996 Olympics, 242; streaking, 193–194; support for Vietnam War, 192
Columbus Guards, 13, 32, 81–82
Columbus Land Company, 12–13, 16, 18, 19, 27. *See also* Fontaine, John; Howard, John H.; Jones, Seaborn; Shorter, Eli
Columbus Stockade, 138, 140
Columbus Symphony Orchestra, 220, 243
Columbus Technical College (originally Muscogee Area Vocational-Technical School

and Columbus Area Vocational-Technical College), 189, 247, 260

Comer, Laura Beecher, 38, 47

Commerce and trade, 16, 17–18, 21, 24, 63, 77, 81, 202, 249, 261; antebellum period, 5, 16, 17, 21, 23, 24; desegregation of stores and restaurants, 183–184; early twentieth century, 256, 257–258, 259, 260–261; Great Depression, 145, 148, 160; late nineteenth century, 63–67, 113–114; late twentieth century, 212–215; 1920s, 125–126, 133, 142–143; Panic of 1837, 18–19; post–Civil War recovery, 49, 56–57; post–World War II growth, 174, 204–205, 210–211; slave trade, 30–31; World War II, 162–163, 166, 167. *See also* Chattahoochee River: riverboats and river trade

—Board of Trade / Chamber of Commerce, 80; advocacy for dams on Chattahoochee, 124; antipoverty program, 251; boosterism/ slogans, 82, 83, 87, 125, 140, 190, 215, 239; city planning, 187, 202, 204; desegregation, 184, 195; downtown revitalization, 238, 240; emphasis on textiles, 209; founded, 63; Ralston Hotel, 67, 129; support for city-county consolidation, 224; support for commission form of government, 121; support for Pratt & Whitney, 260

—cotton warehouses and factors, 2, 21, 23, 45, 46, 57, 61, 238; W. C. Bradley Company, 63, 125, 210, 238

—downtown retail, 56, 63, 81, 125, 142, 174, 175, 183–184, 226, 245; death of, 204–206; revitalization of, 2, 4, 237–239, 257, 261, 263, 265

—drug stores, 63, 126, 133, 134, 162; Eagle Drug and Chemical House, 56, 127

—dry goods, 21, 40, 61, 63–64, 65, 152; David Rothschild Company, 66; J. Kyle's, 63–64; Kirven's Department Store, 64, 140, 184, 205–206

—food products, 21, 166, 209; soft drinks, 127, 128–129, 166, 209 (*see also* Coca-Cola; Industry/manufacturing: food products)

—grocers, wholesale and retail, 65, 66, 67, 94, 95, 125, 129, 133, 145; Sol Loeb, 66; W. C. Bradley Company (Bradley and Carter), 63

—insurance, 49, 71, 112; Aflac, 212–215, 246, 259; Georgia Home Insurance Company, 23, 61

—liquor, wholesale and retail, 263; antebellum era, 9, 27; ban during 1971 riots, 228, 229; end of Prohibition, 159, 160; late nineteenth century, 65, 66, 68, 71; during World War II, 219

—malls and shopping centers, 143, 202, 204–205, 211; Columbus Square, 204, 205, 246, 252, 261; Cross-Country Plaza, 204; the Landings, 211; Main Street Village, 261; Peachtree Mall, 204, 261; St. Elmo Shopping Center, 204

—restaurants and cafés: Big Eddy Club, 111, 204; Columbus Centennial, 140; desegregation, 184, 185, 214; Goetchius House, 236; Goo-Goo Drive-In, 138; owned by African Americans, 67, 133, 162, 173; revitalization of downtown, 237, 238, 245, 261, 263; River Club, 240; Spano's Restaurant, 160

Crawford, Martin J., 31, 39, 48, 123, 235

Creek Indian War (1835–1836), 12–15. *See also* Columbus Land Company

Crime and violence, 2–3, 27, 68, 206, 231, 253; deaths of school superintendents, 233–234; duels and "trials of manhood," 10–12, 69; involving African Americans, 28, 51, 54, 56, 68, 96–98, 161–162, 173–174, 175–178, 197, 200, 217, 227–229, 231–232, 233, 234, 252–255; involving Creek Indians, 13–15; killings of and by police, 68, 177, 227, 233, 253–255; during labor conflicts, 92–93, 150–151, 170; during Reconstruction, 51–53, 54, 56, 68; related to Phenix City, 219 (*see also* Sodom); relationship of honor to violence, 11–12, 27, 69–70; relationship to alcohol, 27, 51, 68; relationship to poverty, 253; riots in summer of 1971, 227–229; during school desegregation, 197, 200; serial killings, 231–232. *See also* Columbus Land Company; Ku Klux Klan; Race relations: lynching

Daniel, Roland, 102, 132
Darby (Tom) & Tarlton (Jimmie), 138–140
de Graffenreid, Edwin L., 6, 9, 12
Dews, George, 98
Dimon, Homer, 121, 122

Education (K–12), 71, 155; antebellum era, 26; Baker High School, 196, 199, 200, 226, 233, 252; Carver High School, 187, 200, 201, 250; city-county schools consolidation, 187; 233–234; Claflin School, 49–50; Columbus High School, 99, 104, 108, 109, 131, 140, 153, 154, 155, 156, 158, 165, 198, 250; deaths of

Education (K–12) (continued)
superintendents, 233–234; desegregation, 175, 181, 187, 194–201, 249–250, 255; Eagle Mill free school, 35; during early twenty-first century, 250–251; establishment of public school system, 50; during Great Depression, 144–145, 147; Hardaway High School, 198; Jordan Vocational High School, 103, 147, 153, 165, 197, 220; Primary Industrial School, 101–102; Secondary Industrial School, 102–103, 158; segregation, 50, 98, 103, 131–132; Spencer High School, 132, 137, 173, 187, 190, 195, 199, 200, 251; sports, 108; during World War I, 103–104; during World War II, 165. *See also* Shaw, William Henry; *and specific educators and administrators*
Eisenhower, Dwight D., 130

Fabiani, Rozell, 153, 220–221
Farley, E. E., 162, 173, 203, 204, 236, 239
Few, Ignatius, 6
fire department, 24–25, 67, 71–72, 146, 228
Flournoy, John F., 116, 131; baseball team, 106; Columbus Railroad Company, 75–76, 87–88, 96; Coweta Power, 78; Jordan duel, 69; real estate development, 76–77; Wildwood Park, 106, 110–111
Fontaine, John, 13, 21, 39
Ford, George, 183, 184, 185, 186, 195, 214, 223, 229
Forrest, Nathan Bedford, 46, 52. *See also* Ku Klux Klan
Fort Benning, 140–141, 143, 158, 215, 240, 242, 264; African American troops, 130, 172, 160–163, 166, 168, 217, 232; desegregation, 182, 196, 200, 217; economic contribution to Columbus, 162–163, 144, 146, 160, 165, 166, 202, 204, 206, 217, 218, 256, 262; female troops, 166, 262; founding, 82–83; growth in 1920s and 1930s, 129–131, 160; School of the Americas/WHINSEC, 214, 262–263; Vietnam War, 206, 217, 220; World War II, 160–162, 164, 165, 166, 166–169, 218. *See also* Museums: National Infantry Museum; Prostitution / venereal disease
Fraternal societies, social and civic clubs, 112–113; for African Americans, 49, 112–113, 132; Big Eddy Club, 111, 204, 214; Columbus Country Club, 25, 90, 111–112, 141, 237, 255; Federation of Women's Clubs, 97, 113, 142–143; Fort Benning, 130, 161; Harmony Club, 112, 211; Kiwanis Club, 218; Masons, 112; Muscogee Club, 111; Prince Hall Masons, 49, 112, 178; River Club, 240; Rotary Club, 107; Social-Civic-25 Club, 133, 145 (*see also* Brewer, Thomas H.); Standard Club, 112; United Daughters of the Confederacy, 46, 113, 118; women's clubs, 74, 108, 140; workers' social clubs, 87, 149

Galer, Mary Jane, 224, 225
Gary, Carlton ("Stocking Strangler"), 231–232
Gibson, Carleton, 99, 101, 103
Girard, Alabama, 13, 14, 17, 27, 36, 43, 68, 106
Godwin, John, 16–17
Golden, Theodore, 62, 106, 107
Goodman, Alfred, 179
Gordon, Frederick B., 78, 85, 90, 91, 99, 101, 103, 123
Great Depression, 107, 126, 129, 136, 138, 155; Civilian Conservation Corps, 147, 160; education, 144–145; entertainment/recreation, 152–154; Federal Emergency Relief Administration, 146, 154, 160; labor, 144, 148–149; National Recovery Administration, 147–148, 151; National Youth Administration, 147; post office and federal court building, 146; poverty, 145, 148, 149; Public Works Administration, 147, 160; racial discrimination, 146, 147–148; Social Security, 145–146; Textile Strike of 1934, 149–152, 158; Works Progress Administration, 146–147. *See also* Fort Benning; Housing Authority
Greene, Prince, 87
Griffin, Anna, 118, 121, 226

Hallam, James, 6
Hardaway, B. H., 74, 77, 79, 80
Hardaway Company, 123, 166, 238
Harris, Julian, 122
Hatcher, Claud, 128–129
Hill, John, 58
Hinkle, Gordon, 122
Historic Columbus Foundation, 236, 238, 243, 246, 257, 263, 265
Historic preservation: adaptive reuse of textile mills, 257; City Market, 142–143; Historic Columbus Foundation, 235–236; Iron Works Convention and Trade Center, 237; Rankin Square, 237–238; revitalization of

downtown, 263; Springer Opera House, 222

Holt, Hines, 19, 30, 31

Hospitals and medical care, 73, 104, 113, 167; African American doctors, 132–133 (*see also* Brewer, Thomas H.); City Hospital / Midtown Medical Center, 73, 82, 133, 174, 203, 215; during Civil War, 39, 127; Pest House, 73; St. Francis Hospital, 203

Hotels, 243, 263; Columbus Hotel (1828), 8; penning of voters, 15, 31, 58; Perry House (also called Racine), 67, 75; Ralston Hotel, 67, 82, 129, 204, 237; Rankin Hotel, 27, 67, 237, 248; segregation, 133, 185; Springer Opera House, 244; Waverly Hotel, 77

Housing Authority, 146, 179, 203–204, 206, 236, 251–252, 263, 264. *See also* Public housing

Howard, H. Augusta, 3, 115–117, 141, 157, 235. *See also* Politics: woman suffrage

Howard, John H., 13, 15, 19–20, 21, 23, 31, 69, 115

Howard, Richard, 69–70, 115, 116, 117, 131

Howard, Robert, 51, 69–70, 96, 115, 116

Howard v. Ingersoll, 23–24

Huston, Tom, 125–126

Illges, A., 62, 74

Illges, John P., 39, 83, 131

Industry/manufacturing, 80, 202, 216; Civil War, 35–36, 39, 45; hydropower for industry, 1, 18–20, 21–22, 86 (*see also* Chattahoochee River: dams and hydropower); Kodak, 260–261; Litho-Krome/Hallmark, 210–211; NCR Technologies, 261; post–Civil War dynasties, 57, 58; 1970s, 209; Pratt & Whitney, 212, 217, 260; Rock Island Paper Mill, 20, 23 (*see also* Mott, Randolph; Winter, John); wood products/furniture, 20, 23, 58, 114; World War II, 165. *See also* Labor unions and strikes; Textiles
—clothing/shoes, 21, 35, 58; Schwobilt, 66
—cotton gins, 20, 58, 114, 125, 165, 210; Lummus Cotton Gin Company, 125, 165, 210
—food products, 21, 58, 125–126, 127, 209–210, 260; Dolly Madison, 209, 260; RC Cola/Nehi, 128–129, 141, 166, 209, 210, 223; Southland Pecan Company, 125, 211; Tom's Peanuts (bought by Snyder's/Lance), 125–126, 166, 209, 260
—gristmills, 23; City Mills, 18, 45, 62, 75, 77, 79, 80, 236, 263; Empire Mills, 39, 45, 62, 140, 237; Palace Mills, 20, 23, 39, 45, 62 (*see also* Mott, Randolph; Winter, John)
—iron foundries, 20, 58, 61, 188; Columbus Iron Works, 20, 35, 46, 51, 56, 61–62, 125, 210, 222, 236, 237 (*see also* Bradley, W. C.); Goldens' Foundry, 39, 62, 106, 165, 210
—labor: African Americans' industrial, 27, 35, 37, 42, 85, 88, 91, 92, 170, 207–209; child, 2, 20, 28, 30, 85, 88, 99, 100, 101, 102, 148, 151; textile, 18, 22, 35–36, 59, 85–86, 87, 88–89, 91–93, 102, 148–152, 158, 165, 169–171, 207–209; women's industrial, 20, 85, 91, 165, 169, 207

Ingersoll, S. M., 16, 23

Iverson, Alfred, 37, 38

Jackson (Civil War ironclad), 45, 222, 235, 245

Jewish community, 21, 97, 112, 113, 179, 237; anti-Semitism, 57, 64, 65, 97, 169, 179, 237; conflict between Germanic and Eastern European Jews, 65, 112; post–Civil War merchants, 64–66; role in civil rights movement, 179; role in Civil War, 36–37, 38, 64. *See also specific Jewish people*

Johnson, James, 31, 51

Johnson, Nunnally, 4, 154–155, 156

Johnston, Evall G. ("Parson Jack"), 169, 173, 175, 180, 194

Jones, Seaborn, 41, 115; attorney for John Milton, 12; Bank of Columbus, 18, 19; Broad Street commercial building, 17; City Mills, 18, 45; city water supply, 25; death, 62; 1828 auction, 8; ferry, 16; state's rights and secession, 15, 31

Jordan, G. Gunby, 71, 77, 141; Bibb Mill, 87; Board of Trade, 67; Columbus Power Company, 78–79; convict labor, 83–84; dueling, 69; Eagle & Phenix Bank / Columbus Savings Bank, 61; Eagle & Phenix Mill, 57, 86; immigrant labor, 85; industrial education, 101, 102, 103; Jordan Company, 77, 124; Jordan High School, 103, 147; Jordan Mills, 116; National Civic Federation, 99; philanthropy, 2, 101, 102, 132; post–Civil War dynasty, 61; railroads, 62; Spencer High School, 132; Third National Bank, 61; woman suffrage, 115, 117

Jordan, G. Gunby, II, 111, 164, 223

Kamensky, Harry, 237–238

Kendrick, Edna, 226, 237

King, Horace, 3, 16, 17, 49, 62, 74

King, Primus, 134, 172–173, 176, 187, 195
Kirven, J. Albert, 64, 71
Ku Klux Klan: during civil rights era, 173, 177, 180; during 1920s, 3, 122; during Reconstruction, 3, 52–56, 64; threat against Carson McCullers, 158
Kyle, Clason, 9, 160, 222
Kyle, James P., 63, 64
Kyle, Joseph, 63, 64

Labor unions and strikes, 86, 148, 212, 260; 1896 Eagle & Phenix weavers' strike, 86, 87; National Union of Textile Workers, 87; Operation Dixie, 169, 170–171; streetcar strikes, 87–88; Textile Strike of 1934, 149–152, 158; textile strikes, 1918–1919, 88–93; Textile Workers Organizing Committee, 152; Textile Workers Union of America, 208–209; United Textile Workers of America, 87, 89, 91–93, 149–151
Lamar, Mirabeau, 7, 15, 34
Leebern, Fate, 160, 219
Lewis, David, 251
Lewis, Ulysses, 8
Liberty District: attempts to revitalize, 206, 243, 263–264; beginnings during Civil War, 35; during civil rights movement 173–175; decline by 1990s, 206, 245; during late nineteenth century, 65, 66; Ma Rainey house, 137, 238; during 1920s, 131, 133, 134; during Reconstruction, 49; during World War II, 166
Libraries, 123, 239; Bradley Library, 159, 187–188, 195, 246; Carnegie Library, 104, 206, 257; Columbus Public Library (2005), 246–247; Eagle & Phenix library, 85, 112; first library, 9; Fourth Avenue / Mildred Terry Library, 175; Schwob Library, 66, 189
Linwood Cemetery, 6, 38, 73, 76, 117, 126, 128, 141, 145
Loeb, Sol, 66, 238
Lunsford, Lizzie, 133, 162, 163, 173, 263
Lunsford, Walter, 162–163

Marshall, George C., 130–131
Martin, Frank ("Butch"), 137, 227, 239–240, 242, 255
Martin, Roy, 104–105, 134, 211
Martin/Carmike Theatres, 105, 134, 184, 211, 238, 261. *See also* Theaters
Massey, Annie V., 165
McClung, A. J., 162, 175, 183, 185, 186, 195, 224, 228, 229, 230, 260

McCullers, Carson, xiv, 4, 144, 155–159, 160
McDougald, Daniel, 13, 27
McGee, Theo, 146, 169, 173, 179, 189, 203–204
McIlhenny, John, 50
McNeill, Robert B., 179–182
Midtown Columbus, Inc., 246, 247
Milton, John, 11–12
Moses, Raphael, 21, 26, 36, 41, 47, 49, 57, 64, 235
Mott, Randolph, 46; Claflin School, 50; mayor pro tem during Reconstruction, 54, 55; Mott house, 23, 206, 257; opposition to secession, 37, 45; Palace Mill, 23, 39, 45, 62; People's Stage Line, 16, 23; Republican Party activism, 51; Rock Island Paper Mill, 23; the *Wanderer*, 31
Museums, 123, 236; Columbus Museum, 153–154, 188, 243; Ma Rainey House Blues Museum, 137; National Civil War Naval Museum / Confederate Naval Museum, 222, 243, 245; National Infantry Museum, 222, 245–246, 265

NAACP (National Association for the Advancement of Colored People), 173, 214; bus desegregation, 183; end of white primary, 172–173; establishment of Columbus chapter, 172; Fort Benning racism, 130, 161, 162; leadership in civil rights movement, 179, 229; school desegregation, 194, 196, 249, 250; theater desegregation, 184. *See also* Brewer, Thomas H.; Farley, E. E.; Ford, George; King, Primus
Nail, Braxton, 200, 233
Nelms, Buddy, 199, 200, 238
Newspapers, 81, 94, 106, 138; antiunion sentiment in, 169; Ashburn murder in, 52, 53, 55, 56; *Columbus Democrat*, 9; *Columbus Times* (African American newspaper), 133; convict labor in, 83; Fort Benning underground newspaper in Vietnam War, 217; Ku Klux Klan in, 52, 173; opposition to Civil War in, 37, 41; opposition to Civil War speculation/profiteering in, 40, 42; runaway slave ads, 28; school desegregation in, 187, 194, 195, 196; support for city-county consolidation, 224; support for commission form of government, 121; support for Confederacy, 32; *Saber*, 189, 191, 192; view of African Americans during Reconstruction, 49, 50, 51; view of black labor during Civil War, 42
—*Columbus Enquirer/Enquirer-Sun*, 71, 124;

conflict during editorship of Calhoun, 60-61; Creek War in, 13; established, 7; Nunnally Johnson's work for, 155; lynching in, 97, 98; merged with *Ledger*, 154; murder of editor Salisbury, 69; opposition to dueling, 11; opposition to Ku Klux Klan, 122; opposition to poll tax, 57; opposition to secession, 32, 45; Pulitzer Prize, 122; support for Christian Commonwealth, 114; support for Jewish community 64, 65; support for property requirements for voting, 41; woman suffrage in, 115, 118, 120
—*Columbus Ledger*, 79; controversy over Columbus High School site in, 131; established, 104; Forces of Evil serial killer letters to, 232; merged with *Enquirer-Sun*, 154; 1971 riots in, 228; Pulitzer Prize, 220; "Shame of Columbus" series in, 203; support for woman suffrage, 117, 118
—*Columbus Ledger-Enquirer*, 153; Broadway building, 160, 206, 249; Columbus Beyond 2000, 239-240; merger of *Enquirer-Sun* and *Ledger*, 154; use of courtesy titles for African Americans, 179
Nolen, John, 123

Patton, George S., 160
Peabody, George Foster, 99, 101, 102, 103, 106, 113, 132
Pearce, George, 62, 77
Pemberton, John, 56, 63, 126-128
Phenix City, Ala., 13, 60, 63; Columbus-Phenix City Religious Council, 179; Darby & Tarlton, 138, 140; Ku Klux Klan, 122, 173; Martin theater, 105; mill housing, 86; 1929 flood, 124; 1996 Olympic softball, 242; Phenix City clean-up, 218-220; prostitution during World War II, 167; textile union, 152
Pierce, Richard, 133, 162
Police / law enforcement, 69, 94, 154, 202, 255, 256; African American officers, 168, 172, 174, 175, 177, 226-227, 230; during civil rights movement, 177, 182, 183, 184, 195; Civil War women's bread riot, 40; connection with Ku Klux Klan, 122, 173; Fort Benning, 161, 162, 217; gang task force, 252-253; killing of citizens, 68, 121, 253-254; 1971 riots, 228-229; officers killed, 68, 233; opposition to unions, 91, 92, 169, 170; in Phenix City, 219; professionalization of, 72; prostitution, 82, 167, 219; during Reconstruction, 48, 51, 54; role in lynching, 97; during school desegregation, 200; school superintendent Jim Burns's murder, 233-234; Sodom, 10, 27; Stocking Strangler serial killings, 231-232; violence against African Americans, 68, 97, 172, 173-174, 175, 227, 253-255. *See also* Crime and Violence; Ku Klux Klan; Labor unions and strikes; Prostitution / venereal disease; Race relations
Politics, 150, 214; African Americans in public office, 51-52, 185, 214, 224, 229, 230, 243, 255; during antebellum era, 8, 11-12, 16; bond issues, 72, 74, 81, 147, 187, 189, 203, 246; during Civil War and Reconstruction, 40-41, 51-53, 54-55, 56, 57-58; commission form of government, 120-122, 123; consolidation of Columbus and Muscogee County, 202, 223-224; disfranchisement of African Americans, 52, 54-55, 57-58, 71, 96, 159, 172-173; during early twentieth century, 255; electoral fraud, 15, 54-55, 58, 96, 219; penning of voters, 15, 58, 71; poll tax, 52, 55, 57-58; private school amendment, 194; during Progressive era, 70-71, 72, 74, 79, 81; secession, 15, 31-33, 34, 37, 45, 55, 141; state's rights, 15, 31-32, 118, 122; woman suffrage, 3, 114-116, 117-119, 120, 121 (*see also* Howard, H. Augusta); women in public office, 121-122, 224-225, 255
Poverty/homelessness, 134, 140, 158, 166, 185; during antebellum era, 22; during Civil War and Reconstruction, 35-36, 40, 46, 49; during early twentieth-first century, 250-252, 264-265; during Progressive era, 99-104. *See also* Great Depression; Housing Authority; Public health; Public housing
Prostitution / venereal disease, 40, 82, 167-169, 206, 218-219, 232
Public health, 72-73, 82, 104, 113, 133, 145, 167-169, 172, 203. *See also* Hospitals and medical care
Public housing, 146, 203, 263; Arbor Pointe, 264; Baker Village, 146, 217, 264; Booker T. Washington Apartments, 146, 206, 264; Columbus Commons, 264; E. E. Farley Homes, 203; Elizabeth Canty Homes, 203; Peabody Apartments, 146; Ralston Towers, 67, 204. *See also* Housing Authority
Public utilities: Columbus Power Company, 77-79, 80, 102, 124, 141; electricity, 58, 59, 67, 73, 75, 77-80, 94, 105, 121, 129, 146, 216; gas works, 25, 78, 79, 80, 88, 102, 124, 240; telephone, 77, 160; water supply / Columbus Water Works, 24-25, 71-72, 76, 80-81,

Public utilities (*continued*):
216, 241–242, 246. *See also* Baldwin, George J.

Quintard, Charles, 43, 47

Race relations: lynching, 3, 96–98, 110, 113, 159, 161–162, 177, 231; during 1920s and 1930s, 3, 68, 130, 131–137, 142, 145–148, 154; during 1990s and early 2000s, 137, 237, 238, 239, 245, 249–251, 252–253, 255, 259, 263–265; police killing of Kenny Walker, 253–255; during Reconstruction, 3, 48–52, 54–56, 58; during slavery, 3, 8, 16, 26, 27–31, 37, 42, 43, 45–46; during World War II, 161–163, 165, 166, 167, 168–169, 170, 207
—during civil rights movement: African American police protest (1971), 226–227, 230 (*see also* Police / law enforcement: African American officers); African American resistance to segregation, 173, 174, 175, 183, 184, 195; city-county consolidation, 223–224; desegregation of Columbus College, 190–192; desegregation of public facilities, 182–184, 185; desegregation of textile mills, 207–208; divisions among African Americans, 185; end of "separate but equal," 174, 175; end of white primary, 172–173 (*see also* Brewer, Thomas H.; King, Primus; Lunsford, Lizzie); at Fort Benning, 217; harassment of Columbus Confederate Yankees, 221; K–12 school desegregation, 187, 194–201; murder of Thomas Brewer, 3, 175, 177; 1971 riots, 228–230; violence against African Americans, 173–174, 177–178 (*see also* Police / law enforcement: violence against African Americans)
—education, 247; during antebellum era, 26; during city-county consolidation, 187; Columbus College desegregation, 190–192; establishment of Spencer High School, 131–132; gangs in schools, 252–252; during Great Depression, 145, 147; K–12 school desegregation, 175, 194–201, 249–250; during late twentieth and early twenty-first centuries, 250–251; during Reconstruction, 49–50; at turn of twentieth century, 98–99, 103; during World War II, 165. *See also* Education; Spencer, William H.
—labor, 94–95; in city government, 226, 255; convict lease, 83–85; desegregation of textile mills, 207–208; at Fort Benning, 130; during Great Depression, 147–148; industrial education training, 103, 131; in police department, 168, 172, 174, 175, 177, 226–227, 230; during Reconstruction, 49; during slavery, 16, 30, 33, 42; at turn of twentieth century, 67, 85, 88, 111; unionization of, 170, 208–209; during World War II, 207. *See also* Labor unions and strikes
—segregation (Jim Crow), 98, 185; Columbus Museum, 188; Fort Benning, 130, 161–162, 217; fraternal societies and clubs, 112–113; during Great Depression, 145–146, 147–148; hospitals, 73, 133, 174; hotels, 133, 185; legal system, 96, 97, 174, 177; libraries, 104, 159, 175, 188; in McCullers's books, 158–159; in professions, 98, 103–104, 133, 174; residential, 95–96, 133, 146, 204, 207; restaurants, 174, 184; sports and leisure, 105, 106, 110, 134, 154, 162, 175, 184; stores, 65, 134, 174, 183; transportation, 96, 110, 162, 182–183, 185; United Way, 191

Radio, 129, 138, 140, 152–153, 162, 181, 221, 242
Rainey, Gertrude ("Ma"), 3, 9, 134–137, 138, 238
Real estate development, 8, 110; acquisition of Creek lands, 12–13, 16; Benning Technology Park, 264; City Village, 263; Jordan Company, 77, 102, 124, 164, 204; Muscogee Real Estate Company / Flournoy Realty, 76, 78, 110–111, 131 (*see also* Flournoy, John F.); W. C. Bradley Company, 2, 210, 240, 257, 263, 265, 266 (*see also* Turner, William B.). *See also* Suburbs
Reconstruction, 3, 48–58, 64, 68, 74; African American education, 49–50; African American voting and office holding, 51–52, 54–55, 57–58; Ashburn assassination and Columbus prisoners, 53–54, 55–56; conflict with African American troops, 51; Freedmen's Bureau / poverty for freedmen, 49, 54, 55; historical memory, 48, 55–56; occupation by federal troops, 48, 49, 51, 52, 54; panic of 1873, 58, 61, 62; return of prosperity, 49, 56–57, 58–59; violence toward / intimidation of African Americans, 52, 54, 56, 58
Richards, Walter, 123, 126, 189
Riverdale Cemetery, 105, 123, 140, 150, 154, 164
RiverWalk, 240, 241, 242, 263, 264, 265
Rothschild, David, 66, 236

Salisbury, William, 61, 69
Schwob, Ruth, 66, 189
Schwob, Simon, 66, 189

Sconiers, John, 66, 133
Shaw, William Henry, 187, 195, 196, 197, 198, 200, 233
Shepherd, Hoyt, 219, 220
Shorter, Edward, 153, 167, 188
Shorter, Eli, 12, 13, 15, 17, 111, 153, 235
Simons, George J., 187, 189, 202, 204
Simons, Max, 65, 125
Simons, Sidney, 65, 125, 211
Sodom (Ala.), 3, 10, 27
Spencer, William H., 50, 98, 103, 132, 238
Sports and recreation: baseball, 106–108, 109, 110, 130, 131, 149, 195, 221–222, 264; football, 108, 130, 153, 195; golf, 108, 111, 154, 175, 204, 240; horse racing, 10, 69, 75; Memorial Stadium, 108, 141, 145, 203, 242, 264; Olympic softball, 1996, 242–243, 264; Villa Reich, 105; YMCAs, 106, 133, 145, 154, 155, 162, 183, 185 (*see also* McClung, A. J.; Peabody, George Foster)
—parks and playgrounds, 113, 203, 238, 240; Carver Park, 175; Columbus Public Library park, 246, 247; 1896 courthouse park, 71; Golden Park, 107, 124, 173, 203, 221–222, 242, 264; Lincoln Park, 110; Mott's Green, 23, 104, 108, 187; North Highlands Park, 110; the Promenade, 236; Recreation Department, 108, 110, 154; segregation, 110, 174, 175, 184, 185, 195; Wildwood/Weracoba/Lakebottom Park, 76, 106, 107, 110–111, 126, 128, 131, 139, 153, 195, 204, 233, 246; Woodruff Park, 240, 265
Springer Opera House, 9; Columbus Challenge, 243, 244; Confederate Memorial Day, 141; historic preservation, 222, 234, 235; Little Theatre, 153; Ma Rainey, 134; McClure Theatre Academy Education Center, 245; opened, 104; Three Arts League, 140. *See also* Historic preservation
Stanton, George, 216
St. Elmo, 110, 154, 222
Straus family, 39, 64, 97–98
Strong, Rose, 226
Suburbs, 76, 198, 202, 204, 261; Bibb City, 92, 112, 148–149, 151, 170, 207, 223, 256 (*see also* Textiles: Bibb Mill); Carver Heights, 204 (*see also* Farley, E. E.); East Highlands, 75, 76, 77, 110, 145 (*see also* Flournoy, John F.); Green Island Hills, 124, 204, 214 (*see also* Jordan, G. Gunby); Waverly Terrace, 77, 102 (*see also* Jordan, G. Gunby); Willis Plaza, 204 (*see also* Farley, E. E.)
—North Highlands: Camp Conrad, 81; "City Beautiful" movement, 74; first motion picture, 105; North Highlands Park, 110; Primary Industrial School, 102; slum clearance, 203; streetcar to, 75; textile strike (1919), 89, 91; textile strike (1934), 151
—Rose Hill, 38, 111, 137; annexation of, 71; Battle of Columbus in, 47; City Hospital, 73; controversy over Columbus High School site, 131; demolition of historic houses, 235; Jewish merchant in, 64; Lincoln Park, 110; Royal Theatre, 105; streetcar to, 75, 96
—Wynnton, 16, 41, 76, 95, 156; Aflac tower, 213; annexation of, 123; Bradley Library, 188; first automobile, 74; golf links, 111; Macon-Dixon dividing line, 247; post–Civil War violence, 51; Stocking Strangler, 231; streetcar to, 75; viaduct to, 123; Wynnton Academy, 26
Swift, George Parker, 39, 57, 59, 89, 153, 160, 222
Swift, Jack, 239

Television, 153, 220–221
Temperance Hall: African American Cotillion party, 49; "Blind Tom" Wiggins, 30; Civil War meetings, 37, 41, 42; first African American public school, 50; opened, 26; Radical Republican rally, 53; secession meeting, 31; Swift Manufacturing's start in, 59
Textiles: Christian Commonwealth, 114; Civil War destruction, 45; Civil War profiteering, 39; Clapp's Factory, 18, 20, 57, 78, 81, 204, 216; Columbus Manufacturing, 78, 85, 99, 100, 125, 188, 206, 257 (*see also* Gordon, Frederick B.); Coweta Falls Factory, 20; Eagle Mill, 21, 22–23, 35–36, 39, 45, 57; effect of World War II, 165; electrification, 77–78; Howard Factory, 20, 22; Jordan Mills, 116; Meritas Mill, 91, 92, 152; mill closings at turn of twentieth century, 256–257; post–Civil War growth, 58–59; post–World War II changes, 206–208; Shannon Hosiery Mill, 189, 248. *See also* Labor unions and strikes
—Bibb Mill, 110; closed, 256; corporate welfare, 144, 148–149, 168–170, 207; destroyed by fire, 256; effect of World War II, 165, 207; established, 87; growth in 1920s, 125; historic designation, 236; labor conflict, 88, 92, 112, 149–151, 170; powered by North Highlands dam, 77–78, 79; purchased Meritas Mills, 152

Textiles (*continued*)
—Eagle & Phenix Mill, 77, 80, 188; bankruptcy (1896), 86; child labor, 100; corporate welfare, 85, 112, 149; dam removed, 265; early twentieth-century growth, 86–87; electrification, 79; historic designation, 236; housing in Phenix City, 86; immigrant labor, 85; kindergarten, 101; labor conflict, 87–89, 92, 148, 150, 152, 208; post–Civil War growth, 57, 58–59; post–World War II changes, 206; purchased by Fieldcrest, 206; race conflict, 207–208; renovation into condominiums, 240, 257. *See also* Bradley, W. C.; Jordan, G. Gunby; Young, William H.
—Muscogee Manufacturing, 188; Carnegie Library, 187, 206, 257; Civil War profiteering, 39; closed, 256–257; demolished, 257; electrification, 59, 77, 79; established, 57; growth in 1920s, 125; historic designation, 236; labor conflict, 89, 151; Mott House, 206, 257; post–Civil War dynasty, 57; sold to Fieldcrest, 206. *See also* Swift, George Parker
—Swift Manufacturing / Swift Spinning: burned, 257; Civil War profiteering, 39; closed, 257; established, 59; growth in 1920s, 125; labor conflict, 89, 91, 92, 150, 152, 169, 170, 208; renovated into apartments, 257; sold, 206–207
Theaters (live and motion picture): AMC purchases Carmike Theaters, 261; amphitheater on Promenade, 236; antebellum era, 26–27; Civil War theater troupe, 38; desegregation of, 184; downtown theater district, 245; Fort Benning, 130, 161; growth of Martin/Carmike Theatres, 211, 238; Liberty Theatre, 105, 134, 206, 243, 245, 263, 264; RiverCenter, 243–244, 245, 246, 248; Royal Theatre / Three Arts Theatre, 105, 140, 152, 220 (*see also* Radio; Three Arts League); Sol Smith and His Dramatic Company, 9–10. *See also* Martin, Roy; Martin/Carmike Theatres; Springer Opera House; Temperance Hall
Thomas, Alma, 137
Thomas, Edward Lloyd, 6
Thompson, Albert, 174, 183, 185, 186, 224
Three Arts League, 140, 153, 220, 243
Tolbert, Love, 121–122, 224
Toles, Alex, 66, 97
Toombs, Robert, 39

Tourism, 16, 27, 66, 67, 133, 138, 216, 235, 243, 246, 265
Townsend, John, 190
Transportation, 94; airports, 123, 154, 164, 182, 203, 215; buses, 80, 162, 164, 174, 182–183, 185; for homeless, 252; during 1996 Olympics, 242; stagecoaches, 16; during World War I, 82. *See also* Chattahoochee River
—automobiles, 120, 185, 208; city planning for parking and traffic, 123, 142, 205, 256; Columbus Centennial parade, 141; first automobiles, 74–75; funeral procession during 1934 textile strike, 150; gas rationing in World War II, 166; growth of suburbs, 204; suffrage parade, 117; taxis, 162; urban sprawl, 261
—Columbus Railroad Company (streetcars): acquired by Columbus Electric and Power Company, 80; electrification of, 77–78; end of, 80; establishment of, 75; hazards of, 76; labor conflict, 87–88; parks, 106, 110, 126; purchase by George Baldwin, 78–79; Ralston Hotel, 67; rivalry with North Highlands Electric Railroad Company, 75; route, 75, 76; segregation, 96; use in lynching, 97. *See also* Baldwin, George J.; Flournoy, John F.; Suburbs: East Highlands
—railroads, 2, 21, 37, 57, 62, 64, 83–84, 154; circus train wreck, 105; convict labor, 83–84; cotton transport, 63; dedication of Goat Rock dam, 80; failure of Tom Huston's frozen peaches, 126; first railroad, 24; post–Civil War growth, 58, 62; rail tracks and yard in city, 123; resistance to, 3, 24; segregation, 96, 185; Sixth Avenue passenger depot, 238; slave labor, 27, 42
—roads and highways, 16, 73–74, 83, 123, 164, 205, 215; I-185, 211, 215, 247; Macon Road, 82, 173, 204, 246; Manchester Expressway, 204, 215; Thirteenth Street viaduct, 123, 124, 156, 174, 211; Victory Drive, 164, 260, 264, 265
TSYS/Total System Services, 212, 238, 247–248, 257–258, 263
Turner, D. Abbott, 128, 149, 188, 189, 210, 212, 235, 236
Turner, Edwin, 133
Turner, John, 265
Turner, William B. (Bill), 244; Coca-Cola board, 128; Columbus Challenge, 243, 245; Columbus Public Library, 246; county-city

consolidation, 223; 1971 riots, 229; Uptown Columbus, 238

Uptown Columbus / downtown revitalization, 202–203, 204–205, 236–239, 243–245, 248–249, 257, 261, 264–266

Wadkins, Mary Jane, 192
Wetherington, Jim, 234, 255
Whitley, Thomas Y., 189, 190–192, 193, 194, 223, 248
Wiggins, Thomas Bethune ("Blind Tom"), 3, 29–30, 40
Wildwood/Weracoba/Lakebottom Park, 76, 106, 107, 110–111, 126, 128, 131, 139, 153, 195, 204, 233, 246
Willcox, Cyprian, 5, 26, 27
Wilson, Augusta Evans, 110, 115, 118
Wilson, James H., 42–46, 47, 81
Winter, John, 2, 19, 20, 23, 32, 33, 37, 46, 235
Wood, Edwina, 108, 110
Woodruff, George Waldo, 39, 45, 62, 140
Woodruff, J. W., 140, 215–216
Woodruff, J. W., Jr., 152, 220
Woolfolk, John, 10, 17, 30, 82
Woolfolk, Sowell, 11
World War I, 83, 107, 108, 113, 118; effects on education, 103–104; textile strikes during, 149–152, 158; women's contributions, 82. *See also* Columbus Guards; Fort Benning; Prostitution / venereal disease

World War II, 55, 144, 235; effect on education, 165; housing shortages, 164; industry, 59, 152, 165–166, 202, 207, 256; Phenix City, 218; racial discrimination, 161, 165, 168, 172, 182; rationing, 166; recreation, 154, 162; time zone change, 163–164; women's contributions, 165, 166–167. *See also* Fort Benning; Prostitution / venereal disease

Wright, Robert, 184, 185, 223, 224, 225, 226, 228, 229

Young, William H.: acquires Howard Mill, 22–23; Bank of Columbus / Eagle & Phenix Bank, 23, 61, 86; Civil War speculation/ profiteering, 35, 39; corporate capitalism, 85; Eagle & Phenix Mill, 57–59, 85; Eagle Mill, 21, 35, 45; first free public school, 2, 35–36; forced resignation from Eagle & Phenix, 86; Georgia Home Insurance Company, 23; immigrant labor, 85; importance, 21; philanthropy, 2, 35–36; post–Civil War dynasty, 57; post–Civil War growth, 58–59; support for Confederacy, 32, 35. *See also* Banking: Bank of Columbus; Textiles: Eagle & Phenix Mill

www.ingramcontent.com/pod-product-compliance
Lightning Source LLC
Chambersburg PA
CBHW010926180426
43192CB00043B/2782